CREATIVITY TWELVE

A PHOTOGRAPHIC REVIEW EDITED BY DON BARRON
ART DIRECTION BOOK COMPANY New York, N.Y. 10016

Advertising Directions, Volume 16

Designed by Stanley Stellar

Copyright © 1983 by Art Direction Book Company
10 East 39th Street, New York, N.Y. 10016
All rights reserved

No part of this book may be reproduced, stored in a retrieval system, or transmitted in any form by any means, electronic, mechanical, photocopying, recording or otherwise, without the prior permission of the publishers.

ISBN: 0-910158-99-1
ISBN for Creativity Annuals Standing Orders: 0-910158-10-X
Library of Congress Catalog Card#74-168254

Printed in the United States of America

Distributors:
USA and Canada: Art Direction Book Company
Foreign Distributor: Fleetbooks, c/o Feffer & Simons, Inc.
               100 Park Avenue, New York, N.Y. 10017

Contents

Publisher's Statement
   A Cross Section of Creativity 12 in Color

PRINT

Consumer Single Unit	1-44
Consumer Campaign	45-64
Consumer Fractional Page	65-79
Trade Single Unit	80-106
Trade Campaign	107-128
Posters	129-164
Brochures / Catalogs	165-236
Book Jackets	237-269
Record Album Covers	270-290
Magazine Covers	291-324
Package Deisgn	325-375
Calendars	376-394
Annual Reports	395-437
House Organs	438-453
Editorial Design Single Unit	454-486
Editorial Multiple Unit	487-498
Trademarks & Logotypes	499-551
Letterheads / Envelopes	552-570
Letterhead Sets	571-589
Corporate Identity	590-594
Promotional Pieces	595-651
Self-Promo	652-705
Public Service Advertising	706-719
TV Graphics	720-734

TELEVISION / FILM

Consumer Single Unit	735-768
Consumer Campaign	769-782
Corporate Commercials	783-787
Public Service	788-793
Political	794
Show Openings / ID's / Titles	795-796
Animation	797-802

SPECIAL CREATIVE ACHIEVEMENT

Art Illustration	803-836
Photography	837-864
Typography	865-910
Radio	911-920
Index	

CREATIVITY TWELVE

...THE ART DIRECTOR IS THE GENRE ARTIST OF OUR TIMES. HIS TALENT IS HIS EYE AND MIND FOR THE CONTEMPORARY SCENE, AND HIS SKILL THE ABILITY TO DEPICT HIS CLIENT'S PRODUCT IN TERMS OF THE IMMEDIATE MOMENT.

FROM THE ANNOUNCEMENT FOR THE FIRST CREATIVITY SHOW, 1970

This Creativity Show proved without quesiton that advertising design is now where most art directors and graphic designers thought it was, had been, would be, or should be...more or less...sooner or later. And that is, television graphics is now the dominant influence.

It's a design trend that has been developing for years. In the beginning, of course, print graphics led the way in all design categories, including TV. This was understandable: most art directors, designers, photographers and animators were recruited for television from print graphics. Only a relatively few came from Hollywood.

But, as the years rolled by, TV developed its own disciplines, its own point of view. And then, with computer animation, TV finally acquired its own personality. Armed with its very own gadgetry, television graphics cut the last remaining strings to print, and rocketed off in uncharted directions, completely independent.

A distinguishing characteristic of TV graphics is its spatial renderings. There are no limitations; anything is possible. This freedom from perspective is accomplishing two results simultaneously. One is the financial effort to milk the new condition for every bizarre visual effect. The other is to reaffirm, via grids, an artist's debt to perspective. In its own way, it's repeating, "The more things change, *the more they stay the same!*"

This fancy-free attitude towards spatial requirements has been visible for some time now. For example, the new wave/no wave school of the last few years certainly is beholden to TV. But what this year's Creativity Show demonstrates is that the freedom to render volume and distance now extends in all directions—size of type, art and photography, design.

And that is only part of the story, for in addition to the clear influence of television, advertising design is being pushed and pulled every which way. New wave freedom is now harnassed into corporate control with flair; old standbys like product-as-star and simple, elegant fashion work are coming back; and other, seemingly set-in-stone approaches are being abandoned, at least for now. In a sense, design has gotten bigger than itself. Today its field of play is the entire realm of possibility—and that includes micro-chips as well as human minds.

It is this looseness, this lack of respect, if you will, for the more formal and clasic concepts of design that is driving advertising management up the wall. This particular echelon of executive has always exhibited an extraordinary inability to judge advertising art. Their current blasts denouncing a lack of creativity is the latest evidence that they simply do not understand the violent changes occurring in the field of advertising design. The rules, principles, and traditions of art, some hundreds of years old, are being reviewed through radically new lenses. And the new measures, if such yardsticks are indeed possible in the 1980s, are yet to be created.

You get an even sharper picture of what's going on, particularly here in New York, if you study the entries from around the world. Overseas—with Japanese illustration being the only innovative exception—creativity in the classic sense is highly visible. The work is dramtic, clean, bold, exciting—which explains all the carping by the U.S. advertising establishment: "There's no creativity here...it's only overseas...that's where the good stuff is being done today..."

This verdict, of course, exposes their utter lack of understanding of current advertising design. They simply do not comprehend that the New York design community is fighting with all its strength to stay afloat in a strange new world, while practically everyone else is having a joyride fine tuning American ad design circa 1965-75. The basic point of this show is that while no one is 100% right, neither is anyone 100% wrong. Design today is whatever you say it is.

This lack of uniformity is in itself not especially noteworthy; its been building up ever since the late 1970's. The Creativity Annuals of the last five years have each commented on this development.

What is new about this show is now the total uncoupling of design trends. It's one thing to see an art director here or there starting to lead his own parade, even if these are parades of only one. It's quite another situation to realize that that's exactly what every art director and designer is doing.

The result is total creativity or no creativity. It depends on your point of view. It's not easily understandable. Many clients are actually angry and feel they are being betrayed. It's really bizarre. While art directors are going far beyond the call of duty to satisfy their responsibilities to their clients, these same clients are beating them over the heads for coming up with trash. What an odd and eerie coincidence that New York in late 1982 put on a theatrical production of "Alice in Wonderland," with the queen screaming, of course, "Off with their heads."

As readers of Creativity Annuals know, we also chart each year's visual developments by design cateogry. Here is this year's analysis:

CONSUMER ADS As in illustration—although rarely used here—this category was people oriented. There was a very strong effort by clients to identify their audiences. The consumer campaigns were exceptionally strong all the way from fractionals to spreads. The photography was, of course, excellent.

TV COMMERCIALS It's a commentary of sorts that there was, in the main, less humor this year, and more uncluttered, straight forward product use in commercials. The romance with computer animation is, however, the big story.

BROCHURES, as always, were tremendous. However, for the first time in years, it appears improvement has not been as marked. After all, this discipline has racked up spectacular gains year after year—and it's just not possible to maintain that kind of improvement forever.

POSTERS, for the third year running, continue to improve, not only here, but around the world. Lots of 4-color. Although they've become stronger, there is, strangely enough, a marked increased of art/illustration and a falling off of photography.

TRADE ADS are extremely strong. They work very hard, and successfully, for high visibility and identity. They are direct, clear, simple. Perhaps due to the recession, there is a very definite shift away from 4-color to b/w. The slow change in emphasis from photography to illustration of the recent past is still evident.

ANNUAL REPORTS had a tremendous year. Companies continued the progression of the last few years toward meeting their boasts. Excellent use of type was utilized to aid readership; a wide selection of typefaces, sizes, widths and leading made a favorable impression. The excellent photography of plants, equipment and products was a plus, and b/w shots of employees continue to increase.

COVERS/BOOK JACKETS was another category that moved away from formula solutions and toward individual treatments. While this may not be true for the entire book field, it was for the entries we received. Record albums, now a small cateogry, suddenly turned around this year with a surprising number of very well art directed pieces. There was a slight improvement in magazine covers, although they're now taking on a TV graphic look.

TRADEMARKS/LOGOTYPES The trend toward illustrative corporate symbols, which seemed only tentative a year ago, blossomed. There is now a definite swing away from type as an identifying factor. Interest is developing not only for illustration, but also for color. Also noteworthy is that type is being spaced out. What a development for a design category once known for compacting type!

LETTERHEADS were spectacular. The use of color, color stocks, the handling and selection of type and overall design achieved outstanding results for both client and designer. Quality was everywhere. Overseas, the usual verve toned down a bit and, if anything, marked an improvement.

PACKAGING had an up year. Here is a design category that had been going downhill for 3 to 5 years. It really didn't have any place to go but up, and it did that with a pronounced use of color, and a real effort to achieve originality.

EDITORIAL DESIGN is now in its fourth year of improvement. Editorial art directors have definitely broken away from formula solutions, and are now relying on subject matter to determine their layouts. There's no question that publishers have increased their budgets.

TV GRAPHICS demonstrated another year of marked improvement. However, the really fine work is restricted to a few daring souls.

PUBLIC SERVICE The tough, hard-bitten quality observed in this category in the United States for years is now visible around the world.

SELF-PROMOTION, included for the first time, was a disappointment. Perhaps our expectations were too high, and we wondered if the design community realizes that much of what passes for self-promotion today is nothing more than a tearsheet from one of the vanity books.

PHOTOGRAPHY Let's face it, everyone seems to be imitating everyone else in the vanity books (see self-promotion). The work, while good, is beginning to look alike.

ILLUSTRATION continued its slow, slow progress toward a more competitive posture. Considering how little is actually being used, it's surprising how much is figure work, also experimental. One other development to note is in fashion—the work here is beginning to achieve an individuality that's been missing for decades.

TYPOGRAPHY was a surprise due to its quality. Exhibiting less of the extraordinary exuberance this medium has had for years, it is now settling down to much more discriminating and judicious treatments. It was a real pleasure to see so much good work here.

SUMMARY Two separate and different crosscurrents are beginning to emerge. While television is now dominating the entire design community, it is also true that the highly individualized art directing today is beginning to guide the various design categories into distinct style preferences. Letterheads, for example, are now approaching quality standards that disappeared in the late 1960's. This Annual may mark the start of this new—and exciting—development in advertising design.

650
Richard Haymes Designer
Eric Sutherland Photographer
Richard Haymes & Co. Studio
Leo Castelli Gallery Client
New York NY

BOOKS

WHO'S ON FIRST
Some novelists get it right the first time.

BY WILLIAM PLUMMER

This is about first novels, a subject at once dear and of sore concern to the publishing industry. The simple fact is, first novels don't sell. What with library sales being depressed, the publisher today is lucky if he makes back his advance—not that said advance is any great shakes (most first novels can be had for between $4,000 and $10,000, unless the book is especially commercial or has extra textular appeal). But given that it now costs somewhere around $90,000 just to bring out a book, a well-turned story by a Writer of Promise that will doubtless do no more than 6,000 copies is a risk. Naturally, such sluggards are expected to be carried by more lissome fare with titles like *The Preppy Solution to Rubik's Cube*. Still, even those houses known for their friendliness to first novels (say, Random House) publish no more than half a dozen a year.

The lot of first novels considered in 1981 for The American Book Awards did include fiction by several authors with extra textular appeal. There were books by Jan Kerouac, the illegitimate daughter of the King of the Beats; by comedienne Fannie Flagg; by Tabitha King, wife of Stephen; by Tom McDonough, who shot the Academy Award-winning *Best Boy*, and by Tracy Hotchner, who scripted *Mommie Dearest;* by N.A. Straight, who claims Gore Vidal and Louis Auchincloss as kin, and by Robb Foreman Dew, related to John Crowe Ransom and Robert Penn Warren; by Joyce Maynard, who in 1972 wrote the epochal *Sunday New York Times* piece, "An 18-Year-Old Looks Back on Life"; by celebrated short-story writer Leonard Michaels and by noted poet Dave Smith; and by one Robert Herring, who evidently tricked out his own flap copy: "Like most first novelists, ROBERT HERRING is the son of a Baptist minister, has poured concrete in Missouri, sold mattresses door-to-door in Mississippi, desk-clerked and done construction work in Arkansas, been a guide in the Black Mountains of North Carolina, played piano and trumpet in a jazz band, and taught at various colleges...."

Write about what you know best is the first tenet of first-novel writing. A goodly number of these books are about failed marital unions, messy divorces and putting one's own Humpty Dumpty together again—many of these presumably written by veterans of today's most popular rite of passage (e.g., Benjamin Barber's *Marriage Voices* bio says that "He shares custody of his two children, Jeremy and Rebecca, and lives in New York City, where he was born in 1939"). Several others are about the New West, about strip-mining and riding the range in a Willys. In *Women's Work* Antonia Tolstoi Wallach, a New York City ad agency v.p., rehearses the trials of a female copywriter faced with Madison Avenue macho. Midwife Gay Courter has written a book called *The Midwife*, and psychiatrist Paul Buttenweiser a likable one titled *Free Association*. But, then, Celia Gittelson's *Saving Grace* is about a pope on the lam from the Vatican, and Sally George's *Frog Salad* features a young lady who aspires to grow a penis. One assumes these two books are imaginative constructs.

Clichés, of course, are not lies but truths with fallen arches; many clichés about the difference between male and female authors are given new support by this lot of

In Robert Olen Butler's *The Alleys of Eden* are "young women moving with absolute grace... the silk of their black pantaloons shining like the flanks of sea mammals."

ILLUSTRATED BY VIVIENNE FLESHER

William Plummer, who regularly reviews books for us, judged first novels for The American Book Awards.

STONEHENGE

1982
FEBRUARY
MARCH

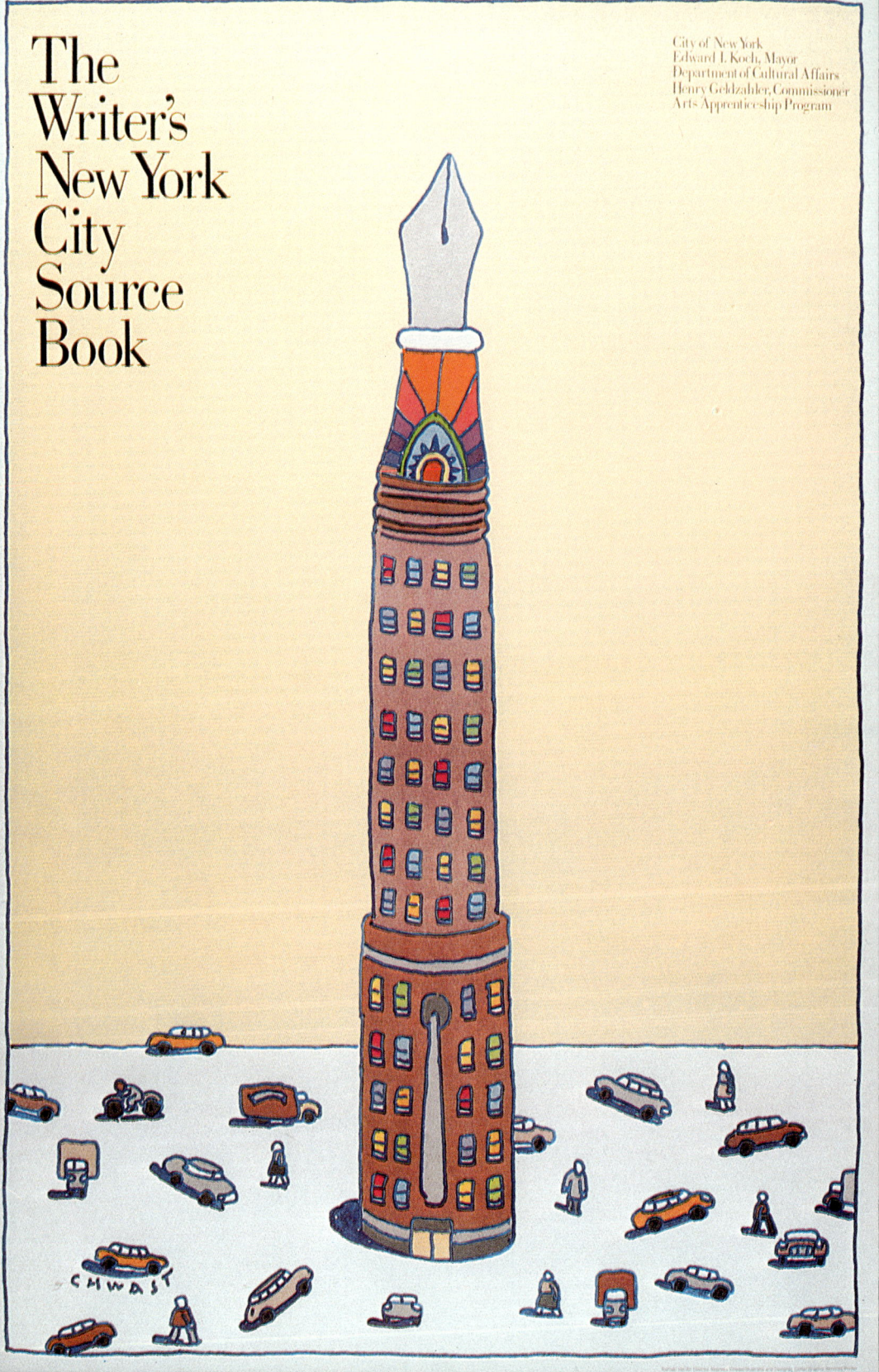

CREATIVE NEWSPAPER
1 9 8 2

CALL FOR ENTRIES

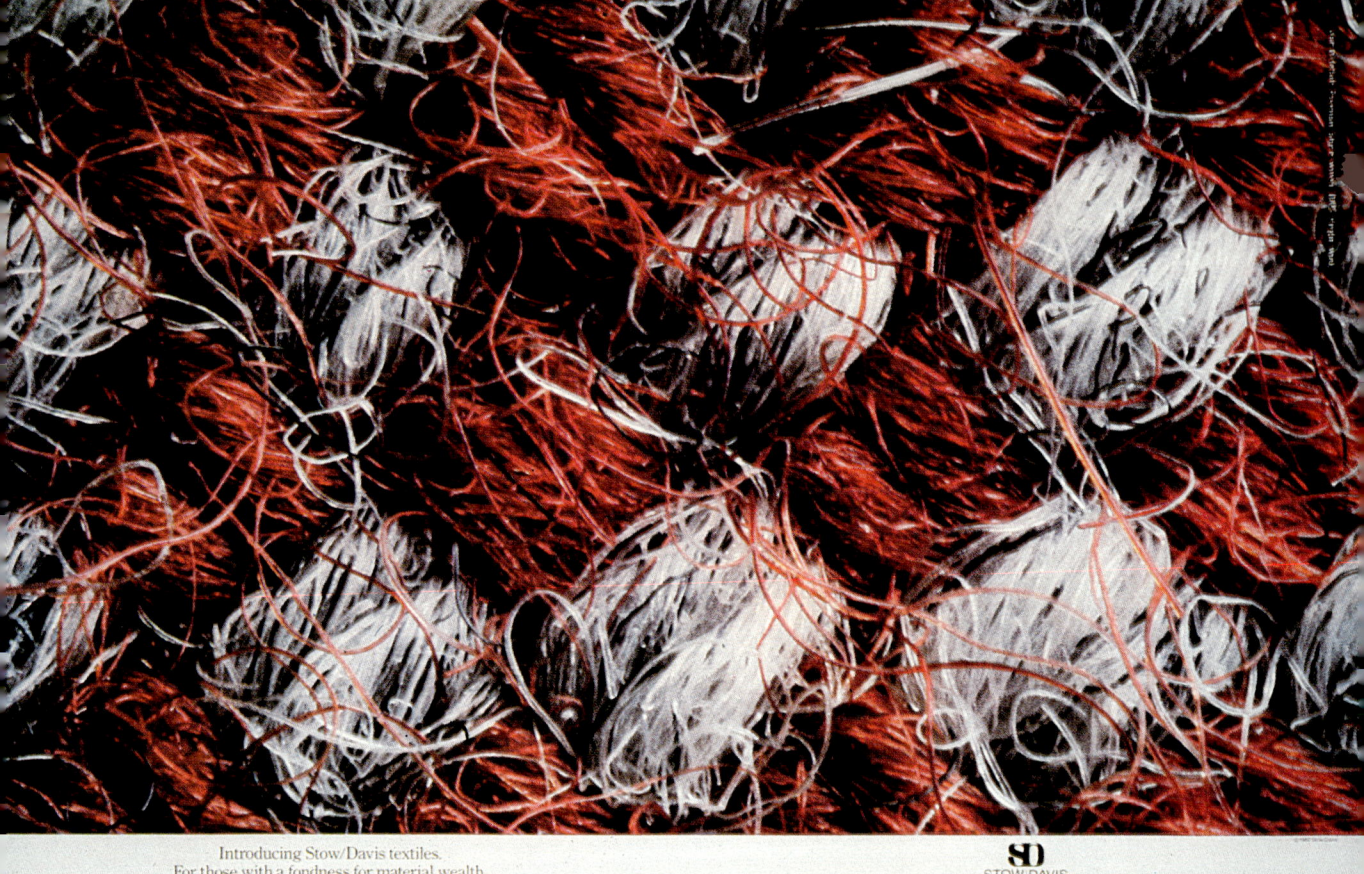

Introducing Stow/Davis textiles.
For those with a fondness for material wealth.

STOW DAVIS

THE NEW KNITS.

They play to your sense of touch. Your love of movement. Your eye for color.

Ingora,® Kashmirri® and Llamette® by Initial Trends blend beautifully with the way you want to live today.

On your body, they feel like the most comfortable fabrics in the world. In your busy life, they offer luxury in combination with the easiest care possible. And, for your sense of style, they present a panorama of fresh new looks that play with your sense of touch, your feel for fabric, your delight in color.

Ingora, Kashmirri, and Llamette were created from yarns spun by Carolina Mills, among the most innovative companies in the industry for over 50 years. They're all blends of Trevira,® the luxurious polyester fiber that insures the durability, versatility, and practicality you must have today.

Look for the Ingora, Kashmirri, and Llamette hang tags when you're in the stores. They're going to be on your favorite fashions this season.

Carolina Mills, 111 West 40 Street, New York, NY 10018.

Initial Trends, 469 7th Avenue, New York, NY 10018.

For further information, write or call Hoechst Fibers Industries, 1515 Broadway, New York, NY 10036 (212) 869-1930.

KASHMIRRI Kashmirri has all the fabled qualities its name suggests. It has the sensuous hand of cashmere, while its sumptuous look gives it a luxury of its own. And because Kashmirri is a blend of Trevira® polyester and rayon, it has the versatility you need today. The hand wash it and it will retain its wonderful color and soft feel. Kashmirri. The exotic look of cashmere with a practical touch.

LLAMETTE Wooly, superssoft, and hairy textured, Llamette is a luxury blend of 85% Trevira® polyester with 15% misansimante rayon. It's a fabulous fabric that keeps inviting you to touch it. Machine wash it as often as you like and it will keep its rich, vibrant color. Llamette. New wooly is even more wonderful.

*M*orning, a quiet escape from the turbulence of the night and the enchantment of the day now begins. A desirable time for a carefree rekindling of spirit and flesh.

*T*he pleasurable assets of leisure and luxury are sweet rewards and privileges of an affluent life style. You have cultivated a taste for things elegantly comfortable but not pretentious or stuffy.

Tranquil diversions at poolside. Warm friendly skies above. Cool ways to stay refreshed and healthy. Privacy with peace of mind. That special feeling of comfort and ease.

"all palm trees shade all but the gentlest rays and temper all winds to a whisper. Magic hours set aside for relaxation and well-chilled drinks in the cheerful Palm Springs sunshine.

Kein Platz für Bakterien.

In einer Badewanne von Kaldewei ist viel Platz für Erwachsene und Kinder. Aber kein Platz für Bakterien.

Das liegt am Material. Denn alle Badewannen und Brausewannen von Kaldewei sind aus Stahl-Email. Und Stahl-Email ist hart gegen alles, was die Wanne strapazieren könnte.

Für die Bakterien bedeutet das, daß ihnen die Oberfläche, die kinderleicht zu reinigen ist, so gut wie keine Angriffsmöglichkeit bietet. Viele bakteriologische Untersuchungen haben bestätigt, daß Stahl-Email im Gegensatz zu Acryl-Kunststoff an der Spitze der Hygieneskala steht.

Und da Badewannen oder Brausewannen nun mal das Hygienezentrum des Haushalts sind, sollte man auch besonderen Wert darauf legen, daß sie die besten hygienischen Eigenschaften besitzen.

Damit auch ihre Pflege ein Kinderspiel ist.

KALDEWEI
Europas Nr. 1 in Badewannen

Fordern Sie den Prospekt „Baden in neuen Farben und Formen" an bei: Kaldewei, Postfach 480, 4730 Ahlen.

Parlez-vous linoleum? Cabaret table tops come in 7 color choices of linoleum. If there's a better material for table top surfaces, we haven't found it or heard about it. Linoleum is a completely natural product that is liquid repellant, antibacterial and easy to clean. So let them eat cake. Or wine or coffee or a gooey fudge sundae and don't worry if they spill it.

Cabaret tables are available in two diameters, 24 inch and 36 inch. Table height is 28 inches. Stand-up versions in the same diameters are also available with a table height of 44 inches. Table frames are laminated beech finished with two coats of acid-hardened lacquer.

Vive le cabaret. *Vive le* Cabaret Tables.

Cabaret Table (24" diam.) with three legs—MO8060
Cabaret Table (24" diam.) with four legs—MO8070
Cabaret Table (36" diam.) with four legs—MO8090

Rudd International 1066 31st Street, N.W. Washington, D.C. 20007, (202) 333-5600

Designed By Rud Thygesen and Johnny Sørensen

205
James Hellmuth Art Director
Mark Greenspun Copywriter
Don Sparks Photography Photographer
Rudd International Client
Atlanta GA

643
Robin Ward Designer
BBC Enterprises Client
London, England

352
Laurie Rosenwald Designer
Bloomingdale's Client
New York NY

Je schräger, desto besser, sagte sich Herr Bach und nahm die Zwillinge.

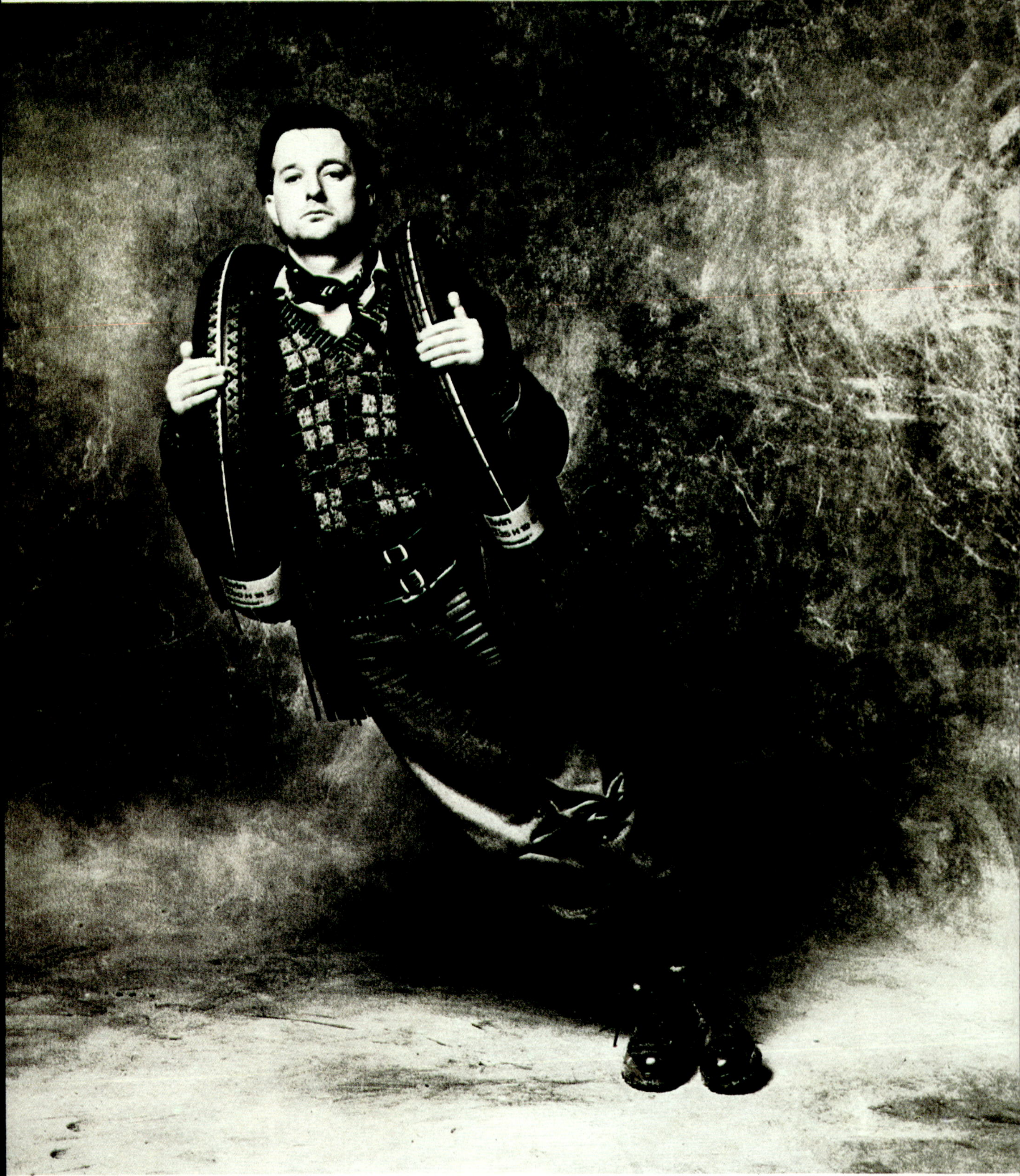

Wer in Kurven gerne besonders schräg liegt und eine Maschine mit 180 Spitze fährt, sollte die Conti Zwillinge aufziehen (Ausführung – und S). Und zwar beide. Denn sie sind gemeinsam entwickelt und haargenau aufeinander abgestimmt worden. Zusammen auf das Motorrad montiert, sind sie für reichlich Schräglage zu haben: Vorne sorgen seitliche Profilblöcke für die notwendige Abstützung in Kurven. Hinten sorgt das Profil mit der soliden Mittelrille für gute Führung.

Continental

Randolph Nolte Art Director
Jan Michael Photographer
GGK/Germany Agency
Continental Tires West Germany Client
Hamburg, W. Germany

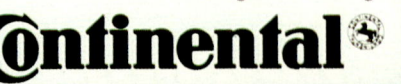

Je schräger, desto besser, sagte sich Herr Knop und nahm die neuen SuperTwin.

Wer, wie Herr Knop, ein neues Superbike sein eigen nennt, ist mit den neuen Conti SuperTwin besser bedient. Sie wurden (gemeinsam!) für Maschinen ab 180 km/h entwickelt (Bereich H und V). Folglich sollte man sie auch gemeinsam aufziehen, wenn man schnell und schräg durch die Kurven gehen will. Außen haben die neuen SuperTwin eine Fangrille. Daneben große, kräftige Profilblöcke. Damit auch in Schräglage die Kraft von 1000 ccm voll auf die Straße kommt.

WOODY HERMAN
FEELIN' SO BLUE

LOCATION

The world's great international cities have their special places: Zona Rosa, Fifth Avenue, Via Condotti, Mayfair, Rive Droit. Each personifies some element of city life: entertainment, living, shopping, dining, lodging.

In Houston three elements come together in one place: the Post Oak area. All the choices Houston has to offer are either here or they are coming here: world class hotels, the Galleria, international cuisine, couture shops, exclusive clubs, entertainment, corporate offices, fine residential neighborhoods.

Now, into this thoroughly urban setting, in the world's newest international city, comes the first truly international residence: Four-Leaf Towers.

A high-rise condominium community set in a quiet, private nine-acre park, Four-Leaf Towers promises to bring a classic style of living to Houston's expansive heart.

Designed by Cesar Pelli and developed by Interfin Corporation, Four-Leaf Towers will be available for occupancy early in 1982. Come, discover its world of choices.

FOUR-LEAF TOWERS

SECURITY

Safety and security are basic needs. And we should expect to have them met, particularly in our homes. This is why Four-Leaf Towers is engineered and built the way it is.

A high-rise condominium community in the heart of Houston, Four-Leaf Towers brings that international city a cosmopolitan style of living that is safe and secure. Its well-lighted grounds are protected by on-premise security patrol. A TV system monitors the entrances and the underground garage which is connected by the main lobbies by shuttle elevators that open in full view of each concierge.

Door keys to the residences cannot be duplicated, and each residence features an emergency call system. The twin, 40-story towers have smoke detectors, automatic sprinkler systems, and emergency power generators. Residences are separated from each other by 15" walls and from public spaces by 12" concrete walls.

Designed by Cesar Pelli, developed by Interfin Corporation, Four-Leaf Towers will be available for occupancy early in 1982. Come, discover the certainty of our world.

FOUR-LEAF TOWERS

LIFESTYLE

The style of living at Four-Leaf Towers begins when you enter the grounds of this formal, nine-acre, private park.

The gracious lifestyle created through carefully planned privacy and accessibility, extends through the richly decorated, wood paneled lobbies, to the doorway of each residence, and beyond, into the residences themselves. Living areas have been given maximum separation from the bedrooms which are well-contained, private suites, with their own bath and closet.

Each tower has forty high-speed passenger elevators and two service elevators. Public corridors are at a minimum. Service lobbies, elevators, and entries are apart from resident and guest areas. The twin, 40-story condominium towers are studies in personal accommodation.

Planned with international experience, designed by Cesar Pelli and developed by Interfin Corporation, Four-Leaf Towers will be available for occupancy early in 1982.

Come, discover this world of graciousness.

FOUR-LEAF TOWERS

LANDSCAPE

Cities offer choices. The more choices you have, the more appealing the setting.

This is why we located Four-Leaf Towers in the heart of Houston's Post Oak area. It is why we surrounded this classic high-rise condominium community with nine acres of greenspace. We wanted residents to be close to the best this city offers, but not too close.

Four-Leaf Towers is a park. It's formal and it's private, with gently rolling lawns, manicured evergreen shrubs, a sunken recreational plaza, and connecting walkways—all enclosed by rows of water oaks and brilliantly colored burgundy sweetgum trees.

From this green pedestal, the twin, 40-story towers rise like sculpture—a quiet, residential landmark on Houston's vigorous skyline.

Designed by Cesar Pelli, developed by Interfin Corporation, Four-Leaf Towers will be available for occupancy early in 1982.

Come, discover gentle urban living in a private park.

FOUR-LEAF TOWERS

811
Sue Coe Illustrator
Louise Kollenbaum Art Director
Dian-Aziza Ooka Designer
Mother Jones Magazine Client
San Francisco CA

8
Michele Leighton, Art Brewer Art Directors
Art Brewer Photographer
Amies and Associates Production House
Off Shore Sportswear Client
Dana Point CA

804
Andrew Holmes Illustrator
George Noordanus Art Director
Gerrit Serne Photographer
Cream Creative Services Studio
Ogilvy & Mather BV Agency
Shell Nederlands Verk, Mij. BV Client
Amsterdam, Holland

452
Richard Hess Art Director
Stuart I. Frolick Editor
Spectrum Composition Svcs. Studio
Champion International Client
New York NY

327
John Coy Art Director
Ardison Philips Artist
COY, Los Angeles Studio
Andrew Quady Vineyards Client
Culver City CA

377
Steve Sessions Art Director
Lee Lee Brazeal, Randy Rogers, Denise Chapman, Jerry Jeanmard Illustrators
Print Resources Client
Houston TX

129
Stephen Frykholm Art Director
Pam Van Dyken Typography
Continental Identification Products Production House
Tulip Time Festival Client

320
George Coderre Art Director
April Greiman Illustrator
Progressive Architecture Client
Stamford CT

636
Carl Mosander Art Director
Arto Hallakorpi Photographer
Seppo Holopainen, Carl Mosander Studio
Aapiset Oy Client
Helsini, Finland

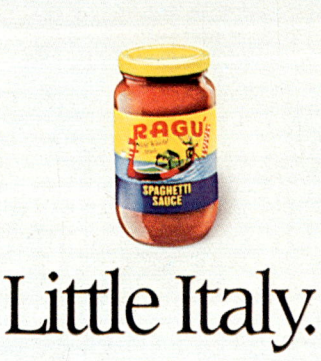

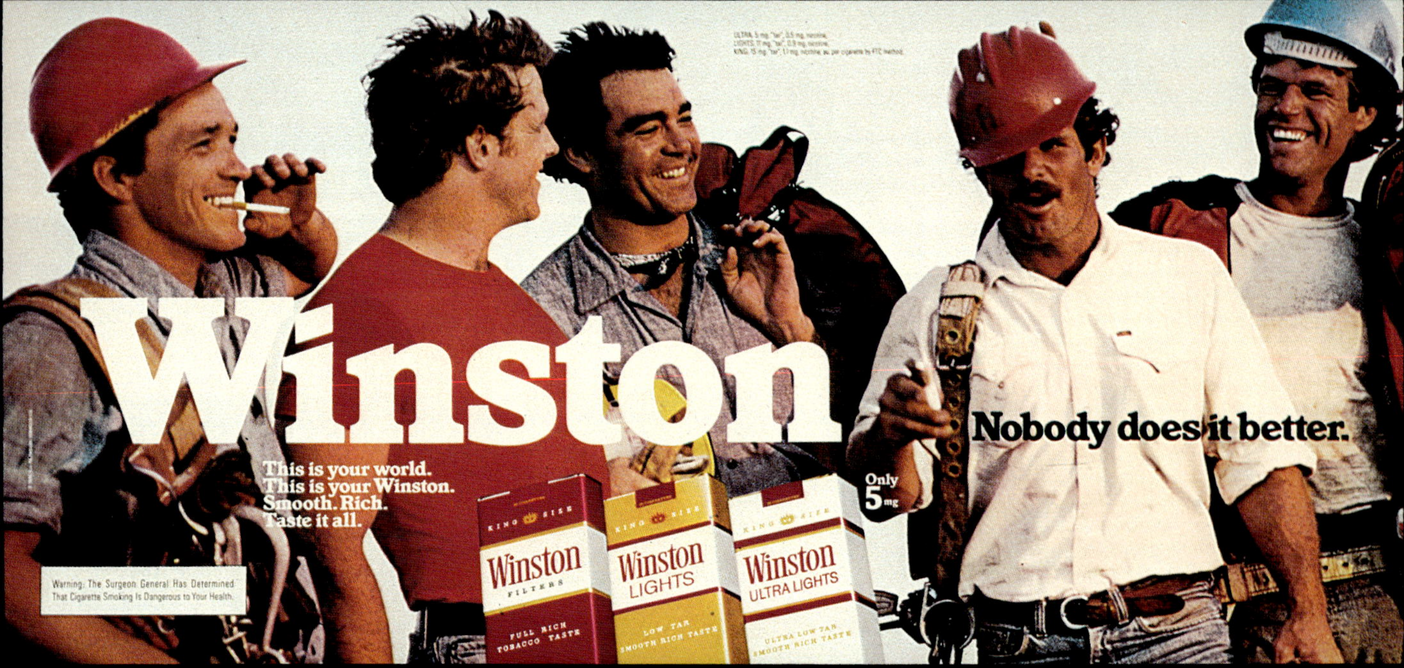
Winston
Nobody does it better.
This is your world.
This is your Winston.
Smooth. Rich.
Taste it all.
Only 5 mg
Warning: The Surgeon General Has Determined That Cigarette Smoking Is Dangerous to Your Health.
King Size
Winston
Filters
Full Rich Tobacco Taste
King Size
Winston
Lights
Low Tar Smooth Rich Taste
King Size
Winston
Ultra Lights
Ultra Low Tar Smooth Rich Taste

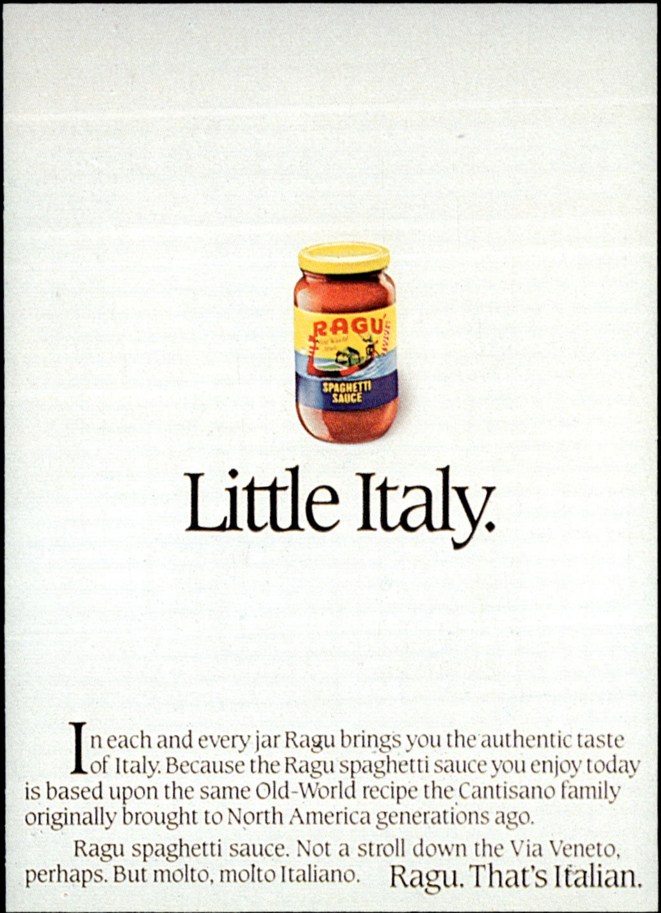
Ragu
Spaghetti Sauce
Little Italy.
In each and every jar Ragu brings you the authentic taste of Italy. Because the Ragu spaghetti sauce you enjoy today is based upon the same Old-World recipe the Cantisano family originally brought to North America generations ago.
Ragu spaghetti sauce. Not a stroll down the Via Veneto, perhaps. But molto, molto Italiano.
Ragu. That's Italian.

26
Emil Dispenza, Cyndi Rishko Art Directors
Bob Day Photographer
Mindy Rosengarten, David Burleigh Copywriters
William Esty Co., Inc. Agency
R.J. Reynolds Tobacco Co. Client
New York NY

25
Steve Thursby Art Director
Bob Hawton Writer
George Simhoni Photographer
F.H. Hayhurst Co. Ltd. Agency
Chesebrough-Pond's (Canada) Inc. Client
Toronto, Canada

PRINT Consumer SINGLE UNIT

1
Tom Devlin Art Director
Bob Higbee Copywriter
Charles Moretz Photographer
Lord, Geller, Federico, Einstein Agency
Hilton International Client
New York NY

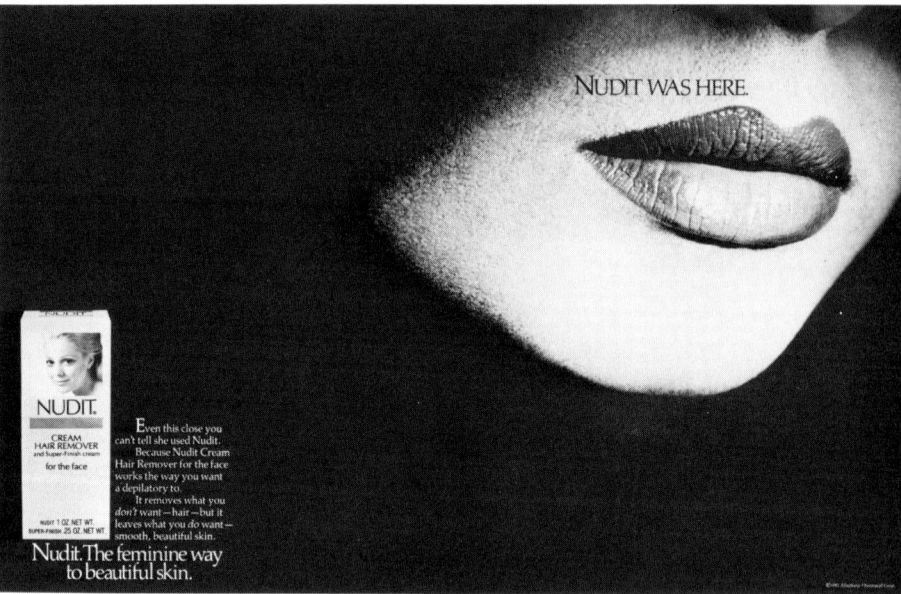

2
Len Favara Art Director
Peter Rogers Associates Agency
Donghia Client
New York NY

3
Harry De Zitter Photographer
Grey-Phillips, Bunton, Mundel & Blake Agency
Moor Life Client
Johannesburg, S. Africa

4
Richard Brown Art Director
James McLoughlin Photography Studio
Alleghany Pharmaceutical Corp. Client
New York NY

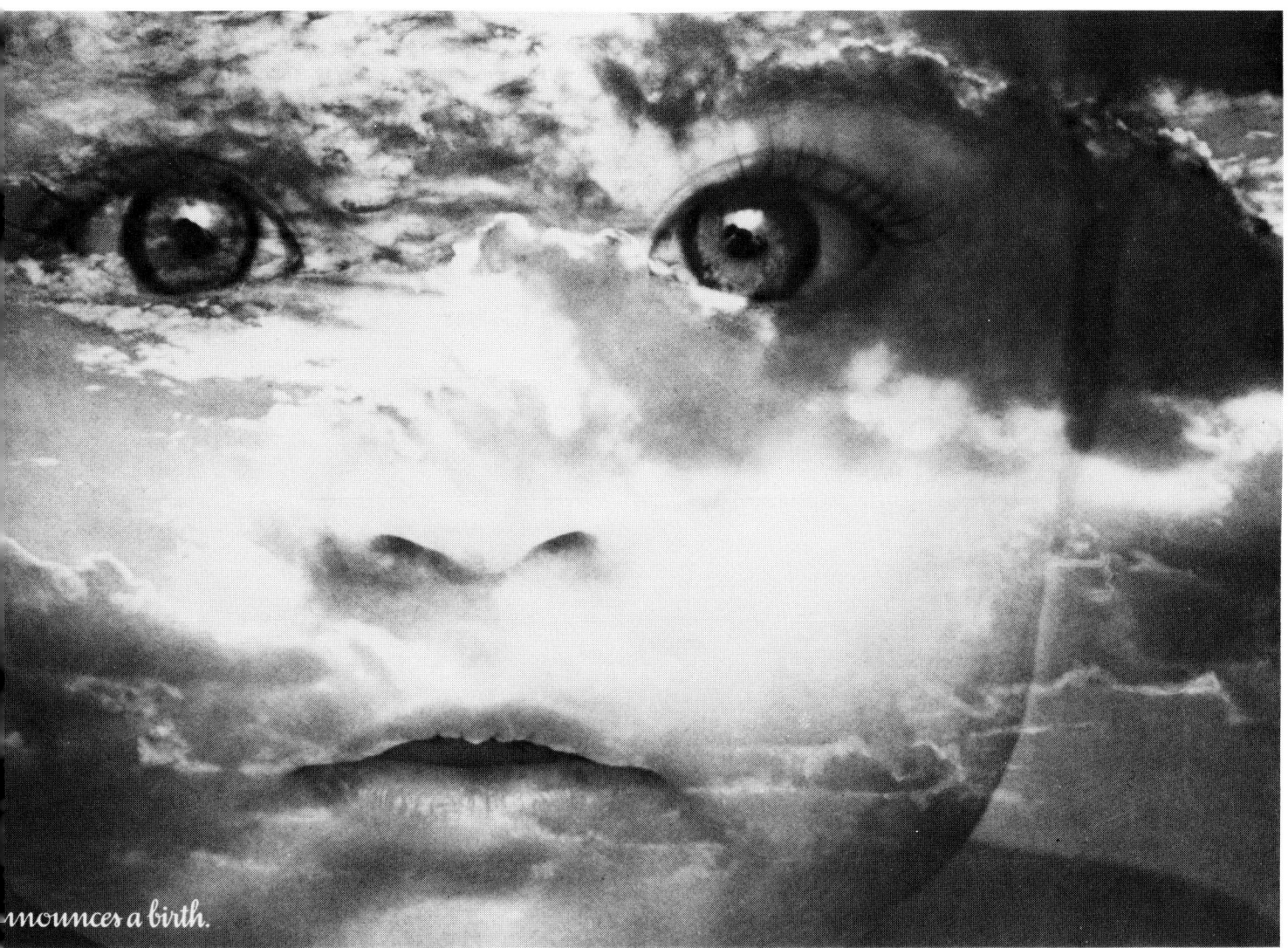

5
P.R. Christensen Art Director
Brown, Christensen & Assoc. Ltd./New
 Zealand Agency
American Express/Air New Zealand Client
Auckland, New Zealand

6
Matt Basile Art Director
Erica Ress Copywriter
Carl Fischer Photographer
Young & Rubicam Agency
Johnson & Johnson Client
New York NY

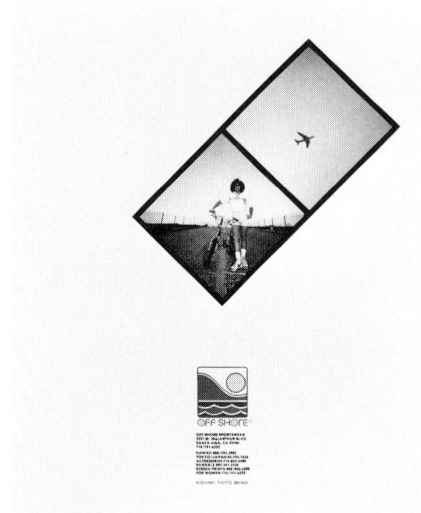

8

7
Glenn Scheuer Art Director
Lance Mald Copywriter
Gary A. Perweiler Photographer
BBD&O, Inc. Agency
General Electric Client
New York, NY

8
Michele Leighton, Art Brewer Art Directors
Art Brewer Photographer
Amies and Associates Production House
Off Shore Sportswear Client
Dana Point

9
Robin Sweet-Wyatt Creative Director
Andrea Blanch Photographer
JoAnn Wolf Copywriter
Olivetti Client
New York NY

10
David Wenman Art Director
Carol Wenman Copy Writer
Gordon Munro Photographer
David Wenman Associates Agency
St. Gillian Client
New York NY

11
Hans Goedicke Art Director
Reg Cartwright Illustrator
KVH/GGK International BV Agency
Brandsteder Electronics BV Client
Amsterdam, Holland

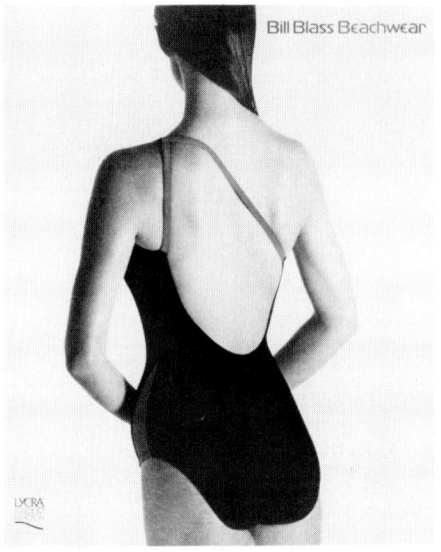
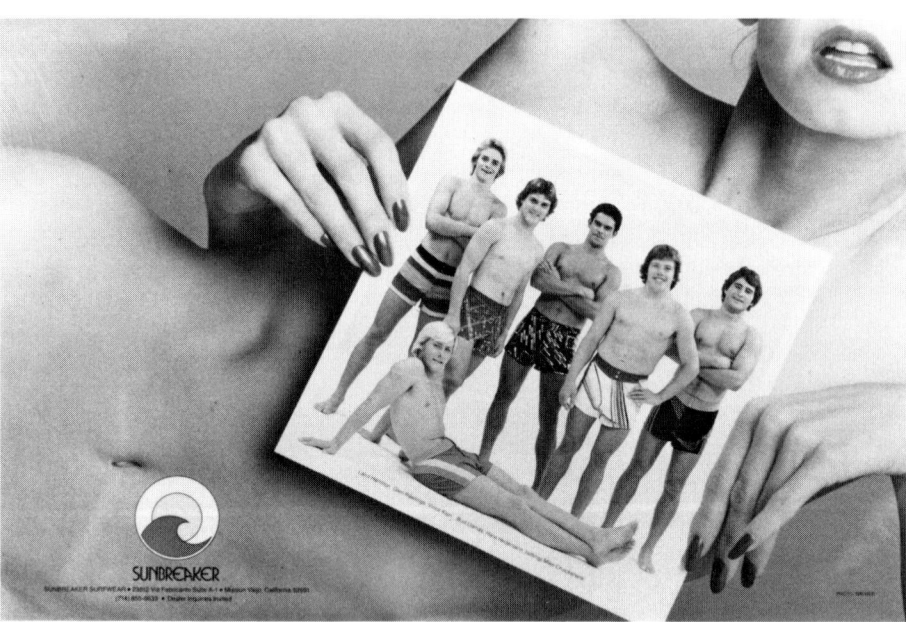

12
Raymond Lee Art Director
Yosh Inouye Photographer
Terry O'Conner Copywriter
Raymond Lee & Associates Agency
McGregor Hosiery Mills Client
Toronto, Canada

13
Len Favara Art Director
Gideon Lewin Photographer
Peter Rogers Associates Agency
Bill Blass Client
New York NY

14
Paul Randolph Haven Art Director
Art Brewer Photographer
Paul Haven Graphics Production House
Sunbreaker Surfwear Client
San Juan Capistrano CA

15
Charma Hawk-James Art Director
Carson Pirie Scott & Co. Client
Chicago, IL

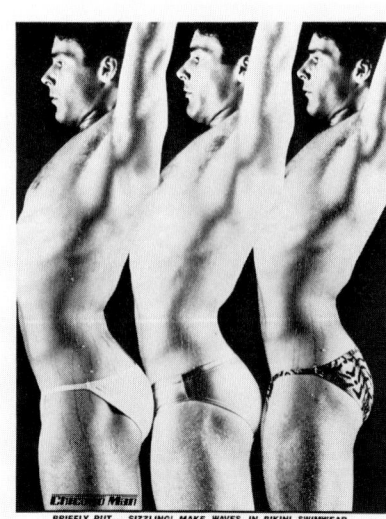

New Chairman of the City Deep Hockey Club, Ian Presley, confirmed that his voice cracked several times during his maiden speech to the club committee last week. "It's quite true," said an embarrassed Mr Presley in the clubhouse afterwards. "One of the guys recorded the proceedings on a Maxell UD cassette tape. They have a gamma ferric oxide formulation that gives them a terrific frequency response and dynamic range. Their performance is outstanding, which is more than you can say for mine. You can hear every crack and tremor in my voice just as it happened." Mr Presley suspects that being hit in the throat with a ball last season is the major cause of his problems. He would not confirm reports that he has been asked to resume his former duties as assistant groundsman.

IT'S ALL REVEALED IN THE MAXELL TAPES.

Maxell UD. C60 & C90 cassettes. Five-second head cleaner, five-second cue in line and lifetime warranty. Also available: Low Noise, Ultra Low Noise, XLIS, XLIIS, Metal and Reel to Reel.

DISTRIBUTED BY MAYFAIR SALES (PTY) LTD.
Trade Enquiries only: Jhb (011) 29-2921 CT (021) 51-8260
Dbn (031) 39-1245 Bloem (051) 8-2272 PE (041) 54-2951

FINE, GEFFEN, SIMKINS & MARRINGTON 5473/2

To make sure you're buying 100% Colombian Coffee, read the fine print.

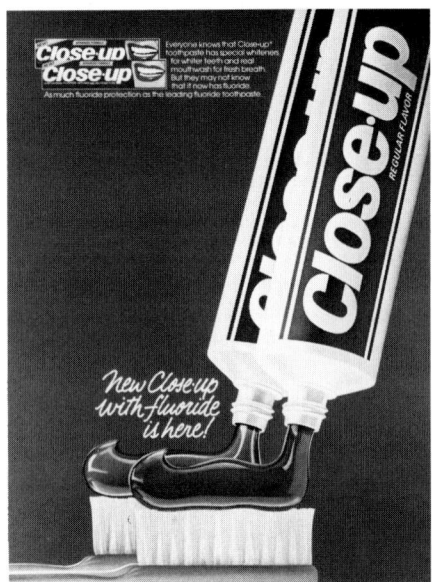
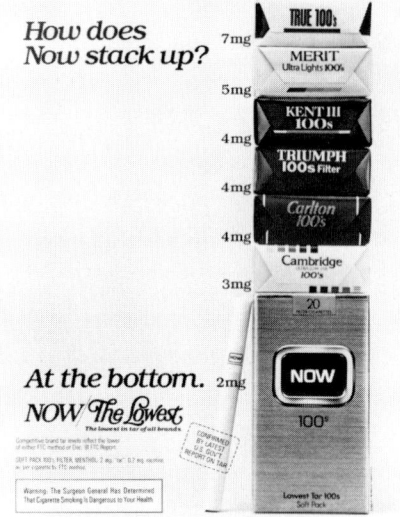

19

25
Steve Thursby Art Director
Bob Hawton Writer
George Simhoni Photographer
F.H. Hayhurst Co. Ltd. Agency
Chesebrough-Pond's (Canada) Inc. Client
Toronto, Canada

22
Corning Designs, Ltd. Designers
Lord, Geller, Federico & Einstein, Inc. Agency
Corning Designs, Ltd. Client
Clinton NJ

23
Danielle Roy Beaudoin Art Director
Jean Tremblay Photographer
Cabana, Seguin-Design Inc. Agency
Labatt Brewing Company Limited Client
Montreal, Canada

24
Omar Guedes Art Director
Jose Daloia Neto Photographer
J.D.N. Estudio de Fotografia S/C Ltda Studio
Volkswagen do Brasil S.A. Client
Sao Paulo, Brazil

19
Susan Rose Art Director
Gary Perweiler Photographer
J. Walter Thompson Agency
Lever Brothers Client
New York NY

20
Ric Cohn Photographer
Leber Katz Partners Agency
RJR-NOW Cigarettes Client
New York NY

21
John Paul Itta, Inc. Agency
Aer Lingus Client
New York NY

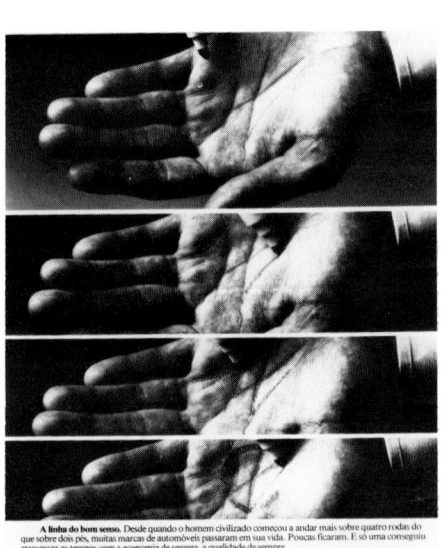

Little Italy.

In each and every jar Ragu brings you the authentic taste of Italy. Because the Ragu spaghetti sauce you enjoy today is based upon the same Old-World recipe the Cantisano family originally brought to North America generations ago.

Ragu spaghetti sauce. Not a stroll down the Via Veneto, perhaps. But molto, molto Italiano.   **Ragu. That's Italian.**

26
Emil Dispenza, Cyndi Rishko Art Directors
Bob Day Photographer
Mindy Rosengarten, David Burleigh Copywriters
William Esty Co., Inc. Agency
R.J. Reynolds Tobacco Co. Client
New York NY

27
Stanley Eisenman, Dennis Dollens Art Directors
John Pilgreen Photographer
Eisenman & Enock Inc. Agency
Susan Bennis/Warren Edwards Client
New York NY

28
Randolph Nolte Art Director
Jan Michael Photographer
GGK/Germany Agency
Continental Tires West Germany Client
Hamburg, W. Germany

30

32

33

30
Andy Edwards Art Director
Louis Koenders Illustrator
Harry deZitter Photographer
BBDO Marketing & Advertising Agency
Stellenbosch Farmers Winery Client
Johannesburg, S. Africa

31
Vickie Gillis Art Director
Steve Bronstein Photographer
Graham Turner Copywriter
TBWA Agency
Absolut Vodka Client
New York NY

32
Jorma Kosunen Art Director
MK, MarknadsKommunikation AB Agency
Pripps Brewery Client
Stockholm, Sweden

33
Stephen Sieler Art Director
John Kubly Photographer
Robert Miles Runyan & Assocs. Studio
Vuarnet, USA Client
Playa del Ray CA

Dobson's Cloth.
First, he made it for his son. Now he makes it for Southwick.

Hamish Dobson manages one of Scotland's finest woolen mills. Not a textile mill, mind you, a woolen mill. This is a man who believes that material without wool is immaterial. If you can imagine a man constructed entirely of tweed, there you have Hamish Dobson.

And had Hamish's son not been at least as stubborn as his father, Dobson's cloth might not exist today.

It all began one Sunday morning in July, when the lad outright refused to put on his jacket. "That jacket happens to be made of the finest wool in the world," roared Hamish, "and you *will* wear it."

"That jacket is too hot," his son fired back. "And *nobody* wears wool jackets in summer, dad. Except you."

"They don't?" The man was genuinely surprised. No one had told him.

"They don't," his son replied. "I'm sorry, Dad," he added.

"Well, they *will*." So Dobson went to work, determined to invent a woolen cloth that his son would find suitable, for even the warmest weather.

And, of course, he did.

Dobson's cloth: 50% silk, 30% wool, 20% linen. Now available to the world, in very attractive Shetland colors tailored in Southwick's classic natural-shoulder tradition, and very comfortable in summer.

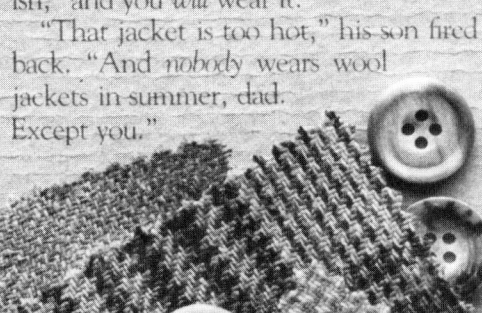

Southwick
A tradition among gentlemen.

For a list of the select stores in your area which carry on the Southwick tradition, write to: Southwick, 115 Newbury St., Boston, MA 02116.

37
Greengage Associates, Inc. Agency
United States Virgin Islands Client
New York NY

38
Jim Cox Art Director
Robert Stevens Photographer
Chiat Day Agency
Yamaha Motor Corp. Client
Los Angeles CA

39
Steven Lester Art Director
Wayne Wanner, Lisa Bell, Melanie Phillips Designers
Eddie Tapp Photographer
Turner Broadcasting Client
Atlanta GA

40
Dan Hackett, Jurij Brezden Art Directors
Bob Tyrrell Illustrator
W.B. Doner & Co. Advertising Agency
Giant Eagle Client
Southfield MI

41
Al Satterwhite Photographer
United States Post Office Client
New York NY

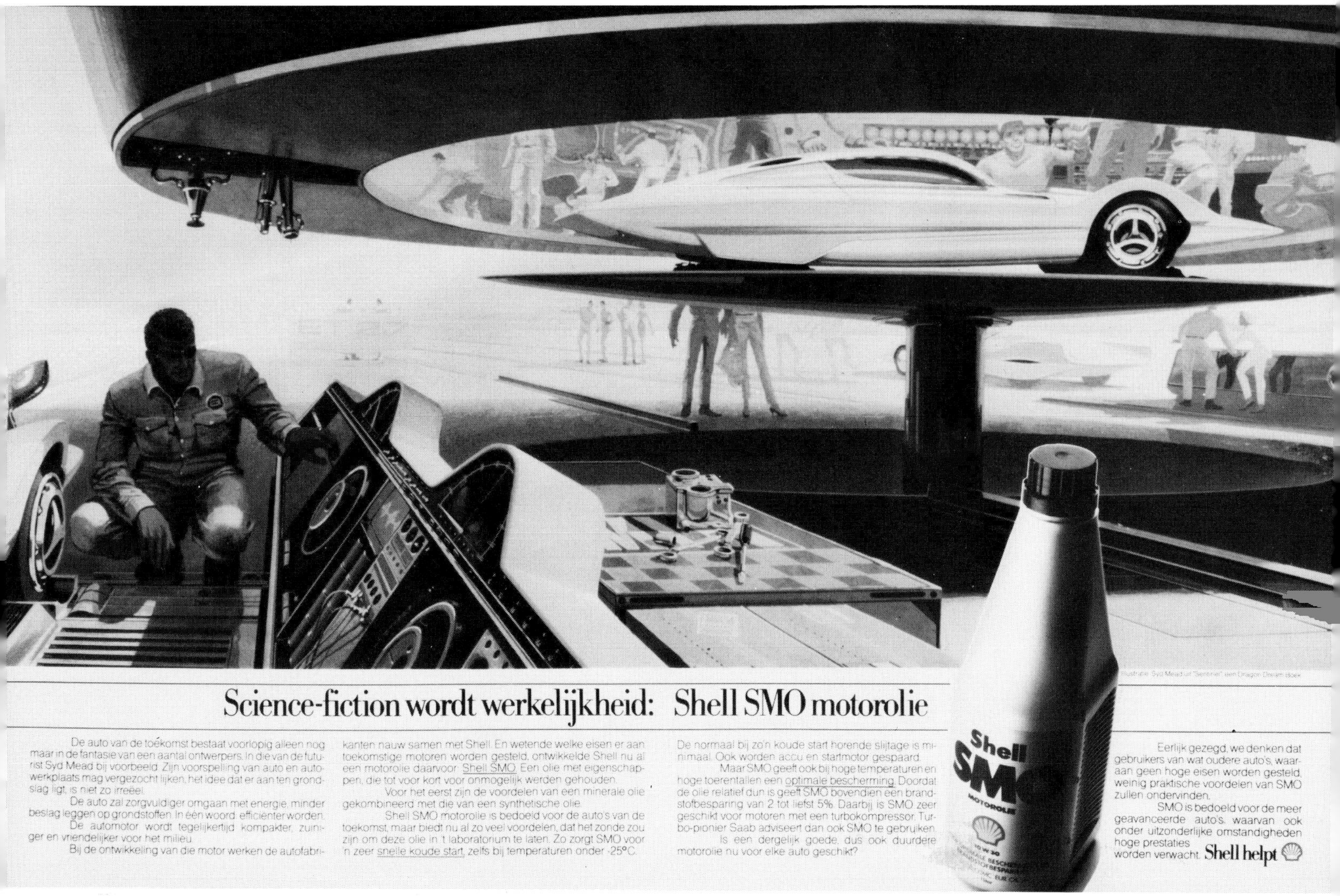
Science-fiction wordt werkelijkheid: Shell SMO motorolie
De auto van de toekomst bestaat voorlopig alleen nog maar in de fantasie van een aantal ontwerpers. In die van de futurist Syd Mead bij voorbeeld. Zijn voorspelling van auto en autowerkplaats mag vergezocht lijken, het idee dat er aan ten grondslag ligt, is niet zo irreëel.
De auto zal zorgvuldiger omgaan met energie, minder beslag leggen op grondstoffen. In één woord: efficiënter worden.
De automotor wordt tegelijkertijd kompakter, zuiniger en vriendelijker voor het milieu.
Bij de ontwikkeling van die motor werken de autofabrikanten nauw samen met Shell. En wetende welke eisen er aan toekomstige motoren worden gesteld, ontwikkelde Shell nu al een motorolie daarvoor: Shell SMO. Een olie met eigenschappen, die tot voor kort voor onmogelijk werden gehouden.
Voor het eerst zijn de voordelen van een minerale olie gekombineerd met die van een synthetische olie.
Shell SMO motorolie is bedoeld voor de auto's van de toekomst, maar biedt nu al zo veel voordelen, dat het zonde zou zijn om deze olie in 't laboratorium te laten. Zo zorgt SMO voor 'n zeer snelle koude start, zelfs bij temperaturen onder -25°C.
De normaal bij zo'n koude start horende slijtage is minimaal. Ook worden accu en startmotor gespaard.
Maar SMO geeft ook bij hoge temperaturen en hoge toerentallen een optimale bescherming. Doordat de olie relatief dun is geeft SMO bovendien een brandstofbesparing van 2 tot liefst 5%. Daarbij is SMO zeer geschikt voor motoren met een turbokompressor. Turbo-pionier Saab adviseert dan ook SMO te gebruiken.
Is een dergelijk goede, dus ook duurdere motorolie nu voor elke auto geschikt?
Eerlijk gezegd, we denken dat gebruikers van wat oudere auto's, waaraan geen hoge eisen worden gesteld, weinig praktische voordelen van SMO zullen ondervinden.
SMO is bedoeld voor de meer geavanceerde auto's, waarvan ook onder uitzonderlijke omstandigheden hoge prestaties worden verwacht.
Shell helpt
Shell
SMO
MOTOROLIE

603
601
CUOIO
cuoio

PASSAT
MASCULINO
SÃO BERNARDO DO CAMPO - SP
VOLKSWAGEN
PASSAPORTE
CONTROLE
Cidadão do mundo.
O Passat, graças à sua alta tecnologia, é o carro que tem o passaporte mais ativo do Brasil, pois no seu visto de saída você vai encontrar mais de 40 países.
E esse sucesso é a comprovação de que o Passat brasileiro reúne soluções técnicas e de estilo como nenhum outro carro de sua classe.
Agora, com o Passat 82, essa preferência por tanta gente lá fora só tende a aumentar, uma vez que ele chega com diversas inovações, próprias para um carro que sempre foi considerado o mais avançado do Brasil, como o novo acabamento de maior luxo nas versões TS e LSE e opcionalmente na versão LS.
Outra novidade é que a Linha Passat 82 não necessitará mais de troca de óleo na transmissão.
Conheça essas e outras inovações da Linha Passat 82 dando uma chegadinha ao Concessionário Volkswagen.
Aproveite as facilidades de compra através do financiamento, leasing ou arrendamento e consórcio para conseguir na hora o seu "visto de saída" para embarcar nesse "Cidadão do Mundo", seja a álcool ou a gasolina.
PASSAT

42
Bart Kuiper Art Director
Ogilvy & Mather BV Agency
Shell Nederlandse Verk. Mij. BV Client
Amsterdam, Holland

43
Mark Kent Art Director
Al Fisher Photographer
Banks & Company Studio
Cuoio Client
Boston MA

44
Deilon Gomes de Lima Art Director
Ramon Chust Photographer
Alcantara Machado, Periscinoto Comunicacoes Ltda. Agency
Volkswagen do Brasil S.A. Client
Sao Paulo, Brazil

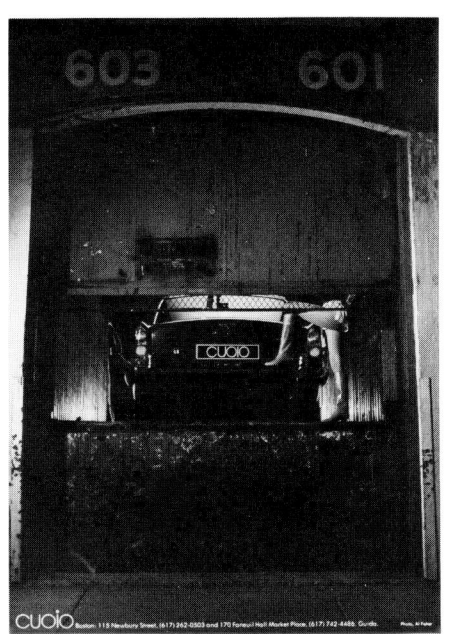

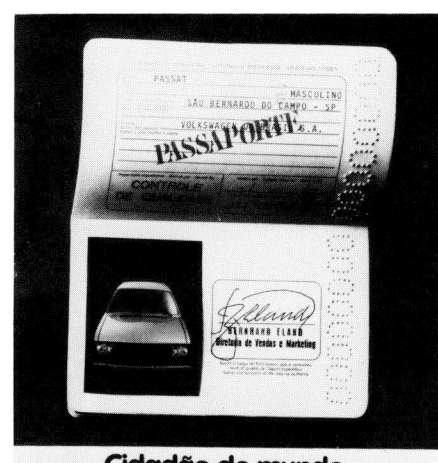

45
Jorma Kosunen Art Director
MK, MarknadsKommunikation AB Agency
Pripps Brewery Client
Stockholm, Sweden

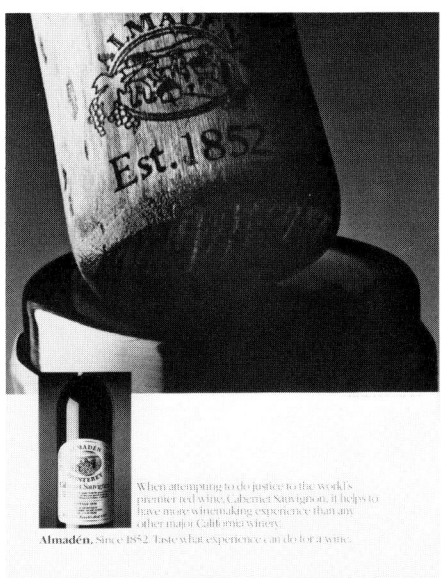

46
Arnold Wicht Art Director
Ron Hills Illustrator
Tony Bliss, Jim Charbonneau, Bill McLeod, Karl Sliva Photographers
Tim Heintzman Copywriter
J & J Typography Production House
Camp Assocs. Advertising Ltd. Agency
Ministry of Tourism & Recreation Province of Ontario Client
Toronto, Canada

47
Tom Freyer Art Director
Gerald Zanetti Photographer
Dan Goldstein Copywriter
Joan Levine Creative Director
Dancer Fitzgerald Sample, Inc. Agency
Almaden Vineyards Client
San Francisco CA

48
Andrew Vuchinich Art Director
Alred Eisenstaedt, Dick Durrance Photographers
Todd Congdon Copywriter
Young & Rubicam Agency
Old Grand Dad Client
New York NY

49
Darrell Wilks Art Director
George I. Parrish, Jr. Illustrator
Larry Volpi Copywriter
J. Walter Thompson Company Agency
Samsonite Client
New York NY

50
Geoffrey Hayes Art Director
Frank Farrelly Photographer
Jim Flaherty Copywriter
TBWA Agency
Bombay Gin Client
New York NY

51
Bernie Fuchs Illustrator
Benton & Bowles Agency
AMF Client
New York NY

52
Hans Goedicke Art Director
Colin Meir Illustrator
KVH/GGK International BV Agency
Dutch Railways Client
Amsterdam, Holland

53
Grey-Phillips, Bunton, Mundel & Blake Agency
La Baguette Bakery Client
Johannesburg, S. Africa

54
John Porter Art Director
Jim Marvy Photographer
Frye-Sills Inc. Agency
American Lamb Council Client
Englewood CO

55
Larry Smith Art Director
Rich Maender Writer
Arthur Beck Photographer
McDonald & Little Agency
The Coca Cola Company Client
Atlanta GA

56
Susan Lloyd Art Director
Bruce Bloch Creative Director
Ulf Skogsbergh Photographer
Patty Rockmore Creative Director/Copy
A C & R Advertising Agency
Ron Chereskin Client
New York NY

"Stripes Descending a Shirt" by Ron Chereskin, August 1981

"Homage to Plaid" by Ron Chereskin, December 1981

"Union of One Part with Another" by Ron Chereskin, April 1982

57
Shelley Heller, Enza Mullen Art Directors
Rainer Laubach Illustrator
McNamara Studio Studio
Grey Advertising Agency
B.F. Goodrich Client
New York NY

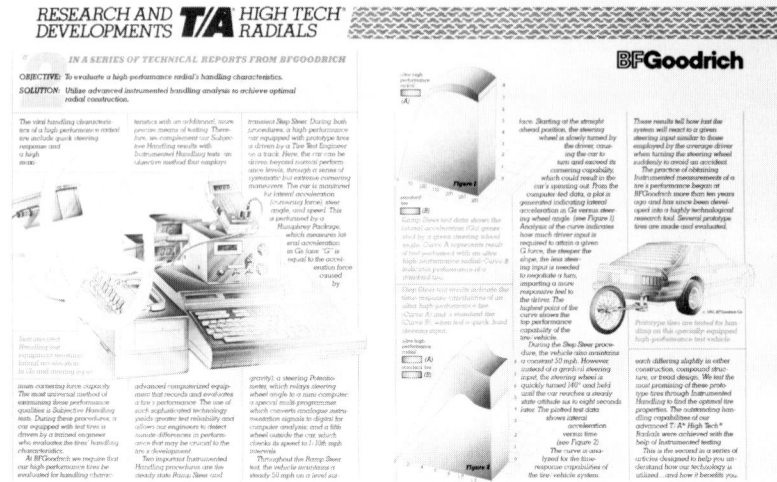

58
Jill Wilkerson Art Director
Wilkerson Advertising Agency
Roland Corporation Client
Beverly Hills CA

59
Jorma Kosunen Art Director
MK, MarksnadsKommunikation AB Agency
National Panasonic Svenska AB Client
Stockholm, Sweden

60
Regina Ovesey Creative Director
Frank Young Designer
Lois Greenfield Photographer
Ovesey & Company, Inc. Agency
Capezio Ballet Makers, Inc. Client
New York NY

CREATE A STAR

Capezio
Capezio

A STAR IN CAPEZIO

STAR
STAR
STAR
STAR

STAR

61
Ina Kahn Art Director
Victor Liebert Designer
Ryszard Horowitz Photographer
Hoechst Fibers Industries Client
New York NY

62
Steven Sessions Art Director
James McMullan, Milton Glaser, John Collier, Charles Schorre, John Hylton Illustrators
Four Leaf Towers Client
Houston TX

LOCATION

The world's great international cities have their special places: Zona Rosa, Fifth Avenue, Via Condotti, Mayfair, Rive Droit. Each personifies some element of city life: entertainment, living, shopping, dining, lodging.

In Houston these elements come together in one place: the Post Oak area. All the choices Houston has to offer are either here or they are coming here: world class hotels, the Galleria, international cuisine, couture shops, exclusive clubs, entertainment, corporate offices, fine residential neighborhoods.

Now, into this thoroughly urban setting, in the world's newest international city, comes the first truly international residence: Four-Leaf Towers.

A high-rise condominium community set in a quiet, private nine-acre park, Four-Leaf Towers promises to bring a classic style of living to Houston's expressive heart.

Designed by Cesar Pelli and developed by Intertin Corporation, Four-Leaf Towers will be available for occupancy early in 1982. Come discover its world of choices.

FOUR-LEAF TOWERS

SECURITY

Safety and security are basic needs. And we should expect to have them met, particularly in our homes. This is why Four-Leaf Towers is engineered and built the way it is.

A high-rise condominium community in the heart of Houston, Four-Leaf Towers brings this international city a classic style of living that is safe and secure. Its well-lighted grounds are protected by on-premise security patrol. A TV system monitors the interiors and the underground garage which is connected to the main lobbies by shuttle elevators that open in full view of each concierge.

Door keys to the residences cannot be duplicated, and each residence features an emergency call system. The twin, 40-story towers have smoke detectors, extensive sprinkler systems, and emergency power generators. Residences are separated from each other by 18" walls and from public spaces by 12" concrete walls.

Designed by Cesar Pelli, developed by Intertin Corporation, Four-Leaf Towers will be available for occupancy early in 1982.

Come, discover the certainty of our world.

FOUR-LEAF TOWERS

LANDSCAPE

Cities offer choices. The more choices you have, the more appealing the setting.

This is why we located Four-Leaf Towers in the heart of Houston's Post Oak area. It is why we surrounded this classic high-rise condominium community with nine acres of greenspace. We wanted residents to be close to the best this city offers, but not too close.

Four-Leaf Towers is a park. It's formal and it's private, with gently rolling lawns, manicured evergreen shrubs, a sunken recreational plaza, and connecting walkways—all enclosed by rows of water oaks and brilliantly colored burgundy sweetgum trees.

From this green pedestal, the twin, 40-story towers rise like sculpture—a quiet, residential landmark on Houston's vigorous skyline.

Designed by Cesar Pelli, developed by Intertin Corporation, Four-Leaf Towers will be available for occupancy early in 1982.

Come, discover gentle urban living in a private park.

FOUR-LEAF TOWERS

63
Bart Kuiper Art Director
Will v.d. Vlugt Photographer
Olgilvy & Mather BV Agency
Hols Donatin Krachtbrokken Client
Amsterdam, Holland

KRACHT GEEFT MACHT

WANDA DRUKT ZICH AL DRIE KEER OP

Wanda is een schat van een beest, we zijn thuis stapelgek op haar.

Maar er is één ding waar we niet tegen kunnen, Wanda is bang en dat is vervelend, want wij zijn thuis geen van allen bepaald bang uitgevallen.

Wanda is zo bang, als Pietje onze kanarie haar iets te lang aankijkt, is ze al weg en laatst werd ze zelfs door een katje achterna gezeten.

Gelukkig gaat dat veranderen. Sinds kort neem ik haar mee naar de sportschool voor een extra stukje krachttraining.

En op aanraden van een vriend, die zelf twee Deense doggen heeft, geef ik Wanda die vernieuwde Hols Krachtbrokken.

Dat is een volledige oergezonde maaltijd, vol vitaminen, mineralen en sporenelementen.

Hols Krachtbrokken zijn licht verteerbaar en toch knapperig, zodat Wanda een sterk gebit houdt en toch niet uit haar bek gaat stinken.

Hols Krachtbrokken bevatten naast plantaardige- ook dierlijke eiwitten, waardoor Wanda naast haar extra training de juiste voeding krijgt om zichzelf sterk en gezond te voelen en voor niemand meer bang hoeft te zijn. En het helpt: laatst zat ze nog een dwergpoedeltje achterna.

Want Hols Krachtbrokken geven kracht en KRACHT GEEFT MACHT.

Onze Krachtbrokken bevatten alle noodzakelijke vitaminen en sporenelementen. Naast plantaardige- bevatten Hols Krachtbrokken ook dierlijke eiwitten. Krachtbrokken vormen een volledige voeding, zonder konserveringsmiddelen. De uitgebalanceerde samenstelling van Hols Krachtbrokken wordt als extra garantie regelmatig onderzocht door het CIVO-TNO.

VOORLOPIG HEEFT HEKTOR HIER NOG 'N ZWARE KLUIF AAN

BOUDEWIJN LOOPT NOG STEEDS ONDER DE HORDEN DOOR

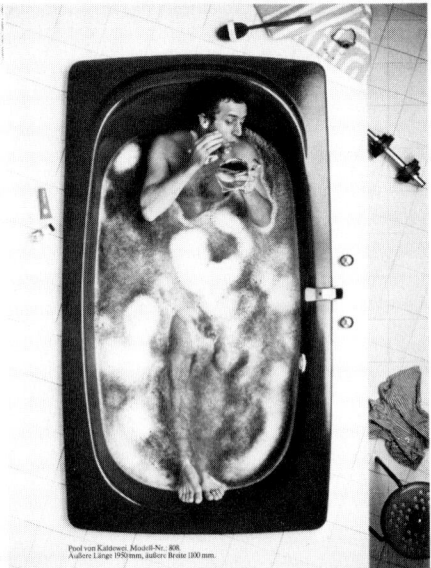

Diese Wanne kriegt so leicht keine Schramme.

In einer Badewanne wird nicht immer nur gebadet. Hier werden auch die Haare gewaschen, die Nägel lackiert, hier duscht man und rasiert sich sogar.
Damit alles glatt geht, sollte die Badewanne von Kaldewei sein. Denn Kaldewei baut seine Wannen aus Stahl-Email. Und Stahl-Email ist hart im Nehmen, weil es eine besonders harte Oberfläche hat.
Das macht die Wannen robust und strapazierfähig.
Und es macht ihnen auch überhaupt nichts aus, wenn sie mit Fleckenwasser, Spiritus oder Kalkentferner in Berührung kommen.
Im Gegenteil, sie strahlen. In den schönsten Farben.
Deshalb ist es wichtig, beim Aussuchen der Wanne das richtige Material zu wählen. Ein Material, das jeden Spaß mitmacht und auch nach Jahren noch sein schönes Äußeres behält.
Stahl-Email von Kaldewei.

KALDEWEI

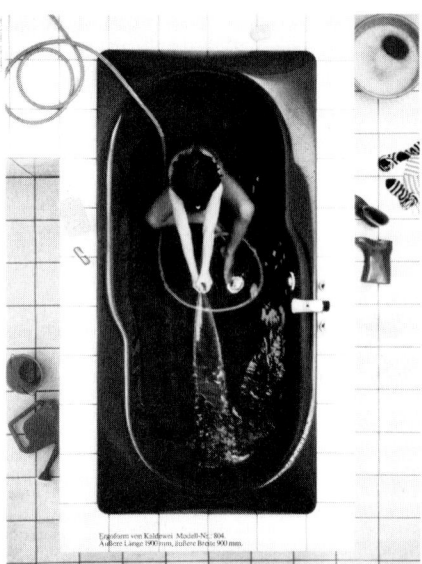

Unsere Wannen kann kein Wässerchen trüben.

Badewannen oder Brausewannen müssen im Laufe der Zeit viel über sich ergehen lassen.
Ob Kinder nun darin herumtoben. Ob Nägel lackiert oder Pflanzen gewässert werden. Ob die Oberfläche mit Fleckenwasser oder Scheuermitteln behandelt wird.
Dies alles darf einer Wanne nichts ausmachen.
Deshalb fertigt Kaldewei seine Bade- und Brausewannen aus hartem, widerstandsfähigem Stahl-Email.
Stahl-Email hat eine besonders harte Oberfläche und steht damit an der Spitze der Hygiene-Skala.
Angenommen also, Sie interessieren sich für eine neue Bade- oder Brausewanne, dann entscheiden Sie sich für Stahl-Email von Kaldewei.
Und damit für ungetrübte Badefreuden.

KALDEWEI

64
Rainer Held Designer
Jan Michael Photographer
Hildmann Simon Rempen & Schmitz Agency
Kaldewei West Germany Client
Hamburg, W. Germany

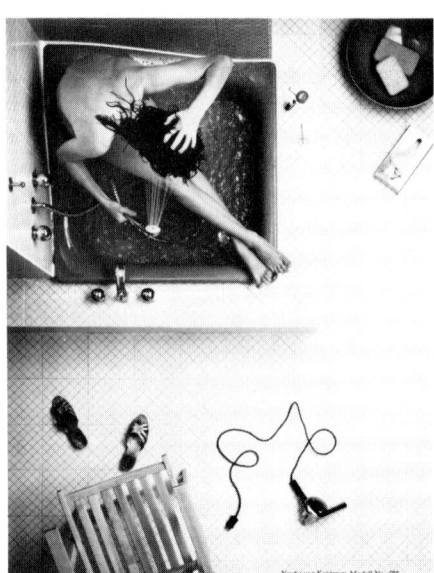

Nehmen Sie Platz zum Duschen.

Wenn Sie die neue „Nautic" Duschwanne von Kaldewei sehen, setzen Sie sich hin.
Einmal, weil Sie das noch nicht gesehen haben. Zum anderen, weil der Sitzplatz sehr bequem ist: Sie sitzen nämlich nicht unten auf dem Rand der Brausewanne, sondern auf dem hochgezogenen Eckteil. Ganz komfortabel.
Das hat natürlich auch eine praktische Seite. Denn Sie können hier im Sitzen und im Stehen bequem Ihre Füße reinigen, ohne daß Sie sich dazu tief bücken müssen.
Diese Duschwanne ist natürlich aus Stahl-Email, wie alles von Kaldewei.
Stahl-Email hat eine besonders harte Oberfläche und ist deshalb hart gegen die Belastungen des Alltags.
Einen schöneren Grund zum Duschen werden Sie nirgendwo finden.

KALDEWEI

Pool von Kaldewei. Modell-Nr. 808.
Äußere Länge 1950 mm, äußere Breite 1100 mm.

CONSUMER FRACTIONAL PAGE

65
Mark Kent Art Director
Al Fisher Photographer
Banks & Company Studio
Cole-Haan Client
Boston MA

66
Sue Wilson Art Director
Young & Rubicam, Inc. Agency
Manufacturers National Bank Client
Detroit MI

67
Muts Yasumura, Joy Greene Art Directors
Joy Greene, Sadat Pakay Photographers
Yasumura & Assoc. Agency
Amiran Corp. Client
New York NY

68
Tobias Moss Art Director
Jerry Sarapociello Photographer
A.I. Friedman, Inc. Client
New York NY

69
Sharon Spence Art Director
Julian Dall Illustrator
Douglas & Barry (Pty) Ltd. Production
Kuper Hands (Pty) Ltd. Agency
Johannesburg, S. Africa

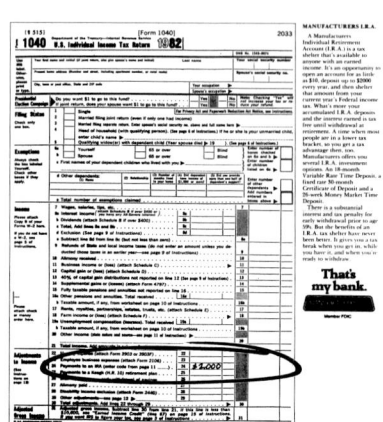

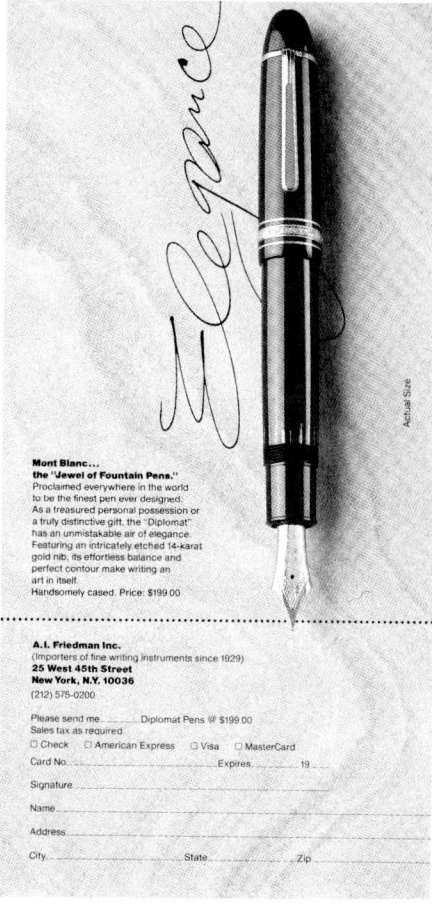

68

at the end of a kilometre a Pilot Fineliner is still a fine-liner.

Fine nylon tip writes up to 1 000 m in black, brown, orange, yellow, green, red, blue and violet.
Available at stationery counters everywhere.

PILOT
Make Pilot your pen friend.
Distributed by Max Frank (Pty) Ltd Tel (011) 29-2711

Kuper Hands 3963

69

70
Gladys Barton Art Director
Stan Baum Copywriter
Wunderman Ricotta & Kline Agency
Columbia Record & Tape Club Client
New York NY

71
Jack de Lange Art Director
Gerard Portengen Designer
DLS Communications BV Agency
Hans Geldof Hairstylist Client
Zaandam, Holland

72
Anita Soos Art Director
Sean Kernan Photographer
Virginia Rudd Copywriter
Gamma One Studio
Hotel Europa Client
Cheshire CT

73
Jordan Krimstein, Barry Udcoff Creative Directors
Tom Albano, Gary Matusek Designers
Marci Iacobucci Copywriter
Campbell-Mithun Agency
Drake Hotel, Chicago Client
Chicago IL

74
Hiroshi Shibata Art Director
Kenro Izu Photographer
Bonni Benstock Copywriter
Cygnus Studio
Dentsu Corp. of America Agency
Mikimoto (America) Co. Ltd. Client
New York NY

75
Connie Blum Art Director
Bob Weaks Photographer
Bozell & Jacobs Agency
Norden Laboratories Client
Omaha NE

76
Stuart Bresner Art Director
Mathieu, Gerfen & Bresner, Inc. Agency
Canadian/Schenley Client
New York NY

77
Alan Gair Art Director
Roger Hill Illustrator
Marty Myers Copywriter
The Gloucester Group Agency
Dare Foods Ltd. Client
Toronto, Canada

78
Christopher Hopkins Art Director
Willardson & White Studio
Niki Client
Los Angeles CA

Right in the middle of bustling downtown Johannesburg is a whole block of sanity. Escape from the ratrace of the Central Business District, visit the Carlton Centre. Fashion shops, sewing shops, gift shops, hi-fi shops, curio shops, jewellers, restaurants, book shops, toy shops, sports shops, parking for 2000 cars and more. The Carlton Centre. It's where Johannesburg's heart beats.

This man wanted a Giorgio Armani suit, a pure silk shirt and Spanish shoes. He found them at the Carlton Centre.

The Carlton Centre has: sewing shops, fashion shops, curio shops, toy shops, sports shops, jewellers, book shops, hi-fi shops, restaurants, gift shops, parking for 2000 cars and more. Or give her a Carlton Centre Gift Voucher and give her the pleasure of doing her own browsing. The Carlton Centre. It's where Johannesburg's heart beats.

Grandma has her heart set on an antique ivory three-pronged crochet thingy this Christmas. You'll find it at the Carlton Centre.

Right in the middle of bustling downtown Johannesburg is a whole block of sanity. Escape from the ratrace of the Central Business District, visit the Carlton Centre. Fashion shops, sewing shops, gift shops, hi-fi shops, curio shops, jewellers, restaurants, book shops, toy shops, sports shops, parking for 2000 cars and more. The Carlton Centre. It's where Johannesburg's heart beats.

This man bought a rare tribal mask at one of the twelve curio shops in the Carlton Centre. No, he's not wearing it.

Right in the middle of bustling downtown Johannesburg is a whole block of sanity. Escape from the ratrace of the Central Business District, visit the Carlton Centre. Fashion shops, sewing shops, gift shops, hi-fi shops, curio shops, jewellers, restaurants, book shops, toy shops, sports shops, parking for 2000 cars and more. The Carlton Centre. It's where Johannesburg's heart beats.

This lady wanted a French suit, a matching Italian handbag and sandals. She found them at the Carlton Centre.

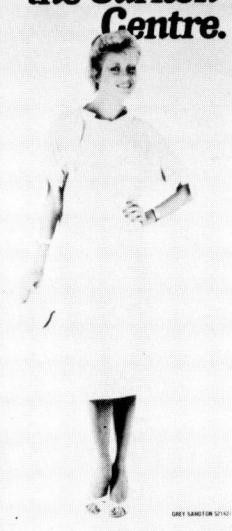

The Carlton Centre has: sewing shops, fashion shops, curio shops, toy shops, sports shops, jewellers, book shops, hi-fi shops, restaurants, gift shops, parking for 2000 cars and more. Or give him a Carlton Centre Gift Voucher and give him the pleasure of doing his own browsing. The Carlton Centre. It's where Johannesburg's heart beats.

Jeremy wants an ultrasonic vacillating radio controlled thingamabob for Christmas. You'll find it at the Carlton Centre.

Gabby Bush Art Director
Horst Klemm Photographer
Howard Smiedt Copywriter
Greysandton Agency
Carlton Centre Merchants Assn. Client
Sandton, S. Africa

TRADE SINGLE

80
Don Harbor Art Director
Freda Shaver Designer
Lynn Blakemore, DonWoodlan Illustrators
Mark McKenna Copywriter
Lawler Ballard Advertising Agency
Virginia Port Authority client
Norfolk Va

81
Al Satterwhite Photographer
AMF Client
New York NY

82
Edward Leighton Art Director
Charles McGovern Copywriter
St. Vincent, Milone & McConnells, Inc. Agency
Door, Oliver Inc. Client
New York NY

83

83
Robert Talarczyk Art Director
Eli Lilly Dista Products Client
Fair Haven NJ

84
Mark Hughes Art Director
Steve Steigman Photographer
Shawne Cooper Copywriter
Doyle Dane Bernbach Agency
Camargo-Weight Watchers Client
New York NY

85
Joe Napurano Art Director
Bruce Pennelton, Dave Hoffman Photographers
Ballotta Napurano & Co. Inc. Studio
Thomas & Betts Corp. Client
Springfield NJ

86
Arthur Vibert Art Director
Bill Tucker Photographer
Mark Aronson Copywriter
Lee King & Partners Agency
Cromwell Paper Client
Chicago IL

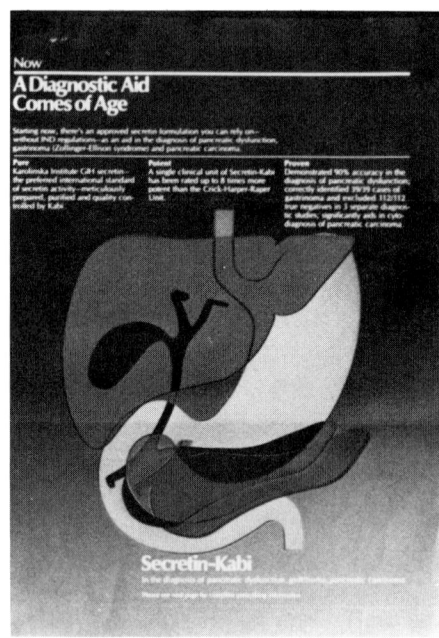

87
David Tomlinson Art Director
Harry Tyler Photographer
Dallas Tomlinson & Assocs. (Pty) Ltd. Studio
Paxit Pipekor Client
Randburg, S. Africa

88
William Vollers, Joan Dugan Art Directors
Sally Andersen Bruce Photographer
Kimmich & Company Agency
Kabi Group, Inc. Client
S. Norwalk CT

89
Peter Begley Art Director
Larry Robins Photographer
Steven Landsberg Copywriter
Doyle Dane Bernbach Agency
Sherwin Williams Client
New York NY

90
Bob Paganucci Art Director
Larry Stein Photographer
CIBA-Geigy Client
Summit NJ

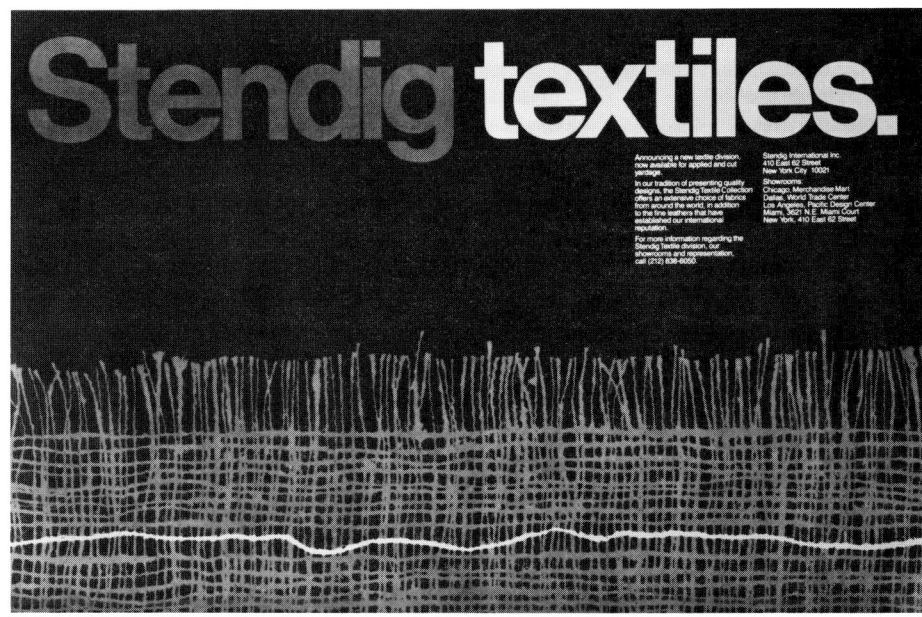

91
Sherry Berne Wallack Designer
Stan Levy Calligrapher
Conceptual Resources Studio
Sun Chemical Export Corp. Client
Great Neck NY

92
Douglass Grimmett Art Director
M & Co. Studio
The Stat Store Client
New York NY

93
Susan Slover Designer
Luckett & Slover Inc. Studio
Stendig International Inc. Client
New York NY

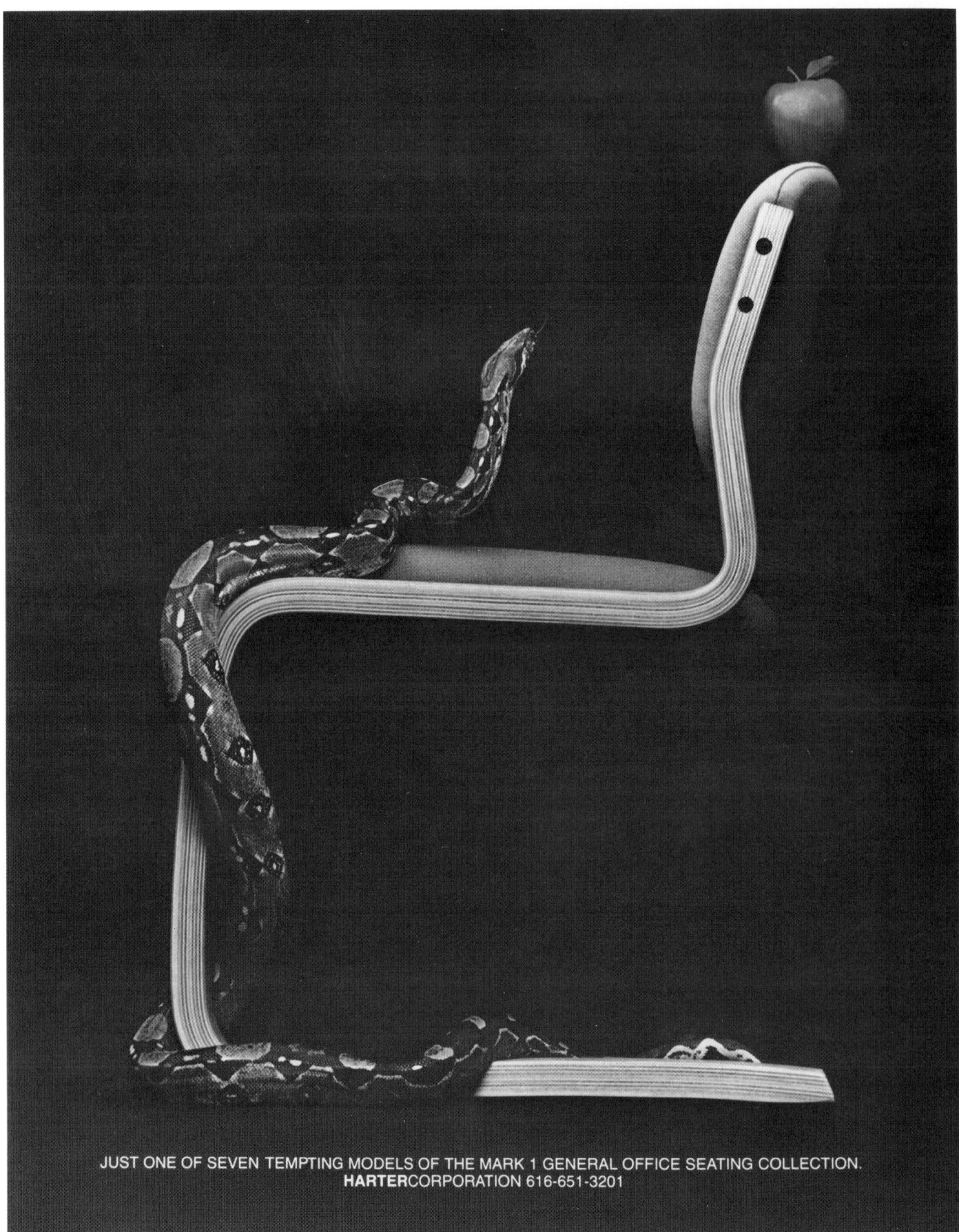

JUST ONE OF SEVEN TEMPTING MODELS OF THE MARK 1 GENERAL OFFICE SEATING COLLECTION.
HARTERCORPORATION 616-651-3201

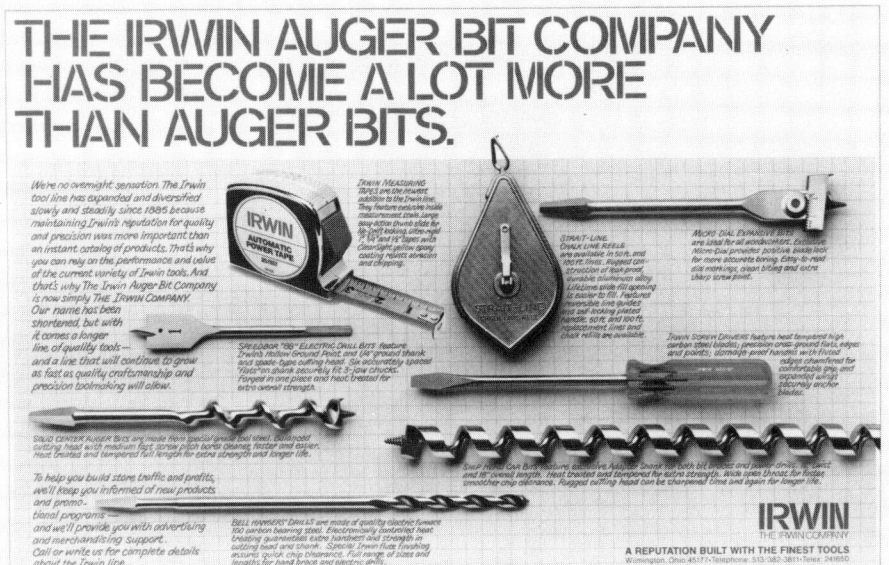

94
Bob Bender, Doug Fisher Art Directors
Hickson-Bender Photographer
Lord, Sullivan & Yoder Adv. Agency
Harter Corp. Client
Marion OH

95
Axel Von Kaenel Art Director
Hickson Bender Photographer
Lord, Sullivan & Yoder Adv. Agency
Irwin Co. Client
Marion OH

96
Charles Hively Art Director
Lyle Metzdorf Designer
Bill Wolfhagen Photographer
Metzdorf Advertising Agency
Texsteam Client
Houston TX

97
Holland S. Macdonald Designer
Christine Olympia Rodin Photographer
CBS Records Client
New York NY

98
Raymond Lee Art Director
Stephen Yeates Photographer
Graziano Palumbo Copywriter
Raymond Lee & Assocs. Studio
Stanfield's Limited Client
Toronto, Canada

99
George Schmidt, Joseph Fazio Art Directors
Chuck Wilkinson Illustrator
Sieber & McIntyre, Inc. Agency
Pennwalt Prescription Products Client
Short Hills NJ

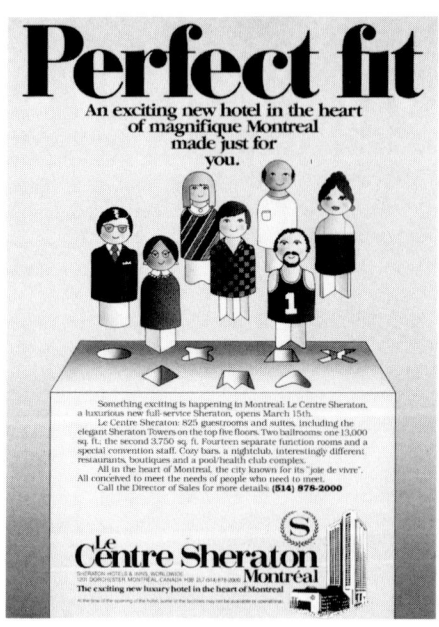

100
John Dolby Art Director
Bob Nardi Photographer
Nick Sirotin Model Maker
David Bender Copywriter
BBDM, Inc. Agency
Ingersoll-Rand Client
Chicago IL

101
Clare Taylor Art Director
Moscovitz & Taylor Adv. Inc. Agency
Le Centre Sheraton Montreal Client
Montreal, Canada

102
Steve Davis Art Director
Howard, Merrell & Boykin Agency
W.R. Grace & Co. Client
Raleigh NC

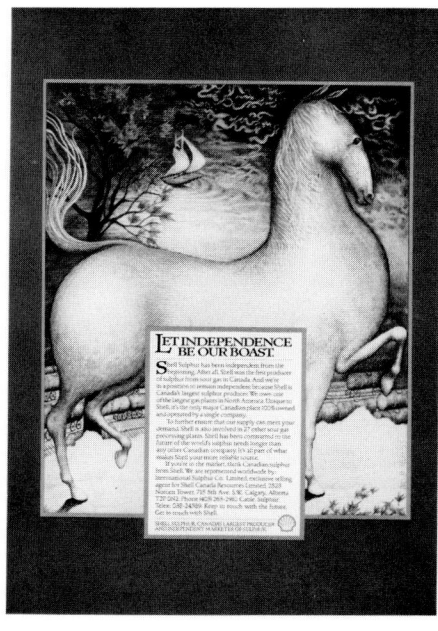

103
Chris Crofton Art Director
Miro Malish Illustrator
Michele Scarff Copywriter
Ogilvy & Mather (Canada) Ltd. Agency
Shell Canada Ltd. Client
Toronto, Canada

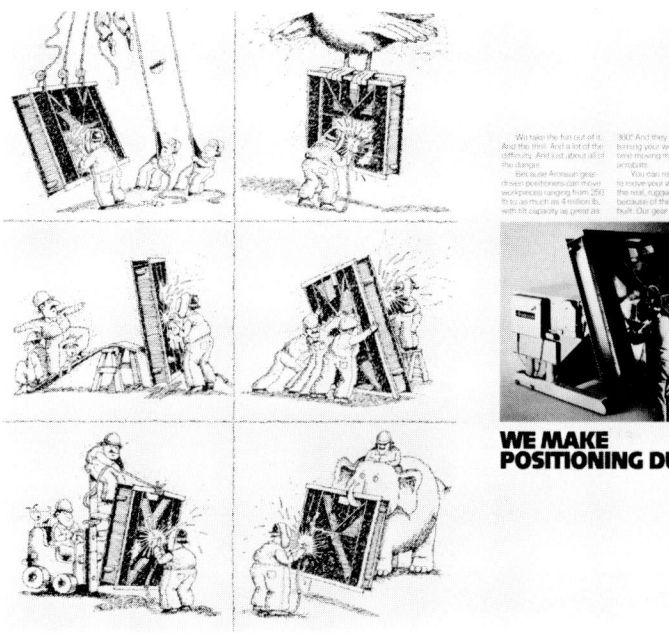

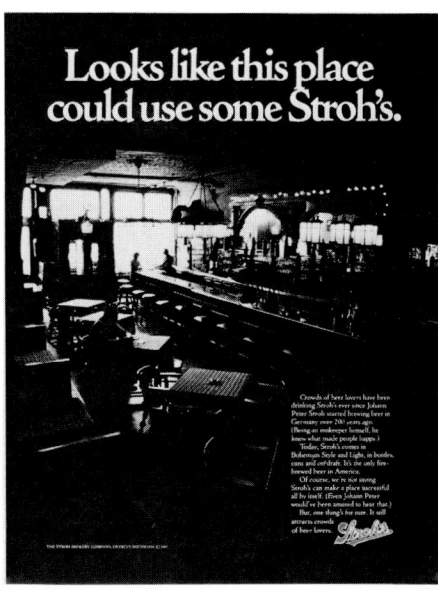

104
Pat Hutt Art Director
Jared Lee Illustrator
Truman Moore Photographer
Hammond Farrell Inc. Agency
Aronson Client
New York NY

105
Mark Hughes Art Director
Steve Steigman Photographer
Steven Landsberg Copywriter
Doyle Dane Bernbach Agency
Colombian Coffee Client
New York NY

106
Mark Hughes Art Director
Jerry Abromowitz Photographer
Steven Landsberg Copywriter
Doyle Dane Bernbach Agency
The Stroh Brewery Client
New York NY

TRADE CAMPAIGN

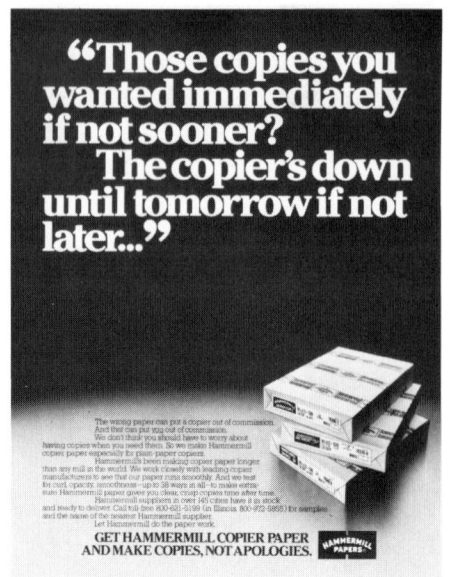

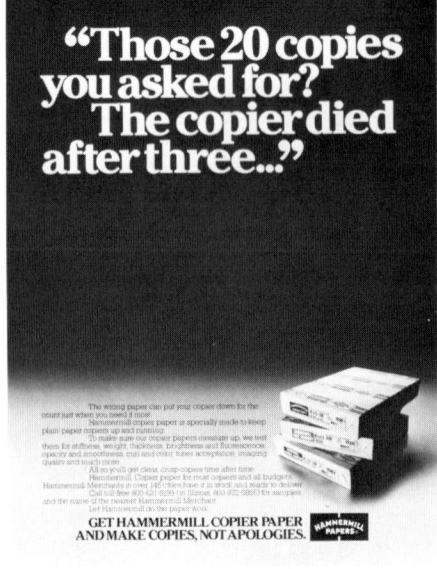

107
Zsuzsa Johnson Art Director
Seymour Mednick Photographer
James A. McDonald Copywriter
Aitkin-Kynett Co., Inc. Agency
NL Chemicals/NL Industries Client
Philadelphia PA

108
Ruthann Richert Art Director
Gary Perweiler, Richard Fried
  Photographers
Terry Scullin Copywriter
BBDO Agency
Hammermill Papers Grp. Client
New York NY

109
Ted McNeil, John Woldin Art Directors
Phil Marco Photographer
Westvaco Client
New Canaan CT

110
Steve Rousso Art Director
Jerry Burns Photographer
Joe Conwell Copywriter
Garrett/Lewis/Johnson Inc. Agency
Cousins Properties Inc. Client
Atlanta GA

WESTVACO PAPER. PRINTABILITY THAT STANDS TALL. RUNNABILITY THAT GIVES DOWNTIME THE BOOT.

"Oh, bury me not on a long press run..."
With Westvaco's STERLING® Litho Gloss going for you, long runs are no problem. Not even when you're in a showdown with a tight deadline. STERLING Litho Gloss lets you run at optimum press speeds and helps corral higher profits by minimizing waste and cutting downtime.
At the same time, STERLING Litho Gloss gives you printability that's second to none. Just take a long, hard look at the opposite page. If you really concentrate, you may even begin to get the scent of freshly tooled leather.
Next time you're facing a stampeding deadline, why not put STERLING Litho Gloss to the test. Use our PressDate® Service to order. You can order 2,500 to 40,000 pounds of STERLING Litho Gloss (60, 70, 80 and 100 lbs., 25 x 38 basis), finished to your specified size. The odds are better than ten-to-one that we'll have your shipment ready-to-go in five days or less. You can also order STERLING Web Gloss through our PressDate Service. Call your Westvaco representative for complete details.
Photograph by Phil Marco. Lithographed, 8-up, on a 40 by 52 sheet of STERLING Litho Gloss, Printer's White, 80#, 25 x 38 basis. Precision single-roll-sheeted by Westvaco's exclusive AccuTrim™ machines. Westvaco Corporation, Fine Papers Division, 299 Park Avenue, New York, N.Y. 10171.

Westvaco
It works.

THE TRICK IS KNOWING WHICH TRACK TO TAKE.

Cousins Properties has a unique way of keeping our centers on track. We pioneered the industry's first Shopping Center Performance Tracking Program.
This ongoing, sophisticated research program provides us with valuable information on consumer habits and attitudes relating to our centers and their competitors. Opinions are recorded regarding a mall's atmosphere, the merchandise profile, price point and convenience. The mall's advertising and promotional efforts are tested for consumer awareness and level of acceptance. Analysis of this data provides direction and strategy for center management, marketing, leasing and development programs.
Talk with our Leasing Team in Las Vegas to see how our research can help focus your sales efforts with a powerful train that keeps your business on track.

Cousins Properties Incorporated

THE MAGIC OF WESTVACO PAPER. IT HELPS MAKE PROFITS APPEAR AND DOWNTIME VANISH.

There's no illusion about it. When it comes to printability, Westvaco STERLING® Litho Gloss, Printer's White, captures every tone, color, texture, detail...and trick. Note the light bulb at the bottom of the picture. In this case, you believe your eyes. Besides outstanding printability, Westvaco STERLING Litho Gloss gives you runnability that provides a great escape when you're up against tight deadlines and long press runs. And Westvaco paper helps eliminate costly waste and downtime. The result? Presto! Profits appear.
If you need STERLING Litho Gloss to materialize at your door in a hurry, use our exclusive PressDate® Service. Order 2,500 to 40,000 pounds of STERLING Litho Gloss (60, 70, 80 and 100 lbs., 25 x 38 basis), finished to your specified size. We'll have your order ready-to-ship in five days or less. You can also order STERLING Web Gloss through our PressDate Service. Call your Westvaco representative for complete details.
Photographed by Phil Marco. Lithographed, 8-up, on a 40 by 52 sheet of STERLING Litho Gloss, Printer's White paper, 80#, 25 x 38 basis. Precision sheeted by Westvaco's exclusive AccuTrim™ machines. Westvaco Corporation, Fine Papers Division, 299 Park Avenue, New York, N.Y. 10171.

Westvaco
It works.

ALL TOO OFTEN, THERE'S NO BUSINESS IN SHOW BUSINESS.

When a shopping center brings in Bobo the Clown, that may be show biz, but it's not marketing. Marketing, the way we practice it at Cousins Properties, is a consistent, well-planned program designed to highlight store merchandise for customers.
Thorough in-house research targets specific market segments, which we reach with powerful selling events. Multi-media advertising, mall decor, and point-of-purchase visuals are used to guide, motivate and put shoppers in a buying mood. The results of these efforts are measured and examined to help us fine tune our merchandising and advertising to be even more effective.
Oh yes, we do win awards for our marketing programs, but that's as close as we ever come to show business. Talk with our Leasing Team in Las Vegas to see how our marketing efforts can mean more business than show business.

Cousins Properties Incorporated

WESTVACO PAPER. RUNNABILITY WITHOUT ANY TRICKS. PRINTABILITY WITH ALL OF THE TREATS.

The double trouble of a tight schedule against a long run. You probably know this nightmare all too well. But, you have a powerful way to end this curse — Westvaco's STERLING® Web Gloss.
Westvaco's STERLING Web Gloss gives you the kind of runnability that outruns tight deadlines and speeds even the biggest jobs through your press in optimum time. And with less time out for downtime, less waste and higher profits.
At the same time, STERLING Web Gloss casts a spell of 25-inch Web printability that captures tones, colors and details that dazzle the eye and delight the senses. Wouldn't dunking for those apples be delicious fun?
And one more thing. Next time you don't think you have a ghost of a chance against a "witching-hour" deadline, use our PressDate® Service.
Order 5,000 to 40,000 pounds of STERLING Web Gloss (60, 70, 80 lbs., 25 x 38–500 basis) in widths of 23, 23½, 26, 28½, 35 or 35¾ inches. We'll have your order ready to ship in five days or less. Call your Westvaco representative for complete details.
Photography by Phil Marco. Lithographed, 4-up, on STERLING Web Gloss, Printer's White, 80#, 25 x 38 basis. A five-color Harris M200 was used running at 18,000 IPH. Westvaco Corporation, 299 Park Avenue, New York, N.Y. 10171.

Westvaco
It works.

WE CREATE A GOOD FRAME OF MIND BY DESIGN.

A good frame enhances the picture we're looking at becoming the center of attention, much like good shopping center design serves as a backdrop for the stores.
The idea behind a Cousins-designed center is to provide an environment which encourages shoppers to shop. So we use spatial concepts that increase visibility of the stores, traffic patterns that ease pedestrian flow, imaginative signage to focus on the diversity of the shops, and lush landscaping and people places to encourage shoppers to relax longer and return more frequently.
Talk with our Leasing Team in Las Vegas and find out how a Cousins designed center can help ensure your profit picture. That conversation should leave you in a great frame of mind.

Cousins Properties Incorporated

111
Larry Keenan Photographer
Michael Pearce Designer
Wylie Wilson & Munn Agency
Tandom Computers Client
Oakland CA

112
Roger M. Cortani Art Director
Norman Orr Illustrator
Jack Christiansen Photographer
Cortani, Brown, Rigoli Agency
Siliconix, Inc. Client
Mountain View CA

113
Ruthann Richert Art Director
Gary Perweiler Photographer
Terry Scullin Copywriter
BBDO Agency
Timken Client
New York NY

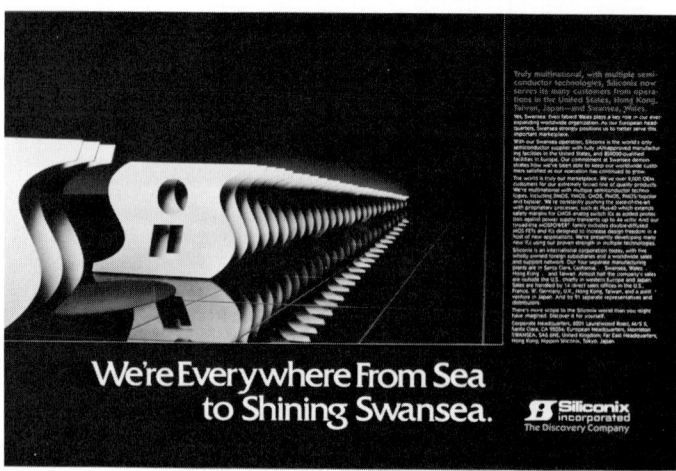

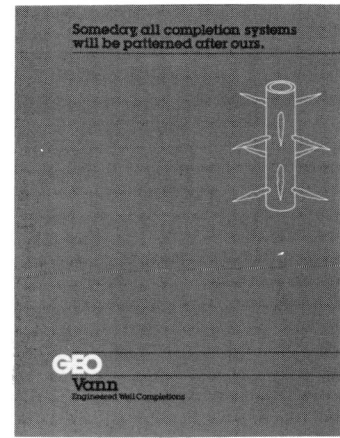

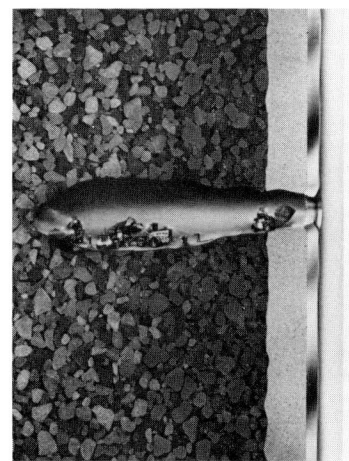
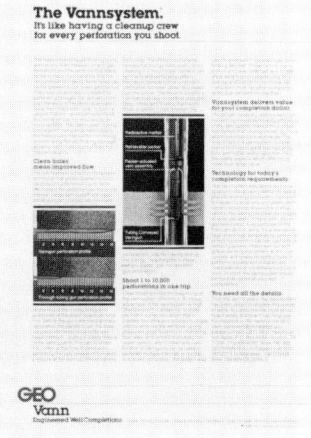

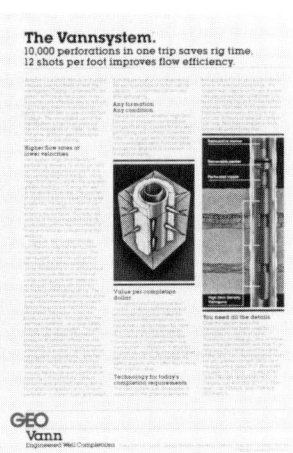

114
John Connolly Art Director
Ken Griffiths Photographer
Ake Bergengron Typographer
Ehrenstrahle Co. Ltd. Agency
Kamasa Tools Ltd. Client
London, England

115
Brenton Stewart Art Director
Jeff Sanson Illustrator
Bob Haworth Copywriter
Bloom Industrial Advertising Agency
Geo Vann Client
Houston TX

116
Mike Rosen Art Director
Joe Ovies Illustrator
Hammond Farrell Inc. Agency
Thomson Industries Client
New York NY

117
Erica Skioldebrand Art Director
Anderson & Lembke Danderydsgatan
  Agency
Wirsbo Bruks AB Client
Stockholm, Sweden

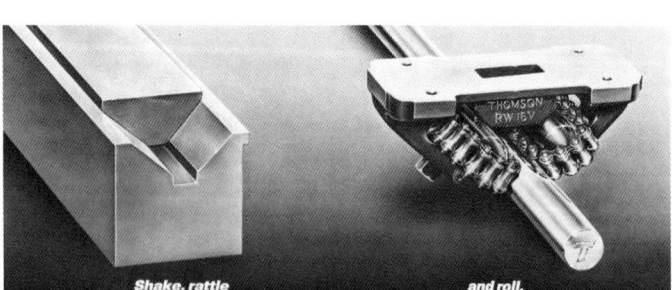

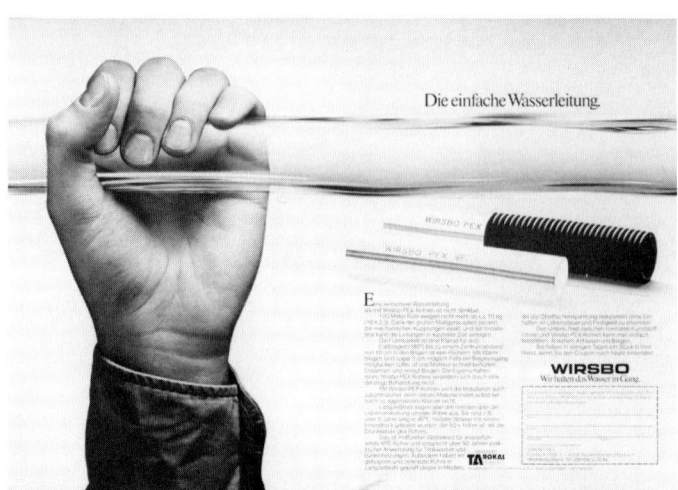
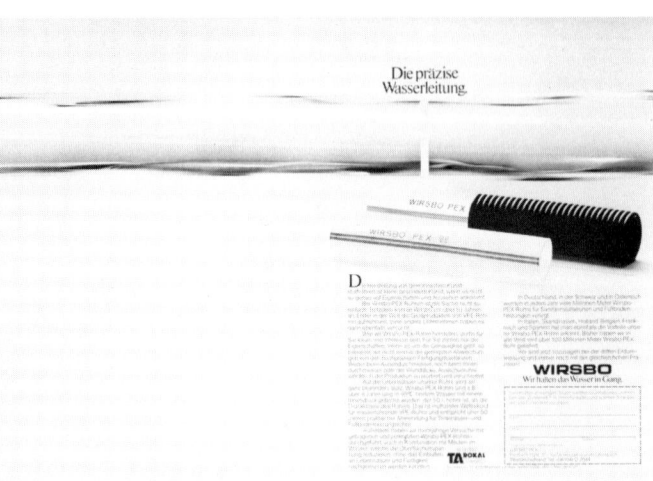

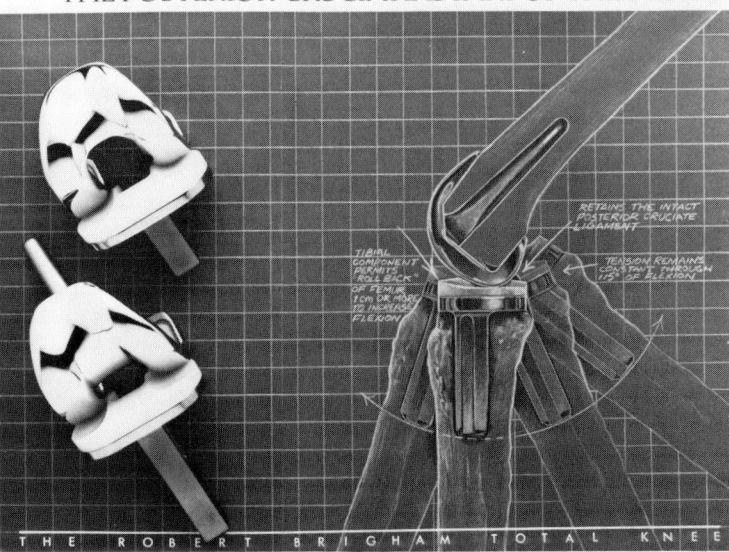

118
Rocco Volpe, William C. Beauchamp
 Art Directors
William C. Beauchamp Illustrator
Michael Furman Photographer
Simms & McIvor, Inc. Agency
Johnson & Johnson, Orthopaedic Client
Bridgewater NJ

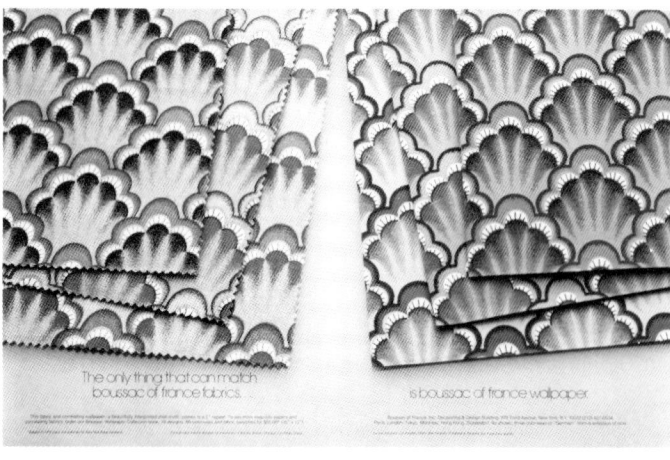
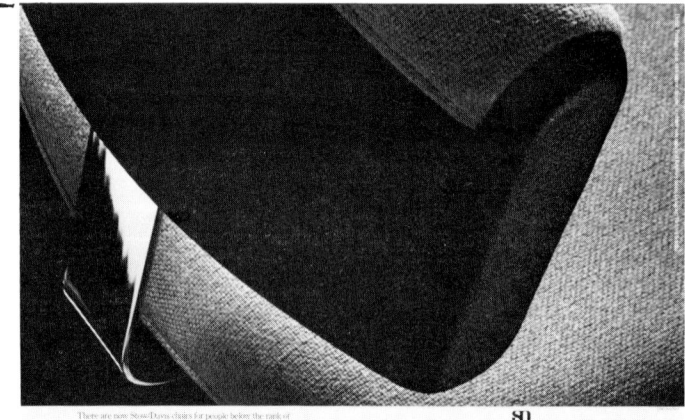

119
Stanley Eisenman, Dennis Dollens Art Directors
John Pilgreen Photographer
Curvon O'Reilly Copywriter
Eisenman & Enoch Inc. Agency
Stow/Davis Client
New York NY

120
David Wenman Art Director
Carol Wenman Copywriter
Andrew Unangst Photographer
David Wenman Associates Agency
Boussac of France Client
New York NY

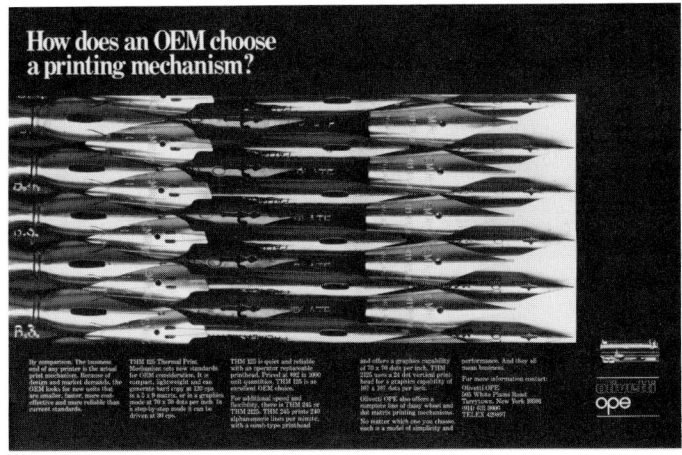

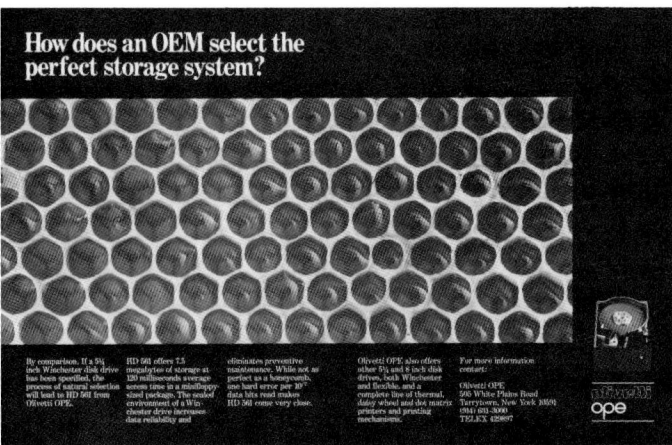

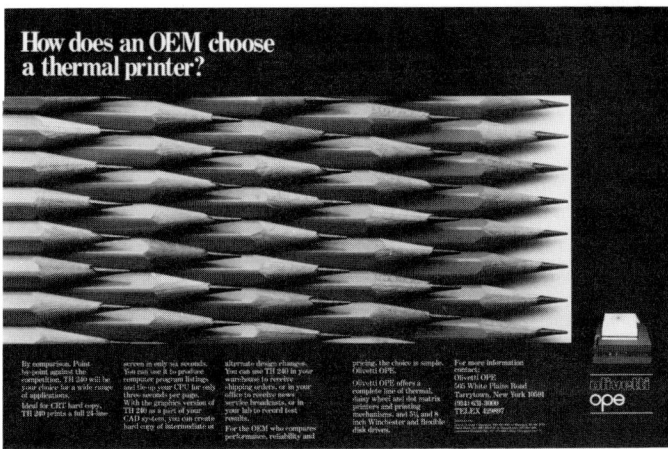

122
Jane Zash, Michael Donovan Art Directors
Steve Ogilvy Photographer
Donovan & Green Studio
Brickel Assoc. Inc. Client
New York NY

123
Charles Hively Art Director
Sherri Oldham Designer
Jay Maisel, Gary Braasch, David Muench
  Photographers
Metzdorf Advertising Agency
Dresser Industries Client
Houston TX

121
Thomas J. Weisz Art Director
Armando Milani Designer
White Light Photographer
Weisz/Greco Inc. Agency
Olivetti OPE Client
New Paltz NY

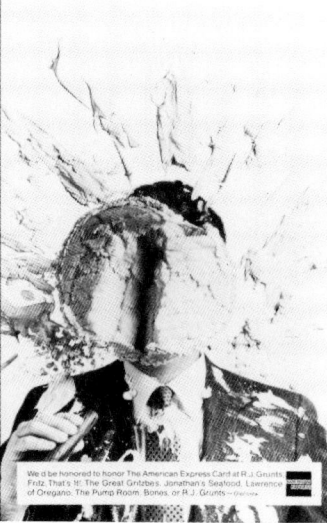

124
Robert Qually Art Director
Denis Scott Photographer
Ken Bailey Copywriter
Qually & Co., Inc. Agency
Rich Melman Client
Evanston IL

125
Charles Fillhardt Art Director
Tom Tracy, Becker Bishop Studios Photographers
Lynne Bowman Copywriter
Bergthold, Fillhardt & Wright Agency
Branson/IPC Client
San Jose CA

126
Dave Hartzell, Russ Hirth Art Directors
Lad Trepal Photographer
John Pierce Copywriter
Studio L Studio
Carr Liggett Inc. Agency
The Ridge Tool Co. Client
Cleveland OH

127
Linda Berg Art Director
Steven Moskowitz Illustrator
Rumrill Hoyt Agency
Agway Client
Rochester NY

128
Paul Petersen Art Director
Mathieu, Gerfen & Bresner, Inc. Agency
All Brand Importers Client
New York NY

POSTERS

129
Stephen Frykholm Art Director
Pam Van Dyken Typography
Continental Identification Products
 Production House
Tulip Time Festival Client
Zeeland MI

130
Colleen Leonhard, Greg Moy Art Directors
Gary Shortt Designer
McNamara Assocs. Studio
Young & Rubicam Inc. Agency
Detroit Renaissance Client
Troy MI

131
Richard Radke Art Director
Martin Cooke Copywriter
Intermarco Advertising Agency
Cointreau America Client
New York NY

132
Marvin Berk Art Director
Steve Levine Illustrator
Creative Images Inc. Studio
The Foundation of the Dramatists Guild Client
New York NY

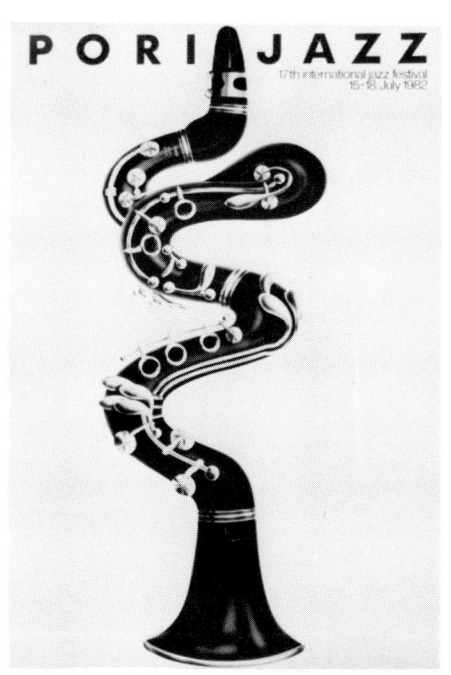
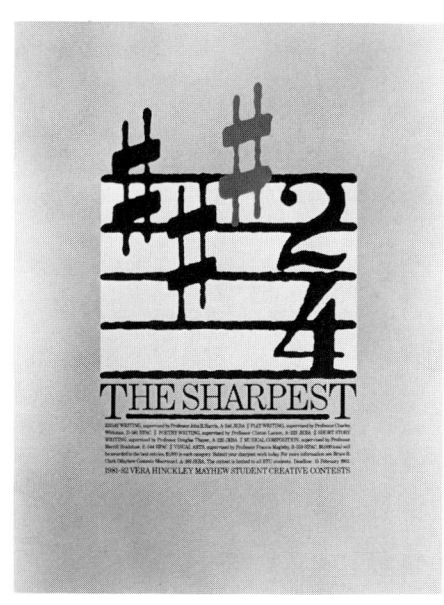

134

133
Kyosti Varis Designer
Matti Sivonen Illustrator
Kyosti Varis/VPV Oy Studio
Porin Jazz 66 ry Client
Helsinki, Finland

134
Bryan L. Peterson Art Director
Graphic Communications-B.Y.U. Studio
Brigham Young University Client
Provo UT

135
Kurt Tausche Art Director
Leland Klanderman Illustrator
Jeanne Shorter Copywriter
Brandt-Barringmann Inc. Agency
Powers Client
Minneapolis MN

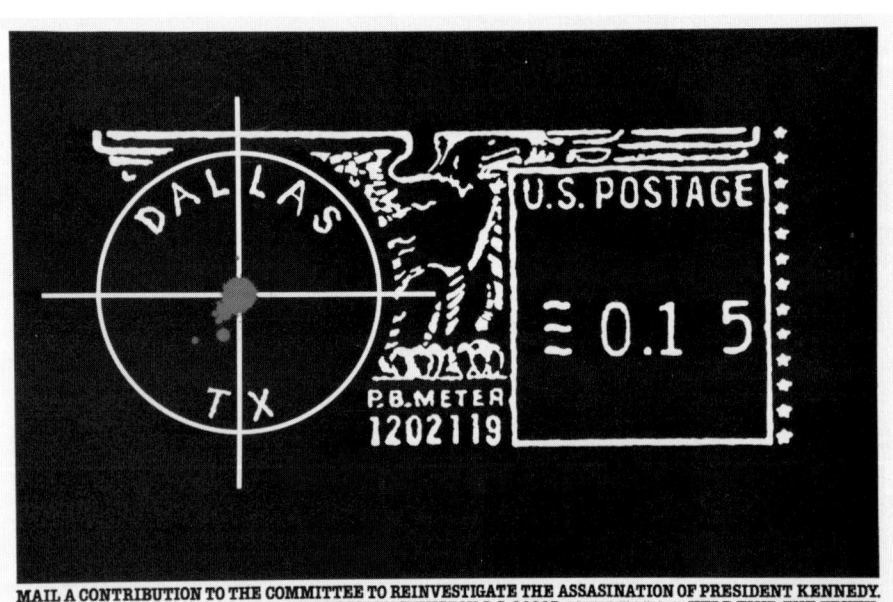

136
William Hemmer Art Director
Michael Norton Studioes photographers
Chenoweth Ellis & Faulkner Agency
Sidewalk Art Festival Client
Tampa FL

137
Charles Blake, Elaine Zeitsoff, Vasken Kalayjian Art Directors
Richard Williams Illustrator
NBC Sports Client
New York NY

138
David B. Wright Creative Director
Steve Tanner Designer
David Wright & Associates Studio
Sandi Smith Client
Marietta GA

139
Dick Kaiser Photographer
Western Landscape Construction Client
Los Angeles CA

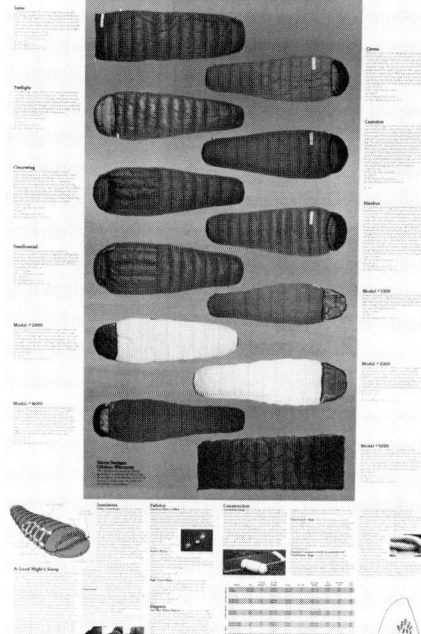

140
Tom Antista Art Director
Rusty Kay & Assocs. Studio
So. Calif. Antique Motorcycle Club Client
Santa Monica CA

141
David Gauger Art Director
Robert Ankers, Mary Rudnicki Orr Designers
Michael Jensen Illustrator
John Horvers, Kim Momb Photographers
Susan Van Epps Copywriter
Gauger Sparks Silva, Inc. Agency
Sierra Designs Client
San Francisco CA

142
Ron Wolin Art Director
Ignacio Gomez Illustrator
Dancer, Fitzgerald Sample Agency
Toyota Client
Los Angeles CA

143
Joseph J. Mango, Shelley Heller Art Directors
Don Wieland Illustrator
Gary Shortt Designer
McNamara Assocs. Studio
BF Goodrich Client
Troy MI

144
Ed Koslow, David Bartels Art Directors
David McMacken Illustrator
Strandel Baker Typography
The Hanley Partnership Agency
Anheuser Busch Inc. Client
St. Louis MO

145
Charles Hively Art Director
Sherri Oldham Designer
Seymour Chwast Illustrator
Metzdorf Advertising Agency
Anchorage Restaurant Client
Houston TX

146
Sharon Streger, Yukio Kondo Art Directors
Alex Tiani Illustrator
Kasica & Brown, Inc. Studio
Continental Insurance Client
New York NY

147
Russell Hardin Art Director
Hecht's Client
Washington D.C.

148
Kirk Hinshaw Art Director
Raul del Rio Illustrator
John Casado Design Studio
Dancer Fitzgerald Sample Agency
San Francisco Zoo Client
San Francisco CA

SAN FRANCISCO ZOOLOGICAL SOCIETY

149
Ralph Burch Art Director
Stuart Block Photographer
Roger Myers Copywriter
Burch Myers Cuttie, Inc. Agency
Kieffer-Nolde, Inc. Client
Chicago IL

151
Paul Hodgson Art Director
John Martin Illustrator
Fifty Fingers Inc. Studio
Ontario Science Centre Client
Toronto, Canada

152
Diana Graham Art Director
Al Lorenz Illustrator
Gips Balkind Associates Studio
Fearon O'Leary client
New York NY

153
Roland Lacher Art Director
Konstantin Jacoby Creative Director
Jan Michael Photographer
GGK-Dusseldorf Agency
Volkswagen Germany Client
Hamburg, Germany

154
David Morris Art Director
Bonni Benstock Copywriter
Dentsu Corp. of America Agency
Nintendo of America Inc. Client
New York NY

155
Stephen Bleinberger Art Director
Stephen Longley Photographer
Stuart Miller Copywriter
Cat's Paw Heels & Soles Client
Baltimore MD

156
Marty Neumeier, Byron Glaser Art Directors
V. Courtlandt Johnson Illustrator
Neumeier Design Team Studio
Creative Education, Inc. Client
Santa Barbara CA

157
Erkki Ruuhinen Art Director
Anderson & Lembke Oy Agency
Svenska Film Institute Client
Helsinki, Finland

Avskedet

En kvinnas väg till frihet.
Regi Tuija-Maija Niskanen.
Foto Esa Vuorinen. I huvudrollerna:
Pirkko Nurmi, Carl-Axel Heiknert,
Stina Ekblad och Sanna Hultman.
Produktion Cinematograph för SFI/SF.
Distribution SF.

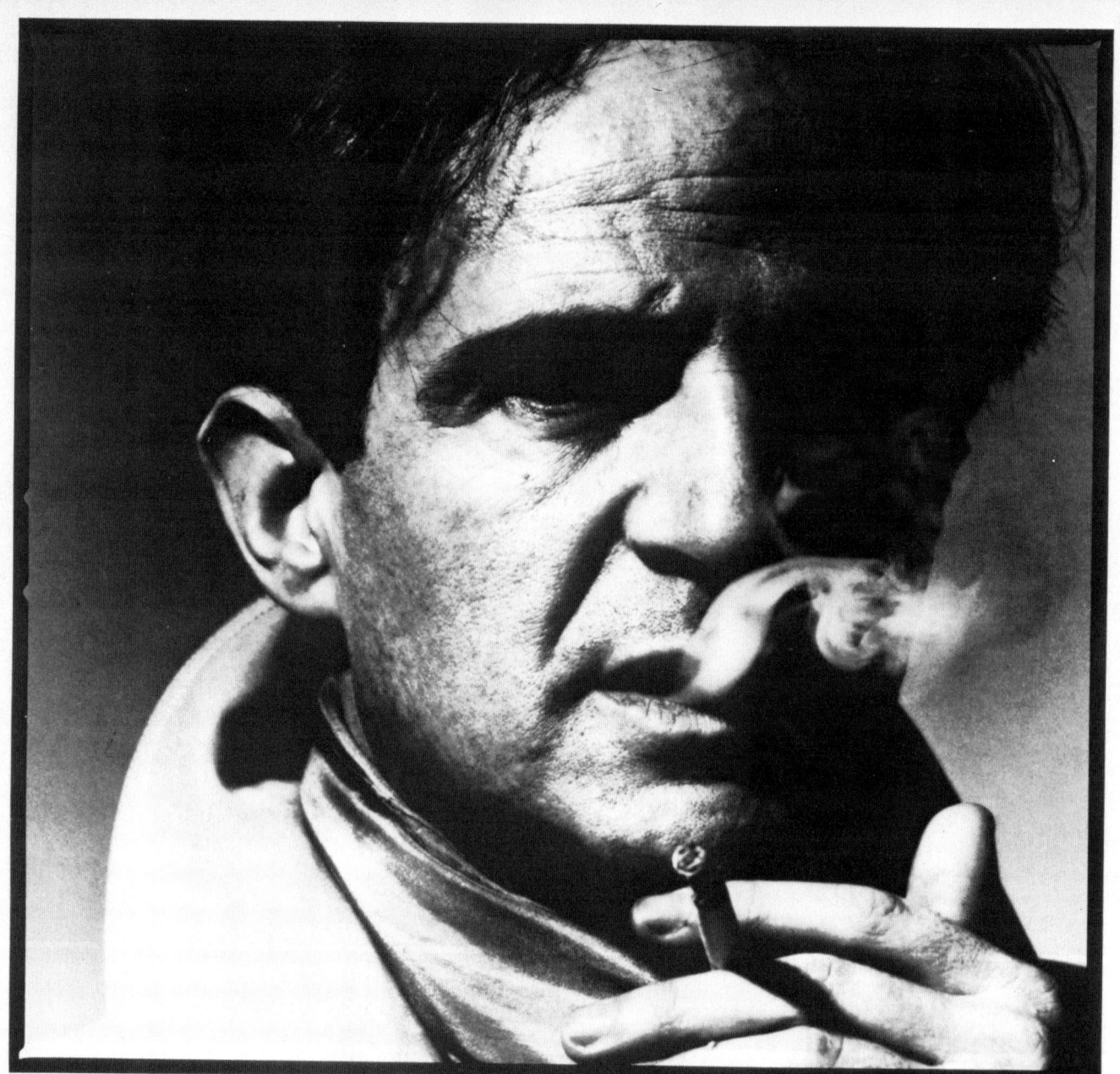

159
Tom Clemente Art Director
Milton Glaser Illustrator
Newspaper Advertising Bureau Client
New York NY

160

160
Bill Caldwell Art Director
Just Imagine Studio
International Communications Agcy. Client
McLean VA

161
Andy Malcolm Designer
Suzanne Lantagne Photographer
Omnibus Client
Toronto, Canada

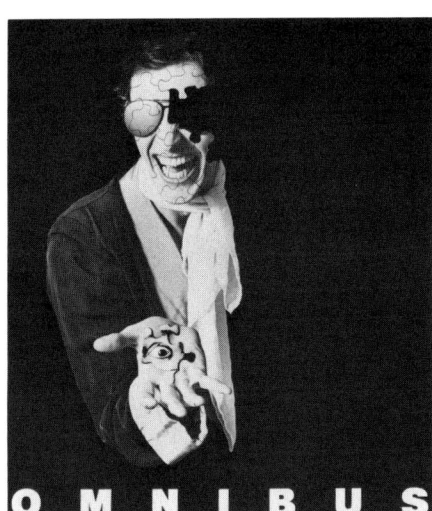

158
Michael Kutza Art Director
Skrebneski Photographer
Chicago International Film Festival Client
Chicago IL

162
Josephine DiDonato Art Director
David Gahr Photographer
CBS Records Client
New York NY

163
Wayne Salo Art Director
Mort Engel Photographer
Paul Crifo Illustrator
T.J. Callahan Copywriter
Diener/Hauser/Bates Agency
Paramount Pictures Client
New York NY

164
Tom Foerstel Art Director
Cline Inc. Agency
Idaho Potato Commission Client
Boise ID

Brochures / Catalogs

165
John Coy Art Director
Tracey Shiffman Designer
Sidney B. Felsen, Douglas Parker
  Photographers
Coy, Los Angeles Studio
Gemini G.E.L. Client
Culver City CA

166
Gene Rosner, Rachel Schreiber Levitan
  Art Directors
Ron Seymour Photographer
Brown & Rosner Inc. Studio
Luther and Pedersen, Inc. Client
Chicago IL

165

168

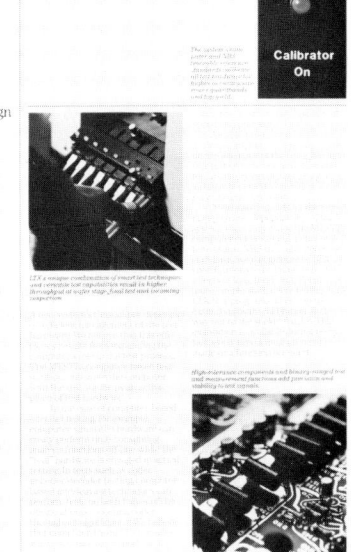

167
Arnold Jones Art Director
Tim Bieber Photographer
Mendenhall Jones & Leistra Agency
Kysor Industrial Corporation Client
Grand Rapids MI

168
John Dolby, Lisa Miller Art Directors
Bill Graham; Phase II Illustrator
Paul Gremmler Photographer
BBDM, Inc. Agency
Ingersoll-Rand Client
Chicago IL

169
David Lizotte Art Director
Eric Simmons Photographer
Gunn Associates Studio
LTX Client
Boston MA

170
Christor Laurent Art Director
Ken Griffiths Photographer
Ake Bergengren Typography
Ehrenstrahle & Co. Agency
SKF JBD AB Client
London, England

170

172

171

171
Becky Adolphson Garvey Art Director
Jerry LaRocca Photographer
Morton Advertising Inc. Agency
Long Machinery Client
Portland OR

172
Robert Ankers, David Gauger, Mark Decena
  Designers
Kevin Yarbrough Copywriter
Barbeau Engh Photographer
Don Gentry, Robert Ankers Illustrators
Gauger Sparks Silva, Inc. Agency
Dividend Development Corp. Client
New York NY

173
Michael M. Smit Art Director
RSR Associates Illustrator
John H. Anderson Photographer
Michael M. Smit & Assoc., Inc. Studio
Southwest Truck Body Client
Ballwin MO

174
Denise Spaulding Art Director
Denise Spaulding, David E. Carter
  Photographer
David E. Carter Corporate Communications
  Agency
Davis & Burton Contractors, Inc. Client
Ashland KY

175
Richard Duffy Art Director
Michael John Assoc. Inc. Agency
Pittston Coal Co. Client
Greenwich CT

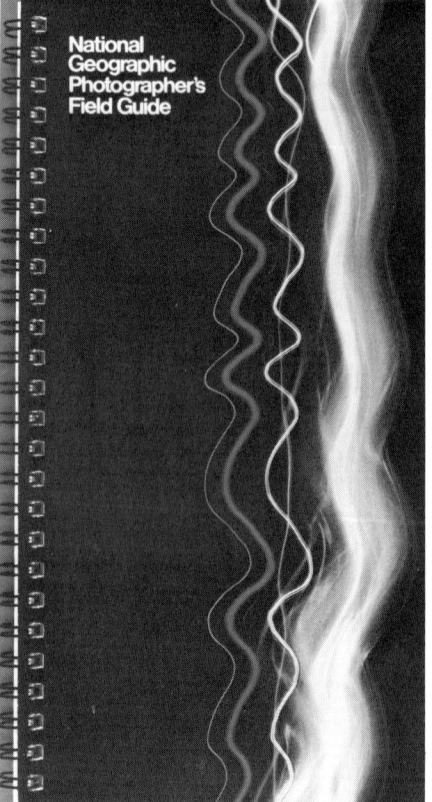

176
Larry A. Profancik Art Director
Charles Spizzari, Joe Boone Photographers
Sam Miszewski Copywriter
PW Incorporated Studio
International Harvester Client
Louisville KY

177
David M. Seager Art Director
Jim Sugar Photographer
Anne D. Kobor Editor
National Geographic Society Client
Washington DC

178
Steve Brennan Art Director
John M. Wright Illustrator
Amikin (Bristol Laboratories) Client
East Syracuse NY

179
Thomas J. Weisz Art Director
Armando Milani Designer
White Light Photographer
Weisz/Greco Inc. Agency
IBM World Trade Client
New Paltz NY

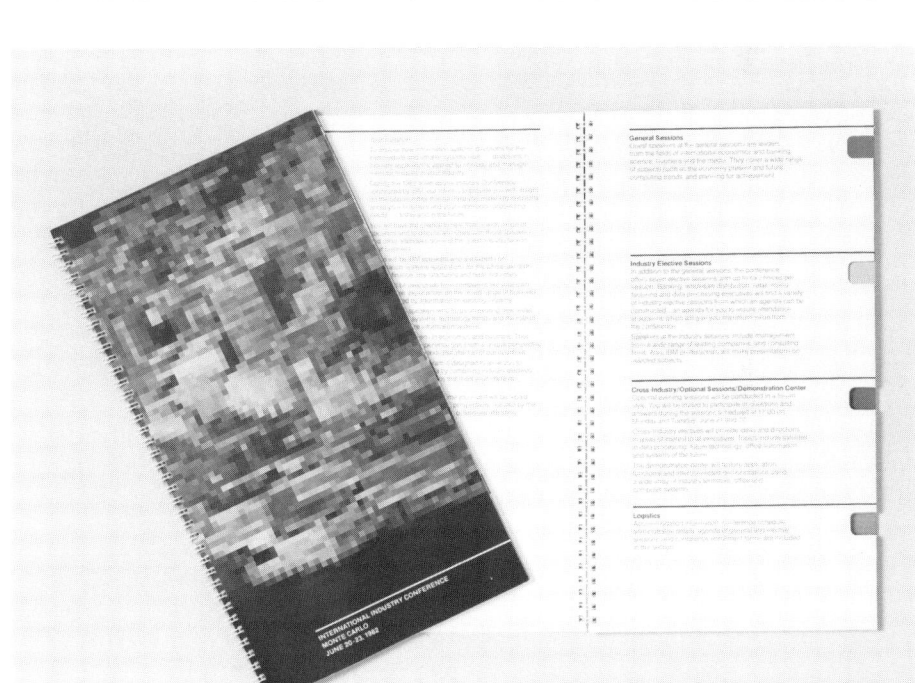

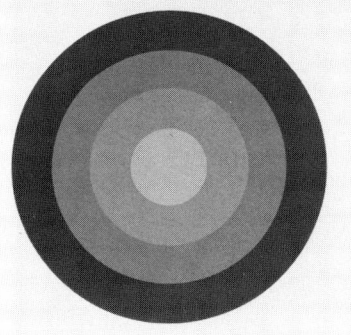

180
Jerry Lieberman Art Director
Rich Chiorando Illustrator
Presentations Services Grumman Aerospace Corporation Studio
Grumman Energy Systems Co. Client
Bethpage NY

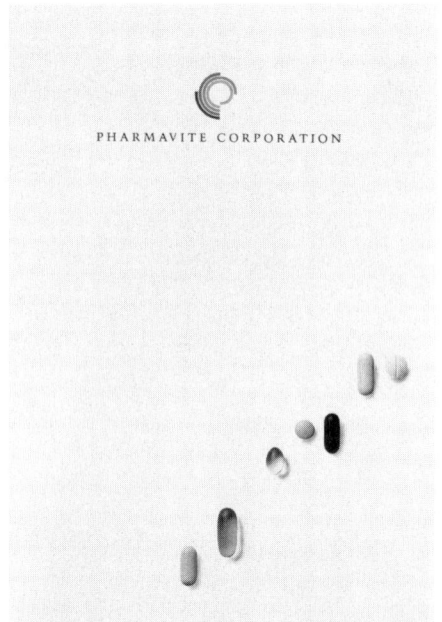

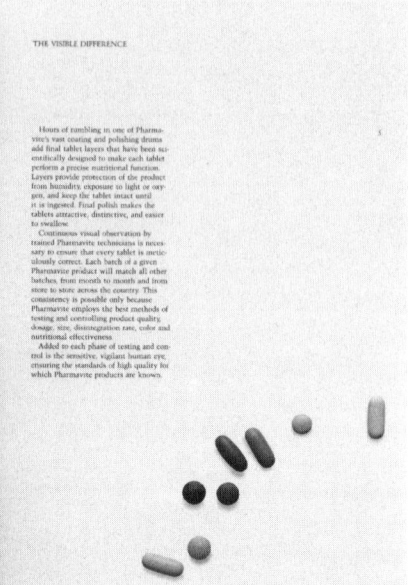

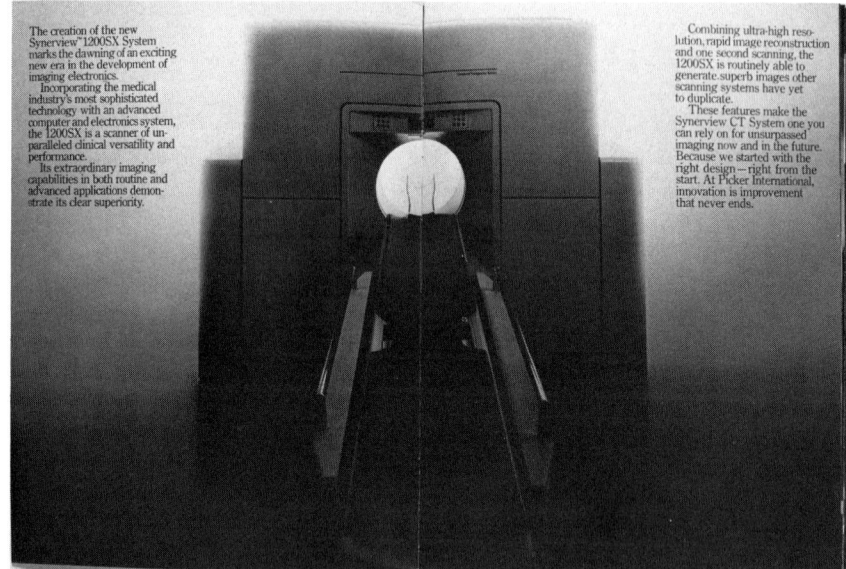
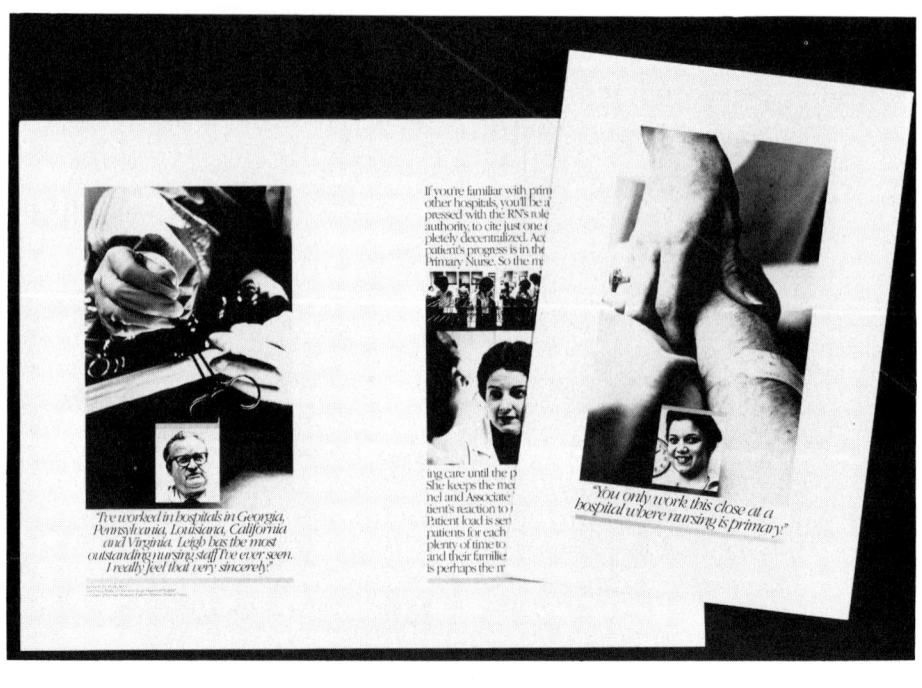

181
Dennis Tani Art Director
Ken Whitmore Photographer
Robert Miles Runyun & Assoc. Studio
Pharmavite Corporation Client
Playa del Rey CA

182
Russ Hirth Art Director
Chris Lee Copywriter
Lad Trepal/Charlie Coppins Photographers
Car Liggett Agency
Picker International Client
Cleveland OH

183
Don Harbor Art Director
Mike McMahon Designer
John Whitehead Photographer
Ken Kines Copywriter
Lawler Ballard Advertising Agency
Leigh Memorial Hospital Client
Norfolk VA

184
Lauren Squashic Art Director
Intermedics, Inc. Client
Freeport TX

185
Edyce Hall Art Director
R.J. Reynolds Industries Client
Winson-Salem NC

186
Tyler Smith Art Director
C. Genuzio/Myron Taplin Photographers
Tyler Smith Art Direction Studio
Danielle Prosciutto Client
Providence RI

187
Bob Paganucci Art Director
Ciba-Geigy Client
Summit NJ

188
Erkki Ruuhinen Art Director
Ilmari Kostiainen Photographer
Anderson & Lembke Oy Agency
Pohjola-Yhtiot Client
Helsinki, Finland

189
Rudolph de Harak, John D. Branigan, Stewart Siskind Art Directors
Stanford Golob Photographer
Rudolph de Harak & Assoc., Inc. Design Firm
River Tower Assoc. Client
New York NY

190
Torbjorn Winckler Art Director
Johnny Johansson Photographer
Stendahls Vasagatan Studio
Volvo RS Client
Gothenburg, Sweden

191
Gregg Sibert Art Director
R.A. Cooney, Inc. Studio
The Rowland Co. & The Scotch Whisky Information Center Client
New York NY

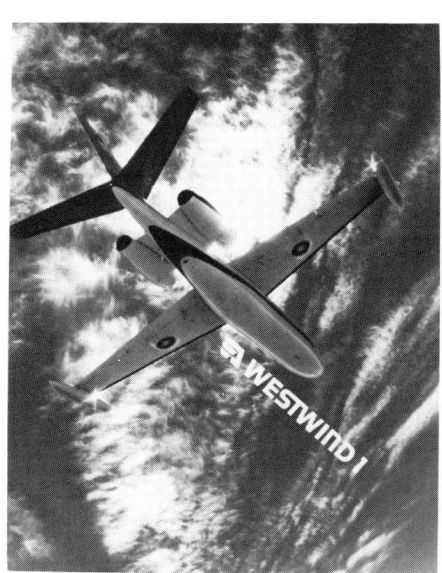

192
Clement Mok Art Director
Richard Baehr, Bon Hui-Uy Illustrators
Bo Parker, Jack Horner Photographers
Donovan & Green Studio
Cooper, Eckstut Assoc. Client
New York NY

193
Michael Tedesco Art Director
Atlantic Aviation Client
New York NY

194
Morton Goldsholl Art Director
**David Clifton/Lee Balterman
 Hedrich-Blessing/Edward Lee**
  Photographers
Goldsholl Associates Studio
Metropolitan Structure Client
Northfield IL

195
Michael Souter Art Director
Tim Girvin Illustrator
Communications Design Studio
Kaiser Permanente Federal Credit Union
  Client
Sacramento CA

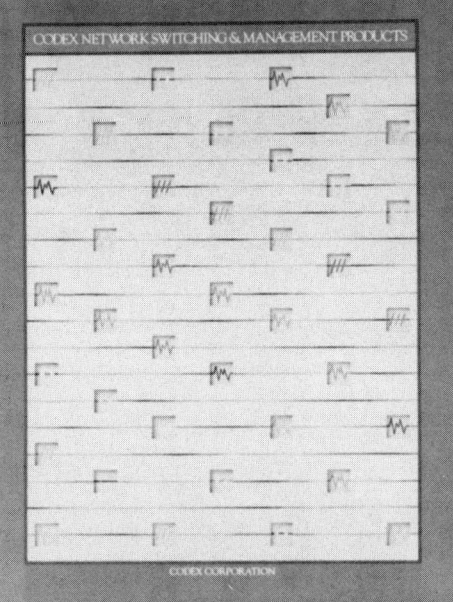

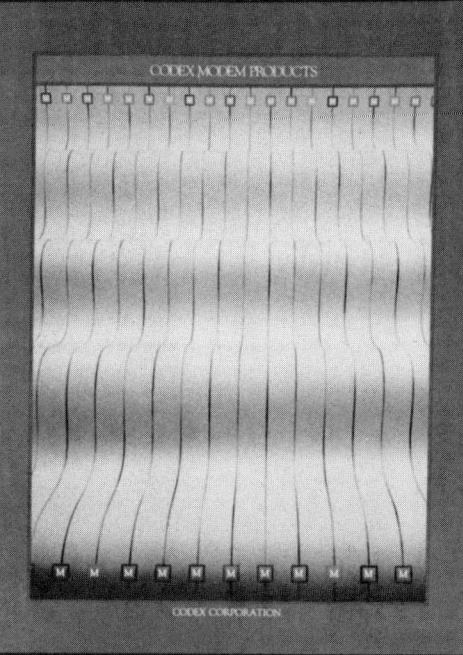

196
Marty Neumeier, Sandra Higashi Art
  Directors
Neumeier Design Team Studio
U.S. Invest Client
Santa Barbara CA

197
Cheryl Heller Art Director
Michael Orzech Illustrator
Jack Richmond Photographer
HBM Design Group Studio
Codex Client
Boston MA

198
Jack Odette Art Director
Steve Hodowsky Designer
Citibank Client
New York NY

199
Kathleen Trainer Art Director
Richard Barre Copywriter
James Chen Photographer
John M. Alexander-Barre Adv. Agency
Santa Barbara Designs Client
Santa Barbara CA

200
Bob Salpeter Art Director
IBM Client
New York NY

In any business, you have to measure

to manage

IBM

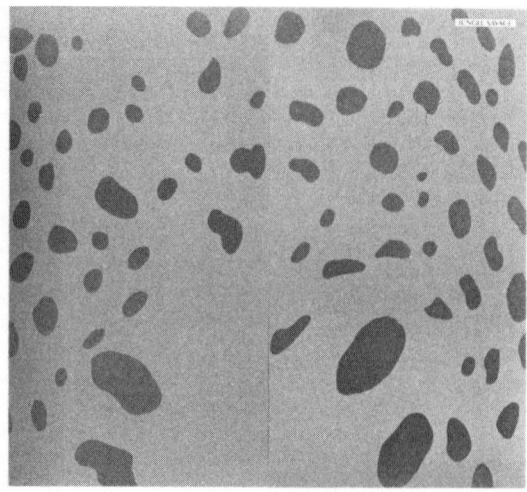
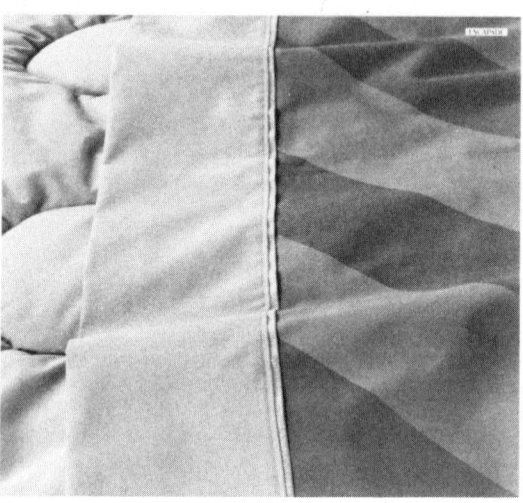

201
James Sebastian Art Director
Joe Standart, Elizabeth Heyert
  Photographers
James Sebastian, Michael Laurentano
  Designers
Crafton Graphic Co. Inc. Production
Martex/West Point Pepperell Client
New York NY

202
Harry Gutman Art Director
Herbert Migal Photographer
Mark Pollack Production Coordinator
Steelograph Co. Inc. Production
Jack Lenoir Larsen Client
New York NY

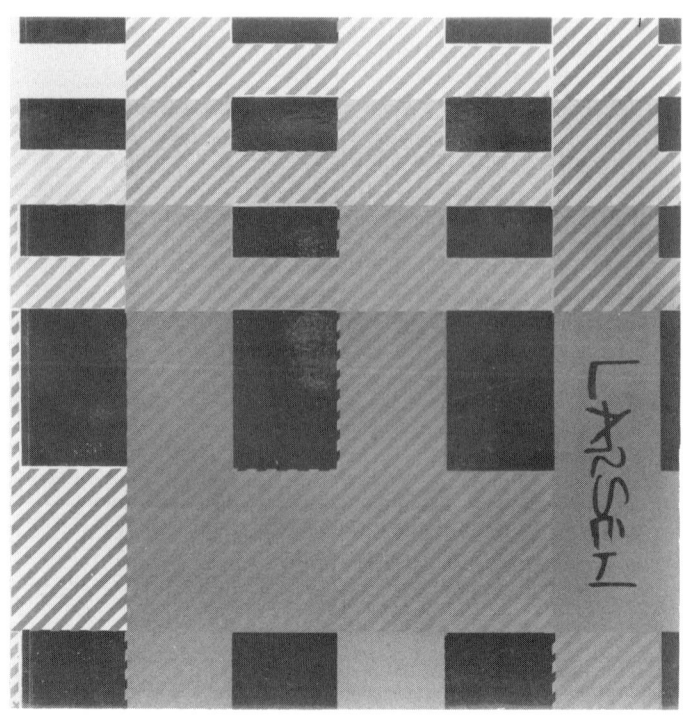

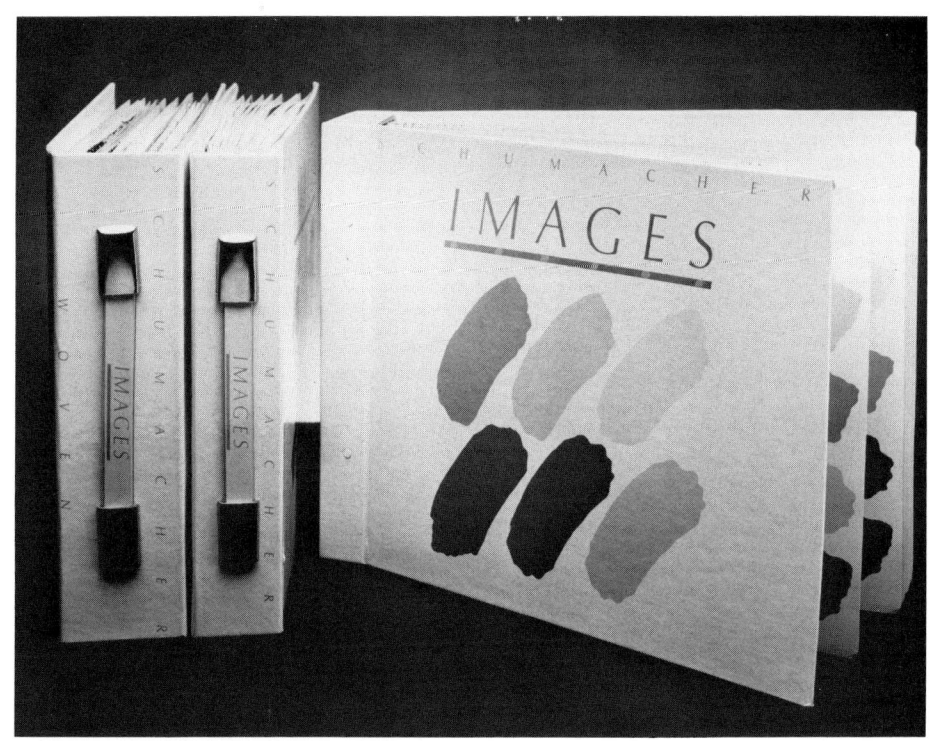

Raymond Waites, Cheryl Lewin Art Directors
Bruce Wolf Photographer
Gear Studio
Schumacher Client
New York NY

CRAFTSMANSHIP TELLS

DECLARATION 1
NICHOLS & STONE

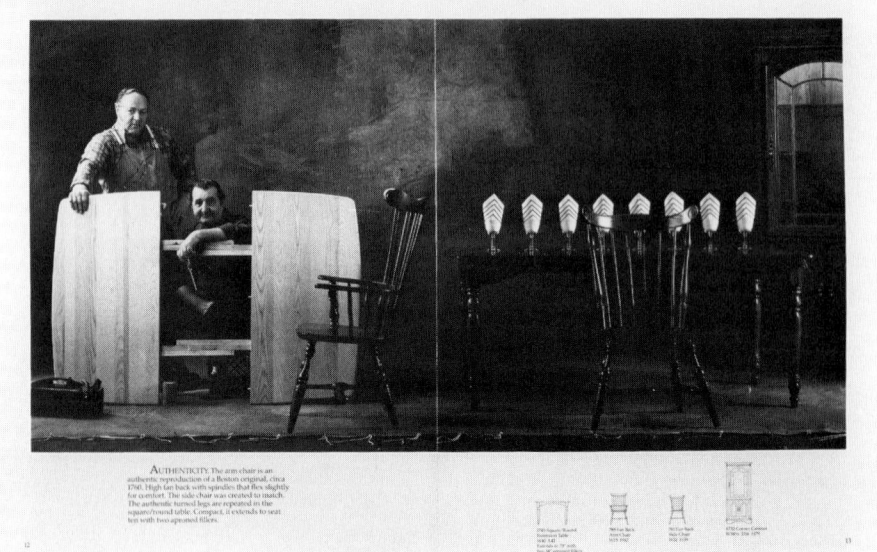

204
Marie McGinley Art Director
Alderman's Illustrator
Al Fisher Photographer
June Agranat Copywriter
Harcomm Assocs. Agency
Nichols & Stone Client
Cambridge MA

205
James Hellmuth Art Director
Mark Greenspun Copywriter
Don Sparks Photography Photographer
Rudd International Client
Atlanta GA

206
Terry Lesniewicz/Al Navarre Designers
Owens Corning Photo Services
   Photographers
Lesniewicz/Navarre Studio
Owens-Corning Fiberglas Corp. Client
Toledo OH

207
Muts Yasumura/Joy Greene Art Directors
Joy Greene/Sadat Pakay Photographers
Yasumura & Assoc. Agency
Amiran Corp. Client
New York NY

208
Clement Mok Art Director
BRT Photographic Illustrators
Donovan & Green Studio
Litton Business Furniture Client
New York NY

209
Paul Deur Copmpany Designer
John Boucher, Earl Woods Photographers
Haworth, Inc. Client
Grand Rapids MI

210
Eva Martin Art Director
Goran Tell Copywriter
HLR/BBDO Agency
Tarkett AB Client
Stockholm, Sweden

211
Jeff Moriber Art Director
Gabe Palmer Photographer
Hill & Knowlton Inc. Studio
BA Capital Corp. Client
New York NY

212
Gosta Enhammar Art Director
Marten Gullstrand Photographer
Gunnar Ekberg Copywriter
Ogilvy & Mather AB Agency
PLM Pac Client
Malmo, Sweden

213
Jody Famuliner Art Director
Bruce Peterson Photographer
Steven O. Petty, Cathy L. Famuliner
    Copywriters
Zeitgeist/Houston Studio
Pyro Energy Corp. Client
Houston TX

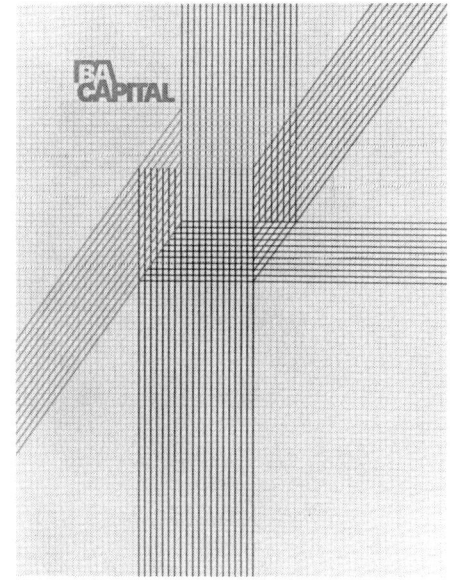

211

213

214
Eva Martin Art Director
Bjorn Keller Photographer
Goran Tell Copywriter
HLR/BBDO Agency
Tarkett AB Client
Stockholm, Sweden

215
Don Denny Art Director
Brent Cavedo Photographer
Sherri Williams Copywriter
Philip Morris Design Group Studio
Philip Morris U.S.A. Client
Richmond VA

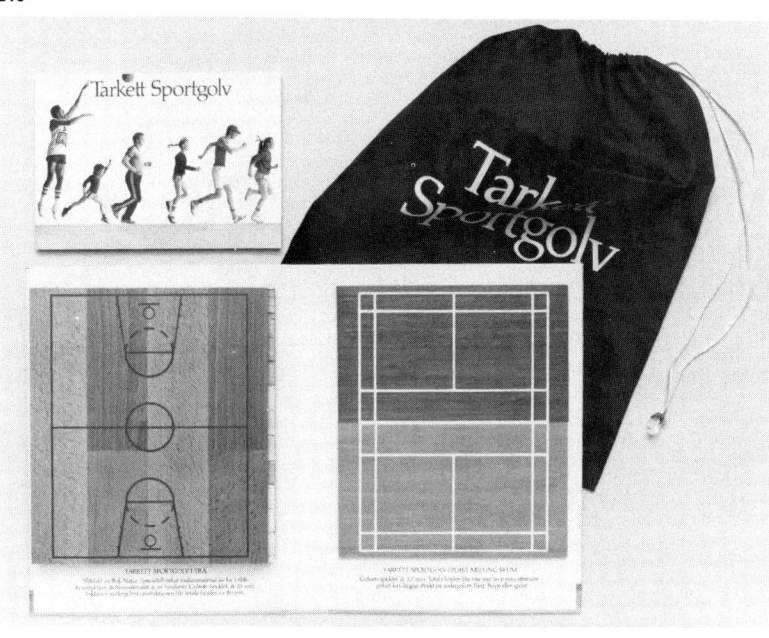

212

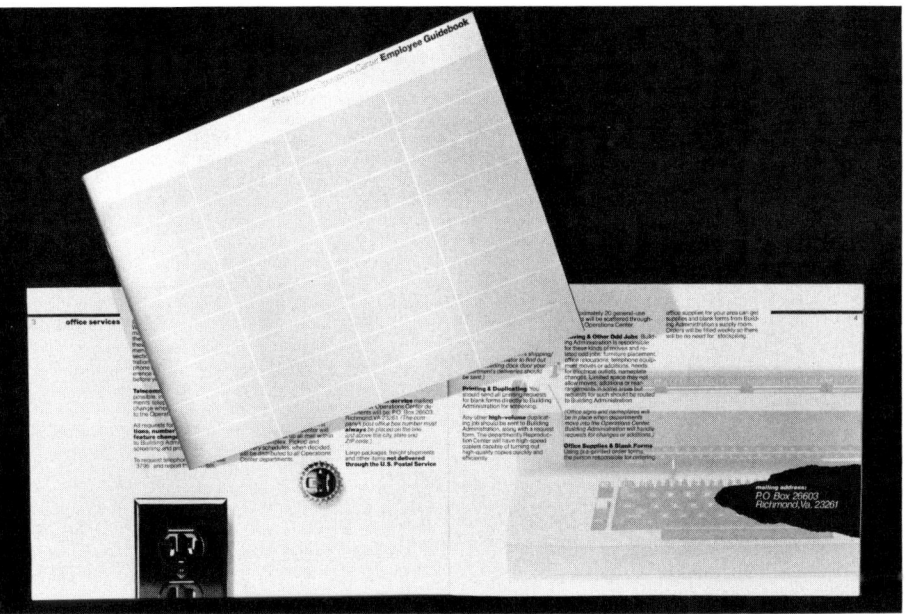

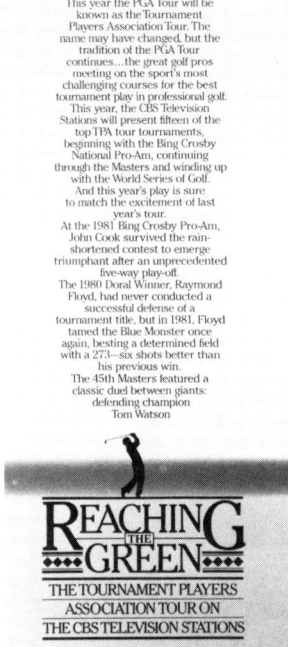

216
Pat Kroutel Art Director
Jim Osborn Photographer
Lawhead Press Studio
Rocky Boots Client
Athens OH

217
Lou Dorfsman, Ted Andresakes Art Directors
Grace Uhlig Designer
CBS Photo Photographers
CBS Advertising & Design Studio
CBS Television Stations Client
New York NY

218
Diana Marshall Art Director
Robert Stevens Photographer
The Designory Studio
Yamaha Parts Distributors Inc. Client
Los Angeles CA

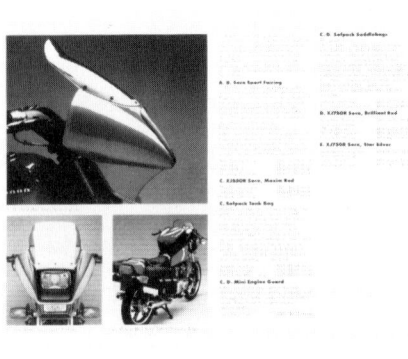

219
Art Riser, Danny Strickland Art Directors
Edward Jett Designer
Jamie Cook Photographer
Art Riser Creative Director
John H. Harland Co. Client
Atlanta GA

220

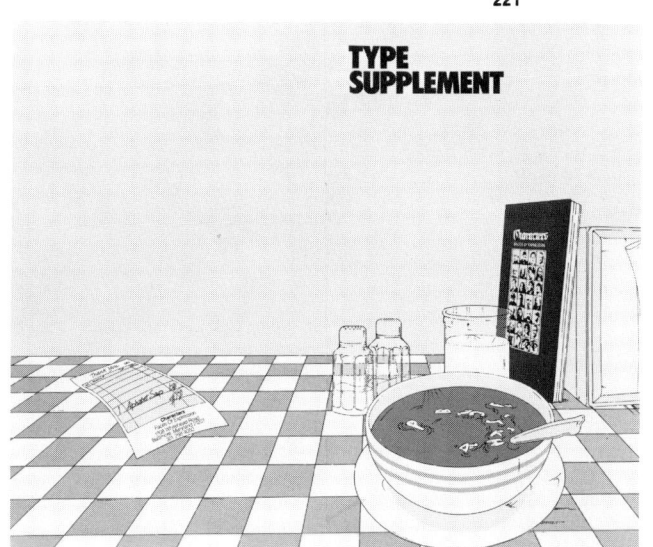

221

220
Kyosti Varis Designer
Kaj. G. Lindholm Photographer
Kyosti Varis/VPV Oy Studio
United Paper Mills Ltd. Jamsankoski Client
Helsinki, Finland

221
Jack de Lange Art Director
Henry Kaein/Jan Woudt Photographers
Cor Visser Illustrator
Gerard Portengen Designer
DLS Communications B.V. Agency
Wessanen Meel B.V. Client
Zaandam Holland

222
Eric Diggs Art Director
The Woods Group Agency
Characters Client
Baltimore MD

223
Jose A. Garcia-Luna, Marcos Rodriguez, Javier Torres Art Directors
Michel Zabe Photographer
Formento Cultural Banamex A.C. Client
Tlalnepantla, Mexico

224
McRay Magleby Art Director
Graphic Comm. Studio
Brigham Young University Client
Provo UT

226
Joel Margulies Art Director
Curtis Davis Writer
American Broadcasting Co. Client
New York NY

225
Kay Sabinson Art Director
Margaret Youngblood Designer
Bernard Collet Photographer
Burson-Marsteller-Paris/France Cartes
  Client
Highland Park IL

227
Russell A. Patrick Art Director
David Barnett, Dennis Barnett Designers
Graphic Solutions, Inc. Studio
HBO National Sales & Planning Client
New York NY

228
Erica Skioldebrand Art Director
Bo Trenter Photographer
Anderson & Lembke Danderydsgatan
  Agency
Soina Offset AB Client
Stockholm, Sweden

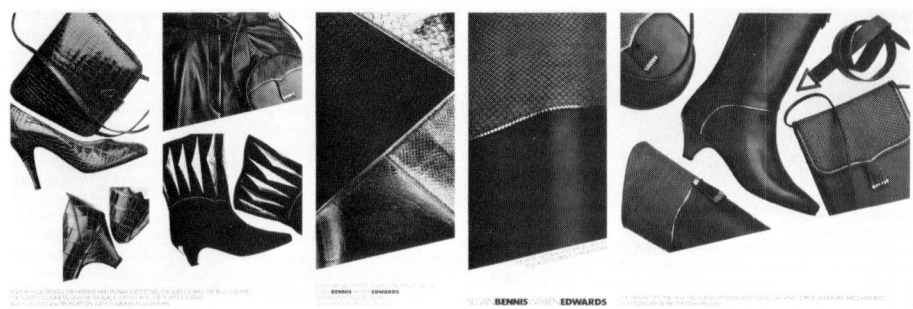

229
Stanley Eisenman, Dennis Dollens Art Directors
John Pilgreen Photographer
Eisenman & Enock Inc. Agency
Susan Bennis/Warren Edwards Client
New York NY

230
Patrick A. Old Art Director
Anne A. Old Illustrator
Oroton/Whiting & Davis Co. Client
Haywards Heath, England

231
Torbjorn Lindgren Art Director
Johan Ronn Photographer
HLR/BBDO, Artillerigatan Agency
Marc O' Polo Client
Stockholm, Sweden

232
Torbjorn Lindgren Art Director
HLR/BBDO Agency
Medisan Client
Stockholm, Sweden

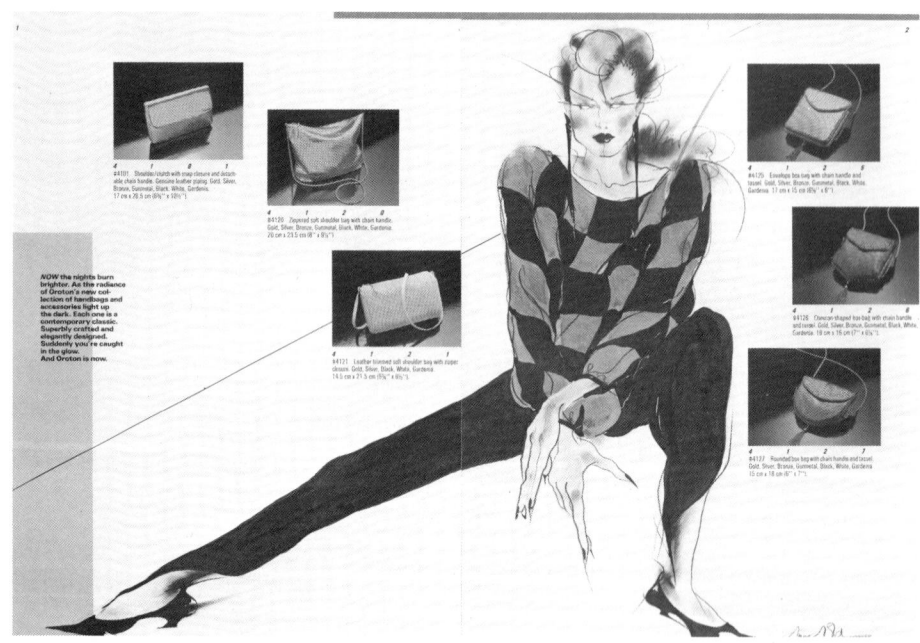

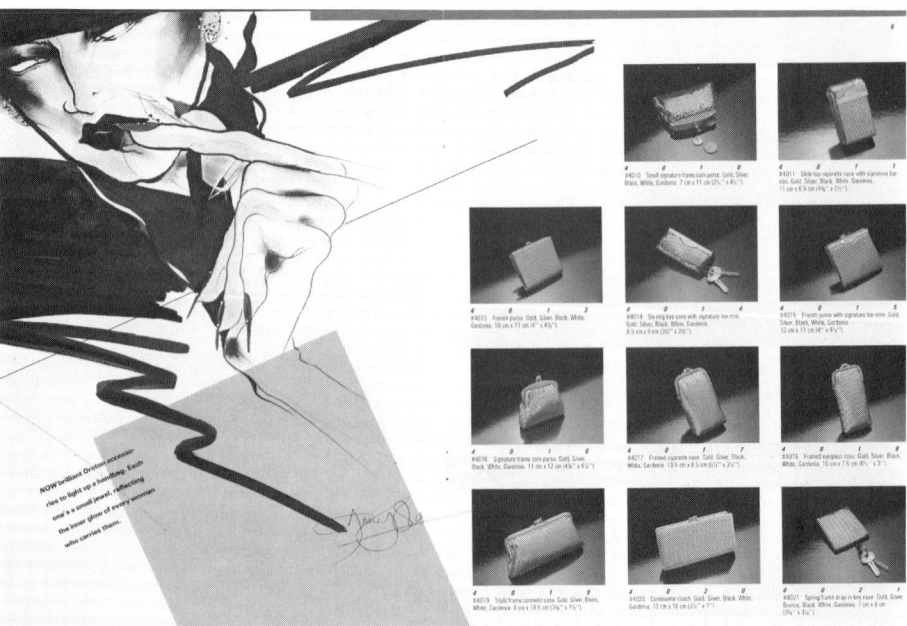

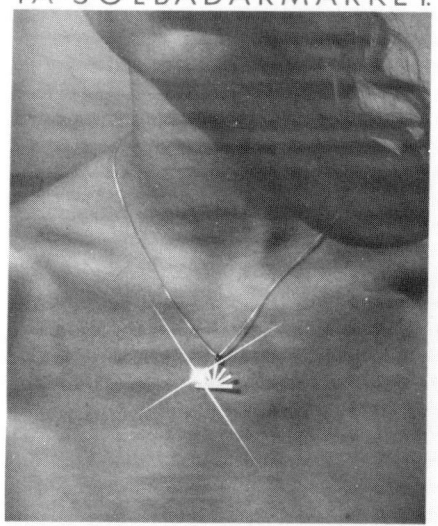

232

233
Tyler Smith Designer
Jacques Malignon Photographer
Tyler Smith, Art Direction Inc. Studio
Ann Taylor Client
Providence RI

234
Leonard Restivo Art Director
Saks Fifth Avenue Client
New York NY

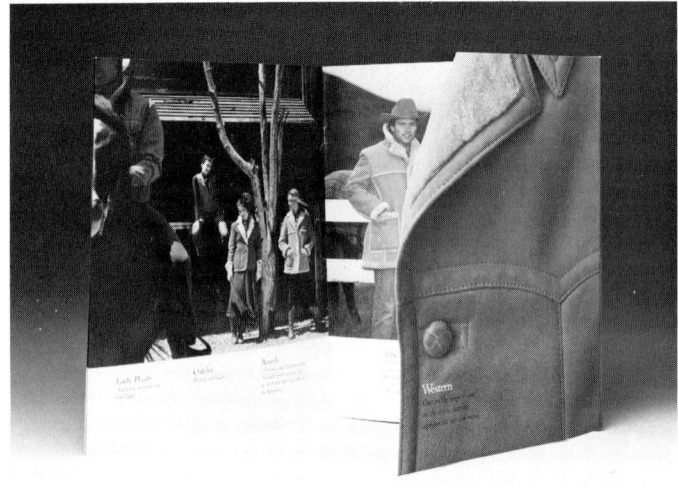

235
David Gauger, Mary Rudnicki Orr, Mark Decena Art Directors
Larry Silva Copywriter
John Horvers Photographer
Gauger Sparks Silva, Inc. Agency
Sawyer of Napa Client
San Francisco CA

236
David Blumenthal Art Director
Henry Wolf Photographer
Ken Hall Copywriter
Henry Wolf Productions Studio
After Six Client
New York NY

Book Jackets

237
Louise Fili Art Director
Dagmar Frinta Illustrator
Louise Fili Letterer
Pantheon Books Client
New York NY

THE BRANDEIS/FRANKFURTER C·O·N·N·E·C·T·I·O·N

The Secret Political Activities of Two Supreme Court Justices
Bruce Allen Murphy

241

241
Don Munson Art Director
Alex Jay Designer & Calligraphy
Ballantine Books Client
New York NY

242
Rubin Pfeffer Art Director
Bascove Illustrator
Harcourt Brace Jovanovich Client
New York NY

239

238
Leonard Levitsky Designer
Elliott Banfield Illustrator
Laura Brown Creative Director Marketing
Oxford University Press Client
New York NY

239
Judith Loeser Art Director
Cathy Saksa Designer
Tony deSpigna Lettering
Random House/Vintage Client
New York NY

240
Richard Adelson Art Director
George W. Sanders Jr. Illustrator
Viking Press Client
New York NY

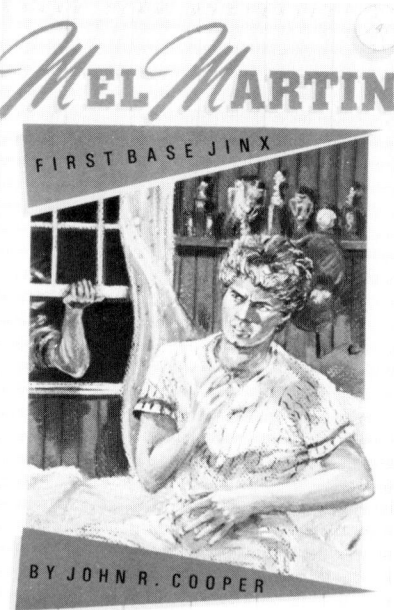

243
Rebecca Tachna Art Director
Barbara Maslen Illustrator
Jonette Jakobson Creative Director
Simon & Schuster/Wanderer Books Client
New York NY

244
Carol Goldenberg Art Director
Diane deGroat Illustrator
Houghton Mifflin Company Client
Yonkers NY

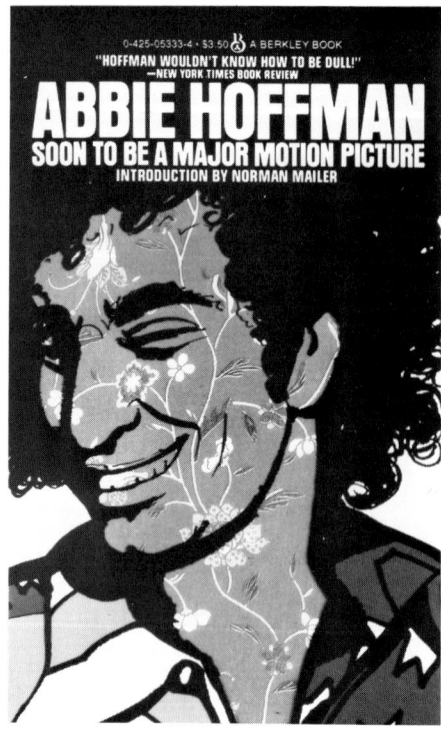

245
Frank Metz Art Director
Wendell Minor Illustrator
Simon & Schuster Client
New York NY

246
Gene Mydlowski Art Director
Milton Glaser Illustrator
Berkley Books Client
New York NY

248
Michael Less Art Director
AWE/Gebers Client
Copenhagen, Denmark

249
Steven Hoffman Designer
Performing Arts Journal Publications Client
New York NY

250
Iska Rothovius Art Director
Michael Dudash Illustrator
New York Telephone Client
New York NY

249

Queens

247
Charles A. Carson Art Director
McGraw-Hill Book Co. Client
New York NY

251
Linda V. Rettich Art Director
Arnold Katz Photographer
Peter Borrell Copywriter
John Wiley & Sons Inc. Client
New York NY

252
Tom Clemente, Lynne Anderson Art Directors
Jim Richards Photographer
Newspaper Advertising Bureau Client
New York NY

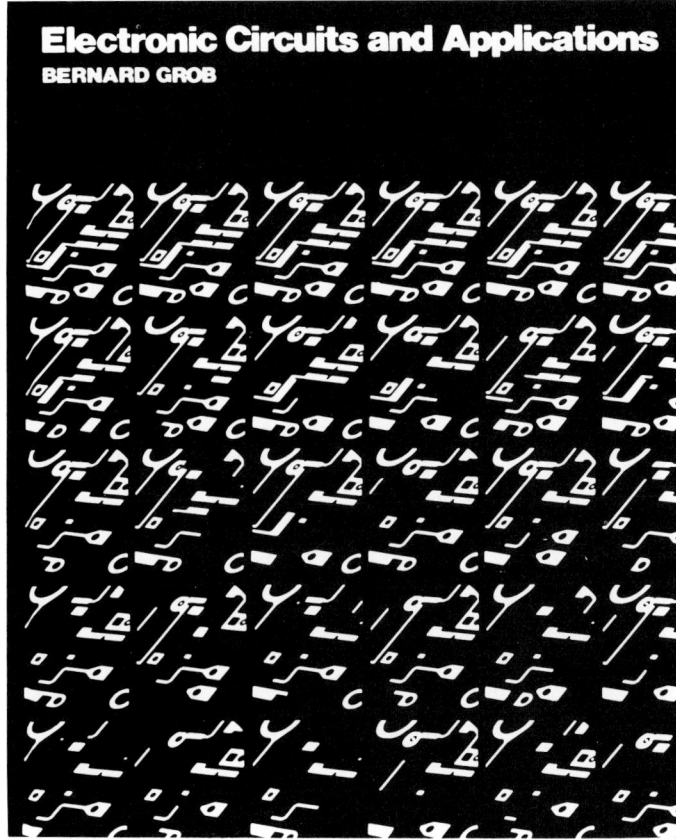

253
Karen Tureck Art Director
Patricia Lowy Designer
Lehigh/Autoscreen Production
Gregg Div. McGraw Hill Book Co. Client
New York NY

254
Toshiaki Ide Art Director
Seymour Chwast Illustrator
Push Pin Studio
NYC Dept. of Cultural Affairs Client
New York NY

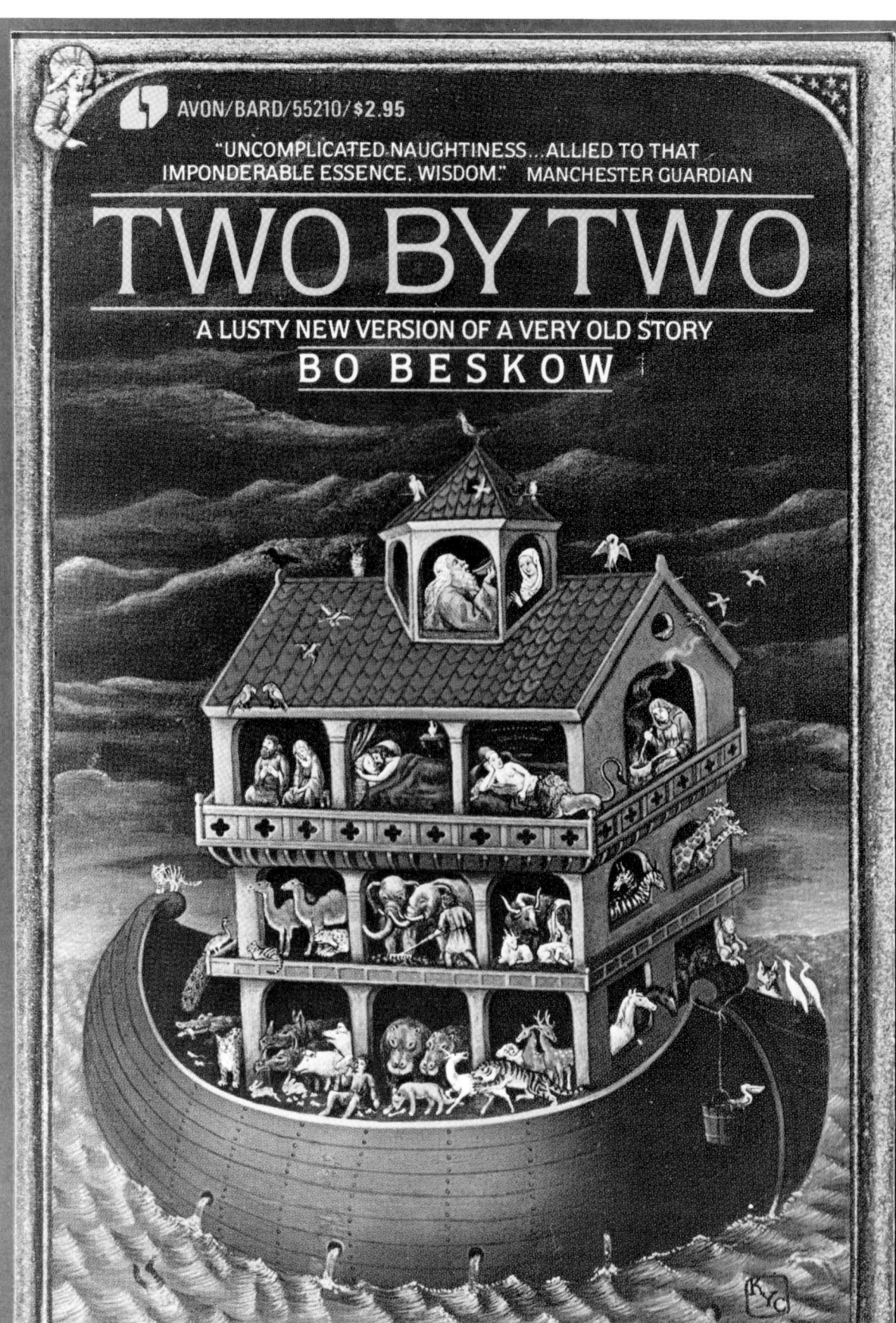

257

258

257
Judith Loeser Art Director
Bascove Illustrator
Vintage Client
New York NY

258
Marty Neumeier, Sandra Higashi Art Directors
Sandra Higashi Illustrator
Neumeler Design Team Studio
Creative Education Inc. Client
Santa Barbara CA

259
David Corbett Illustrator
Fodor's Travel Guides Client
New York NY

255
Carol Inouye Art Director
Kinuko Craft Illustrator
Avon Books Client
New York NY

256
Frank Metz Art Director
Wendell Minor Illustrator
Summit Books Client
New York NY

256

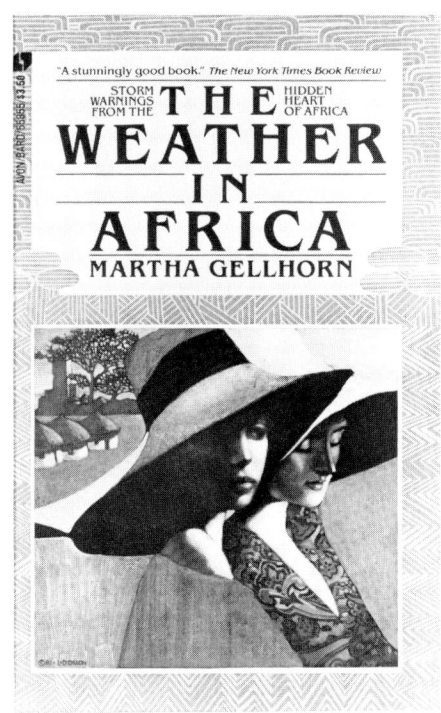

260
Les Meyers Art Director
Steven C. Wilson Photographer
Entheos Client
Bainbridge Island WA

261
Barbara Bertoli Art Director
Leo & Diane Dillon Illustrators
Avon Books Client
New York NY

262
J. Porter, John White Art Directors
Gordon Heckman, Jim Lamothe Illustrators
Yankee Books Client
Dublin NH

263
R. D. Scudellari Designer
John Gruen Photographer
Alfred A. Knopf Client
New York NY

264

265

266

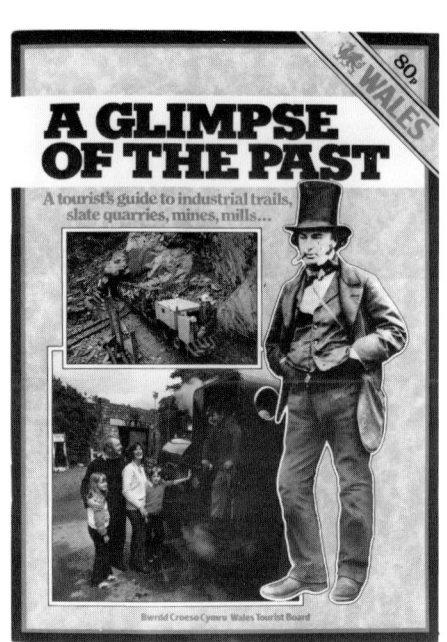
267

268

264
Louise Fili Art Director
Robert Crawford Illustrator
Pantheon Books Client
New York, NY

265
Mary Mietzelfeld Designer
Lynn Hollyn Associates Studio
Perigee Books Client
New York NY

266
Merrill Haber Art Director
McGraw-Hill Book Co. Client
New York NY

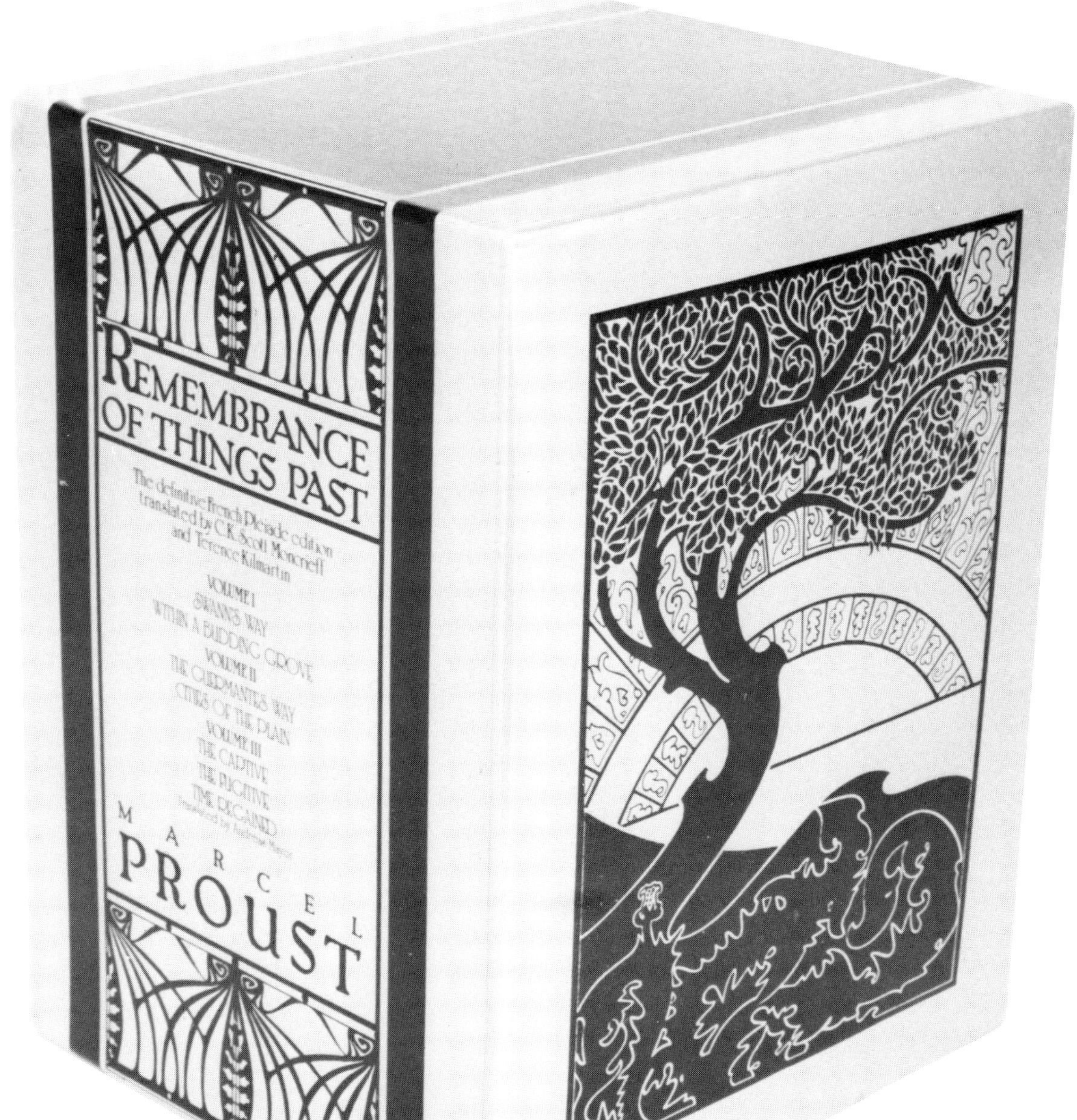

267
Tom Morgan Art Director
Colin Molyneux, Harry Williams
 Photographers
Wales Tourist Board Client
Cardiff, Wales

268
David Bullen Art Director
Larry Keenan Photographer
North Point Press Client
Oakland CA

269
Janet Odgis Designer
Guenet Abraham Art Director
Random House Client
New York NY

Record Album Covers

270

271

270
John Berg Designer
Trudy Schlachter Photographer
Inventive Eye Ltd. Studio
CBS Records Client
New York NY

271
Ron Coro Art Director
Kathy Morphesis Designer
Beth Bergman Photographer
Elektra/Asylum Records Client
Los Angeles CA

272
Ron Coro, Denise Minobe Art Directors
Marshall Arisman Illustrator
Elektra/Asylum Records Client
Los Angeles CA

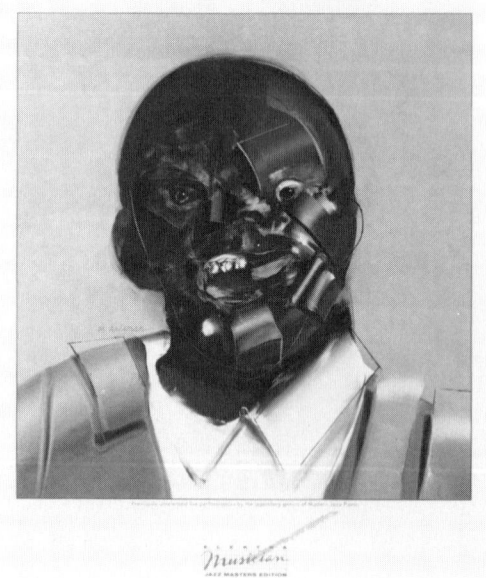

272

273
Ron Coro, Norm Ung Art Directors
Denise Minobe, Designer
Diane Lawrence, Illustrator
Elektra/Asylym Records Client
Los Angeles CA

274
Carol Bokuniewicz, Tibor Kalman Art Directors
Larry Kazal Designer
M & Company Studio
Hannibal Records Client
New York NY

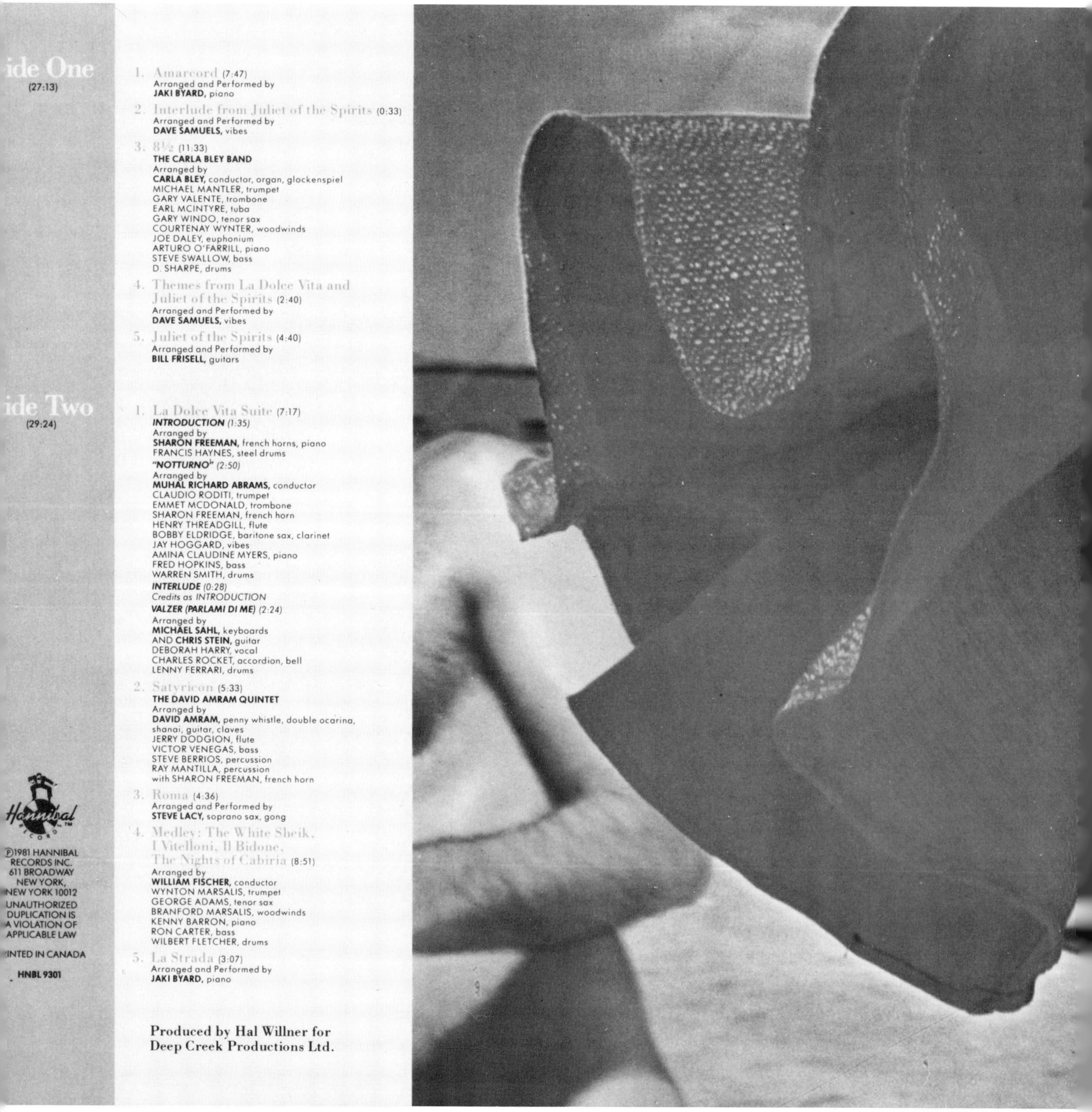

Side One (27:13)

1. *Amarcord* (7:47)
   Arranged and Performed by
   JAKI BYARD, piano
2. *Interlude from Juliet of the Spirits* (0:33)
   Arranged and Performed by
   DAVE SAMUELS, vibes
3. *8½* (11:33)
   THE CARLA BLEY BAND
   Arranged by
   CARLA BLEY, conductor, organ, glockenspiel
   MICHAEL MANTLER, trumpet
   GARY VALENTE, trombone
   EARL MCINTYRE, tuba
   GARY WINDO, tenor sax
   COURTENAY WYNTER, woodwinds
   JOE DALEY, euphonium
   ARTURO O'FARRILL, piano
   STEVE SWALLOW, bass
   D. SHARPE, drums
4. *Themes from La Dolce Vita and Juliet of the Spirits* (2:40)
   Arranged and Performed by
   DAVE SAMUELS, vibes
5. *Juliet of the Spirits* (4:40)
   Arranged and Performed by
   BILL FRISELL, guitars

Side Two (29:24)

1. *La Dolce Vita Suite* (7:17)
   INTRODUCTION (1:35)
   Arranged by
   SHARON FREEMAN, french horns, piano
   FRANCIS HAYNES, steel drums
   "NOTTURNO" (2:50)
   Arranged by
   MUHAL RICHARD ABRAMS, conductor
   CLAUDIO RODITI, trumpet
   EMMET MCDONALD, trombone
   SHARON FREEMAN, french horn
   HENRY THREADGILL, flute
   BOBBY ELDRIDGE, baritone sax, clarinet
   JAY HOGGARD, vibes
   AMINA CLAUDINE MYERS, piano
   FRED HOPKINS, bass
   WARREN SMITH, drums
   INTERLUDE (0:28)
   Credits as INTRODUCTION
   VALZER (PARLAMI DI ME) (2:24)
   Arranged by
   MICHAEL SAHL, keyboards
   AND **CHRIS STEIN**, guitar
   DEBORAH HARRY, vocal
   CHARLES ROCKET, accordion, bell
   LENNY FERRARI, drums
2. *Satyricon* (5:33)
   THE DAVID AMRAM QUINTET
   Arranged by
   DAVID AMRAM, penny whistle, double ocarina, shanai, guitar, claves
   JERRY DODGION, flute
   VICTOR VENEGAS, bass
   STEVE BERRIOS, percussion
   RAY MANTILLA, percussion
   with SHARON FREEMAN, french horn
3. *Roma* (4:36)
   Arranged and Performed by
   STEVE LACY, soprano sax, gong
4. *Medley: The White Sheik, I Vitelloni, Il Bidone, The Nights of Cabiria* (8:51)
   Arranged by
   WILLIAM FISCHER, conductor
   WYNTON MARSALIS, trumpet
   GEORGE ADAMS, tenor sax
   BRANFORD MARSALIS, woodwinds
   KENNY BARRON, piano
   RON CARTER, bass
   WILBERT FLETCHER, drums
5. *La Strada* (3:07)
   Arranged and Performed by
   JAKI BYARD, piano

℗1981 HANNIBAL RECORDS INC.
611 BROADWAY
NEW YORK,
NEW YORK 10012
UNAUTHORIZED
DUPLICATION IS
A VIOLATION OF
APPLICABLE LAW

PRINTED IN CANADA

HNBL 9301

Produced by Hal Willner for Deep Creek Productions Ltd.

275
Chuck Beeson, Jeff Ayeroff Art Directors
Melanie Nissen Designer
A & M Records Client
Los Angeles CA

276
Ron Coro Art Director
Kristen Nikosey Designer
James McMullan Illustrator
Elektra/Asylum Records Client
Los Angeles CA

277
Christopher Austopchuk Art Director
Seymour Chwast Illustrator
CBS Records Client
New York NY

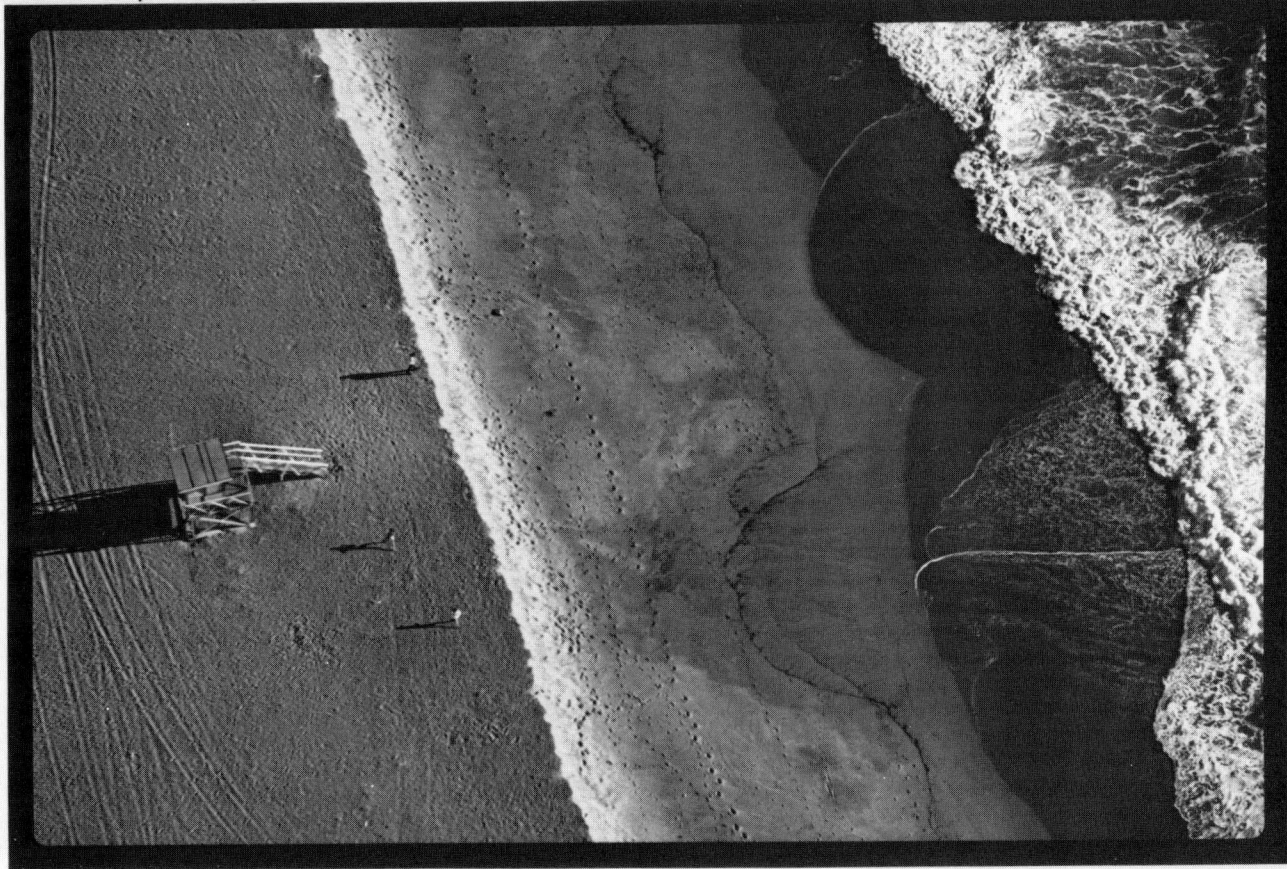

279
Phil Carroll Art Director
Jamie Putnam Designer
Theresa Weedy Photographer
Fantasy Records Client
Berkeley CA

281
Phil Carroll Art Director
Jamie Putnam Designer
Steve Fitch Photographer
Fantasy Records Client
Berkeley CA

280
Ron Coro, Norm Ung Art Directors
Daniel Schwartz Illustrator
Elektra/Asylum Records Client
Los Angeles CA

282
Dian-Aziza Ooka Art Director
Paddy Reynolds Photographer
Adolescent Records Client
San Francisco CA

283
Joan Hall Illustrator
Atco Records Client
New York NY

285
Christopher Austopchuk Art Director
CBS Records Client
New York NY

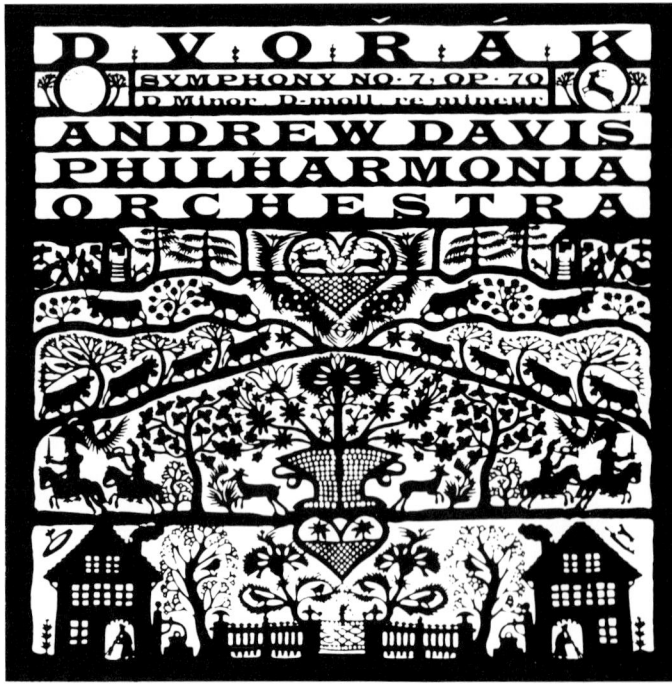

284
Linda Crockett-Hanzel Illustrator
RCA Records Client
Romeo MI

286
Bill Johnson, Virginia Team Art Directors
Deb Mahalanobis Illustrator
Barnes & Company Studio
CBS Records Client
Nashville TN

288
Dian-Aziza Ooka, Martha Geering Art Directors
Adolescent Records Client
San Francisco CA

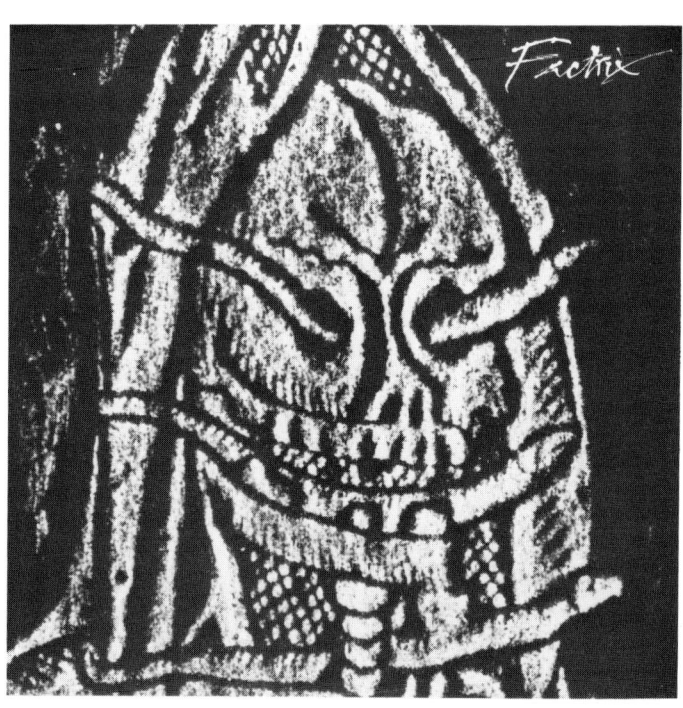

287
Maira Berman, Tibor Kalman Art Directors
Maira Berman Illustrator
M & Company Studio
Warner Brothers Records Client
New York NY

289
Phil Carroll Art Director
Jamie Putnam Photographer
Prestige Records Client
Berkeley CA

290
Bob Heimall Art Director
Montxo Algora Illustrator
Polygram Records Client
New York NY

Magazine Covers

291
Carol Bokuniewicz, Tibor Kalman Art
  Directors
Carol Bokuniewicz Illustrator
M & Company Studio
Art Direction Client
New York NY

292
Robert J. Post Art Director
Eraldo Carugati Illustrator
Chicago Magazine Client
Chicago IL

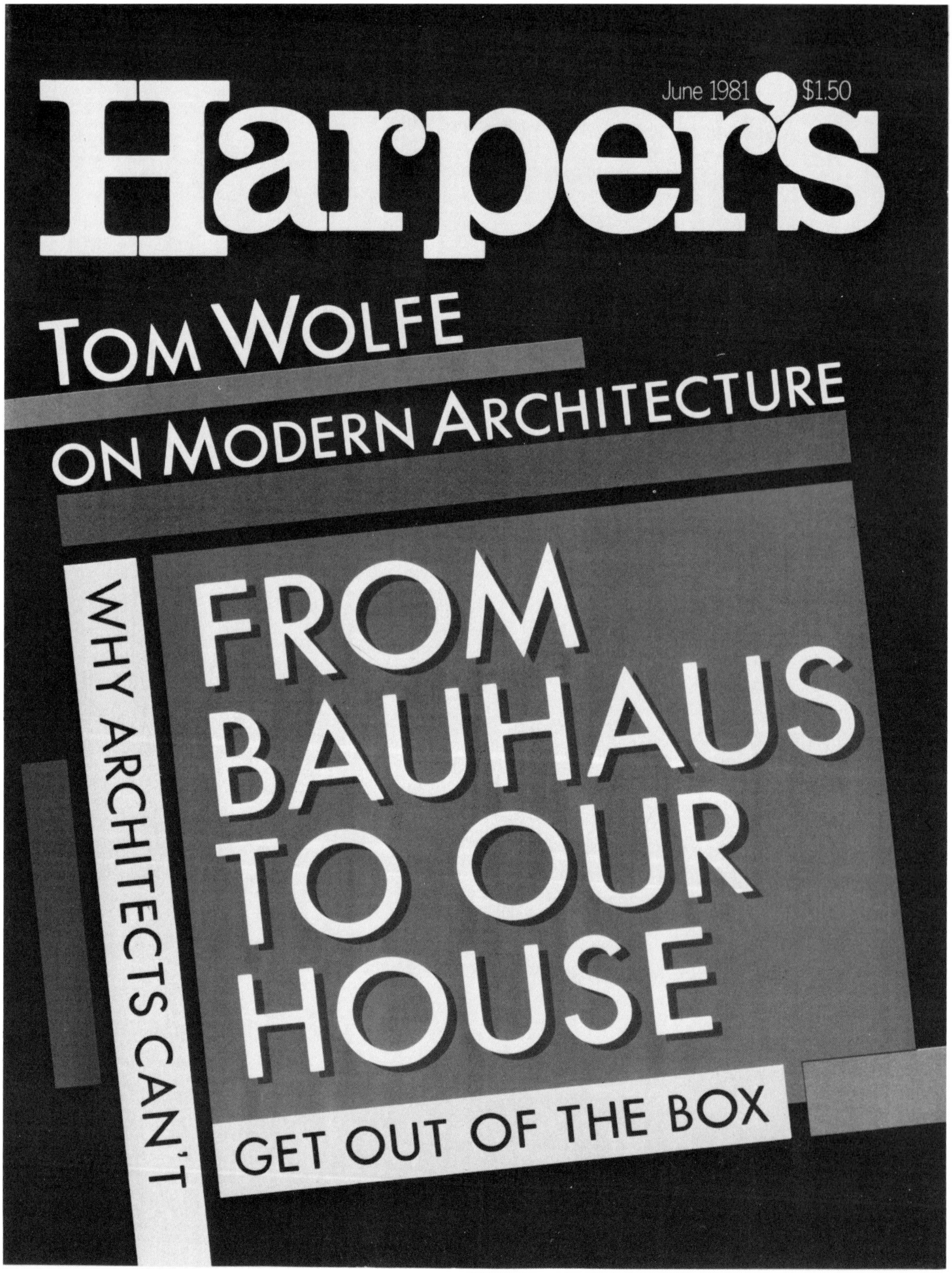

Harper's

June 1981 $1.50

Tom Wolfe on Modern Architecture

From Bauhaus to Our House

Why Architects Can't Get Out of the Box

293
Deborah Rust Art Director
Harper's Magazine Client
New York NY

294
Michael Grossman Art Director
Ronald G. Harris Photographer
National Lampoon Client
New York NY

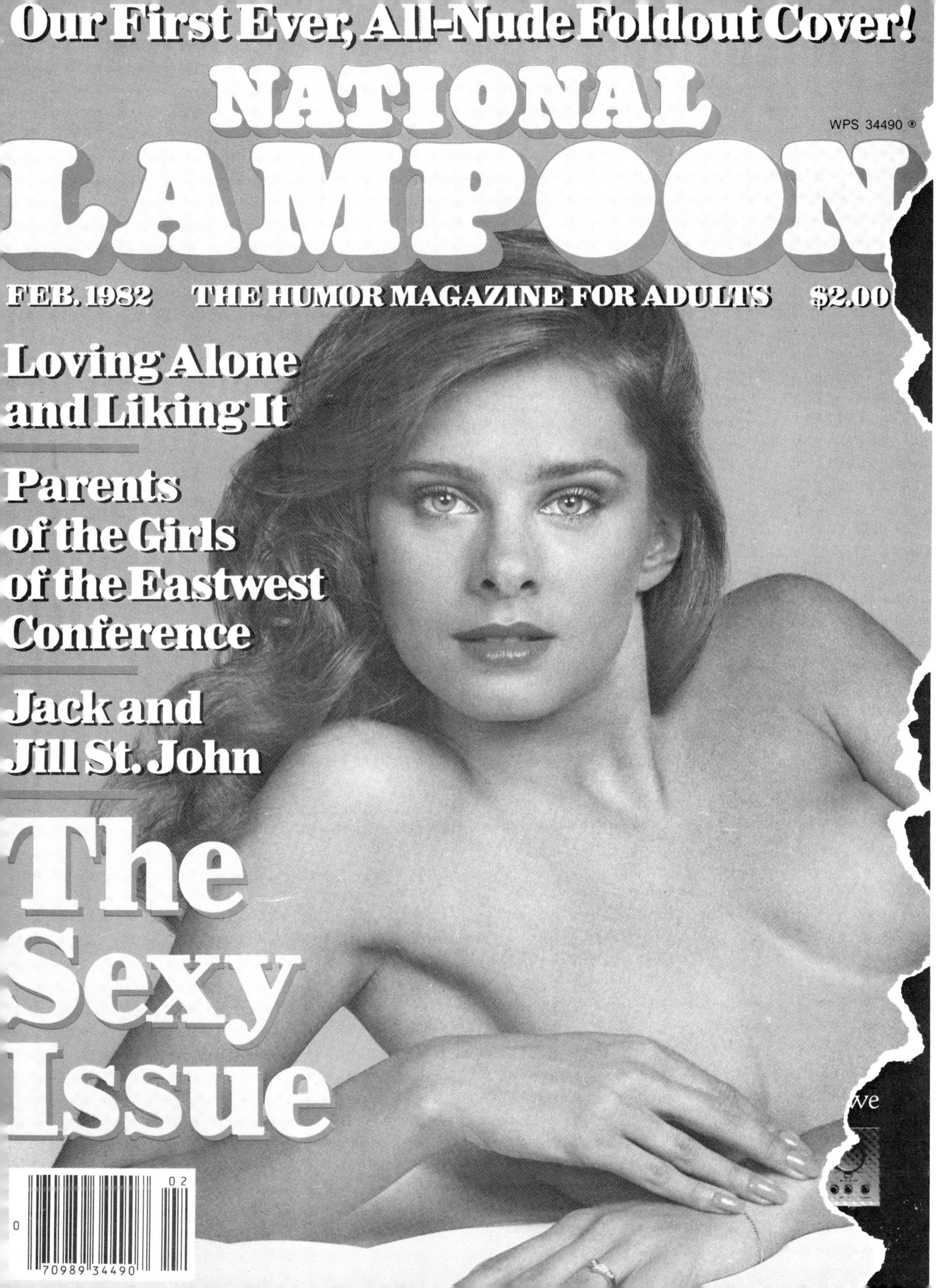
Our First Ever, All-Nude Foldout Cover!
NATIONAL LAMPOON
WPS 34490 ®
FEB. 1982
THE HUMOR MAGAZINE FOR ADULTS
$2.00
Loving Alone and Liking It
Parents of the Girls of the Eastwest Conference
Jack and Jill St. John
The Sexy Issue
02
0
70989 34490

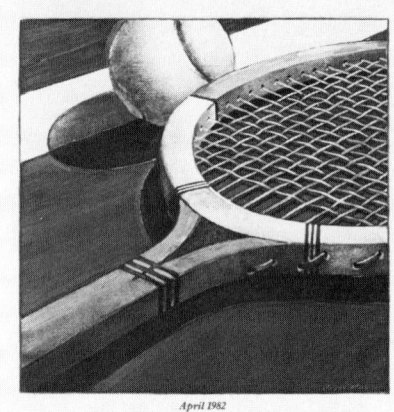

295
Georges Haroutiun, Rod Della-Vedova Art Directors
Roger Hill Illustrator
Joanna Bain Designer
M.A.G. Graphics Ltd. Studio
Bloor Publishing Client
Toronto, Canada

296
Bart Kuiper Art Director
George Noordanus Designer
Andrew Holmes Illustrator
Gerrit Serne Photographer
Ogilvy & Mather BV Agency
Shell Nederlandse Verk. Mij. BV Client
Amsterdam, Holland

297
Greg Paul Art Director
Nancy Niles Illustrator
The Plain Dealer Magazine Client
Cleveland OH

298
Ed Davis Art Director
Footwear News Client
New York NY

299
Maynard Dixon Illustrator
Smitherman Graphic Design Studio
Hundred Arrows Press Client
Austin TX

300
Wayne Burkart Art Director
Tom Sizemore Designer
David Deahl Photographer
Deere & Company Client
Moline IL

JD JOURNAL

PUMPING IRON:
EIGHT EMPLOYEES
WHO WORK
HARD AT PLAY
ALSO:
ENGLAND, STRESS,
1980, AND MONDAYPHOBIA

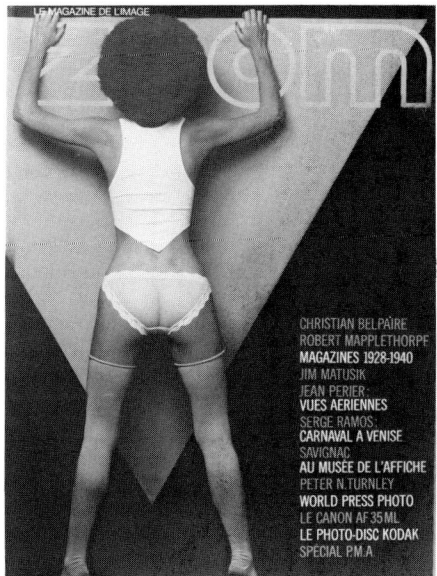

301
Jeff Barnes Art Director
Dennis Manarchy Photographer
Alexander Communications Studio
Chicago Talent Inc. Client
Wheaton IL

302
Patricia Gipple Art Director
Warner Brothers Records, Inc.
 Photographers
America Illustrated Client
Washington D.C.

303
Nick Melillo Photographer
Zoom Magazine Client
New York NY

304
Jim Lienhart Art Director
Tom Chambers Photographer
Savings & Loan News Client
Chicago IL

305
Rudy Hoglund Art Director
Henry Wolf Photographer
Henry Wolf Productions Studio
Time Magazine Client
New York NY

306
Jack J. Podell Art Director
Herbert Jackson Photographer
Catherine Cahan Editor
Student Lawyer Client
Chicago IL

307
Lee Ann Jaffee Art Director
Michael Garland Illustrator
View Magazine Client
New York NY

308
Joseph Davis Art Director
Bil Plummer Photographer
Housing Magazine Client
New York NY

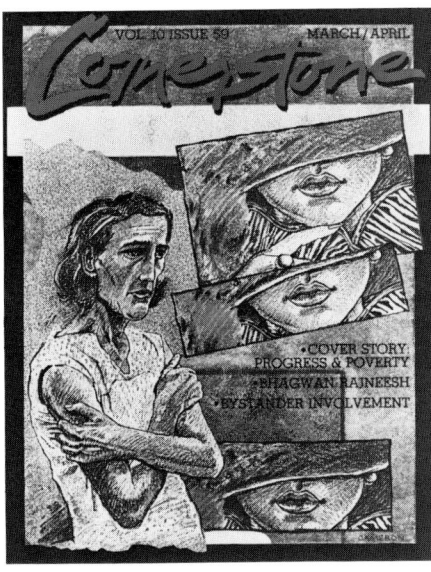

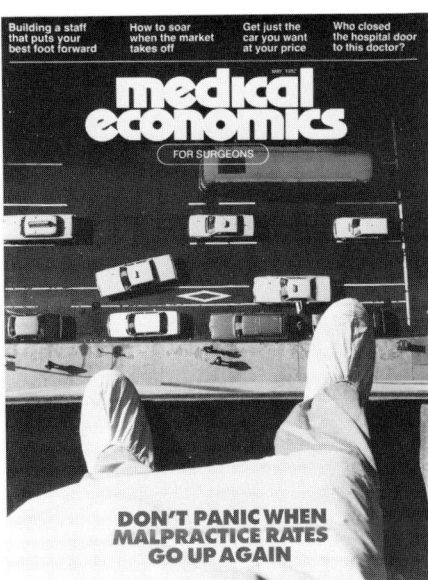

309
Janet Cameron Art Director
J.P.U.S.A. Graphics Studio
Cornerstone Magazine Client
Chicago IL

310
George Obremski Art Director
Avenue Magazine Client
New York NY

311
Pelayia Limbos Art Director
Ron Dicianni Illustrator
The Rotarian Magazine Client
Evanston IL

312
Marty Eggerding Art Director
Toni Santo Regis Illustrator
Cincinnati Enquirer Magazine Client
Cincinnati OH

313
John Newcomb Art Director
Walter Wick Photographer
Medical Economics for Surgeons Client
Oradell NJ

 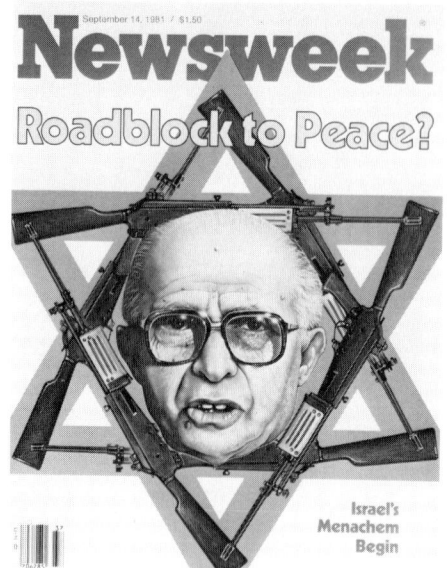 

314
Milton Glaser Illustrator
Jeff Babitz Graphics Studio
A.D. Magazine Client
Corona NY

315
Bob Engle, Ron Meyerson Art Directors
Wayne McLoughlin Illustrator
Newsweek Client
New York NY

316
K.W. Henschel/Bengt Fosshag Art Directors
Leonid Kamarowsky Photographer
Wirtschaftswoche Client
Frankfurt/Maine West Germany

317
Albert N. Garland Art Director
Mary Ann Norton Illustrator
Infantry Magazine Client
Ft. Benning GA

318
Hrair Vartanian Art Director
Wang Laboratories Client
Lowell MA

319
Louise Kollenbaum Art Director
Dian-Aziza Ooka Designer
Richard Hess Illustrator
Mother Jones Magazine Client
San Francisco CA

APRIL 1982 — $1.75

Sperm Count Crisis

MOTHER JONES

On Board The World's Biggest Warship

The Clash: Rock And Revolution

Sweet Sinsemilla

READY FOR WAR

Progressive Architecture

September 1981

Interior design:
An archaeological dig into the present

320
George Coderre Art Director
April Greiman Illustrator
Progressive Architecture Client
Stamford CT

321
Fred B. Eiseman Jr. Photographer
Emphasis (Hong Kong) Ltd. Studio
Cathay Pacific Inflight Magazine 'Discovery' Client
Hong Kong

322
Gregory Downer Art Director
Opera News Client
New York NY

323
Howard R. Klein Creative Director
Buddy Jenssen Photographer
Fieldmark Media Inc. Client
New York NY

324
Mauro Filicori Art Director
Eli Barr Designer
Bob Day Photographer
Filicori Visual Communications, Inc. Studio
Texaco, Inc. Client
New York NY

Package Design

325
Wayne Krimston Art Director
Murrie White Drummond Lienhart Studio
Amity Leather Products Client
Chicago IL

326
Ross Carron Art Director
Carron Design Studio
J.W. Morris Wineries Client
San Francisco CA

327
John Coy Art Director
Ardison Phillips Artist
COY, Los Angeles Studio
Andrew Quady Vineyards Client
Culver City CA

329

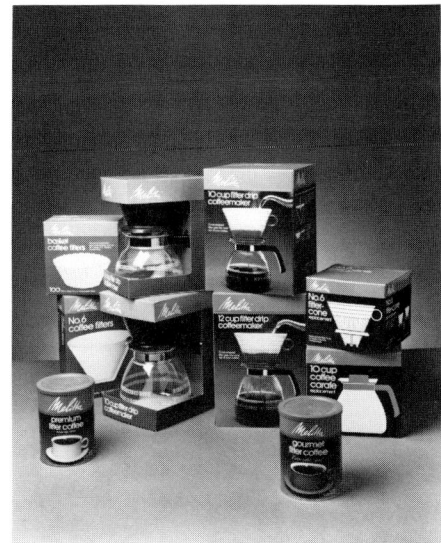

332

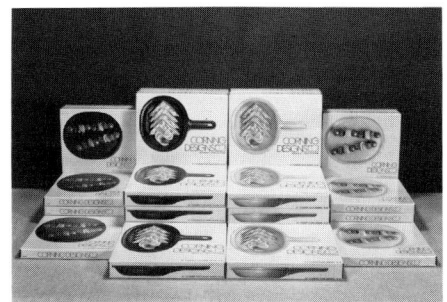

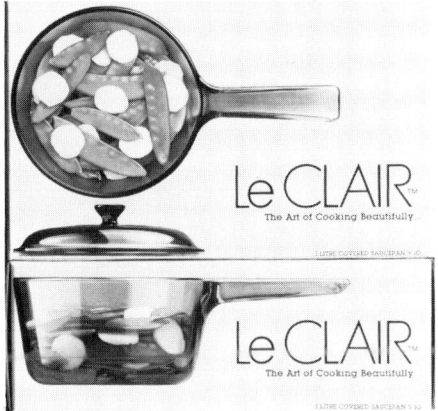

328
Stuart Bresner Art Director
Mathieu, Gerfen & Bresner, Inc. Agency
Canadian/Schenley Client
New York NY

329
Jack Hermsen Art Director
Louis Escobedo Illustrator
Michael Morris Photographer
Hermsen Design Associates Studio
Aguas Minerales Client
Dallas TX

330
Larry Riddell Art Director
David Pruitt Photographer
Julia Noonan, Elias Marge, Barney Plotkin
  Illustrators
Gersten & Meyers Inc. Studio
Melitta Inc. Client
New York NY

331
Alvin H. Schechter, Ronald Wong Art
  Directors
The Schechter Group Studio
R.J. Reynolds Tobacco Company Client
New York NY

332
John Schwarz Art Director
Jim Friedland Copywriter
Pluzynski & Associates Studio
New York NY

333
Charles Ireland, Keith Bevins Art Directors
Steve Sortino Photographer
Mark Color Studio
Corning Designs, Ltd. Client
Clinton NJ

334
Dana Bauer, Keith Bevans, Roger Butz,
  Charles Ireland Art Directors
Steve Sortino Photographer
Mark Color Studio
Corning Designs Ltd. Client
Baltimore MD

335
Michael Fountain Art Director
Michael Doret Designer
Leslie Carbarga Illustrator
Rumrill Hoyt Agency
Remington Client
Rochester NY

336
Primo Angeli Art Director
Primo Angeli Graphics Studio
Pabst Brewing Company Client
San Francisco CA

337
Michael Tieman Art Director
George Juhasz Illustrator
Joe Lederer Photographer
McKim Advertising Agency
Old Fort Brewing Company Client
Vancouver, Canada

338
John A. Flesch Art Director
Horst Mickler Calligrapher
Don Tate Illustrator
Murrie White Drummond Lienhart Studio
The Quaker Oats Company Client
Chicago IL

339
Lyle Metzdorf Creative Director
Lance Brown, Charles Hively Art Directors
Richard Hess, Al Bates Illustrators
Metzdorf Advertising Agency
Blue Bell Creameries Client
Houston TX

340
Bob Taylor Art Director
Robert Horn Lettering Designer
David Cunningham Illustrator
Ficho & Corley Studio
J. Walter Thompson Agency
Kellogg's Client
Chicago IL

341
Harry Murphy, Stanton Klose Art Directors
Harry Murphy & Friends Studio
The Small Things Company Client
Mill Valley CA

342
Ralph Miolia, Paul Port Art Directors
Nancy Stahl Illustrator
Port Miolia Associates Inc. Studio
The Nestle Company Client
Stamford CT

343
Lou Grasso & Associates Designers
Maurice Joseph Creative Director
Laszlo Photographer
Nabisco Brands Inc. Client
New York NY

344
Keith McConnell Illustrator
Mark Wood & Associates Studio
Smith's Vitamins Client
LaCanada CA

345
Gianninoto Associates Designers
Thomas J. Lipton Inc. Client
New York NY

341

343

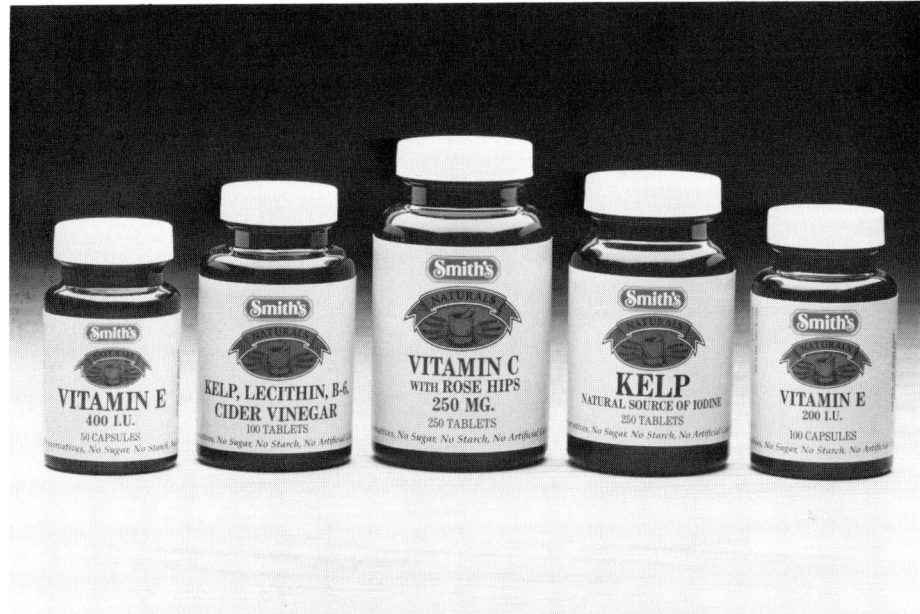

345

346
Mike Downey Designer
Nick Nolten Photographer
Sue Gregerowski Typographer
BBDO Marketing & Advertising Agency
Merck Pharmaceuticals Client
Johannesburg, S. Africa

347
Heather Cooper Art Director
Heather Cooper Illustrator
Burns, Cooper, Hynes Ltd. Studio
Crabtree & Evelyn Client
Toronto, Canada

348
Josh Taylor Art Director
Caswell-Massey Co. Ltd. Client
New York NY

349
Adrienne Y. Carlin Art Director
Alice Cheung Designer
AYC Graphics Studio
J. Winn/Powell Client
New York NY

350
Yutaka Matsushita Art Director
The Design House Inc. Studio
Fujitsu Kogyo Inc. Client
Tokyo, Japan

351
Kan Tai-Keung, Cheung Shu-Sun Art Directors
SS Design & Production Studio
Vanessa Jewelry Client
Hong Kong

352
Laurie Rosenwald Designer
Bloomingdale's Client
New York NY

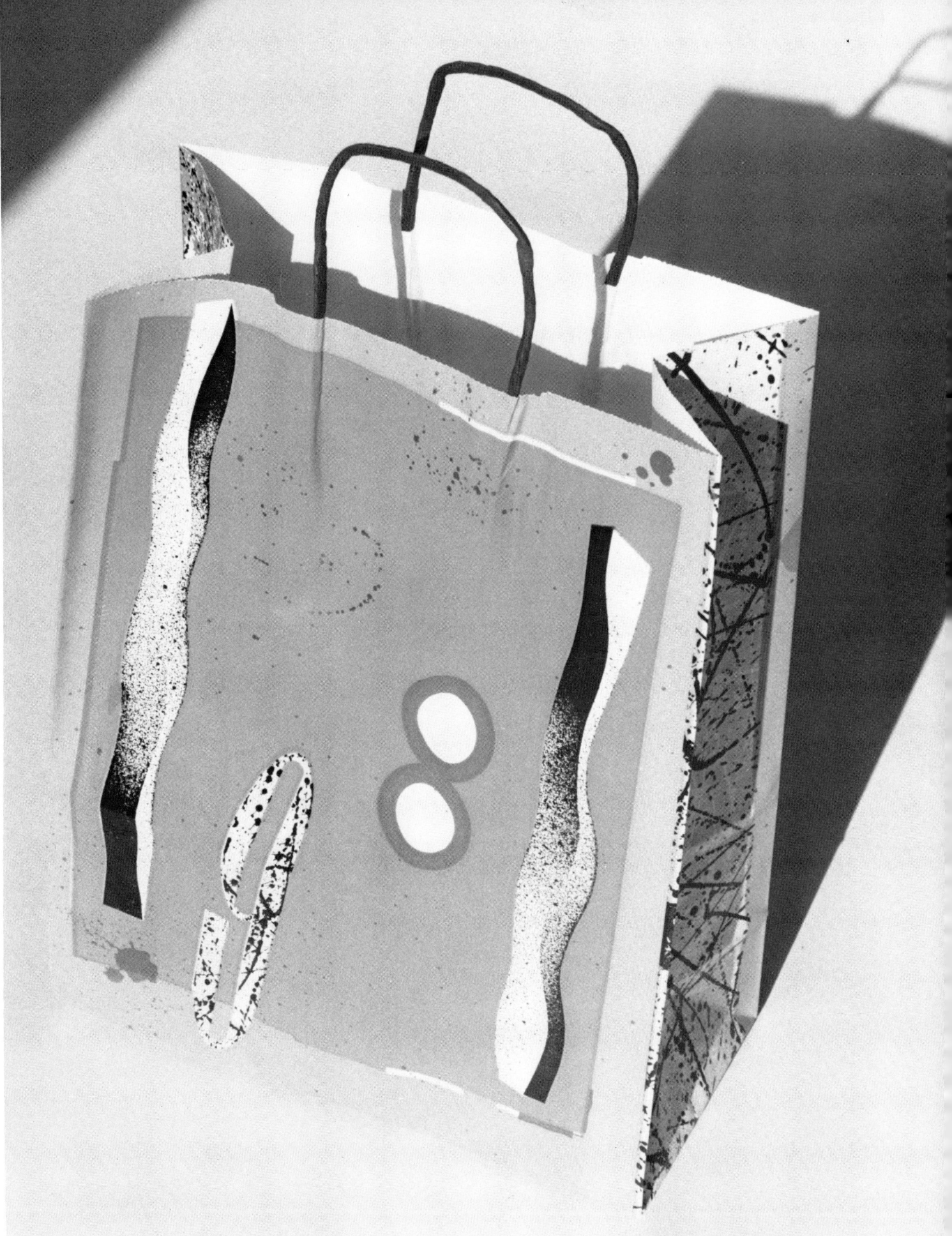

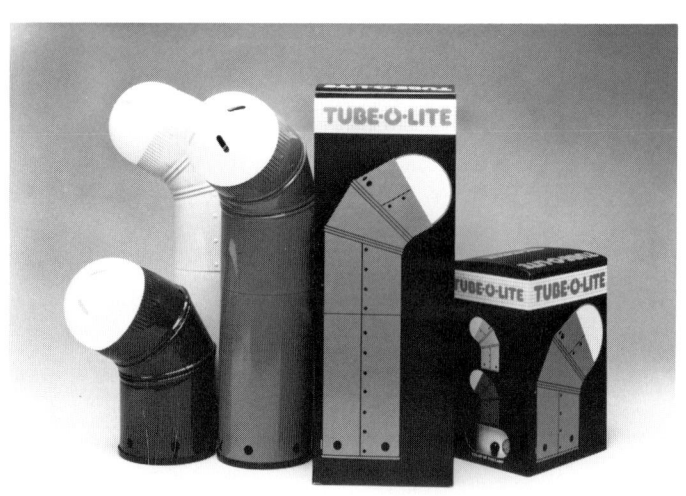

353
Zengo Yoshida Art Director
Zenn Graphic Design Studio
Neo-Art Inc. Client
Los Angeles CA

354
Ferris W. Crane Art Director
City Slickers Client
San Francisco CA

355
Bob Dorfman, Ken Dupey Art Directors
Donna Bassano Illustrator
Ken Dupey Graphics Studio
The Joseph Dixon Crucible Company Client
Bayonne NJ

356
Clare Taylor Art Director
Moscovitz & Taylor Advertising Inc. Agency
Crestar Ltee. Client
Montreal, Canada

357
Barbara Montgomery, Atsutochi Ohyi, Pete Glasheen Art Directors
Harris Haft Photographer
Glasheen Advertising Agency
Uchida of America Corp. Client
New York NY

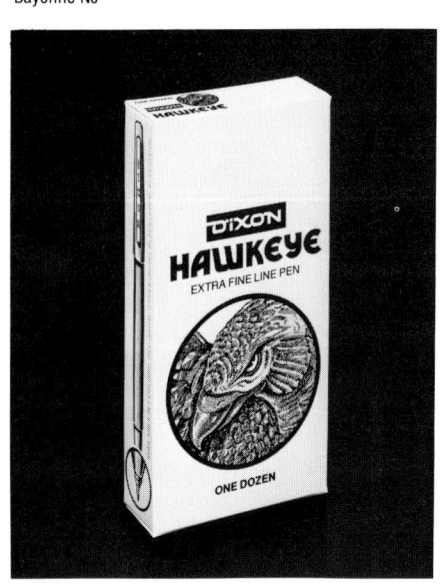

361
Robert P. Gersin Design Director
Charles Totaro Project Director
General Electric Company Client
New York NY

362
Graham Edwards Art Director
Ruben Padova Photographer
Carton y Papel de Mexico s.a. de C.V. Studio
Mexico, D.F.

362

358
Thomas Garber Art Director
James Scherzi Photographer
Evans, Garber & Paige Inc. Agency
R.E. Dietz Company Client
Utica NY

359
Julien Behaeghei Art Director
Marianne Walther Designer
Cato Yasumura Behaeghel Agency
Purina Belgium Client
Brussels, Belgium

360
Gary Palumbo, Michael Zambelli Art Directors
Ron Contarsy Photographer
Palumbo Associates Inc. Studio
Victory Optical/Geoffrey Beene Client
Milington NJ

359

358

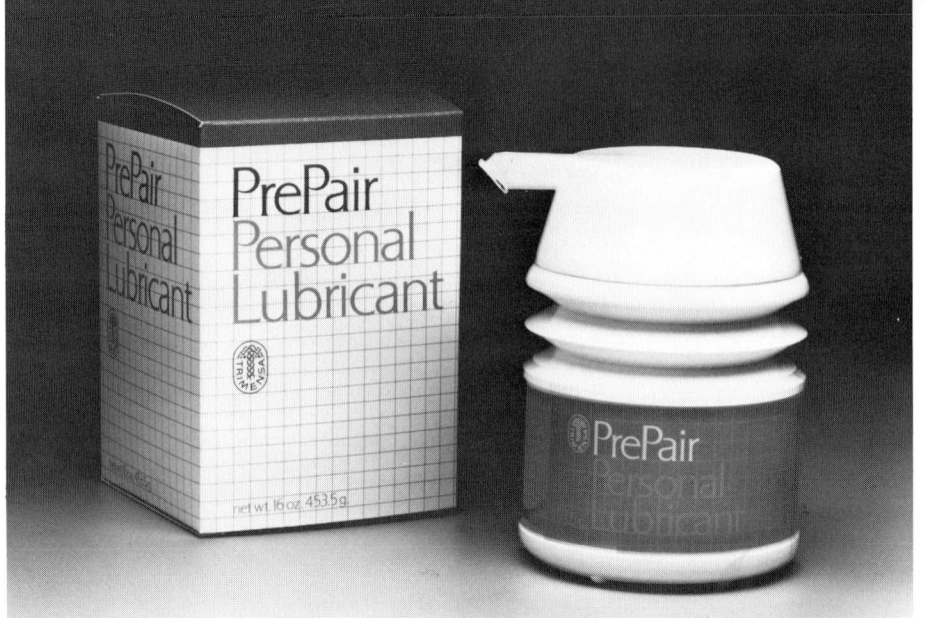

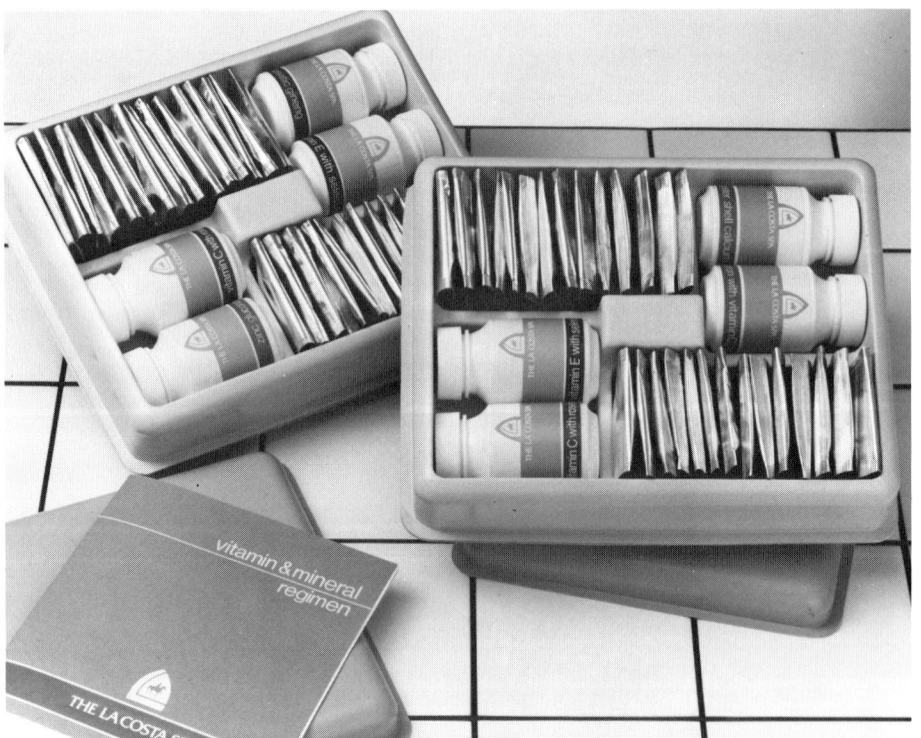

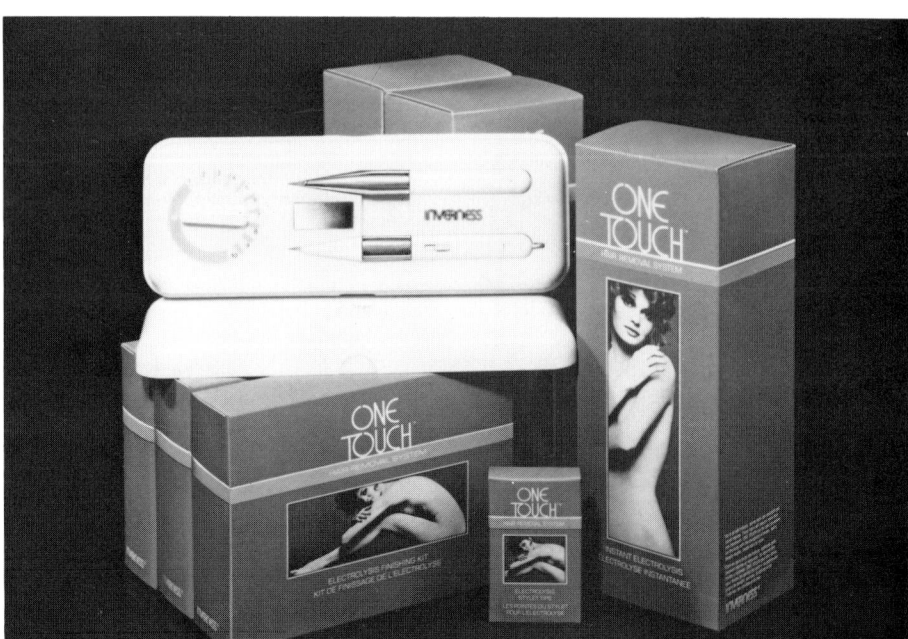

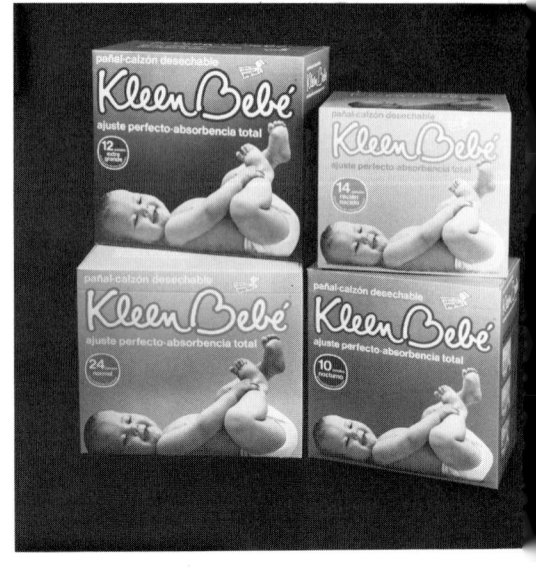

363
Ken Parkhurst Art Director
Peter Sargent Designer
Bright & Associates Studio
The Trimensa Company Client
Los Angeles CA

364
David Mocarski Art Director
Mark MacKinnon Photographer
Nielsen & David Design Studio
LaCosta Products International Client
Irvine CA

365
Bob Wallack Art Director
Wallack & Harris, Inc. Studio
Inverness Int. Corp. Client
New York NY

366
Arie J. Geurts Art Director
Kimberly Clark (Mexico) Client
Cincnnati OH

367
Cinda Katz Bonk Art Director
Kathleen Sullivan Kaska Designer
Del Herman Photographer
Brown & Rosner Inc. Studio
Enterprise Client
Chicago IL

368
Don Weller Art Director
Leland Music Client
Los Angeles CA

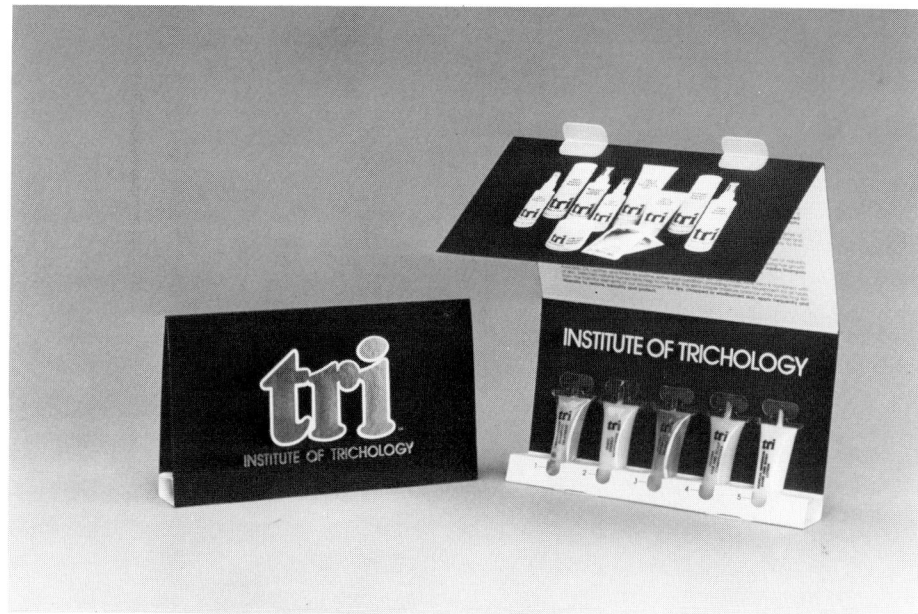

369
Chuck Waldman Art Director
Diagnostics & Designs Inc. Studio
Institute of Trichology Client
Wilmington CA

370
Fernando Medina Art Director
Gillette Espanola Client
Madrid, Spain

371
Jack de Lange Art Director
Cor Visser Designer
DLS Communications BV Agency
Agu Sport BV Client
Zaandam, Holland

372
Christopher Holland, Rob Leyko Art Directors
Holland Advertising Inc. Agency
Audio Dynamics Corp. Client
New York NY

373
Randye E.K. Edwin Art Director
Hector Garrido Illustrator
Stewart Mosberg Design Associates Inc. Studio
Durham Industries Inc. Client
New York NY

374
Ted Bick, Linda Bick Art Directors
Bunny Carter Illustrator
Parker Brothers Client
Beverly MA

375
Mark Setteducati Art Director
Astra Trading Corp. Client
Emerson NJ

375

CALENDARS

376
Doug Fisher Art Director
Lord, Sullivan & Yoder Advertising Agency
Nevamar Client
Marion OH

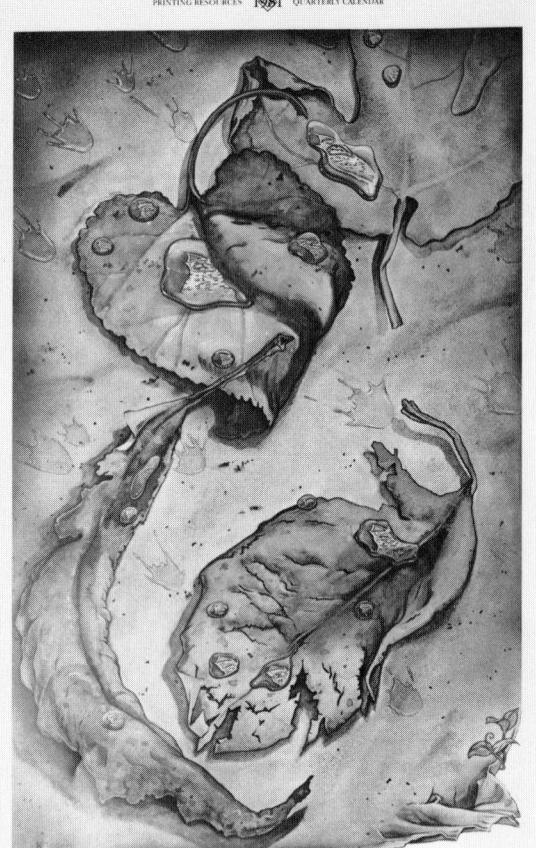

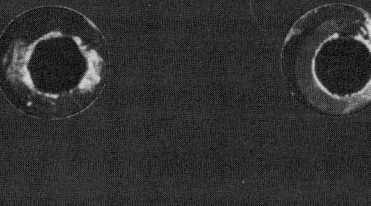

377
Steve Sessions Art Director
Lee Lee Brazeal, Randy Rogers, Denise Chapman, Jerry Jeanmard Illustrators
Print Resources Client
Houston TX

378
Anna Lee Wilson Art Director
Kaeser & Wilson Design Ltd. Studio
Enterprise Press/Smithsonian Client
New York NY

379
John Coy Designer
COY, Los Angeles Studio
Art Institute of Chicago Client
Culver City CA

380
Leonard Restivo Art Director
Saks Fifth Avenue Client
New York NY

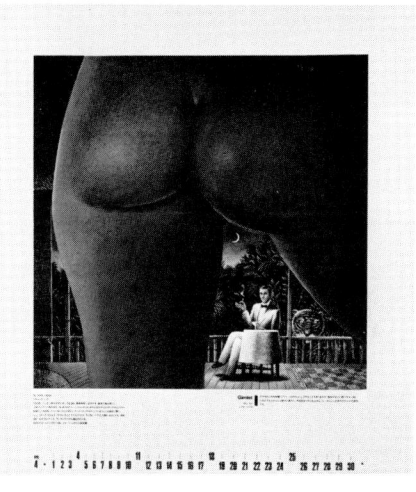

381
Shinichiro Tora, Yasuharu Nakahara, Mitsutochi Hosaka Art Directors
Mitsuo Katsui Designer
Dai Nippon Printing Production
Hotel Barmen's Association Client
New York NY

382
Robert N. Leppert Art Director
R.H. Yates, Donna M. Mayo, Fran Drennan Designers
Cathy A. McDougall Typographer
American McGaw Marketing Communications Client
Irvine CA

383
Tracey Smith-Avery Designer
Franklin Avery Photographer
Trace Elements Design Studio
Grade A Graphics Production
Bruce Kravetz Concept/Client
Santa Cruz CA

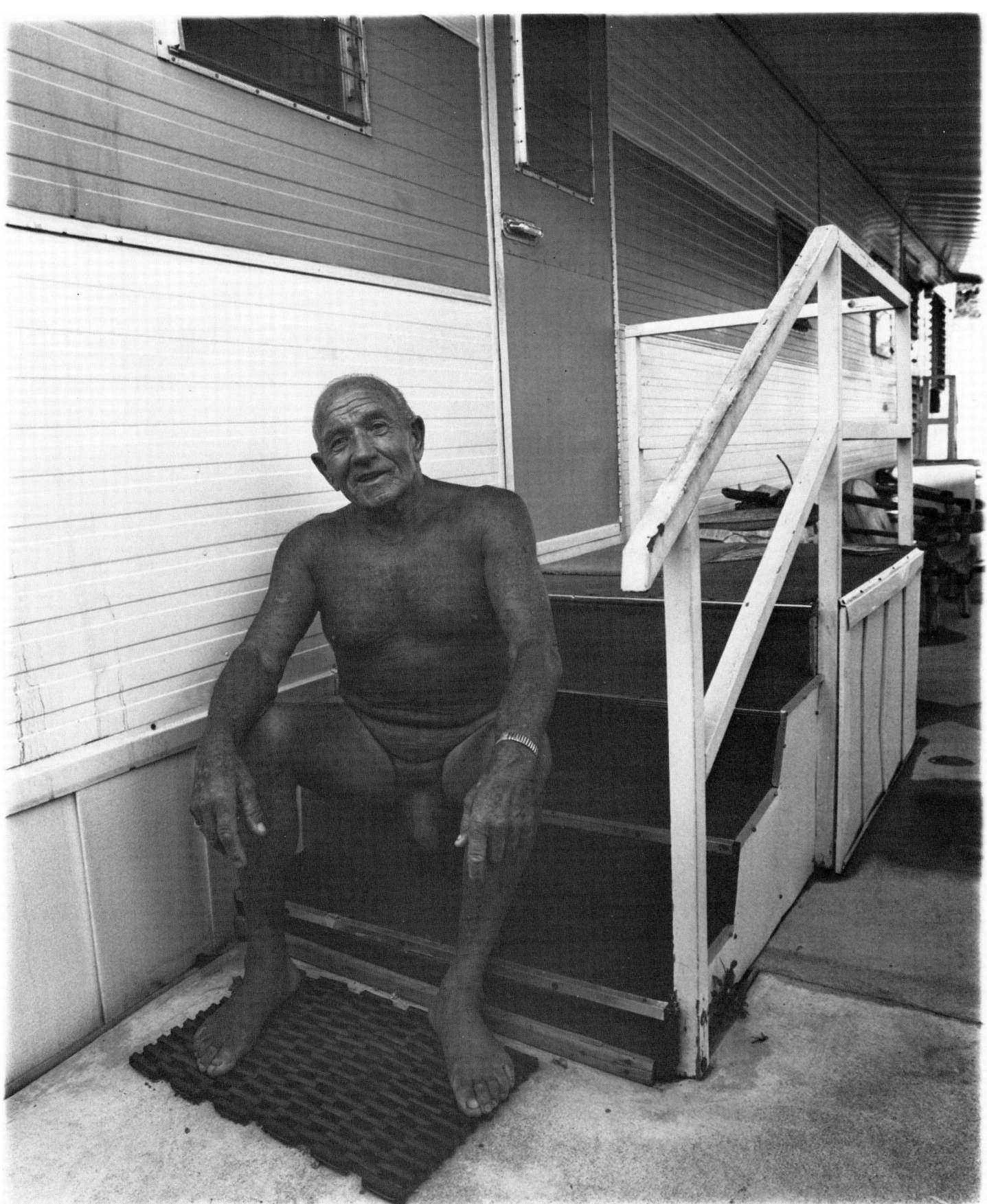

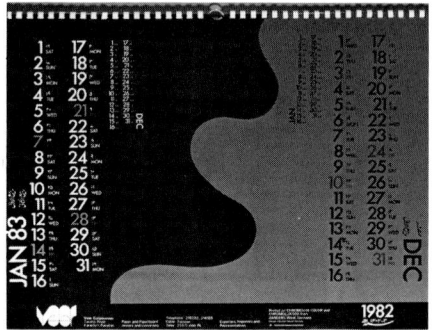

384
Kathy Forsythe Art Director
CCA Marketing Comminications Client
Chicago IL

385
Farzana Adamjee Art Director
Pakistan Design Institute Studio
Veer Corporation Client
Karachi, Pakistan

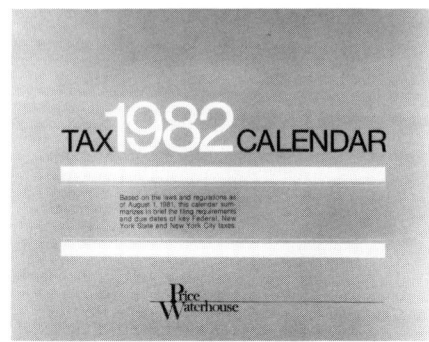

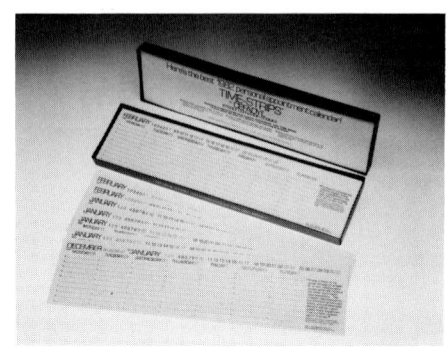

386
Harry Guttman Art Director
Asger Jerrild Designer
Steelograph Co. Inc. Production
Price Waterhouse Client
New York NY

387
Steve Brennan Art Director
John M. Wright Illustrator
Cefadyl/(Bristol Laboratories) Client
E. Syracuse NY

388
Jerry Dadds Designer
Alan Polansky Photographer
Eucalyptus Tree Studio
Allen Advertising Agency
Davison Chemical Client
Baltimore MD

389
Tord Elfwendahl Art Director
Eva Omfors Copywriter
Claes Westlin Photographer
Ogilvy & Mather AB Agency
Allmanna Brand Client
Malmo, Sweden

390
Timothy E. Urban Art Director
Freeman, Huenick, Zilbert Inc. Staff Illustrators
Fox River Paper Company Client
Brookfield WI

391
Tony Huggett Art Director
Michael Foreman Illustrator
Lansdowne Marketing Agency
Commercial Bank of Kuwait Client
London, England

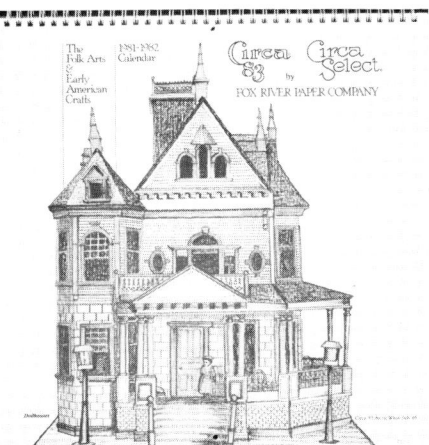

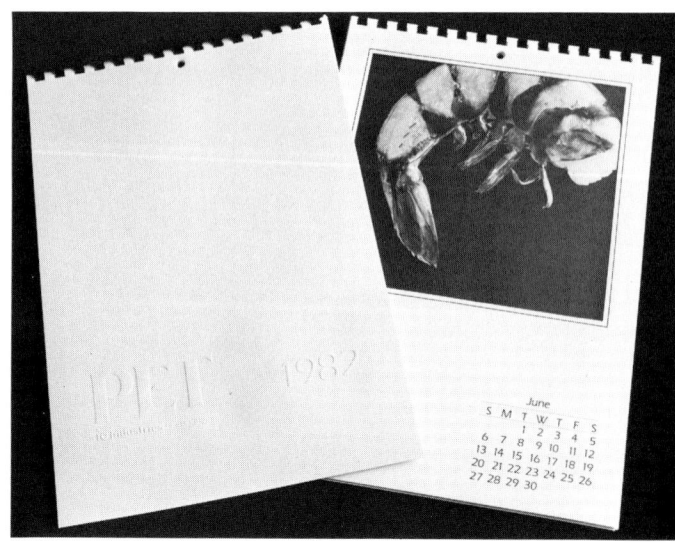

392
Mogens Sorensen Designer
Claus Bruun Art Director
Bergsoe 1I/s Studio
ScanDutch I/s Client
Copenhagen, Denmark

393
Tetsuya Tanaka Art Director
Benihana of Tokyo Inc. Client
Miami FL

394
Carol L. Dunn, Les L. Landes, Donald J. McKenna Art Directors
Donald J. McKenna Photographer
Pet Incorporated Client
St. Louis MO

Annual Reports

395
John Williamson Art Director
Bob Wilson Photographer
Ross M. Harvey Editor
Outcrop Ltd. Studio
Gov't. of the Northwest Territories
　Client
Yellow Knife NWT Canada

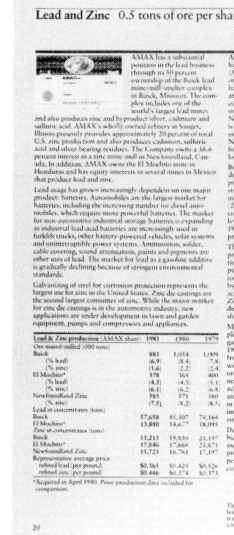

396
M. Badler Art Director
CorpCom Inc. Studio
AMAX Inc. Client
Greenwich, CT

397
Jerry Pavey Designer
Jan Good Illustrator
Jerry Pavey Design Studio Studio
Fiscal Agency for the Farm Credit Banks
   Client
Rockville MD

398
Vickie Sawyer, Kathy D'Amanda Designers
Yolanda Sprinz Illustrator
**Craig Aurness, Marv Wolf, M. Manheim,
   M. Arnold, Rene Sheret** Photographers
Rene Sheret Design Studio
Farr Company Client
Los Angeles CA

399
Barry Ostrie Art Director
John Heiney & Associates, Inc. Studio
Irving Bank Corporation Client
New York NY

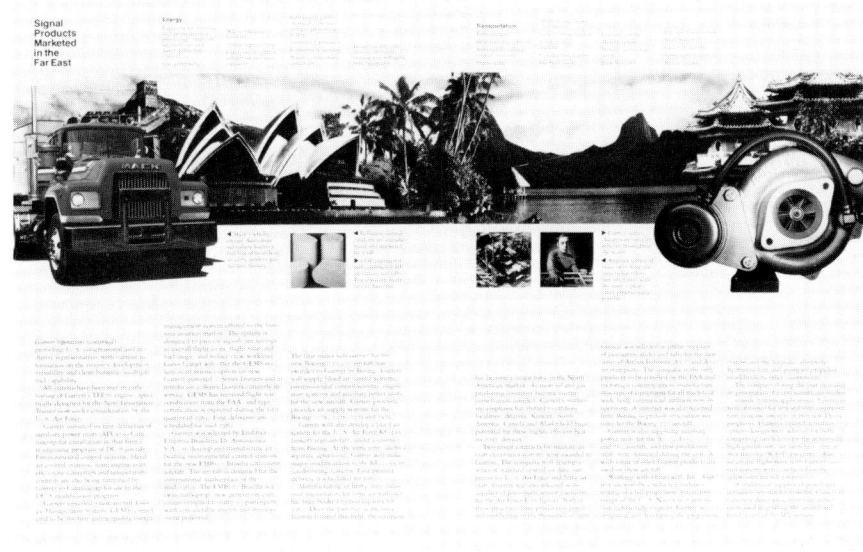

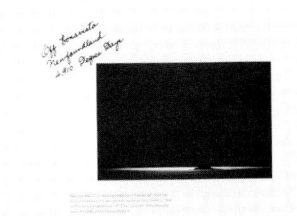

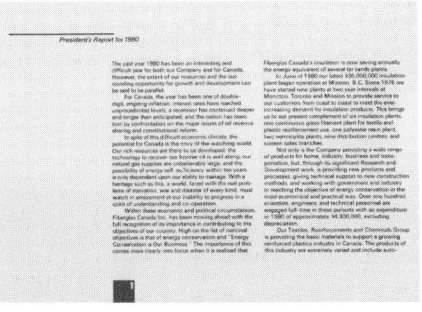

400
Ron Jefferies, C. Claudia Jefferies Designers
Marty Gunsaullus Illustrator
The Jefferies Association Studio
The Signal Companies Client
Los Angeles CA

401
Malcolm Waddell Art Director
Eskind Waddell Studio
Fiberglas Canada Inc. Client
Toronto, Canada

402
David Lizotte Art Director
George Sakmanoff Photographer
Gunn Associates Studio
EPSCO Incorporated Client
Boston MA

403
Leslie Silva, Chris Hill Designers
Arthur Meyerson Photographer
Louis Benito Advertising Agency
Hillsborough County Aviation Authority
  Client
Tampa FL

404
John Cleveland Art Director
Michael Skeji Designer
Jay Freis Photographer
John Cleveland Inc. Studio
First L.A. Bank Client
Sausalito CA

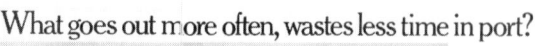

405

John Waters, Beth Story Designers
Yvonne Buchanan Illustrator
Ronald M. Blank Copywriter
John Waters Associates, Inc. Studio
Curtiss-Wright Corp. Client
New York NY

Curtiss-Wright Corporation
1981 Annual Report

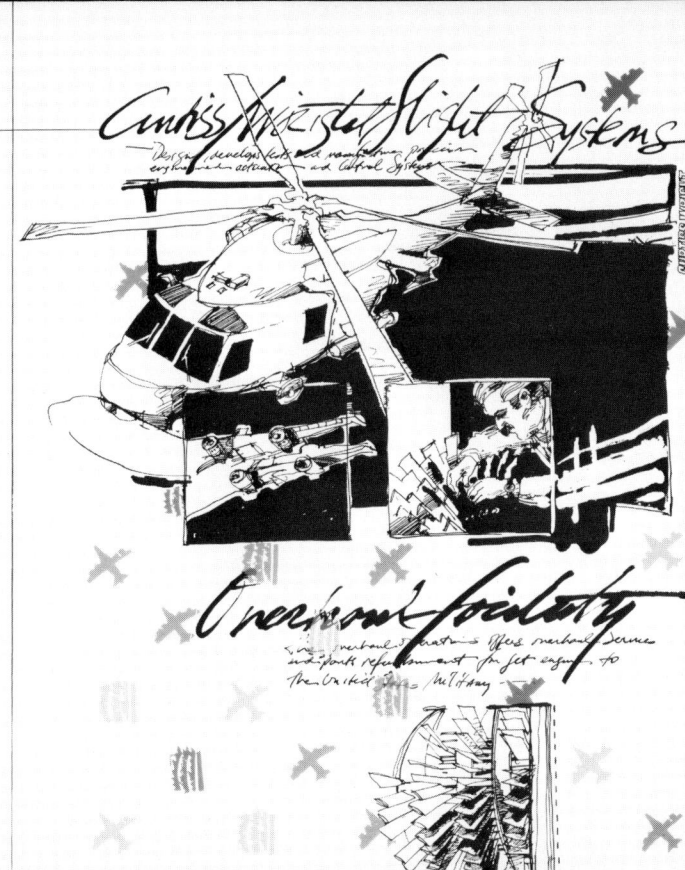

Overhaul Facility
Curtiss-Wright Flight Systems

propagation of surface cracks in metal parts. In peen-forming compound curvatures can be formed in large, panel shape metal parts, to very exacting tolerances. These panels are used as the "wing skins" for some of the largest commercial aircraft in service today.

Numerical control shot-peening is used on complex and intricate critical parts, such as certain aerospace parts, where this accuracy is economically practical.

The entrepreneurial challenge is not limited to growing small businesses into market leaders. Curtiss-Wright Flight Systems, Inc. (formerly the Caldwell Facility and now a wholly-owned subsidiary) and the Overhaul Facility at Wood-Ridge are both textbook examples of how to survive in business when your market disappears.

The rapid decline of Curtiss-Wright's piston engine business in the late 1950's had a severe impact on the Caldwell Facility, whose sole business activity up to that point was the manufacture of propellers, propeller transmissions and related spare parts for those engines.

Decades of expertise in precision design, engineering and machining in propellers and transmission systems were redirected to the engineering and production of mechanical, hydraulic and electromechanical control and actuation systems for aerospace and defense applications.

The facility was successful in becoming the supplier of actuation systems for the nose gear doors, main landing gear and landing gear doors for the giant C5A military transport. The facility was also selected to provide giant power hinge systems for the primary control wing fold system of the Supersonic B-70 Bomber.

In the early 1970's, another downturn struck. Production of the C5A ceased. The B-70 had been cancelled. Commercial programs just beginning, such as the outboard leading edge flap drive system for the Boeing 747 Jumbo Jet, looked uncertain.

The challenge of technological transformation became a challenge of financial survival. The workforce and physical facilities were streamlined, and pointed to the future under a program of management by objectives.

Today, Curtiss-Wright Flight Systems is meeting those objectives and is well positioned for the foreseeable future as a supplier of commercial and military actuation and control systems.

Curtiss-Wright Flight Systems is the supplier of the leading edge flap drive system for the Boeing 747 Jumbo Jet and the trailing edge flap gear boxes for the short range Boeing 737 Jet Transport, and also provides the entire trailing edge control system for the Lockheed L-1011 Tristar Jumbo Jet. This last system will be produced in declining volumes in the future.

In addition to new orders, a large spare parts market is developing for the hundreds of 737's, 747's and L-1011's already in service worldwide.

Military programs include actuation and control systems and components for the F-14 Tomcat Fighter, the Blackhawk (Army) and Seahawk (Navy) Helicopters, the F-18 Fighter, the F-111 Fighter/Bomber and the C5A Transport.

Curtiss-Wright Flight Systems has developed and is manufacturing for Sikorsky, a "roll" and "yaw" actuation and control system—a primary flight control for both the U.S. Army's Blackhawk and U.S. Navy's Seahawk Helicopters. These systems assist the pilot by controlling "roll" (rotation on a horizontal axis) and "yaw" (rotation on a vertical axis) through a complex of actuation and electronic sensing devices, in effect providing a "third hand" to control these flight attitudes.

Curtiss-Wright Flight Systems is manufacturing the canopy actuator for the F-18 Fighter, and cargo door actuators for the new generation Boeing 757 Transport Program and the Space Shuttle program.

Curtiss-Wright's Overhaul Facility faced a similar market deterioration with the decline of the Company's own engine business. Again, the decision was made to take the skills bank, and physical facili-

406
Jim Makstaller, Arie J. Geurts Art Directors
George Tassian Photographer
Benchmark, Inc. Studio
The Timken Company Client
Cincinnati OH

407
Stephen Ferrari Art Director
Lee Dawkins Designer
Dana Duke Photographer
The Graphic Expression, Inc. Studio
Dillon Read & Co., Inc. Client
New York NY

408
David Bloch, Irwin N. Graulich Art Directors
Bloch Graulich Whelan Inc. Studio
Viacom International Inc. Client
New York NY

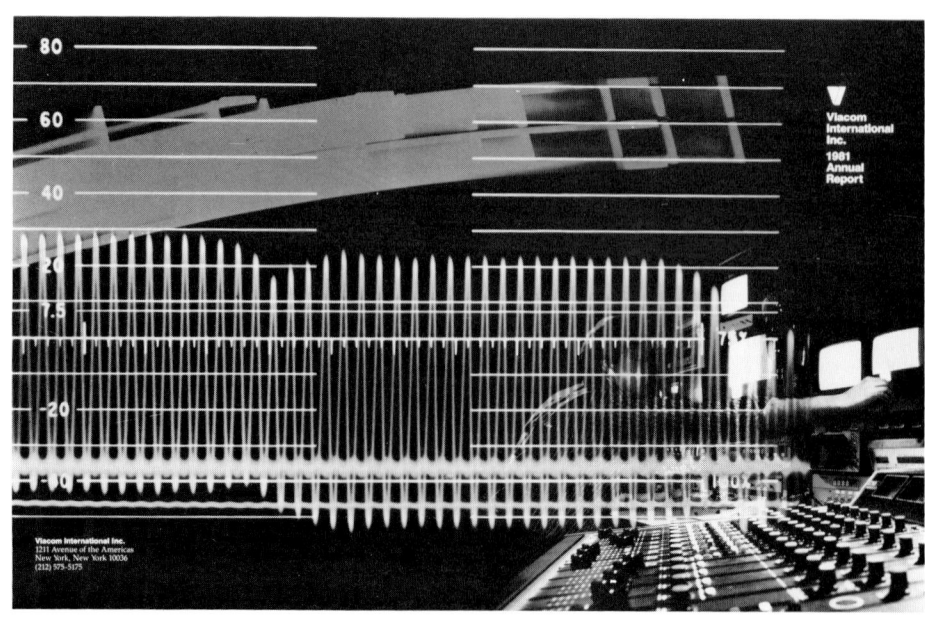

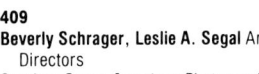
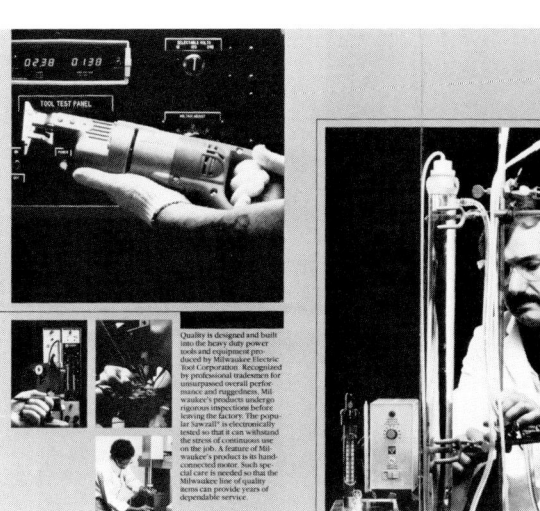

409
Beverly Schrager, Leslie A. Segal Art Directors
Stephen Green-Armytage Photographer
Corporate Annual Reports Studio
Olin Corporation Client
New York NY

410
Edwards Broderick, Robert Pellegrini Art Directors
Pellegrini & Associates Inc. Studio
Amstar Corporation Client
New York NY

411
Jorge Alonso Art Director
Roger Marshutz Photographer
Foutouhi Alonso, Inc. Studio
Products Research & Chemical Corp. Client
Los Angeles CA

412
B. Martin Pedersen Art Director
Nancy Stahl Illustrator
Cheryl Rossum Photographer
Jonson Pedersen Hinrichs & Shakery Studio
Dow Jones & Company, Inc. Client
New York NY

413
Randee R. Rubin, George Shakespear Art
 Directors
Paul Elfenbein Photographer
James Orlandi & Assoc. Studio
R. Rafkin-Rubin Inc. Agency
Biotech Capital Corporation Client
New York NY

Biotech, as a business development company, provides active scientific, managerial, marketing or financial assistance as each portfolio company requires.

1981 Review of the Year

Biotech has adopted and followed a program of investing in areas of high technology, principally in the biotechnological and scientific areas. The potential for explosive growth exists in emerging companies which are developing or applying these types of new technology which may have significant commercial applications.

Industrial microbiology is in a state of flux. Recent advances have generated a wave of excitement about the prospective applications of microbiological techniques in a wide range of industrial and medical roles. The achievements of the artificial recombination of DNA, or "gene splicing," have been highly publicized. This technology involves the insertion of segments of DNA containing specific genetic information into microorganisms which then are able to reproduce in a matter of hours. A ready supply of the desired genetic material or the desired biochemical products is rapidly produced. This technology has produced experimental quantities of human growth hormone, a number of vaccines, various foods and other proteins, human interferon and human insulin. Many believe these substances and others like them have the potential for being made in commercial quantities. Other areas of advancement include development of organisms to convert certain raw materials into alcohol and the creation of organisms to produce protein or other food substances more efficiently.

The ability of recombinant DNA technology to make substances available at a reasonable cost can be appreciated by exam-

Biotech's commitment to biotechnology is evidenced by its investment in Clinical Sciences Inc. After taking a patient's specimen, CSI's diagnostic kits are used to tag certain protein elements in the specimen which then can be examined under a fluorescent microscope for diagnosis of diseases, such as arthritis and infectious diseases.

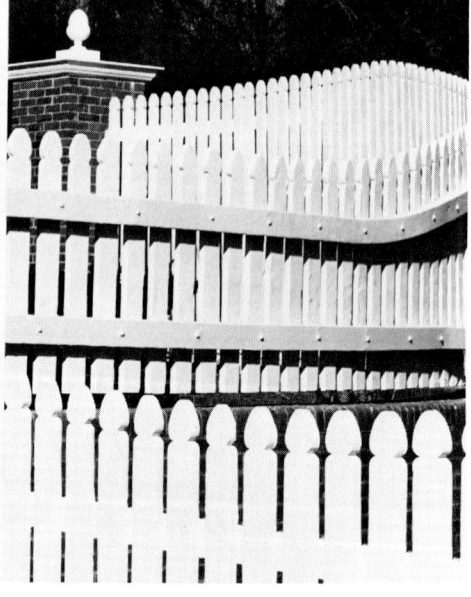

414
Eric Diggs Art Director
The Woods Group Studio
Maryland National Bank Client
Baltimore MD

415
Bennett Robinson, Paula Zographos, Naomi Burstein Designers
Kim Steele Photographer
Corporate Graphics Inc. Studio
Amerada Hess Client
New York NY

416
Bob Newman, Les Segal Art Directors
Karl Hartig Illustrator
Shorty Wilcox Photographer
Newman Design Assoc. Inc. Studio
Corpcom, Inc. Client
New York NY

417
Craig Sheumaker Art Director
Robert Heindel Illustrator
Unigraphics Studio
Homestake Mining Company Client
San Francisco CA

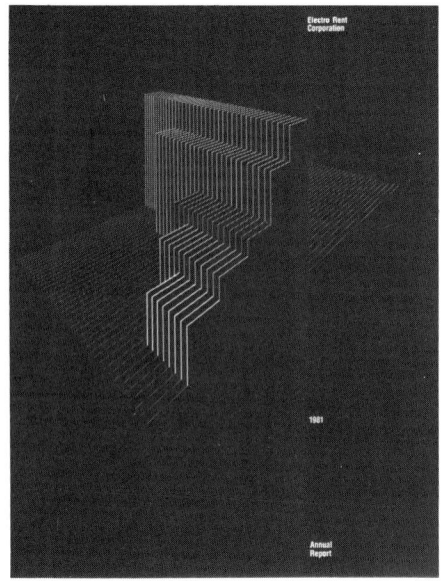
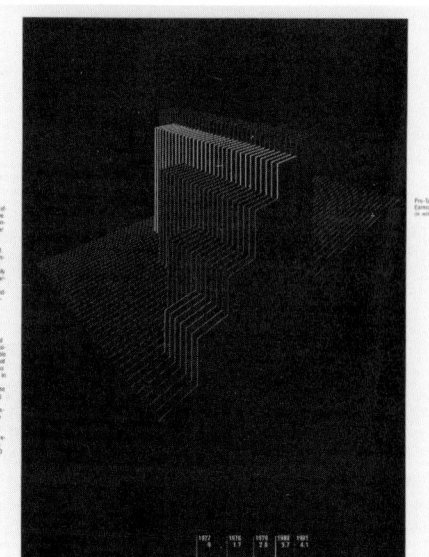
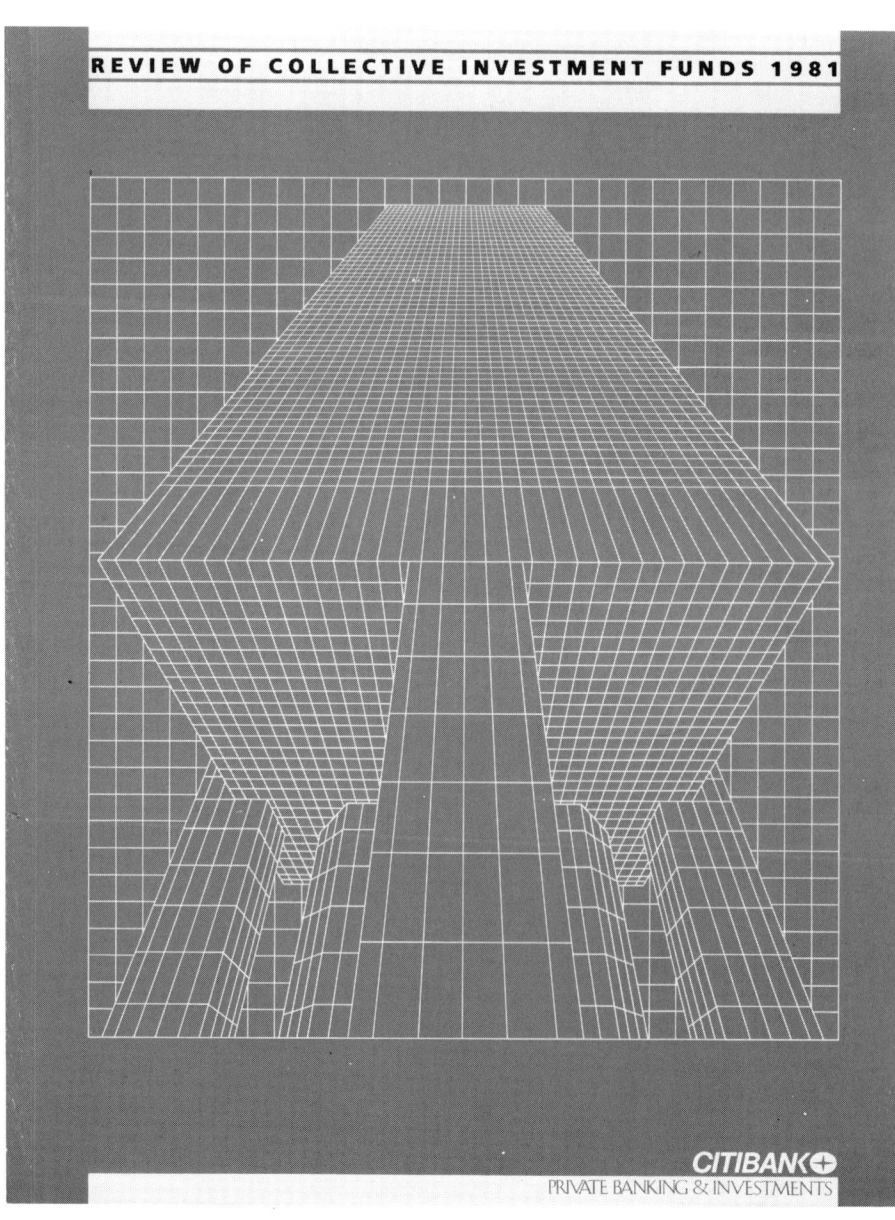

418
Rik Besser Designer
Paul Bice, Kenji Matsumoto Illustrator
Robert Miles Runyan & Assoc. Studio
Electro Rent Corporation Client
Playa del Rey CA

419
Jack Odette Art Director
Mike Focar Designer
Citibank Client
New York NY

420
Heidi Schmeck Art Director
The Associated Press Client
New York NY

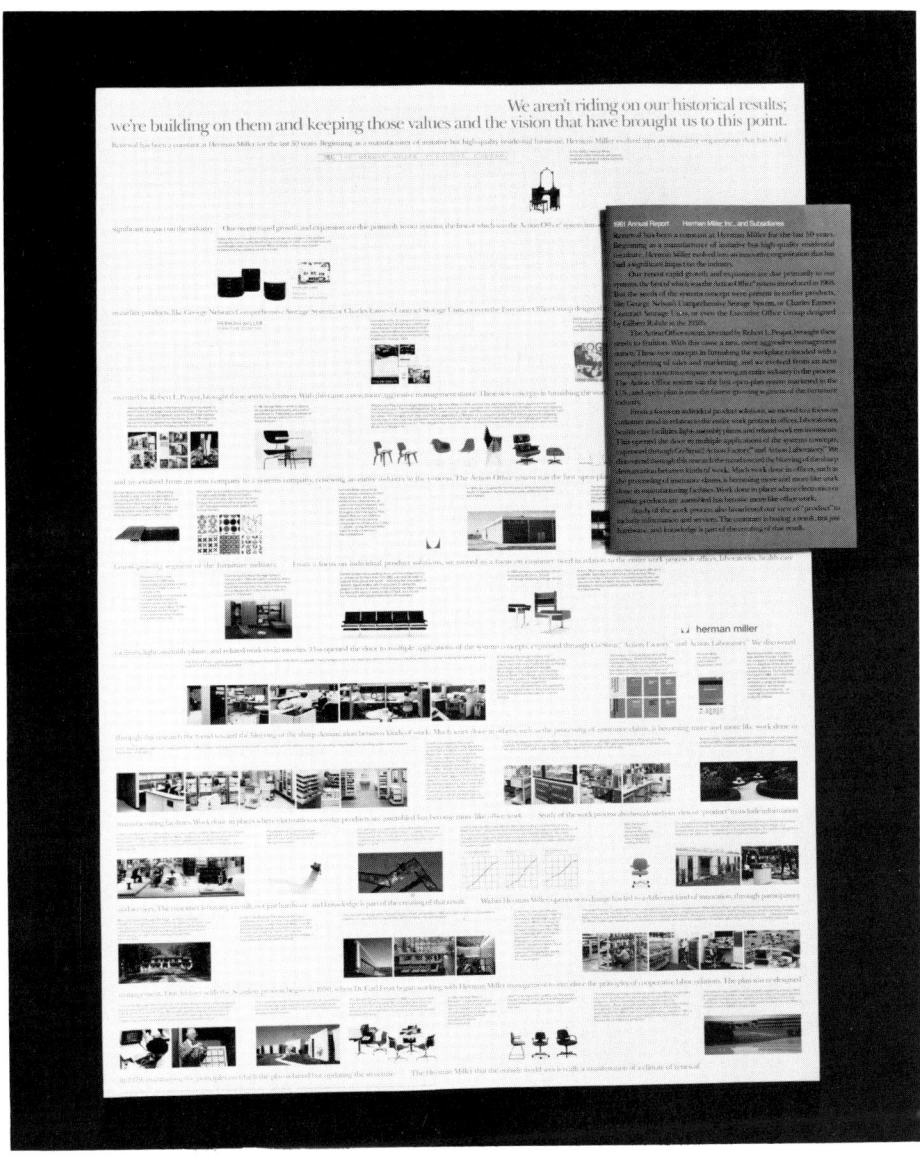

421
Ricardo Salas Art Director
Alfonso Capetillo y Asociados Agency
Banco B.C.H. Client
Mexico DF

422
Stephen Frykholm Art Director
Earl Woods, Bill Sharpe Photographers
Typehouse Typographers
Herman Miller, Inc. Client
Zeeland MI

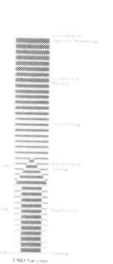

424

425

423
Tony Huggett Art Director
The Curwen Press Production House
Lansdowne Marketing Agency
Commercial Bank of Kuwait Client
London, England

424
Kay Woon, George E. Brown Designers
Larry Keenan Photographer
George E. Browne & Associates Studio
Genentech, Inc. Client
Oakland CA

425
Jack de Lange Art Director
Gerard Portengen Designer
Henry Kaem, Jan Woudt, Dale Banburry Photographers
DLS Communications B.V. Studio
Kominklyke Wessanen B.V. Client
Zaandam, Holland

426
Peter Harrison, Susan Hochbaum Designers
Pentagram Design Studio
The News Corporation Ltd. Client
New York NY

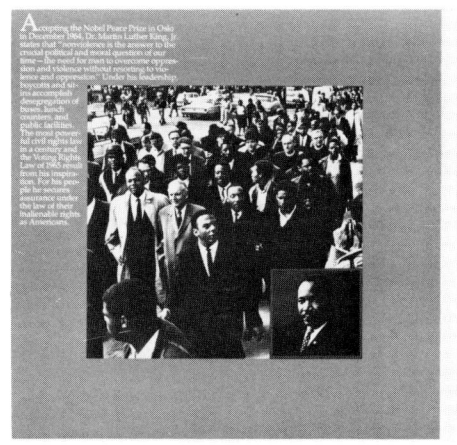

427
Robert Cipriani ARt Director
Al Fisher, Pete Turner, Gary Koepke
    Photographers
Catherine Flannery Copywriter
Robert Cipriani Associates Studio
Charles Stark Draper Labs, Inc. Client
Boston MA

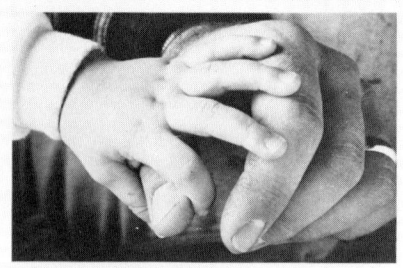
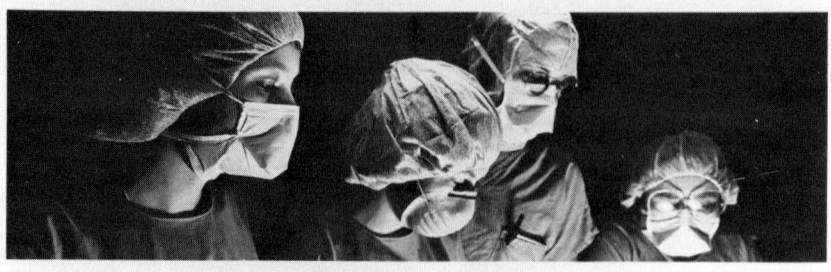
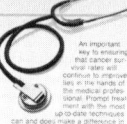

428
Kendall L. Witherspoon Art Director
David Jackson Photographer
Nordstrom/Cox Marketing Agency
American Cancer Society Client
Grand Rapids MI

429
Robert Ethier Art Director
Cabana, Seguin-Design Inc. Studio
The Prudential Assurance Company, Ltd. Client
Montreal Canada

430
David Torme Art Director
Jay Frieze Photographer
Lyn Christenson, Kathleen Hyland Copywriters
David Torme Design Studio
Syntex Client
San Francisco CA

431
Philip Gips, Jane Cullen Designers
John Hill, Greg Edwards Photographers
Gips + Balkind + Associates Studio
Macmilan, Inc. Client
New York NY

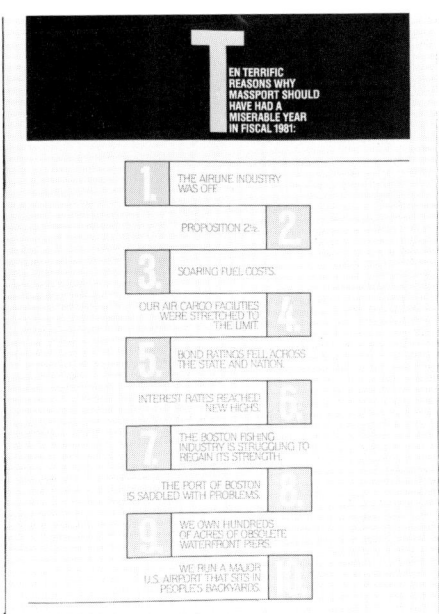

432
Cheryl Heller, David Lopes Designers
Michael Orzech Illustrator
Nubar Alexanian Photographer
HBM Design Group Studio
Massport Client
Boston MA

433
Bennett Robinson, Paula Zographos Designers
Bruce Davidson Photographer
Corporate Graphics Inc. Studio
Eli Lilly Client
New York NY

434
Reginald Jones Art Director
Wilson McClain Illustrator
Fred Stimson, Frank Wing Photographers
Unigraphics Studio
Di Giorgio Corporation Client
San Francisco CA

435
Sheryl Checkman Art Director
William F. Timmins Illustrator
Steven Langerman Photographer
Burson-Marsteller Agency
The J.M. Smucker Company Client
New York NY

436
Tom Wood, Susan Templeton Art Directors
Charles Lathem Photographer
Creative Services, Inc. Studio
Morrisons Client
Atlanta GA

437
Diane F. Dudeck Art Director
Jack Nichols Illustrator
Andrew McKinney, Paul Fairchild
  Photographers
Pizza Time Theatre Client
Sunnyvale CA

House Organs

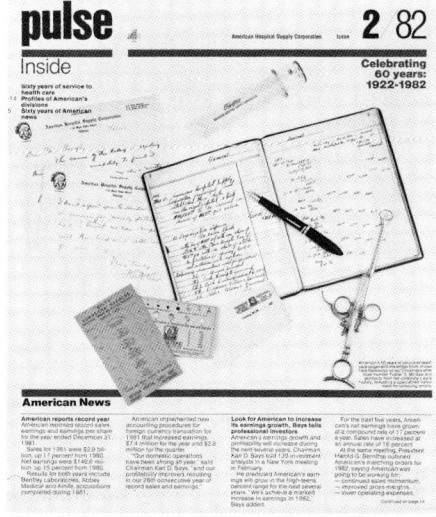

438
Robert Mynster Art Director
John Hines, Butch Hale Photographers
Studiographix Studio
Associates Corp. of North America Client
Irving TX

439
David Bates, Kerry Bierman, Barbara
  Wasserman Art Directors
Judy Benoit, Joe Sterling Photographers
Barbara Sickenberger, John Sandford, Carl
  Koke Illustrators
American Hospital Supply Corp. Client
Evanston IL

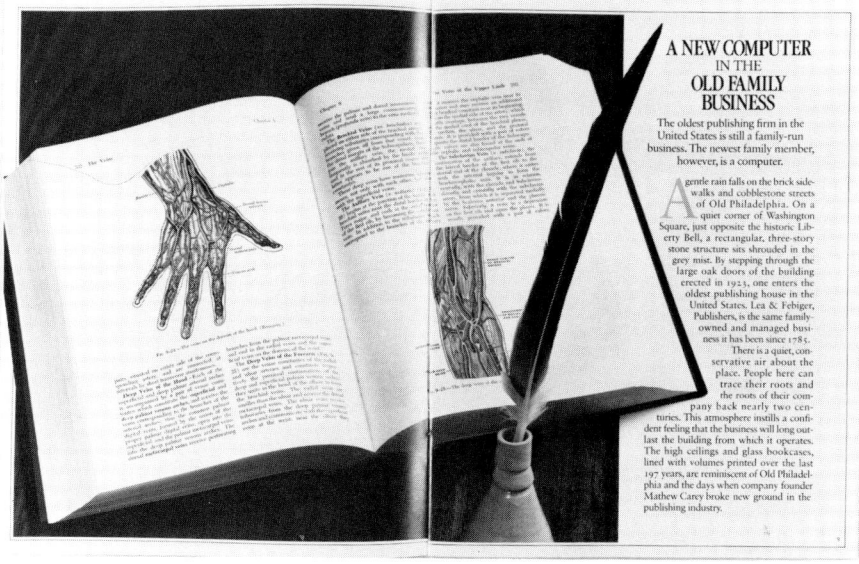

440
Hrair Vartanian Art Director
John Gamache Illustrator
George Disario, Phil Bailey, Steven Dahlgren
  Photographers
Wang Laboratories Inc. Client
Lowell MA

441
David J. Linton Graphics Dri.
Blaine Rose Editor
Sun Company Inc. Client
Radnor PA

442
Herbert M. Rosenthal Art Director
Geoffrey Moss Illustrator
Your Corporate Look Studio
Art Directors Club Client
New York NY

443
Mark Ulrich, Guy Salvato Art Directors
Dan Miller Photographer
Salvato & Cove Associates Studio
St. Joseph Hospital Client
Columbus OH

444
Robert Cooney Art Director
Bob Day Photographer
R.A. Cooney, Inc. Studio
MOAC/Continental Insurance Client
New York NY

445
Harry Gutman Art Director
Asger Jerrild Designer
Steelograph Co. Inc. Production
Price Waterhouse Client
New York NY

446
Judy Amenola Art Director
Graphics Plus Studio
Genrad, Inc. Client
Waltham MA

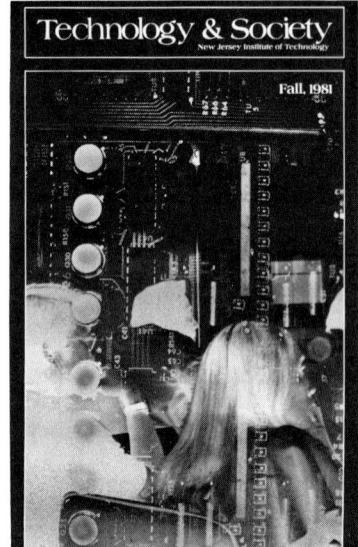
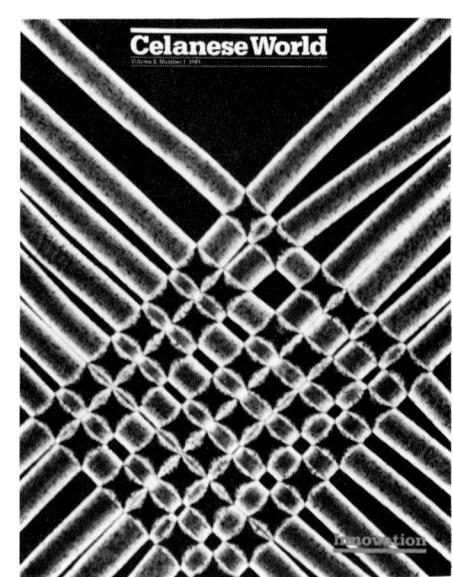

451

447
Linda Grimm Art Director
John Waters Associates, Inc. Studio
National Distillers & Chemical Corp. Client
New York NY

448
Albert J. Battista Art Director
Saxton Communications Group, Ltd. Studio
New Jersey Institute of Technology Client
New York NY

449
Tom Pritzker Art Director
Corpcom Services Studio
Celanese Corporation Client
New York NY

450
Mel Po Hon Art Director
Chase Manhattan Bank N.A. Client
New York NY

451
Bruce Mau Art Director
Fifty Fingers Inc. Studio
Gulf Canada Client
Toronto, Canada

452
Richard Hess Art Director
Stuart I. Frolick Editor
Spectrum Composition Svcs. Studio
Champion International Client
New York NY

453
James Guerard Art Director
Hinsche & Associates Studio
Fluor Corporation Client
Santa Monica CA

Editorial Design
Single Unit

454
Frank B. Marshall III Art Director
GAF Broadcasting Inc. Client
New York NY

455
Frank M. Devino Art Director
Tony Giuccione Photographer
Omni Magazine Client
New York NY

456
Tom Staebler Art Director
Playboy Magazine Client
Chicago IL

457
Melissa Tardiff Art Director
Cy Gross Photographer
Town & Country Magazine Client
New York NY

458
Louise Kollenbaum Art Director
Martha Geering Designer
Marshall Arisman Illustrator
Mother Jones Magazine Client
San Francisco CA

459
Al Braverman Art Director
Jan Schoonover Designer
Al Alexander Illustrator
The Hearst Corp. Client
New York NY

Fanatics Who Want The Wheel
TEAMSTER MADNESS
BY DOUGLAS FOSTER

This is the story of how a bizarre cult called the U.S. Labor Party penetrated the largest labor union in the U.S. to indoctrinate members in the party's brand of right-wing politics. Through its success with the Teamsters, it has gained a frightening foothold in the labor movement.

Shortly before he died of cancer last May, Frank Fitzsimmons, then president of the Teamsters, sent an urgent message to his underlings about a nefarious conspiracy to rip his organization asunder. The "intelligence report" Fitzsimmons sent along to his international executive board warned of a "full-blown freakout from the entire 'Get the Teamsters' network." The report said this "freakout" had been sparked by the election of Teamster ally Ronald Reagan. It described the anti-Teamster network as a Big Business/Red Menace combine that included Wall Street financiers, "press prostitutes" and international Socialists—all prepared to join hands and spend "countless millions of dollars on the war against [the Teamsters] to stop their role for economic development and improved standards of living."

As shocked as they were by the Fitzsimmons mailing, sent along with a personal cover letter, most of the officials who received it ignored the most salient fact: the report had

ILLUSTRATION BY MARSHALL ARISMAN

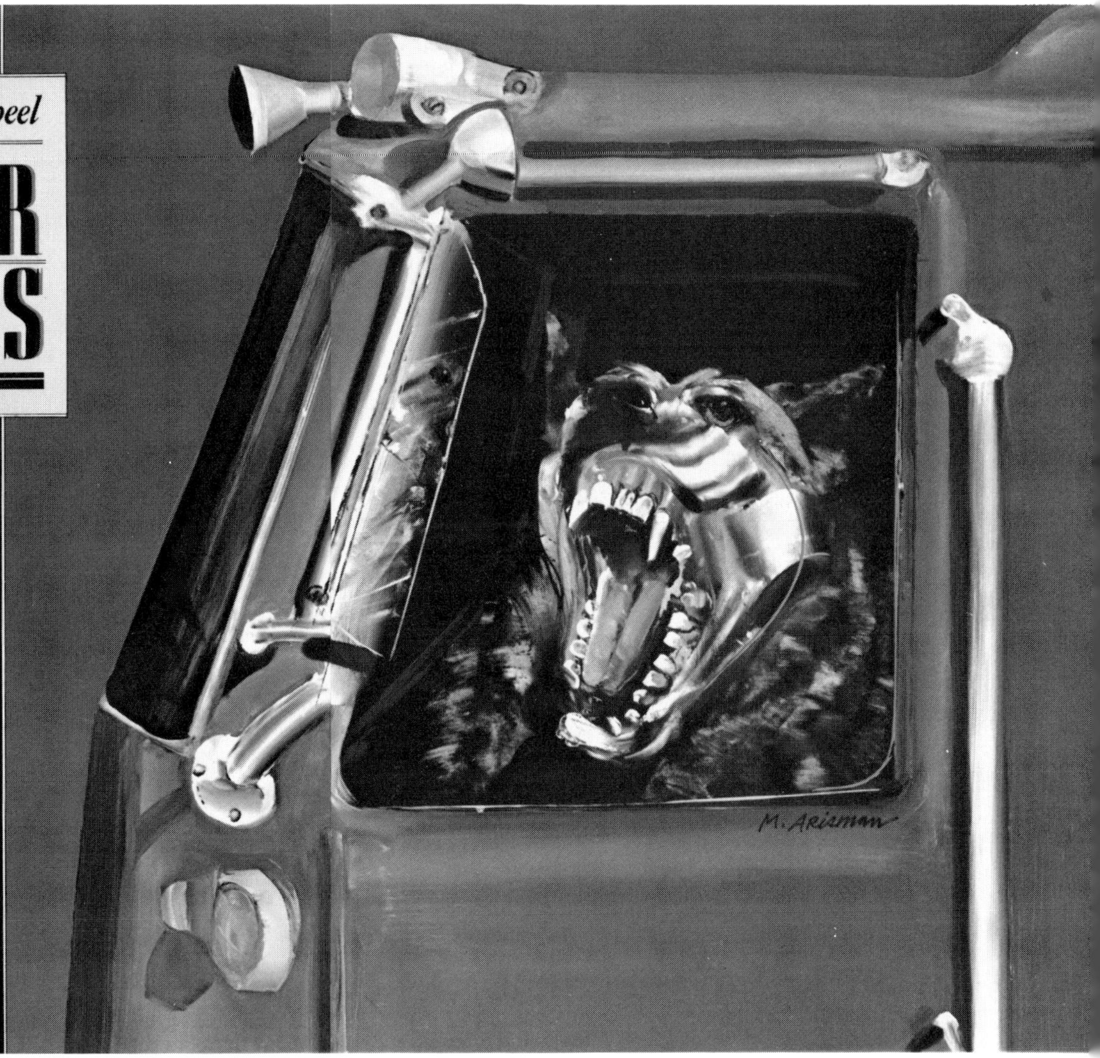

RUN DOWN
A TRAGIC INCIDENT ON LONG ISLAND SOUND BRINGS INTO QUESTION THE "HELP IN DISTRESS" ETHIC SO TRADITIONAL AMONG AMERICAN YACHTSMEN.
By JOANNE A. FISHMAN

THE NEMATODE CHRONICLES

BY EHUD YONAY

IN WHICH *a miracle potion becomes the savior of agriculture and then, through means fair and foul, is banned throughout the land.*

AT FIRST THERE was talk, men's talk about things men don't talk about, and then there was suspicion. In early 1975 Dennis Haight (not his real name) and his wife, Elizabeth, got tired of arguing over whose fault it was that they could not have children. Elizabeth went to her doctor, but he could find nothing wrong with her. Then Dennis went to see his doctor, and what he discovered fueled the men's talk during lunch breaks at Occidental's Ag Chem Division in Lathrop, halfway between Stockton and Modesto. Dennis's sperm contained practically no sperm cells, those tiny tailed creatures without which life cannot begin. "When he told us about it we had a suspicion that there might be something chemical that caused it, but it was only a suspicion," recalls Ted Bricker, a chemical operator, like Dennis, at Oxy. "Sometime after that I was poisoned by parathion at the plant, which was nothing new, because I'd been poisoned nine times in thirteen years. But when my doctor ran follow-up tests on me he suggested doing a sperm test, and I said okay. So we did a sperm test, and I came out zero. Now, that made two of us at the Ag Chem division, and this time I was sure we had a problem."

When additional medical tests revealed that other workers at the same division were either sterile or had inordinately low sperm counts, the news made headlines across the country, and the workers from Lathrop became the center of a new environmental storm. The cause of the problem was pegged as DBCP, an amber-colored liquid used by farmers to control tiny soil-dwelling roundworms called nematodes. As intense media coverage stirred up the specter of collusion and cover-up by ruthless farmers and greedy chemical manufacturers, regulatory agencies began to grind overtime. Several tons of paperwork later, DBCP was banned for use in agricultural fields throughout the country, with the exception of Hawaii's pineapple fields.

On the surface the Lathrop affair had the makings of a first-class scandal: a chemical-agribusiness cabal protects its pet poi-

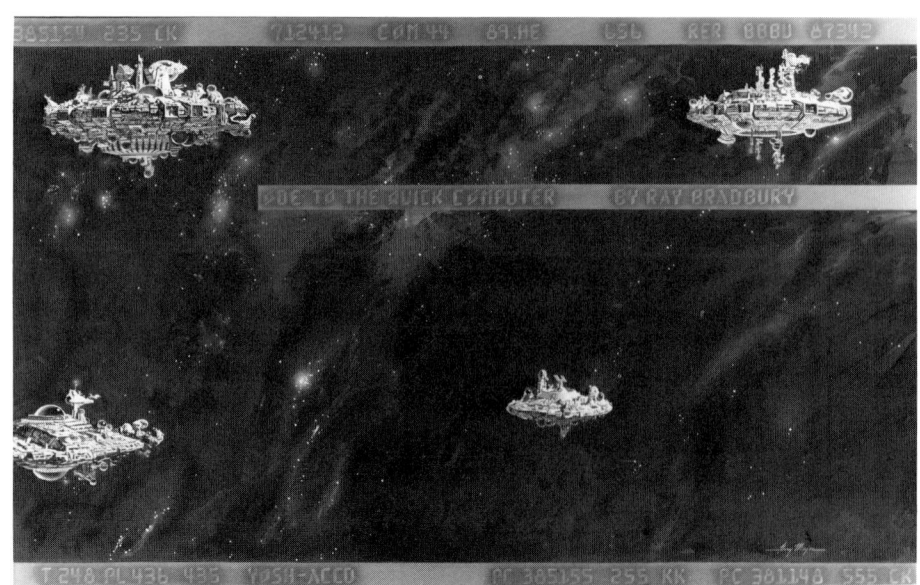

ENERGY

460
Nancy Duckworth Art Director
Rocco Gioffre Illustrator
New West Magazine Client
Los Angeles CA

461
Mauricio Arias Art Director
Gary Meyer Illustrator
Apple Computer Magazine Client
Santa Monica CA

462
Richard M. Ference Art Director
Geoge Kemper, Ed Eng, Mike Donovan
   Photographers
Exxon Chemical Client
Westport CT

463
Greg Paul Art Director
Dagmar Frinta Illustrator
The Plain Dealer Magazine Client
Cleveland OH

464
Bryan Canniff Art Director
Skip Gandy Photographer
Boating Client
New York NY

465
Ralph Stello, Jr. Art Director
Nicolas Furlotte Editor
Spectra II Studio
Cable Marketing Magazine Client
New York NY

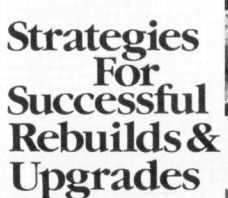

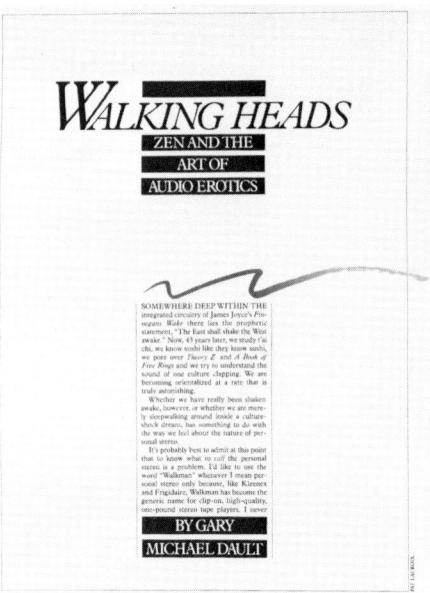

466

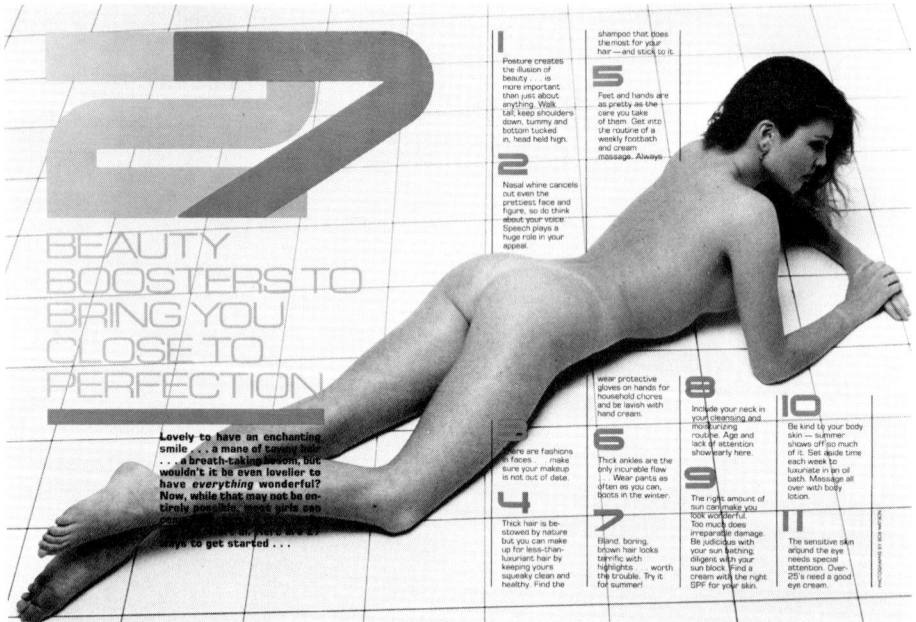
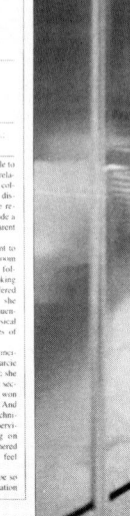

467

466
Mary Opper Art Director
Pat Lacroix Photographer
Quest Magazine Client
Toronto, Ontario Canada

467
Irene Carpelis, Sylvain Michaelis Art Directors
Bob Watson Photographer
Hearst Publishing Client
New York NY

468
Steven Hoffman, Phyllis Schefer Art Directors
Seth Jaben Illustrator
Spring Magazine Client
New York NY

469
Al Foti Art Director
Hans-Peter Dimke Photographer
MD Magazine Client
New York NY

470
John Newcomb Art Director
Stephen E. Munz Photographer
Medical Laboratory Observer Client
Oradell NJ

471
Ursula Kaiser Art Director
Michel Pilon Photographer
Homemaker's Magazine Client
Toronto, Canada

472
Ron A Albrecht Art Director
Stan Shaffer Photographer
Essence Magazine Client
New York NY

473
Wayne Burkart Art Director
Tom Sizemore Designer
John Gerstner Photographer
Deere & Company Client
Moline IL

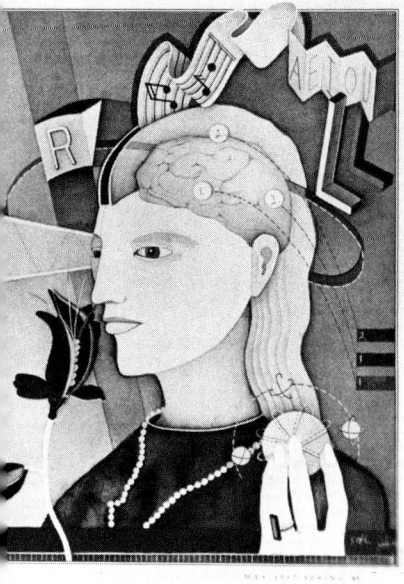

468

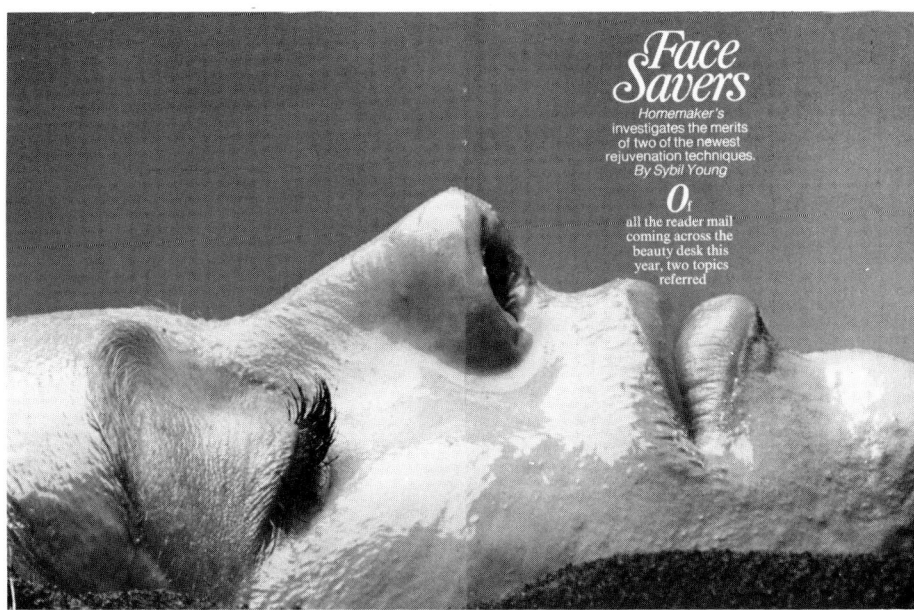

Face Savers

Homemaker's investigates the merits of two of the newest rejuvenation techniques. By Sybil Young

Of all the reader mail coming across the beauty desk this year, two topics referred

471

CREATIVITY AS ENIGMA
INFINITE REASONS FOR WONDER

469

REPLENISH!
MOISTURIZE

472

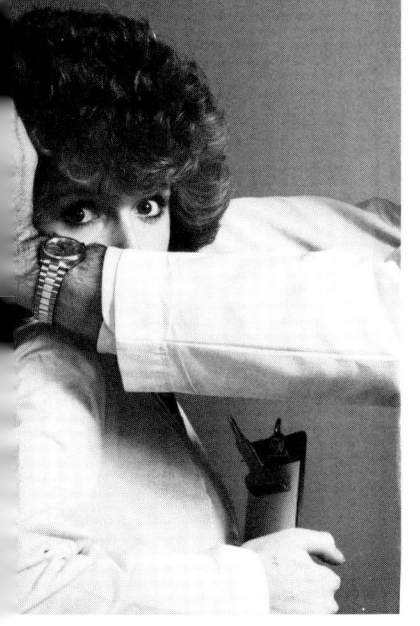

470

GLORIA STEINEM: PUTTING WOMEN IN THEIR PLACE

473

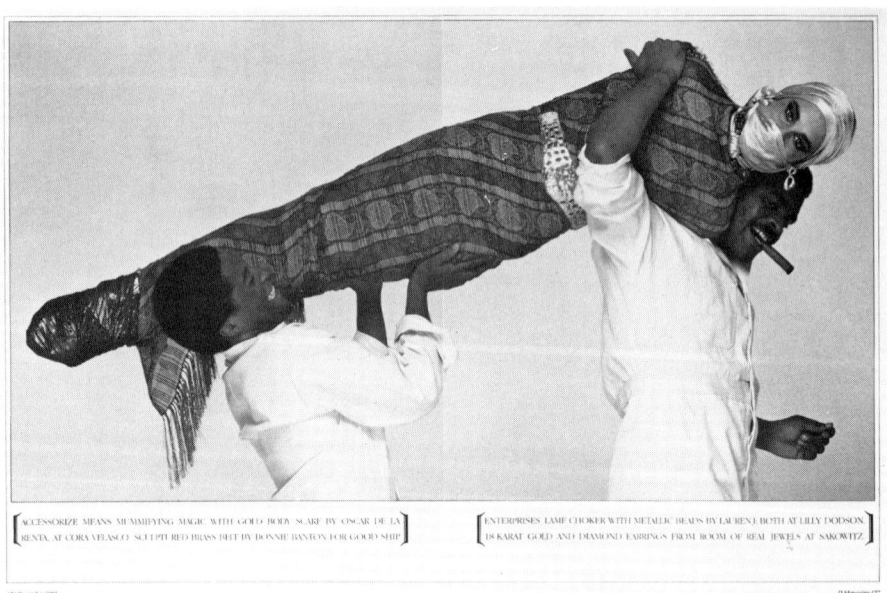

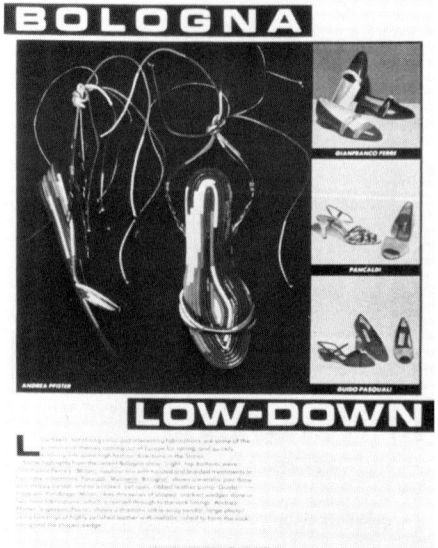

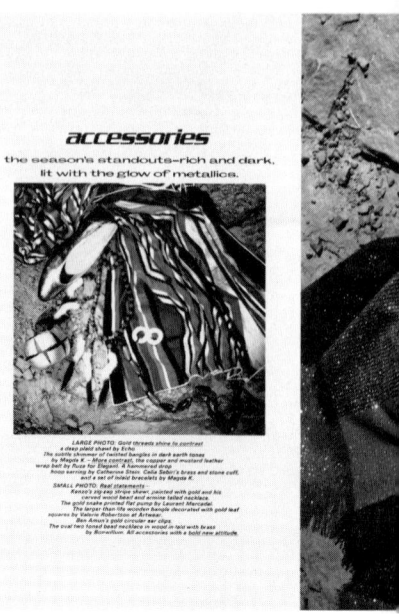

474
Gregory Downer Art Director
Bill Hayward Photography
Opera News Client
New York NY

475
Fred Woodward Art Director
Kent Barker Photographer
D Magazine Client
Dallas TX

476
Susan B. Gallo Designer
Thomas Iannaccone Photographer
Footwear News Magazine Client
New York NY

477
Sally Bruner-Johns Art Director
Sally Bruner-Johns Design Studio Studio
Carolina Arts Magazine Client
Raleigh NC

478
Anthony Devino Art Director
Georgia Candemeres Designer
Tony Lattari Photographer
Julia Schon Editor
The McCall Pattern Co. Client
New York NY

479
Robert J. Post Art Director
Jack Lund Designer
Chicago Magazine Client
Chicago IL

480
George Coderre Art Director
Progressive Architecture Client
Stamford CT

481
Marcia Wright Art Director
Barbara Koster Designer
John Craig Illustrator
The Webb Co. Production House
Trans World Airlines Client
St. Paul MN

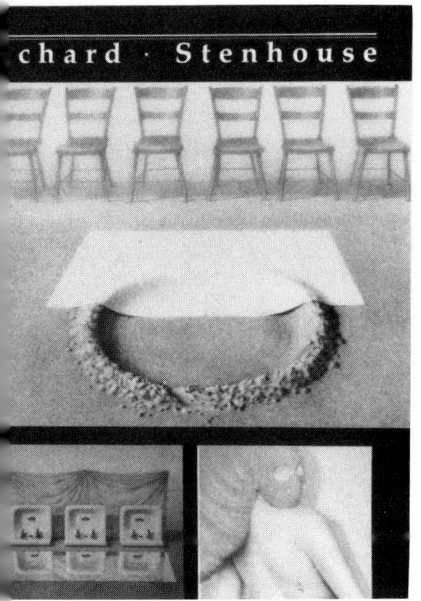

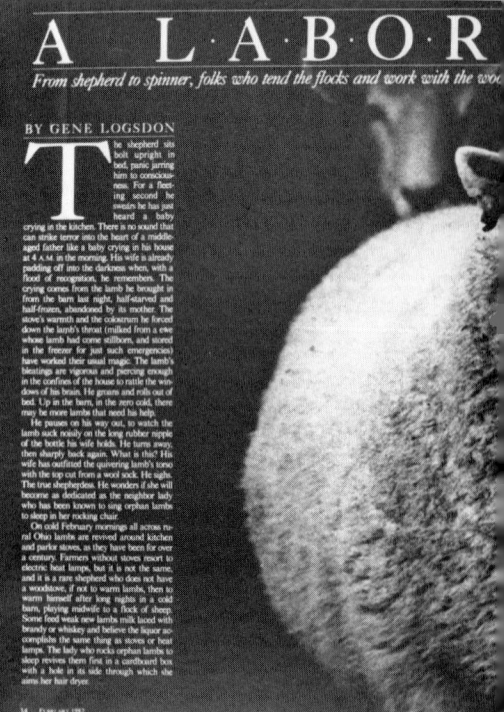

EDUCATION IS FAILING INDUSTRY

Companies rely on the "products" of the nation's educational institutions. And they express growing dissatisfaction with what they've been getting. But they're doing more than grumbling. They're becoming more involved—at all levels.

By Margaret Price

In the eyes of many, America's educational system is failing. Certainly, it failed Jose L., who sat miserably one day in a New York employment agency, unable to fill out an application form. Jose had graduated from high school without ever mastering basic English skills. Nonetheless, he eventually managed to land an entry-level job with a Manhattan bank. But, once hired, he functioned so poorly that the bank ordered him to attend its in-house remedial reading and writing classes.

As he entered the classroom on the first day, Jose wore an expression of fear. "He thought he was being punished," the instructor recalls. However, within a matter of weeks his reading skills improved.

Jose's story is not uncommon. The bank which employed him has encountered similar deficiencies in many of its entry-level hires. And throughout the business world employers find it necessary to train some new employees, not only in specialized skills but also in the basics.

That includes the nation's colleges. Higher education has been the object of much finger-pointing by people in industry, particularly for its failure to educate an adequate number of people in disciplines needed in the working world. Beginning in the late 1960s, critics lament, many colleges stopped demanding top-quality performances from students and veered toward trendiness and experimentation.

But, today, elementary and secondary education are considered the worst offenders. "Generally speaking, we're very pleased with the college grads we get from the 80-or-so colleges we recruit from. The problem is with grade schools and secondary schools, especially in the inner city," says George J. Yoxall, manager of personnel and training at Inland Steel Co., Chicago. "Many companies in the Chicago area which regularly test incoming applicants have data that show that the average high-school graduate has measurably lower verbal and arithmetic skills than ten or 15 years ago."

And, while literacy levels in urban areas are declining, the complexity of jobs in industry today "requires more literacy than in the past," he stresses. Modern steel mills, for example, use highly sophisticated computerized equipment—and workers have to be able to cope with this new complexity. Further, if an employee hopes to advance to a highly skilled position, "he'll need communications skills as he moves up the ladder," Mr. Yoxall stresses.

Remedial courses. In service industries, like insurance, the deficiencies are equally glaring. "The biggest problem," says Carnie

482
Nick Dankovich Art Director
John Chuldenko Illustrator
Industry Week Magazine Client
Cleveland OH

483
David Carothers Art Director
Black Star Photographer
Catherine Cahan Editor
Jack J. Podell Director
Student Lawyer Client
Chicago IL

484
Stan Corfman Art Director
Marathon World Client
Findlay OH

485
David Williams Art Director
Peggy Callaway Designer
Karl & Steve Masiowski Photographers
North Carolina Wildlife Resources Comm. Client
Raleigh NC

486
Mary Lynn Blasutta Art Director
Jay Paris Photographer
Ohio Magazine Client
Columbus OH

Editorial Design MULTIPLE UNIT

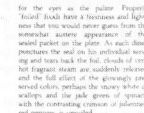

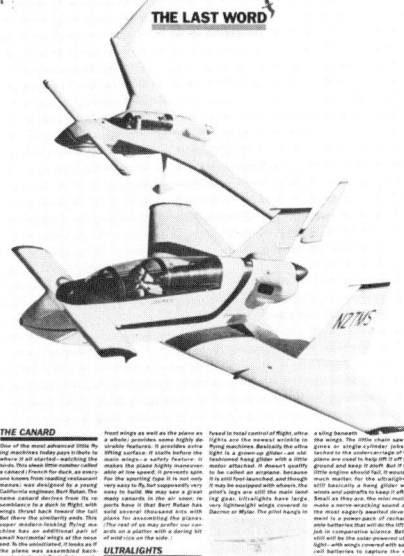

487
Rosslyn Frick Art Director
Michel Tcherevkoff Photographer
Cuisine Magazine Client
New York NY

488
B. Martin Pedersen Art Director
Jonson Pedersen Hinrichs & Shakery Studio
Upper & Lower Case Client
New York NY

489
Patricia Gipple Art Director
David Moore Designer
Martha Swope, Marbeth, Jack Vartoogian, Lois Greenfield Photographers
America Illustrated Client
Washington DC

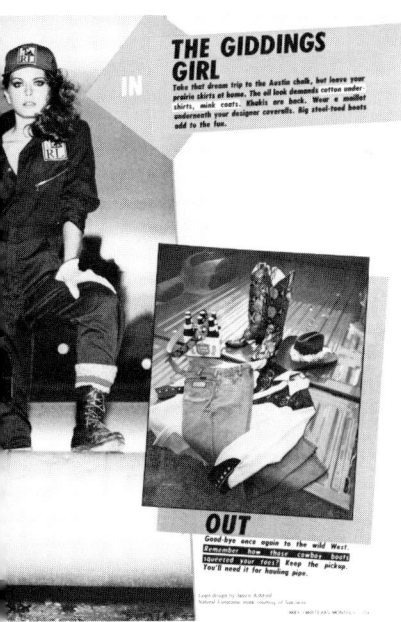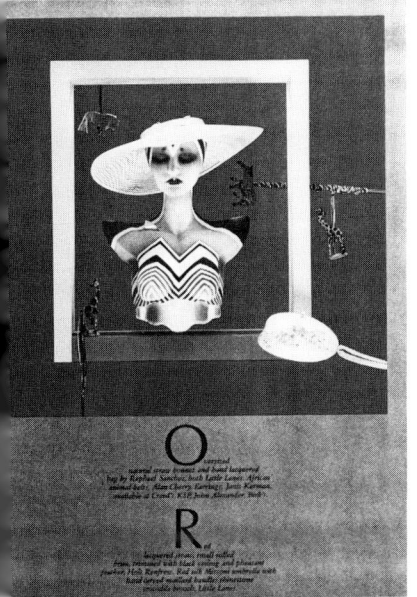

490
Jim Darilek Designer
Kent Kirkley Photographer
Texas Monthly Magazine Client
Austin TX

491
Georges Haroutiun, Rod Della-Vedova Art
   Directors
Joanna Bain Designer
Myron Zabol Photographer
M.A.G. Graphics Ltd. Studio
Bloor Publishing Client
Toronto, Canada

492
Ray Hrynkow Art Director
James LaBounty Photographer
Westworld Publications Client
Vancouver, Canada

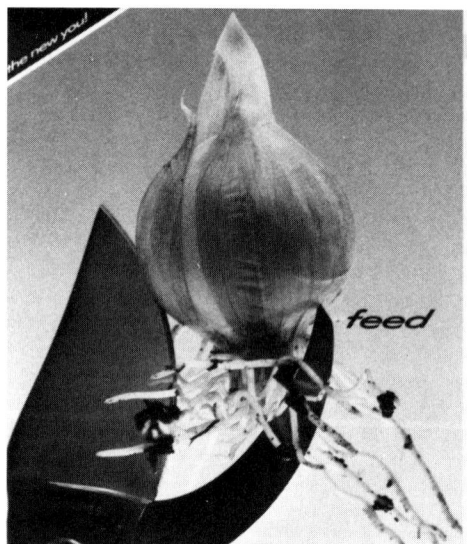
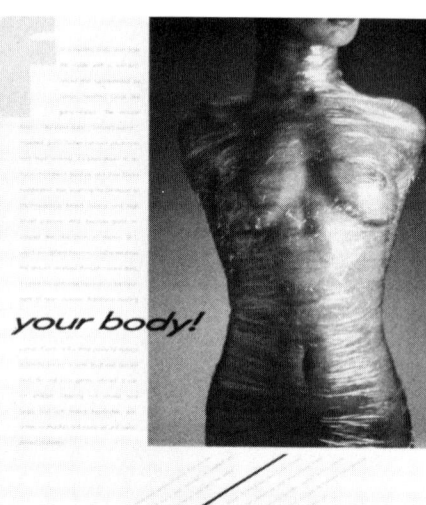
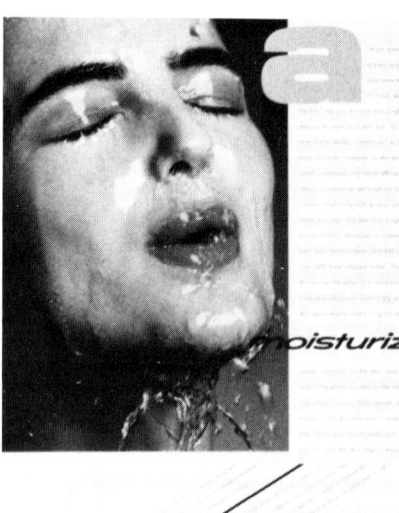

493
Robert Flora Art Director
Hiro Photographer
Harper's Bazaar Client
New York NY

494
Jeffrey L. Dever Art Director
Harry Knox & Associates Studio
Liberty Magazine Client
Laurel MD

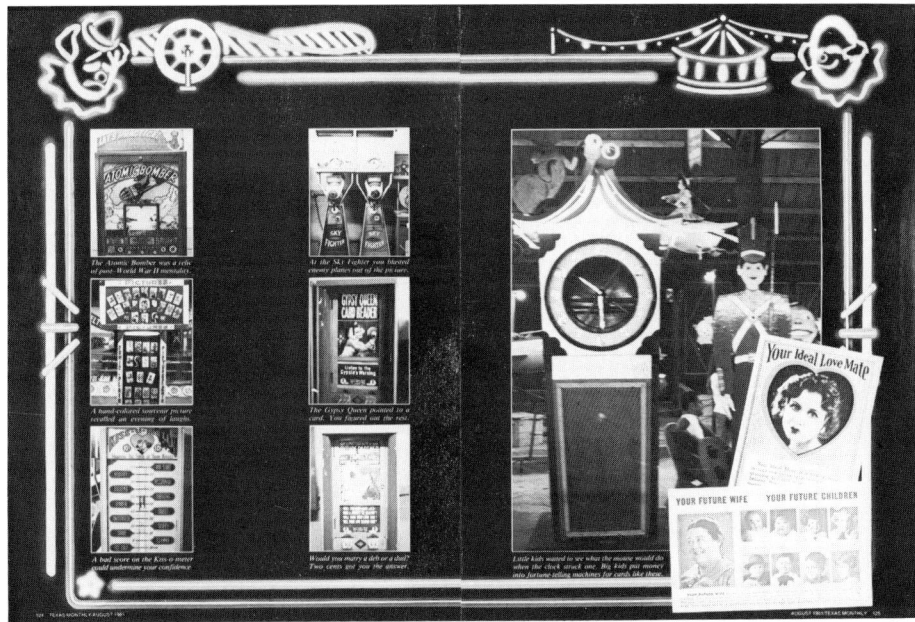

495
Jim Darilek Art Director
Bill Holloway, Patti Heid Photographers
Texas Monthly Magazine Client
Austin TX

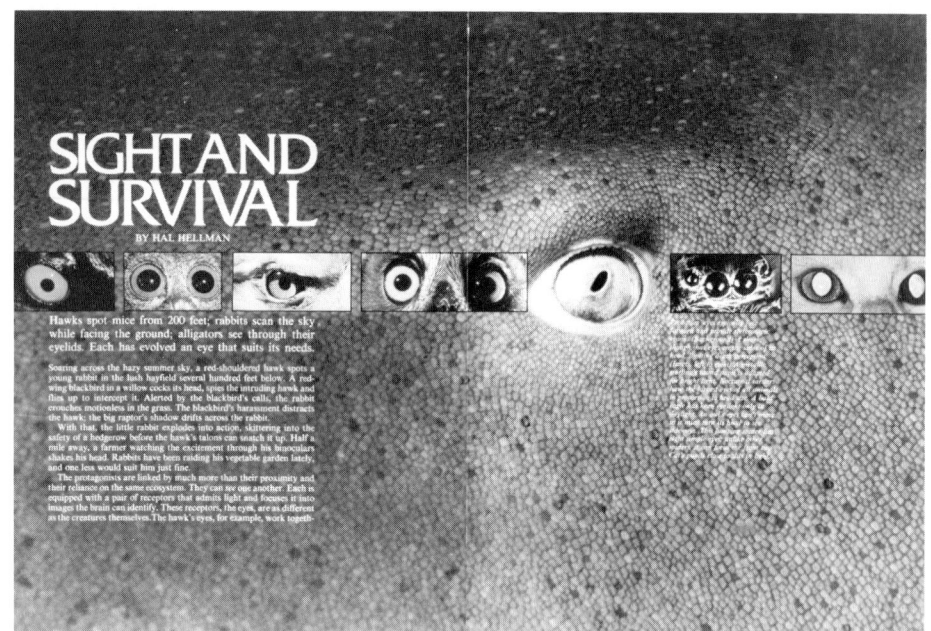

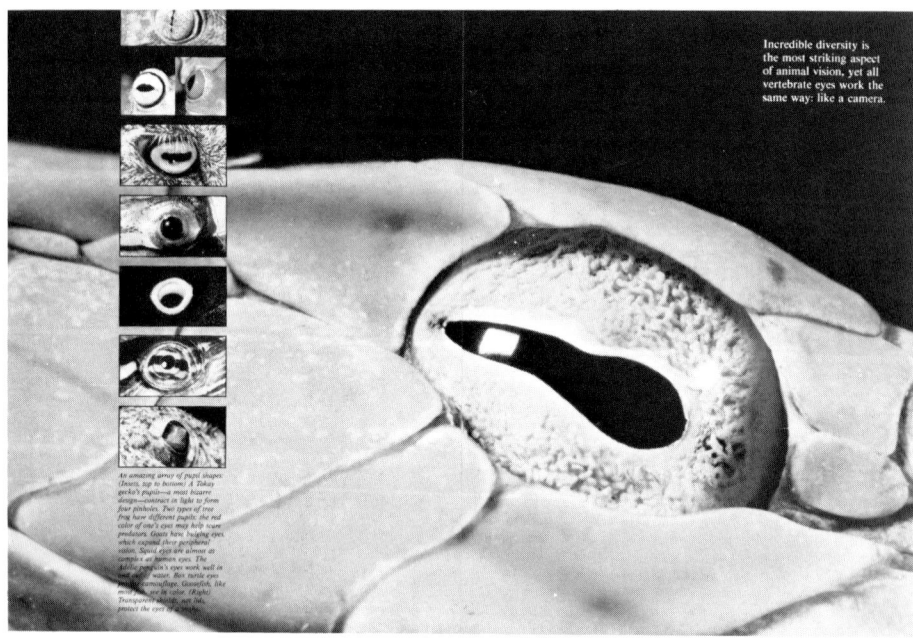

496
Frank Rothmann Art Director
Russell Zolan Designer
Science Digest Magazine Client
New York NY

497
Peter Wong Ming Faye Art Director
Mike Yamashita Photographer
Emphasis (Hong Kong) Ltd. Publishers
Cathay Pacific Client
Central Hong Kong

Some Real Stupid Guys That O.C. and Stiggs Know Go to the Beach

by Harry Beaugereaux

This girl knows where there might be a place to stay where the landlord is an old lady and won't give them any shit.

"The girls on the beach
Are all within reach,
If you know what to do."
—Brian Wilson

"I started to grab her tit
And she took off."
—Harry Beaugereaux

We got some bucks together and figured we'd take a week and go to San Diego or Newport or someplace and get a place on the beach, so I got a new belt and some hoses that my car needed and loaded about three cases of beer in the backseat, and me and Blinn and Burger took off. It was about ten at night, because Blinn didn't get off work at the Safeway until around then, and he was going to run a case of quarts out the loading dock, which would put our brew supply up to about twelve gallons plus a quart of hard stuff and a giant chest full of mixer and more cans of beer. By about one or two we got to Yuma and had drunk about half the beers and Blinn was totally blotto, which was pretty easy to figure out because he'd found a tube of Brite in my stuff, or whatever that toothpaste is that's red, and smeared it all over his lips and chin and his cheeks like fingerpaint because according to him his lips were chapped. He actually said that to a guy at the border inspection station. The guy asks Blinn if he has any fruit or plants and Blinn looks at him with his face all covered with this red shit and says that his lips are chapped and then he says that he's got a couple thousand boll weevils on him, which was not a good thing to say with beer cans all over the car and toothpaste all over his face, plus us drunk and the fact that the inspector is an asshole. So, anyway, we get to San Diego about when the sun was coming up, but it was too early to look for a place on the beach so we went to this guy we know's parents' house near Mission Beach and woke them up to see if we could rack there for a while. We were really fucked up, and just about blew away the guy's mom when she answered the door, especially since I wasn't wearing any shirt and had these powdered soap grains all in my hair from when we spun out on the highway near Winterhaven. Blinn and I had been ripping soap dispensers out of gas stations and we had about ten of them in the car when Burger went to sleep at the wheel and the car started spinning three-sixties and the soap went everywhere just after another car almost totaled us. So, the guy's mom let us in anyway, and we racked until around noon and went looking for an apartment or a house or something at Mission Beach, where we ran into this girl walking along the beachwalk, Sheila, that Burger knew in grade school and jammed once at a party in the seventh grade. Anyway, Sheila says there's this place near there where some guys got thrown out by the landlord and that maybe we could stay there, so we found this woman named Marion who was the landlord and she said the guys she kicked out had put this horrible stuff called Atomic Bomb that they use to fix cuts in football all over her

This is where the guys usually are, if they're not inside or walking around the beach or someplace.

wiener dog, teal thick, and then the dog went rolling in the sand to get the stuff off and got run over by a lifeguard jeep. Somebody put some of that stuff up my ass in P.E. once and it burnt like hell. So the lady was pissed and we had to really bullshit our brains out to convince her we were okay enough to stay in her place, so she finally took my driver's license number and gave us the place for a week. First thing we did was move some stuff to sit on, out in the yard. The house was like all the other places along the beach, with little front yards right up against the beachwalk and about two-foot-high brick walls around them so you could sit on the lawn and look out at the ocean and the beach and all the people walking

One of the guys wonders if they should try to get some girls to come over and try to fuck them.

continued on page 0

This girl might do it because she's fucked up on PCP, one of the guys thinks as he grabs her tit.

Trademarks & Logotypes

499
Jukka Veistola Designer
Veistola Oy Studio
Filmitalli/Film Stable Client
Helsinki, Finland

500
Randi J. Shalit Designer
RL Studio
Eye Institute of New Jersey Client
Atlanta GA

501
Jack Hermsen Designer
Jaime A. Sendra Art Director
Advance Design Center Studio
El Molino Client
Dallas TX

502
Gavin Patterson Designer
Donald Dallas Creative Director
Dallas Tomlinson & Associates Studio
General Business Corp. (Pty) Ltd. Client
Randburg, S. Africa

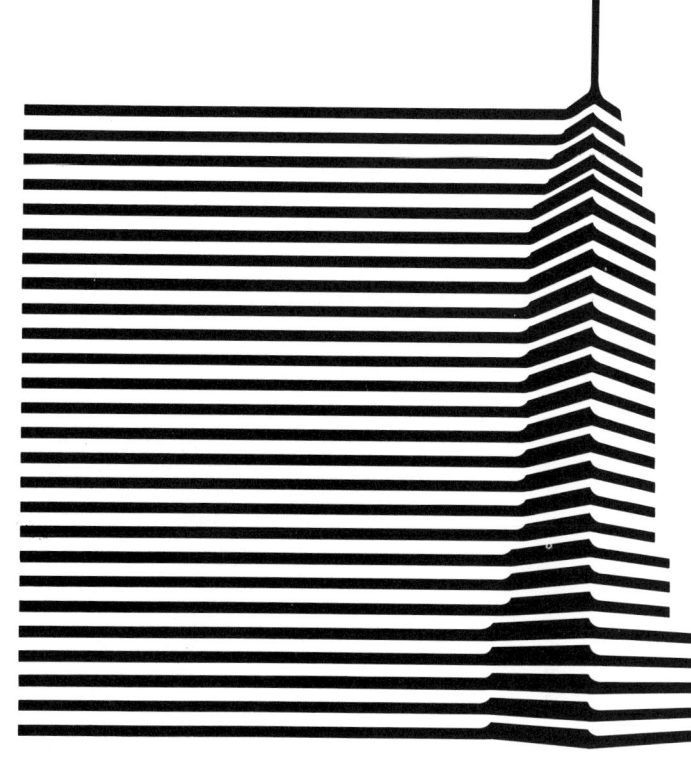

504

503
John DeSieno Designer
Empire State Plaza Convention Center Client
Albany NY

504
Ricardo Salas Art Director
Alfonso Capetillo y Asociados Agency
Latino Americana Seguros S.A. Client
Mexico DF

505
Hoi Ling Chu Designer
H.L. Chu & Company Ltd. Studio
Pellegrini & Kaestle Inc. Agency
SeaQuest Client
New York NY

506
Alan Wood Designer
Ray Barber Lettering
Alan Wood Graphic Design Inc. Studio
Guma Rubber Footwear Ltd. Client
New York NY

THE TYPOGRAPHIC COMMUNICATION JOURNAL. PUBLISHED BY WORLD TYPEFACE CENTER INC., VOLUME ONE, NUMBER ONE, MARCH 1982

507
Tom Carnase, Jason Calfo Designers
Carnase, Inc. Studio
World Typeface Center Inc. Client
New York NY

508
Terry Lesniewicz, Al Navarre Designers
Lesniewicz/Navarre Studio
CEMA Client
Toledo OH

509
Michael Escobedo, Joseph Smith Designers
Burton Advertising Studio
Avco Community Developers Client
Costa Mesa CA

CLEANING EQUIPMENT MANUFACTURERS' ASSOCIATION

510
Fernando Medina Designer
Vias y Transportes Client
Madrid, Spain

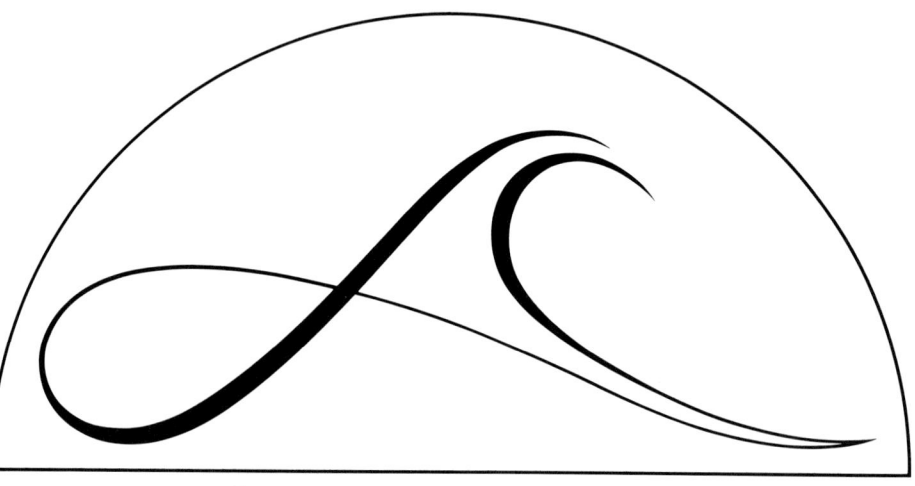

509

510

511
Primo Angeli, Ray Honda, Mark Jones
   Designers
Grid Systems Corporation Client
San Francisco CA

512
Jerry Cowart Designer
Brown, Leifer + Slatkin Client
Los Angeles CA

BROWN LEIFER +SLATKIN
CERTIFIED PUBLIC ACCOUNTANTS

SANDMEYER'S BOOKSTORE

513
Liane Sebastian, Michael Waitsman Designers
Synthesis Studio
Sandmeyer's Bookstore Client
Chicago IL

514
Mitchell Irion Designer
Baney, Gutzmer Inc. Studio
Pacific Fabric Protection Client
Kahului HI

THE
HUNTLEY HOTEL

515
Dan O'Mara Designer
John Anselmo Design Assoc. Studio
The Huntley Hotel Client
Santa Monica CA

516
Dennis P. Moran Designer
Ralph Russini Artist
Adam, Filippo & Moran Studio
Land, Sea & Air Development Corp. Client
Pittsburgh PA

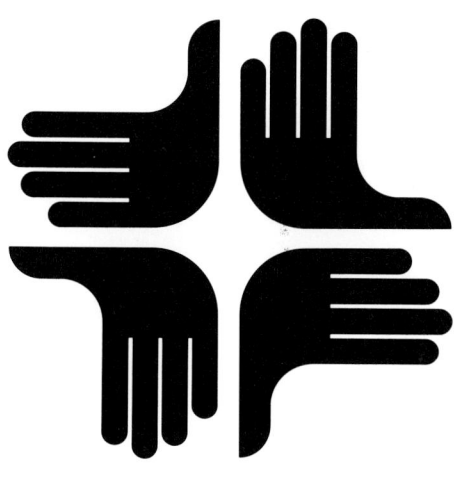

LAND SEA & AIR
DEVELOPMENT CORPORATION

517
Gregory Cutshaw Art Director
Louise Bergman Creative Director
St. Agnes Outreach Client
Dayton OH

518
Al Brandtner Designer
MGA Studio
Ceremony Inc. Client
Birmingham MI

519
Cheryl Lewin Designer
Cheryl Lewin Design Studio
Neuman & Bogdonoff Client
New York NY

520
Marty Neumeier Designer
Neumeier Design Team Studio
Carol Clayton & Associates Client
Santa Barbara CA

521
Susan Rose Designer
Leslie Cabarga Illustrator
J. Walter Thompson Agency
The Company Store Client
New York NY

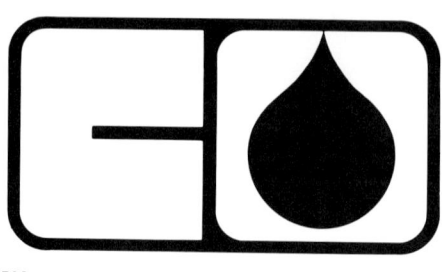
523

522
Robert Burns Designer
Burns, Cooper, Hynes Ltd. Studio
Comus Music Theatre Client
Toronto, Canada

523
Itzhak Beery Designer
Berry Gross Inc. Studio
Cambridge Oil Co. Client
New York NY

524
Diana Garcia de Tolone Art Director
Diana Garcia de Tolone Design Studio
Dipak, S.A. Client
Mexico DF

525
David Brier, Randy Fordyce Designers
David Brier Design Works Studio
Harold Danko Client
New York NY

526
Oswaldo Mendes Filho Designer
Mendes Publicidade Agency
Adao & Eva Client
Belem Brazil

527
Nanette Hucknall Designer
Jewish Reconstructionist Foundation Client
Cliffside Pk. NJ

528
Felix Beltran Designer
Seldon Laboratorios, Madrid Client
Havana, Cuba

529
Gerry Giambattista Designer
Newton Associates Agency
Scholler Chemicals Client
Devon PA

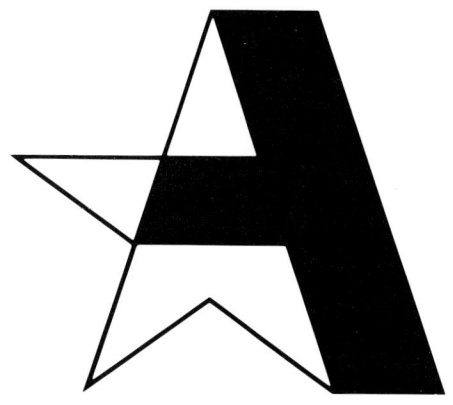

530
Alan Peckolick Designer
Lubalin Peckolick Associates Studio
American Savings Bank Client
New York NY

531
Andrea Binder Designer
Jann Church Adv. & Graphic Design Studio
Trojan Properties Inc. Client
Newport Beach CA

532
Kyosti Varis Designer
Sampo Mutual Insurance Co. Client
Helsinki, Finland

533
Harry Murphy, Diane Levin Designers
Harry Murphy & Friends Studio
William Kreysler & Associates Client
Mill Valley CA

534
Jim Sims Designer
Fibre etc. Weaving Guild Client
Atlanta GA

531   533

535
Gred Resler Art Director
Michael Leidel, David Birdsong Designers
Art Riser Creative Director
John H. Harland Co. Production House
Heritage Bank Client
Atlanta GA

W I N G S

536

536
Diana Graham, Denys Gustafson Designers
Gips + Balkind + Associates Studio
Piedmont Industries Client
New York NY

539

537
Hoi Ling Chu Designer
H.L. Chu & Company Ltd. Studio
Press Brenner Communications Inc. Client
New York NY

538
Gladys Barton Designer
George McGinnis, The Image Factory Concept
B & B Direct Inc. Agency
Showtime Entertainment Agency
New York NY

539
Steven Liska Designer
Liska & Associates Studio
Taylor/Johnson Petrocap Client
Chicago IL

540
Meredith G. Bratt Designer
Ed Gililland Client
Chicago IL

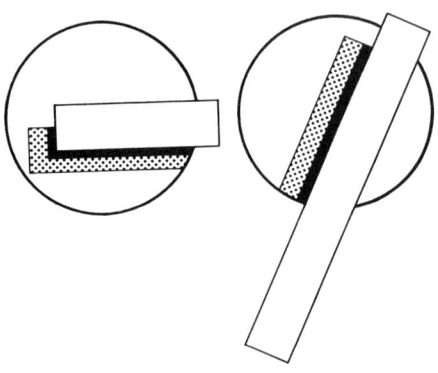
540

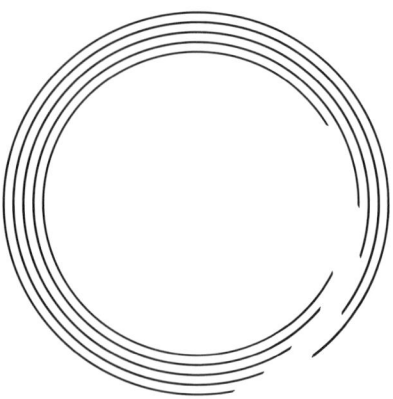

541
Pat Hayes, Joy Yoshikawa Art Directors
Bob Hoffmann Designer
The Design Company Studio
Omann & Co. Hair Designs Client
St. Paul MN

542

543

542
Jean Larcher Designer
Galerie Nina Dausset Client
LaCelle St. Cloud, France

543
Denise Halpin Designer
Dick Davis Client
New York NY

544
David G. Hart Designer
Cos & Co. Hot Air Balloon Flights Client
Atlanta GA

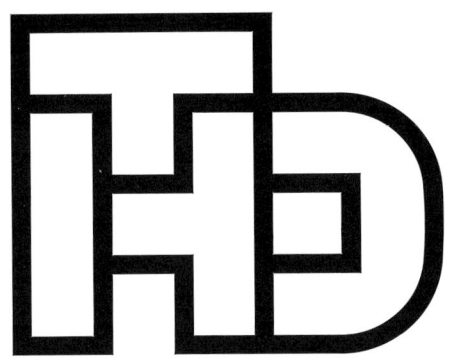

IL CANTONE

545
C.J. Schlosser Designer
Type House & Durograph Client
Minneapolis MN

546
Jose Luis Ortiz Designer
JLO Studio
Restaurant Il Cantone Client
New York NY

547
Gerd F. Setzke Art Director
Kunstschule Alsterdamm Hamburg Studio
Deutsche Shell AG, Hamburg Client
Hamburg, W. Germany

548
Andres Garcia Paz Art Director
Diseno y Communicacion SA Studio
Taller Agricola Mexicano Client
Mexico DF

549
Michael Tobin Designer
Ritta & Associates Inc. Studio
Accudart Client
Englewood NJ

550
Sharon Shayne Designer
The Ground Up Client
Miami FL

551
Robin A. Bugbee, Susan Borgen Designers
Walker/Group Inc. Studio
Rich's Department Stores Client
New York NY

547

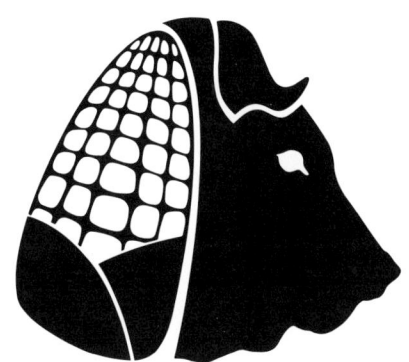

548

549

551

LETTERHEAD / ENVELOPES

552
Carol Bokuniewicz Art Director
Larry Kazal Designer
M & Co. Studio
Crushing Enterprises, Inc. Client
New York NY

553
Harry Murphy, Sheldon Lewis Art Directors
Harry Murphy & Friends Studio
Marin Swim School Client
Mill Valley CA

554
Frank Nichols Art Director
Barbara Harwell Creative Director
Woody Pirtle Inc. Studio
Arnold Harwell McClain & Assoc. Client
Dallas TX

555
Kara Fox Art Director
Mark Matsuno Designer
B.D. Fox & Friends, Inc. Studio
Kara Fox Client
Los Angeles CA

556
Terry O'Connor Designer
Henena O'Connor Illustrator
Terry O Communications Inc. Client
Toronto, Canada

557
Larry S. Paine Designer
Larry Paine & Associates Studio
Carmen Amoras Cabrera Client
Bethesda MD

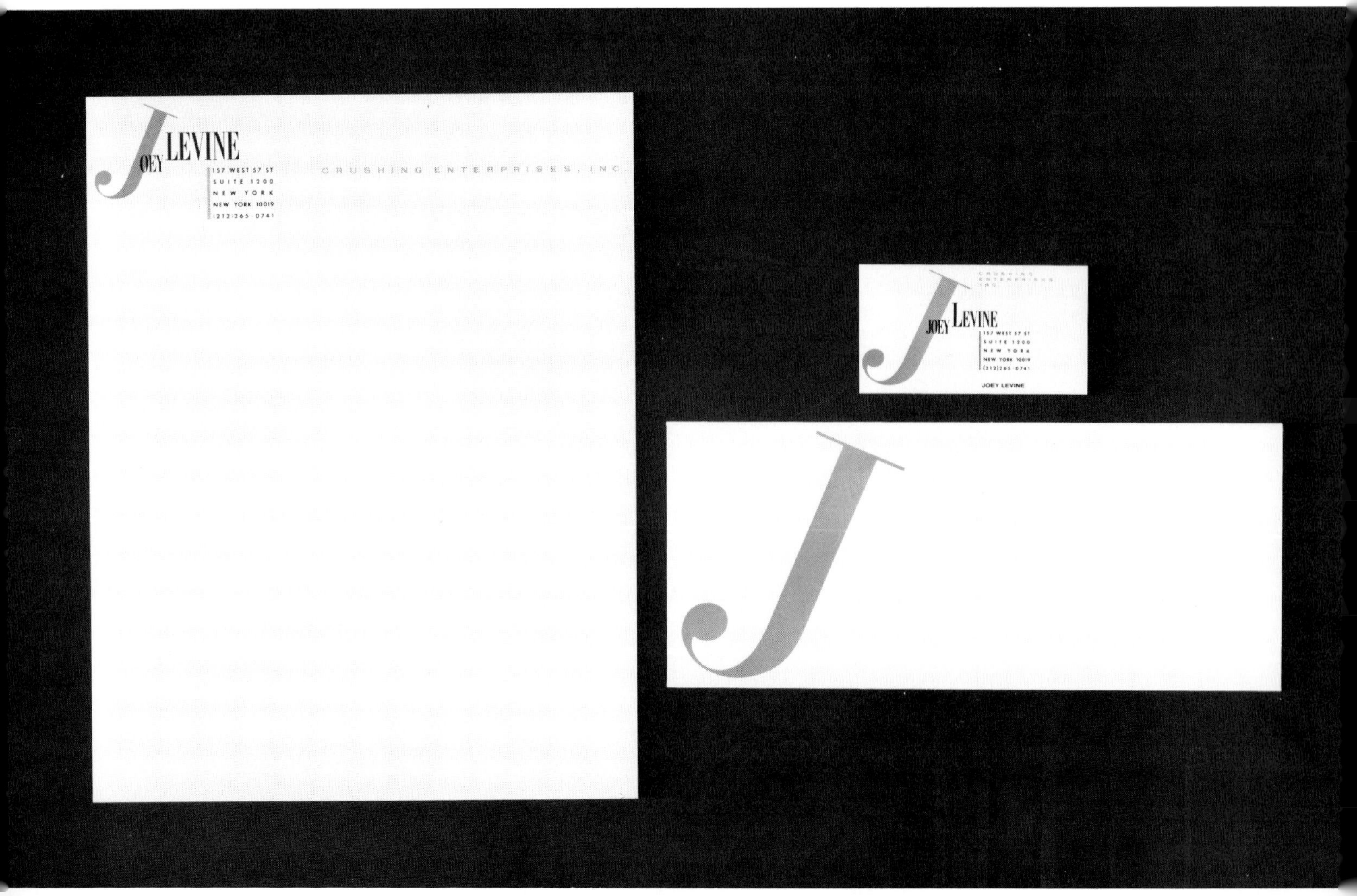

Arnold Harwell McClain & Associates, Inc.
Advertising/Marketing/Public Relations
3434 Fairmount, Dallas, Texas 75219
Arnold Harwell McClain & Associates, Inc.
Advertising/Marketing/Public Relations
3434 Fairmount, Dallas, Texas 75219 (214) 521-6400

554

COLONY VIEW CIRCLE
MALIBU CALIFORNIA 90265

TERRY O COMMUNICATIONS INCORPORATED
T
SILVERWOOD AVENUE, TORONTO, ONTARIO, CANADA

Carmen Amoros Cabrera, L.C.S.W.
2500 Que Street, N.W., Apt. 526
Washington, D.C. 20007
Telephone: 333-9224
For Professional Services Rendered

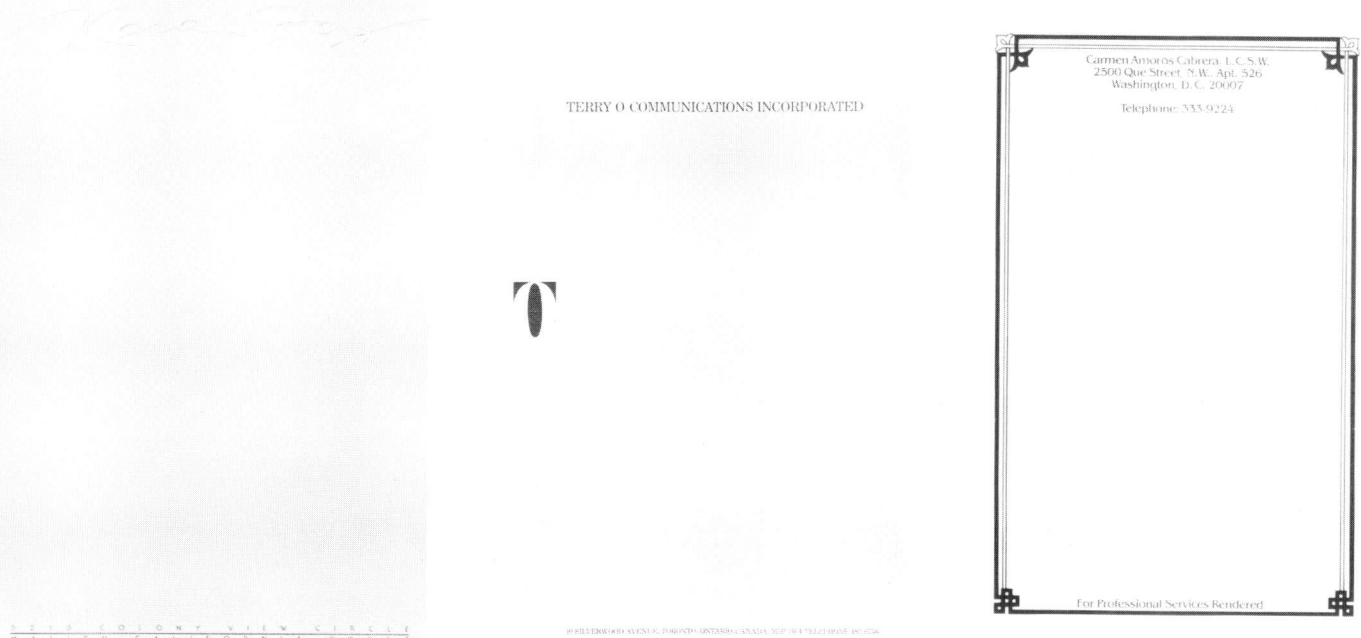

555

558

559

562

558
Dick Lopez Designer
Robert Amen + Associates Client
New York NY

559
Gary G. Polich Art Director
Polich Creative Studio
The Lee Music Center Client
Englewood CO

560
Carol Bokuniewicz, Tibor Kalman Art
  Directors
Joseph Heron Illustrator
M & Co. Studio
Audubon Client
New York NY

561
Arnold Schwartzman Designer
Arnold Schwartzmann Prod. Inc. Client
Santa Monica CA

562
Patrick Florville Designer
Florville Design & Analysis Studio
Guy Romain A.I.A. Client
New York NY

563
Tom Antista Art Director
Rusty Kay and Associates Studio
Heritage Museum Client
Santa Monica CA

565

564
Dan Hyma Art Director
Paul Deur Company Studio
Sandpiper Condominiums Client
E. Grand Rapids MI

568

565
Bill Bundzak Art Director
Earl Lyon Client
Bronxville NY

566
David Olson Art Director
Carl Williams Illustrator
David Olson Design Studio
Susan Moore Lawyer Client
Olympia WA

567
Elizbeth Marks Illustrator
S.C. Peach Council & Promotion Board, Inc. Client
Columbia SC

568
John Kane/Terry Swack Art Directors
John Kane Illustrator
Sametz Blackstone Associates Inc. Agency
Another Season Client
Boston MA

569
Jack R. Anderson Art Director
Cliff Chung Designer
John Hornall Design Works Studio
Susan M. Love Client
Seattle WA

570
Rene Sheret Art Director
Vickie Sawyer Designer
Rene Sheret Design Studio
Intercon Client
Los Angeles CA

571
Bob Newman Art Director
Bonnie Segal Artwork
Newman Design Assoc. Inc. Studio
Susan McCarthy Client
New York NY

LETTERHEAD SET

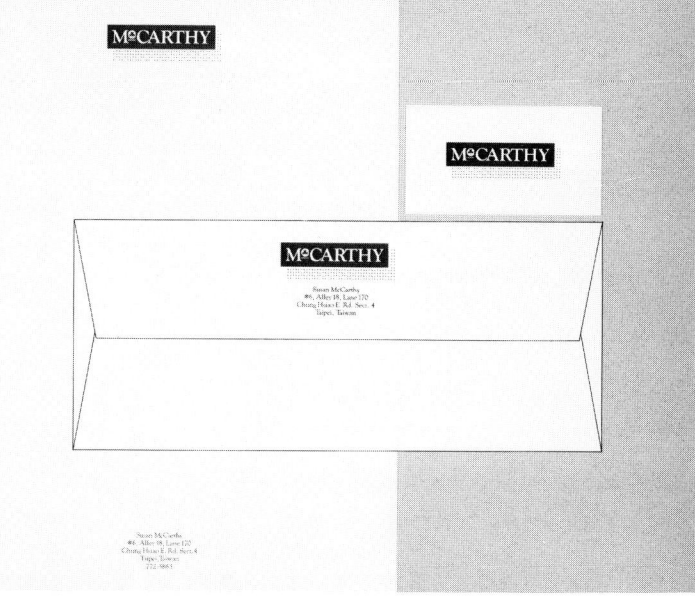

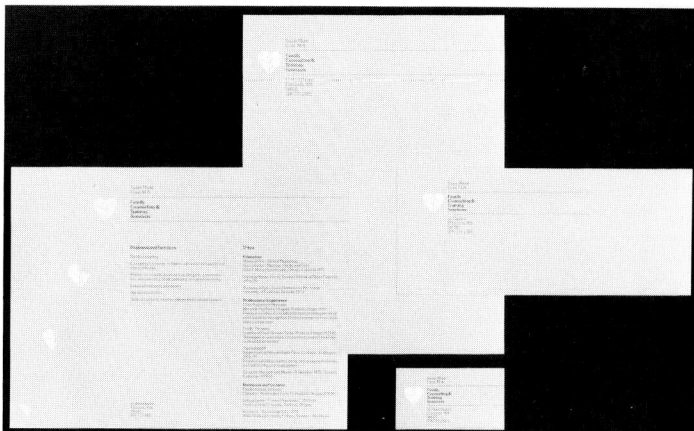
569

572

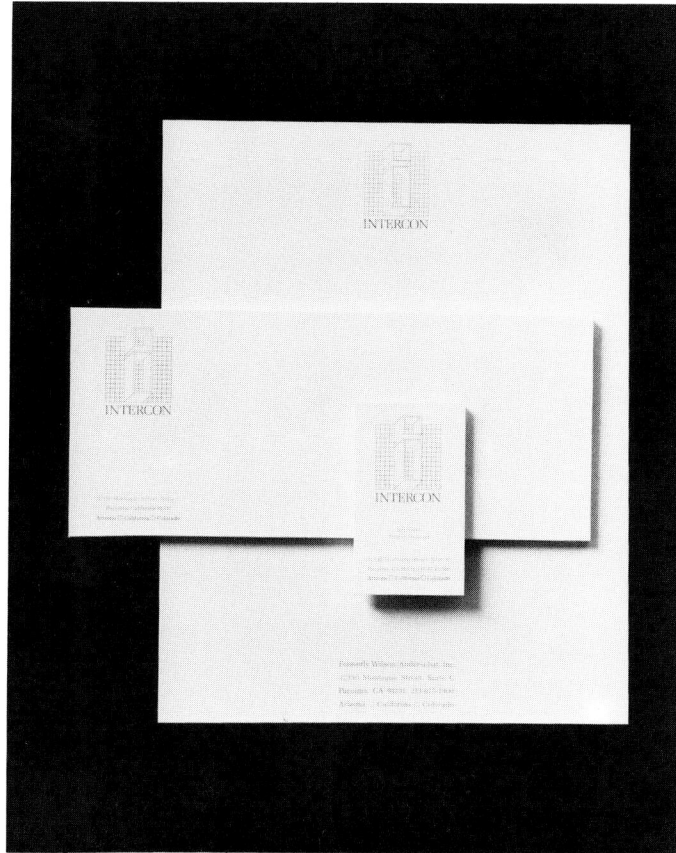

572
Michele Lee Designs Studio
Michele Lee Client
Stanford CA

573
Michael Rowe Art Director
Diamond Art Studio Ltd. Studio
Cinema Projects Inc. Client
New York NY

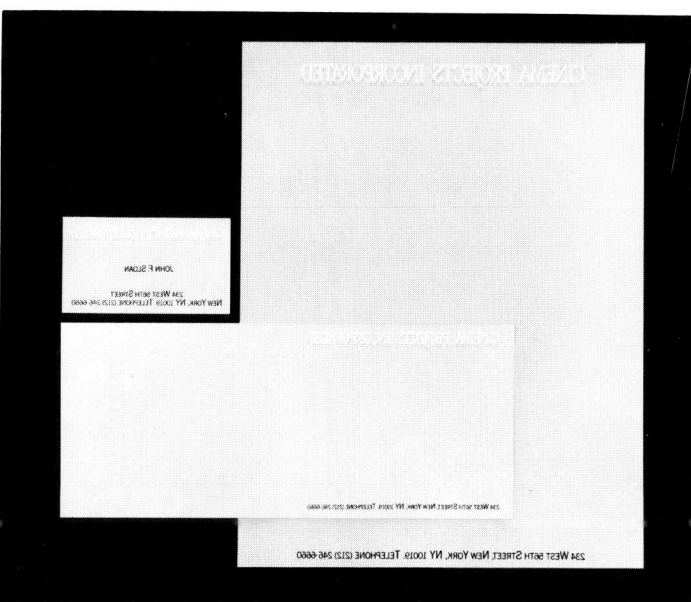
573

574
Anna Amabile Christensen Art Director
Ralph Keefe, Inc. Client
New York NY

575
Gail Blair Creative Director
Naomi Decter Account Services
By Design Studio
Ansearch, Inc. Client
Haddonfield NJ

576
Robert Warkulwiz Designer
Warkulwiz Design Client
Philadelphia PA

577
Tricia & Bill Frost-Buchholz Designers
Frost & Buhholz Graphic Design Studio
Frost & Associates Client
Austin TX

578
Mark Topczewski Designer
Harris & Harris Ltd. Client
Milwaukee WI

579
Alex Gellen Designer
Strathmore Press Client
Cincinnati OH

580
David W. Logan Designer
Black Belt Karate Client
Hermosa Beach CA

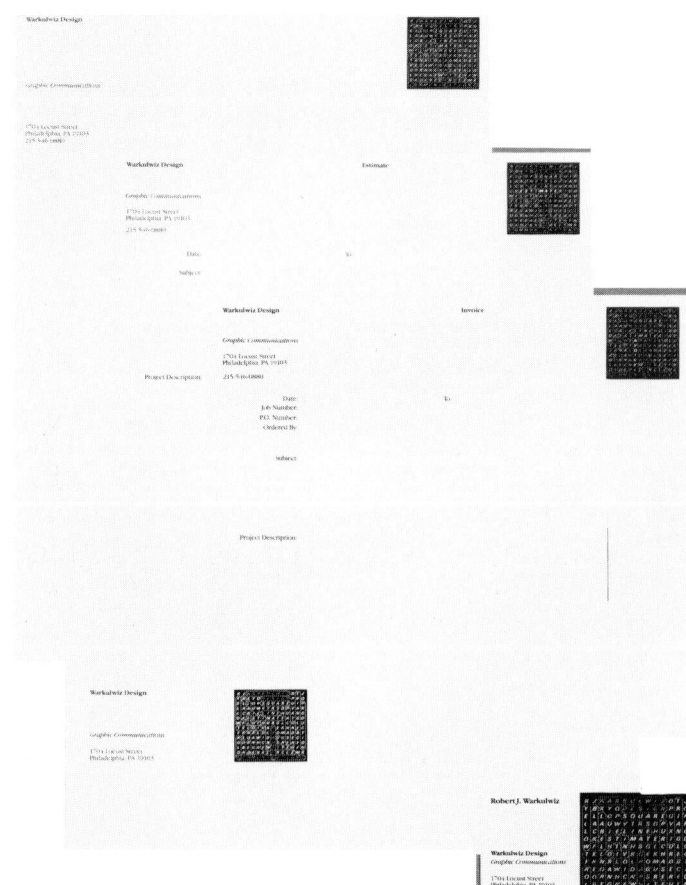

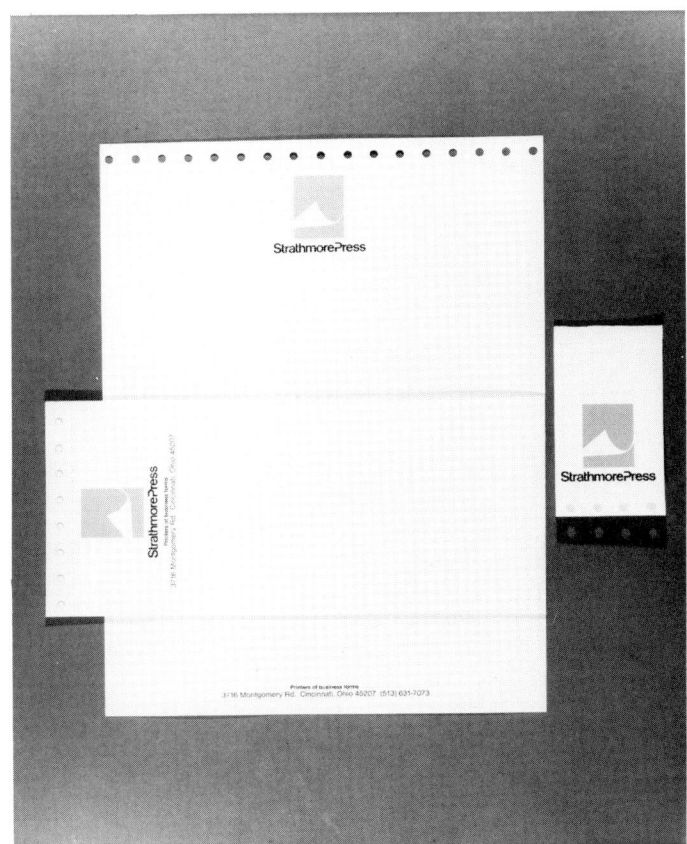

581
Jacklin Pinsler, Bart Crosby Designers
Consolidated Foods Corp. Client
Chicago IL

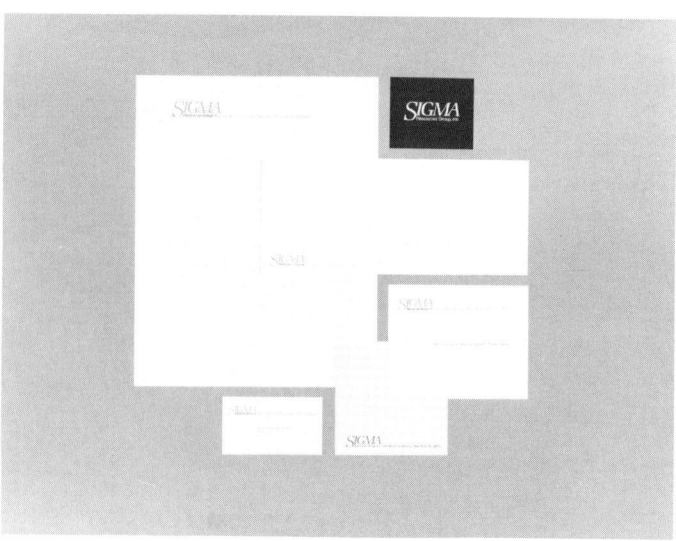

584
Susan Borgen Designer
Robin A. Bugbee Design Director
Walker/Group Studio
Sigma Resources Group, Inc. Client
New York NY

582
Paul Bice Illustrator
Robert Miles Runyan & Assoc. Studio
International Legends, Inc. Client
Playa del Rey CA

583
Danielle Roy Beaudoin Art Director
Cabana, Seguin-Design Inc. Studio
Le Groupe D'Animation Urbaine de Montreal Inc. Client
Montreal, Canada

585
Harold Burch Art Director
Ken White Design Office, Inc. Studio
Housel Precision, Inc. Client
Los Angeles CA

586
Terri Edelman Art Director
Frost Lighting Co. Client
New York NY

587
Jerry Cowart Art Director
Jerry Cowart Design Studio
Klein & Co. Agency
Brown, Leifer + Slatkin Client
Los Angeles CA

588
David Wojdyla Art Director
De Krig Advertising Agency
Tina Lepera Client
New York NY

589
Douglas Joseph Designer
Paul Bice Illustrator
Robert Miles Runyan & Assoc. Studio
A Perfect Setting Client
Playa de Rey CA

Corporate Identity

590
Arie J. Geurts Art Director
Arie J. Geurts Copywriter
Banco de Occidente Client
Cincinnati OH

591
C. Gay, C. Kaminiski, M. Burns, B. Haddon, C. Jones Art Directors
Daimler-Benz (S.A.) Client
Johannesburg R.S.A.

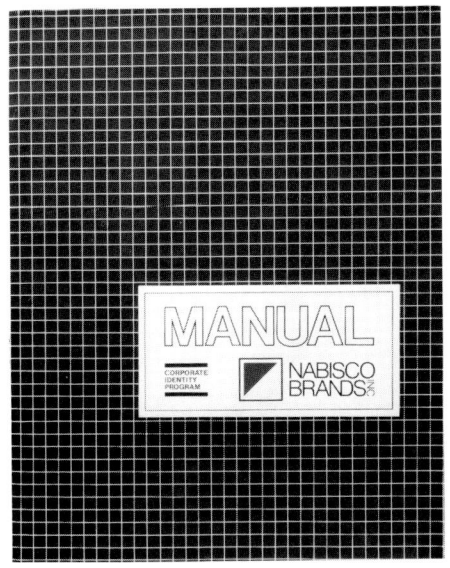

593

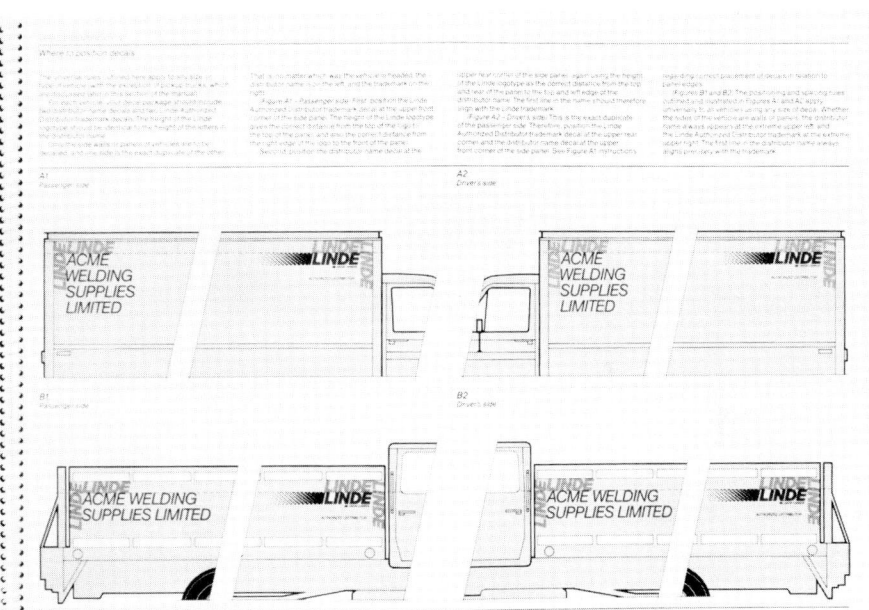

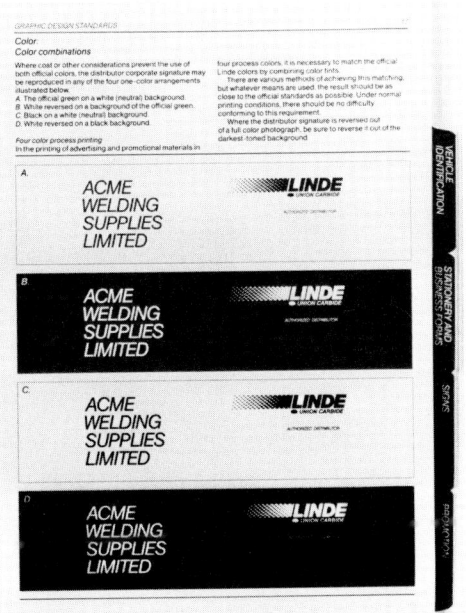

592
Anthony J. Memoli Art Director
J.L.C. Enterprises Copywriter
Visual Services Inc. Studio
Nabisco Brands Inc. Client
Bridgeport CT

593
Jack Anderson, John Hornall Art Directors
Rachel Bard, Debbie Tonkovich Copywriters
Rey Sabado, David Jenks, Mindy Schilperoort, Chris Bulloch Designers
John Hornall Design Works Studio
Westin Hotels Client
Seattle WA

594
Robert Burns Art Director
Ken Kaskin, Diane Mollor Designers
Burns, Cooper, Hynes Ltd. Studio
Union Carbide Canada Client
Toronto Canada

Promotional Pieces, Collateral and Miscellaneous Materials

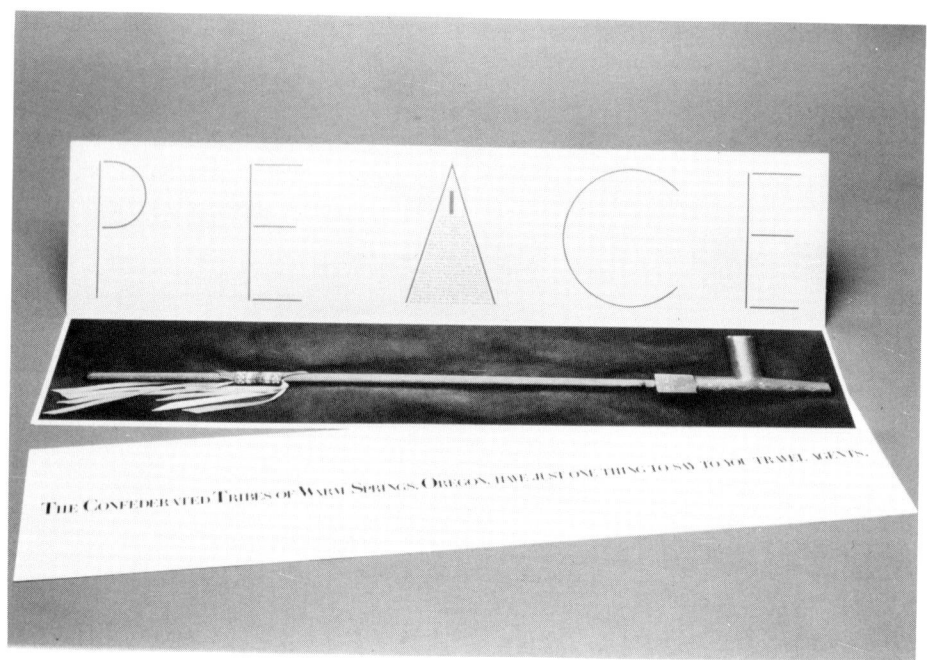

595
Edward Fontecha Tajon Designer
Ford Galbraith Illustrator
Pete Stone Photographer
Borders, Perrin & Norrander Inc. Agency
Kah-Nee-Ta Client
Seattle WA

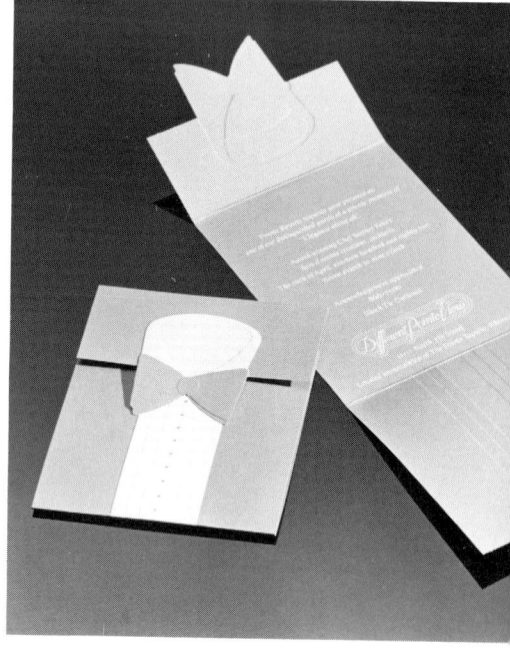

597
Sue Redding Designer
Pointe Communications Studio
Different Pointe of View Restaurant Client
Phoenix AZ

596
Karen Novak Designer
Karen Novak Studio
Madonna Man Boutique Client
New York NY

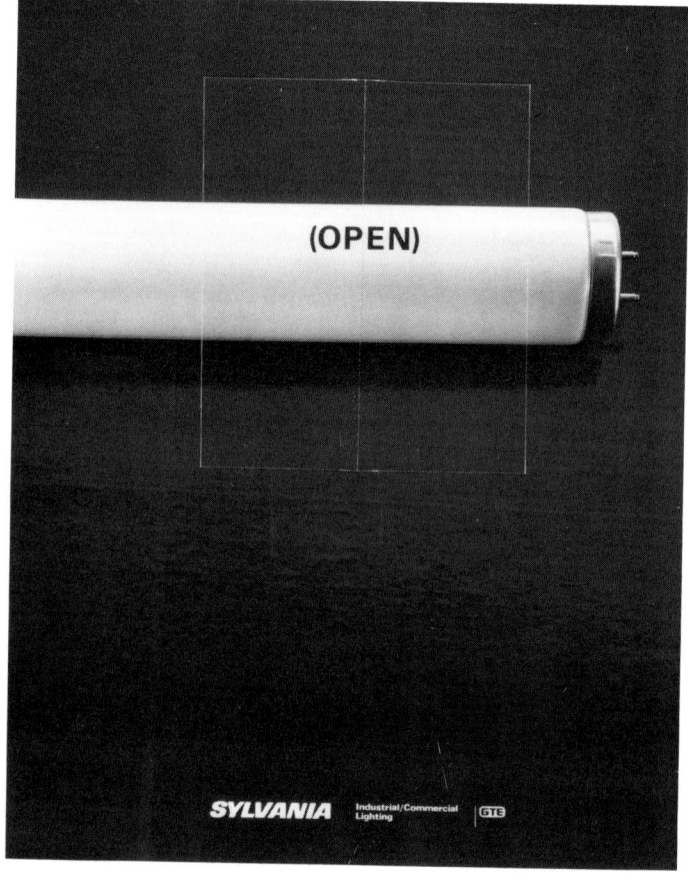

598
Matt Haligman Art Director
James Young Photographer
Doyle Dane Bernbach Agency
Sylvania Client
New York NY

599
Jac Coverdale Art Director
Jerry Fury Copywriter
Bernie Barnett Production House
Clarity Coverdale Advertising Agency
Sealy Mattress Company Client
Minneapolis MN

600
Elaine Crawford, Paul Collins Designers
Maxi Chan Calligrapher
Pfizer Laboratories Client
New York NY

601
Persechini & Moss Designers
Phyllis Persechini/Steven Cerasale Client
Beverly Hills CA

600

601

603

602
Diane J. Hamel Designer
Robert Webster Product Manager
McCormick & Co., Inc. Client
Hunt Valley MD

603
Jim McFarland Art Director
Carmine Photographer
John Lally Copywriter
Lally, McFarland & Pantello Studio
Norwich Eaton Pharmaceuticals Inc. Client
New York NY

604
James Halt Designer
Giulio Michienzi, David Measer Illustrators
David Measer Photographer
Hammermill Paper Co. Client
Tonawanda NY

605
Helaine French Designer
French Advertising Inc. Agency
Celanese Fibers Mktg. Corp. Client
West Caldwell NJ

607
Bill Venn Designer
Robert Lallamant Creative Director
Reg Love Photographer
Sudler & Hennessey Agency
Parke Davis Pty. Ltd. Client
Sydney, Australia

608
G. Stephen Ryan Art Director
Donald N. McKay Photographer
Tegopen (Bristol Laboratories) Client
East Syracuse NY

609
Raon Vareltzis Art Director
Ed Gallucci/Freelance Photographer Guild Photographer
C & G Advertising Studio
Ciba Pharmaceuticals Client
Summit NJ

610
Gene Krackehl Art Director
Waldenbooks Client
Stamford CT

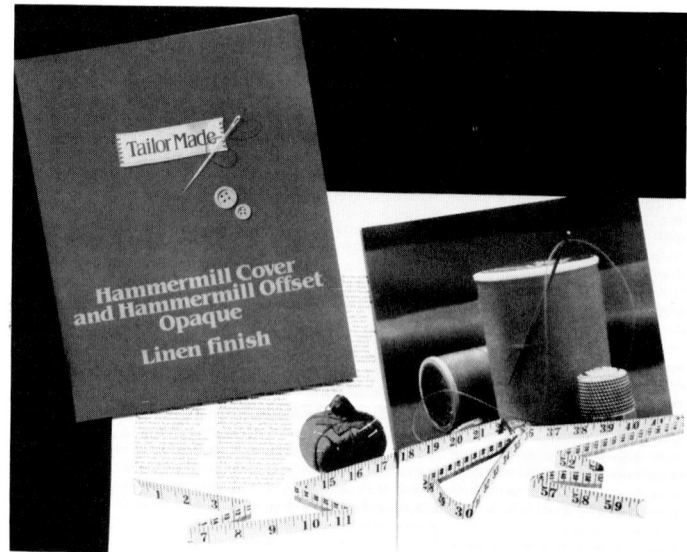

604

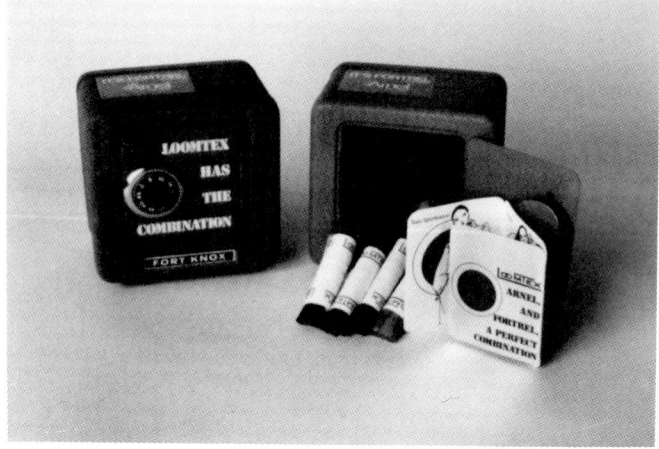

605

606
Ruthann Richert Art Director
George Hausman Photographer
Terry Scullin Copywriter
BBDO Agency
Young President's Organization Client
New York NY

608

609

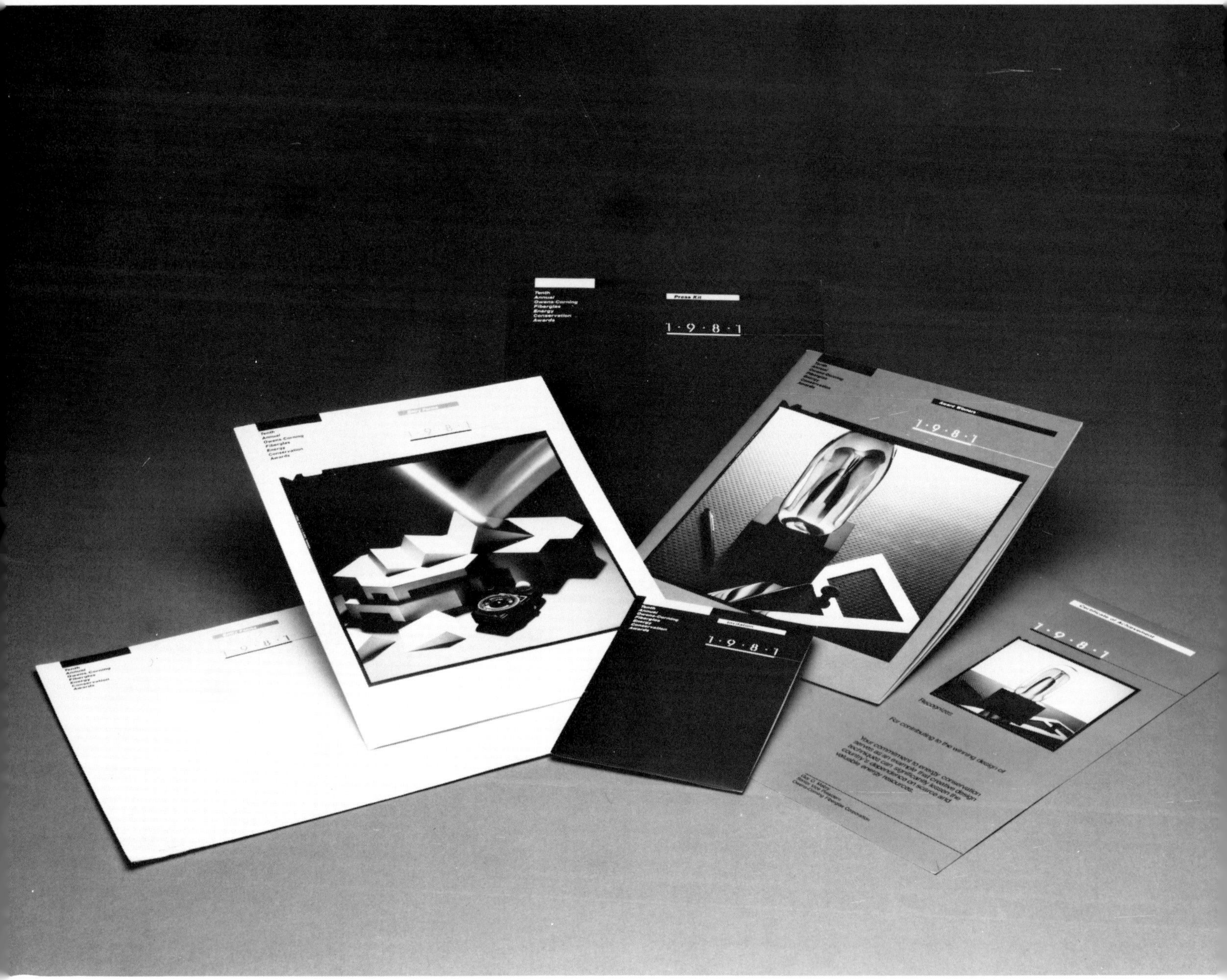

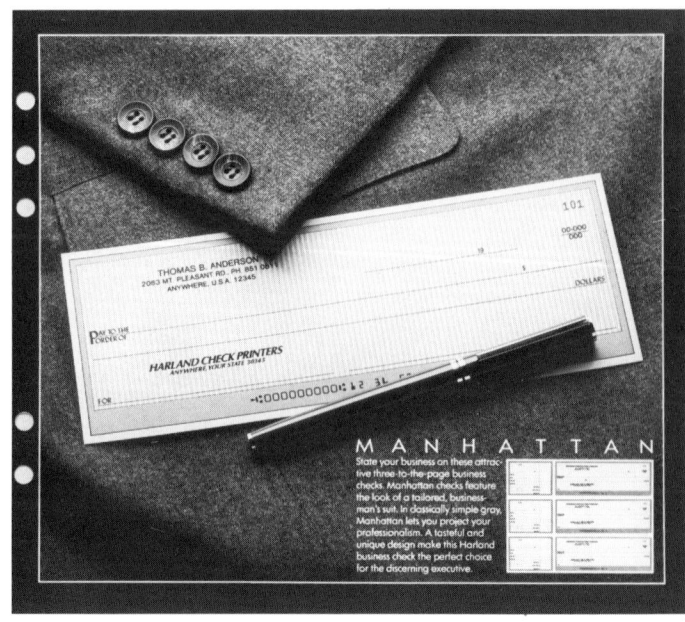

611
Terry Lesniewicz, Al Navarre Designers
Lesniewicz/Navarre Studio
Owens-Corning Fiberglas Corp. Client
Toledo OH

612
Danny Strickland Art Director
Edward Jett Designer
Jamie Cook Photographer
Art Riser Creative Director
John H. Harland Co. Client
Atlanta GA

613

613
Marco De Plano Art Director
Kello Kao, Marco De Plano Designer
Burson Marsteller Agency
Merrill Lynch Client
New York NY

614
John Barnard Art Director
Benn Mitchell Photographer
Bernard: Design Studio
Admatch Corp. Client
New York NY

615
Audrey Geldutis Art Director
Claudia Shadursky Creative Director
Boa Design Inc. Studio
Skiad Inc. Client
Toronto, Canada

616
Anna Lee Wilson Art Director
Kaeser and Wilson Design, Ltd. Studio
E.F. Hutton Client
New York NY

617
Michael Benes, Karen Despo Art Directors
Stephen Grohe Photographer
Joe Nangle, Brian Flood Copywriters
Digital Equipment Corporation Client
Merrimack NH

618
Art Greig Art Director
Stan Fellerman Photographer
LithoArt Client
New York NY

619
Robert M. Herlin Art Director
Graphics 3, Inc. Client
Jupiter FL

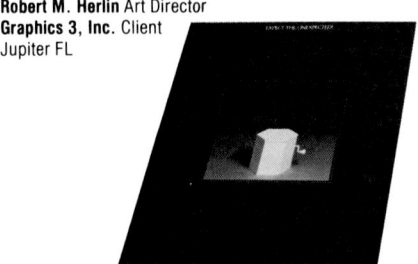

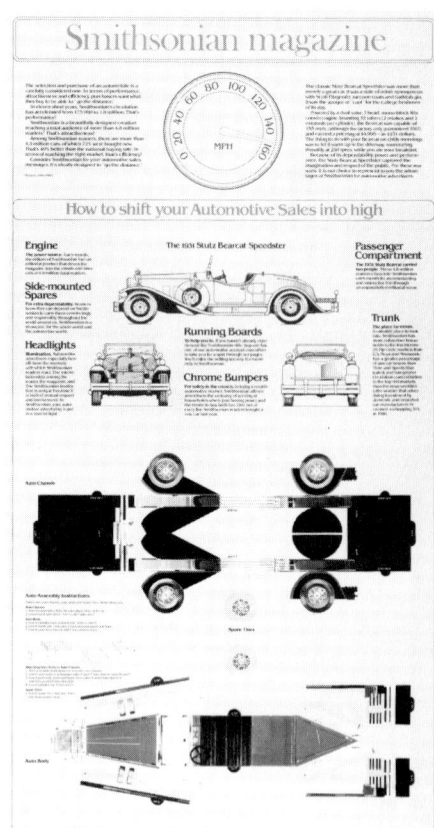

620
Jack de Lange Art Director
Cor Visser Illustrator
DLS Communications BV Studio
Stichting Stoffenbeurs Amsterdam Client
Zaandam, Holland

621
Timothy E. Urban Designer
Freeman, Huenink, Zilbert Inc. (Staff)
  Illustrators
Fox River Paper Company Client
Brookfield WI

622
Erica Skioldebrand Art Director
Bo Trenter Photographer
Anderson & Lembke danderydsgatan
  Agency
Solna Offset AB Client
Stockholm, Sweden

623
Mark Greitzer, Marie Loeber Designers
Bill Wilkinson Illustrator
Millennium Design Comm. Inc. Studio
Smithsonian Magazine Client
New York NY

624
Judy Tipton Creative Director
Martin Leeds Designer
Ric Cohn Photographer
Leber Katz Agency
RJR MacDonald, Canada Client
New York NY

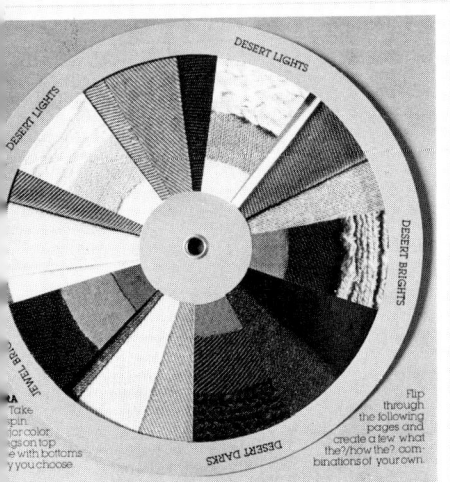

625
David Edelstein, Nancy Borin, Lanny French Designers
Mary K. Bernitt Photographer
Ron Koliha Copywriter
Edelstein-Borin Advertising Studio
Generra Client
Seattle WA

626
William Duevell Designer
Frank Emmi, Bill Duevell Letterers
ABC Art Dept. Studio
ABC Television Network Client
New York NY

627
Orin Kimball Art Director
Susan Culen-Eckrote Designer
Trimensions, Inc. Studio
Gross Townsend Frank, Inc. Studio
CooperVision Pharmaceuticals Client
New York NY

628

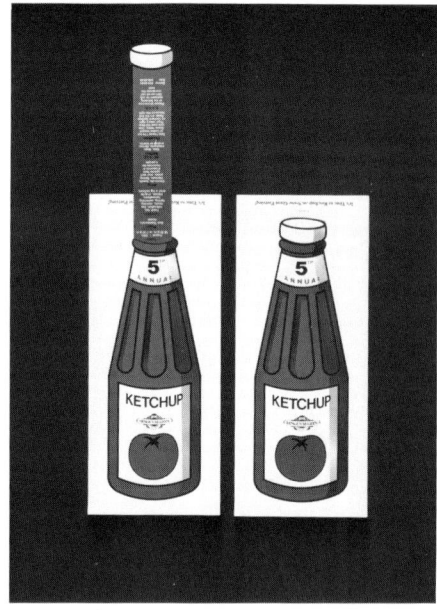
629

630

628
John Kuchera Art Director
Hutchins Y & R Agency
Mobil Chemical Canada Ltd. Client
Rochester NY

629
Michael Kennedy Designer
Chuck Donald Illustrator
William G. Townsend Copywriter
Communications Design Studio
Dingus McGee's Client
Sacramento CA

630
Torbjorn Winchler Designer
Andre Prah Illustrator
Stendahls/Vasagatan AB Studio
Park Avenue Hotel Client
Gothenburg, Sweden

631
Barry Seelig, Stanley Church Designers
Laszlo Stern Photographer
Wallace/Church Assoc. Studio
Package Design Council Client
New York NY

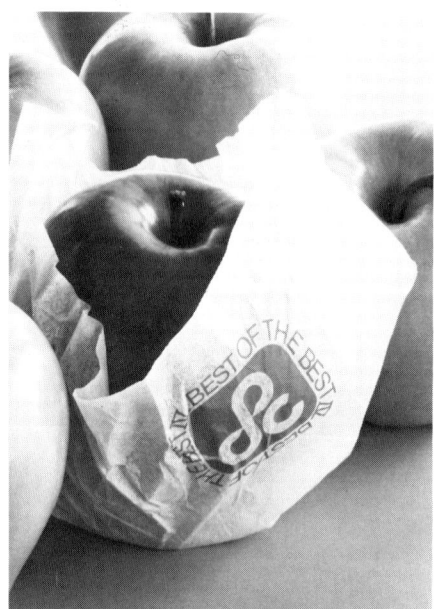
631

632
C. Odeven Art Director
Richard Smith Photographer
Wendover Associates Studio
Ciba-Geigy Client
Greensboro NC

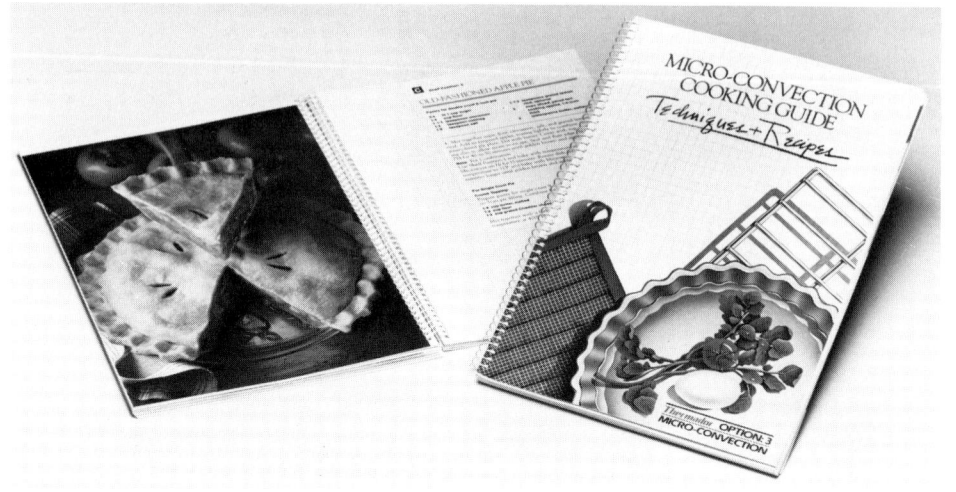
633

634

633
John Coy Art Director
Richard Atkins Designer
Andy Zito Illustrator
George de Gennaro Studio Photographers
Joel Goldstein Marketing Communications Studio
Thermador Client
Culver City CA

634
Cheryl Lewin Designer
Dagmar Frinta Illustrator
Cheryl Lewin Design Studio
Conran's Client
New York NY

635
Jon Adams Art Director
Jim Sims Designer
Postmark Atlanta Production House
Coca-Cola USA Client
Atlanta GA

635

636
Carl Mosander Art Director
Arto Hallakorpi Photographer
Seppo Holopainen, Carl Mosander Studio
Aapiset Oy Client
Helsini, Finland

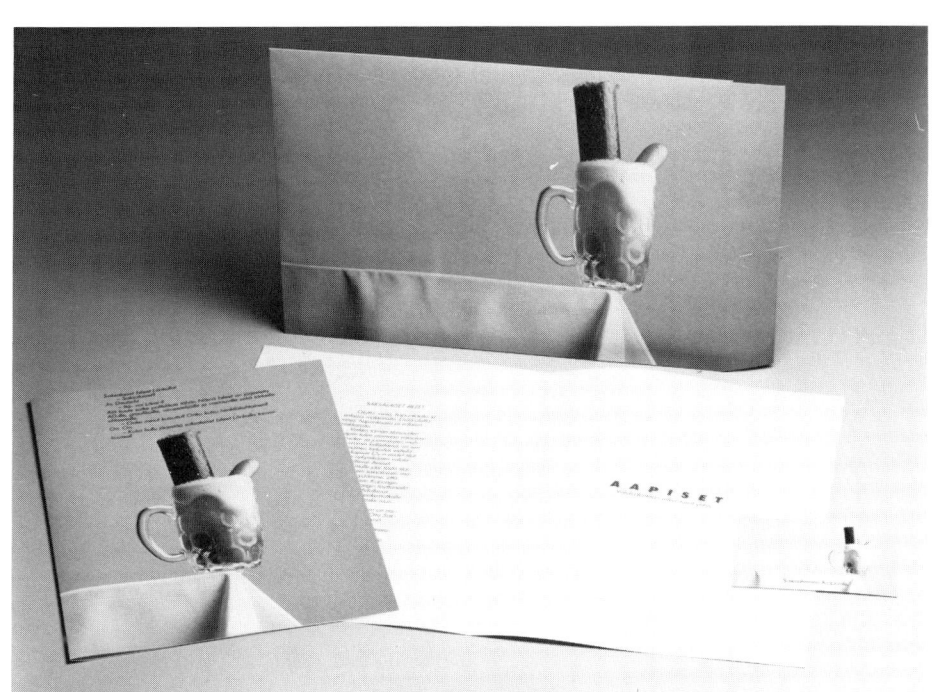

637
Paula Yamasaki Designer
Patrick SooHoo Inc. Studio
Dr. Ernest Nagamatsu Client
Los Angeles CA

638
Luis E. Ramirez Art Director
Lichael Zabe Photographer
Laboratorio de Diseno y Analisis de Mercado-CPM Studio
Litografos Unidos S.A. Production
Grupo Chihuahua Client
Los Angeles CA

639
Charles Blake, E. Zeitsoff, V. Kalayjian, T. Matsuura Art Directors
Jerard Huerta Illustrator
NBC Marketing Client
New York NY

640
Ralph Burch Art Director
Jo Ann Carney Photographer
Roger Myers Copywriter
Burch Myers Cuttie, Inc. Agency
Monogram Models, Inc. Client
Chicago IL

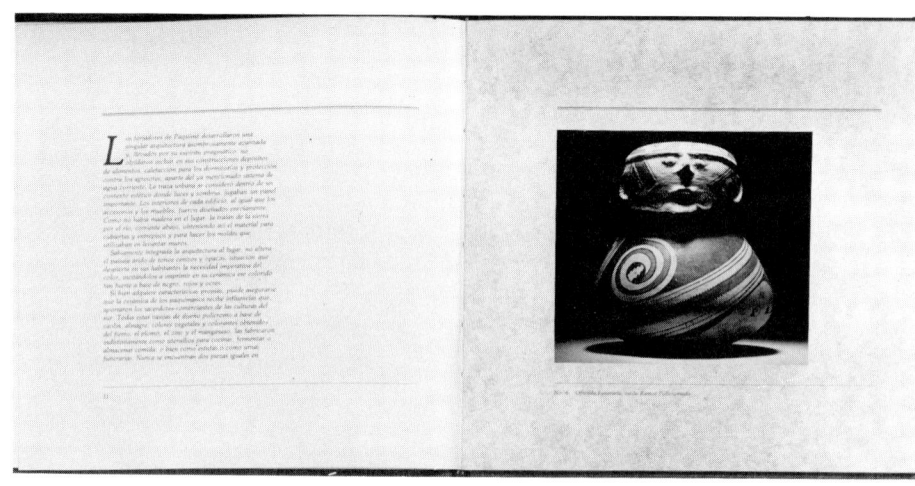

638

642
David B. Waller, Jr. Art Director
Art 'Y Fact Client
Houston TX

643
Robin Ward Designer
BBC Enterprises Client
London, England

641
Jack Odette Art Director
Mike Focar Designer
Citibank Client
New York NY

640

644
Deborah Troxell Designer
Seymour Mednick Photographer
Reliance Insurance Co. Client
Philadelphia PA

645
Steve Bollinger Designer
Admissions Office, Emory University Client
Atlanta GA

646
Dorte Zangenberg Art Director
Stendahls Agency
Politiken Client
Cophenhagen, Denmark

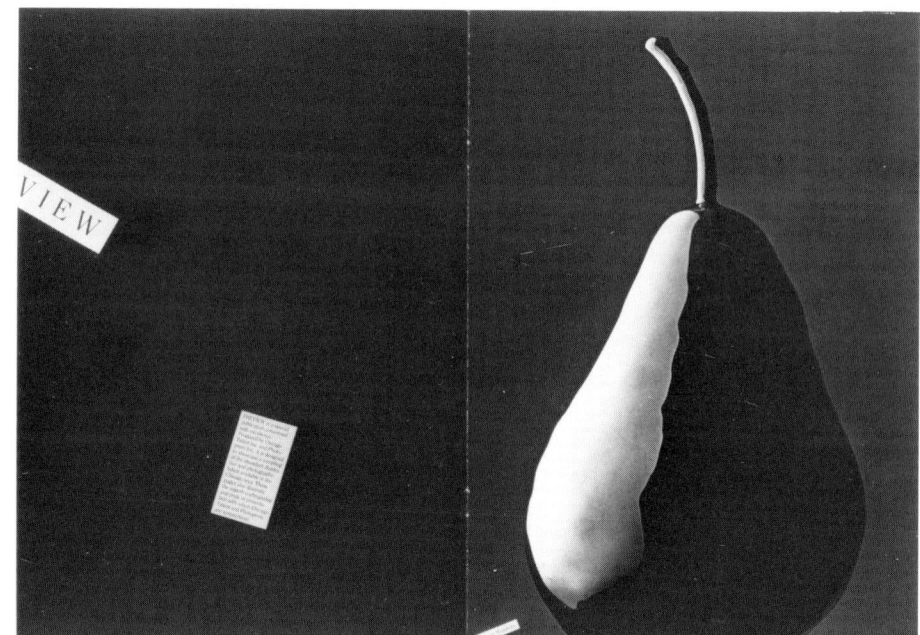

647
Carol Schaeffer Art Director
Schaeffer Boehm Ltd. Studio
Vanity Fair Client
New York NY

648
Mark L. Handler, Gail Rigelhaupt Art Directors
Lee Marshall Photographer
The Handler Group, Inc. Studio
Kate Communications, Inc. Client
New York NY

649
Robert Cooney Designer
R.A. Cooney Inc. Studio
Travel Dynamics Inc. Client
New York NY

650
Richard Haymes Designer
Eric Sutherland Photographer
Richard Haymes & Co. Studio
Leo Castelli Gallery Client
New York NY

651
Carol Bokuniewicz, Tibor Kalman Art Directors
M & Co. Studio
Audubon Client
New York NY

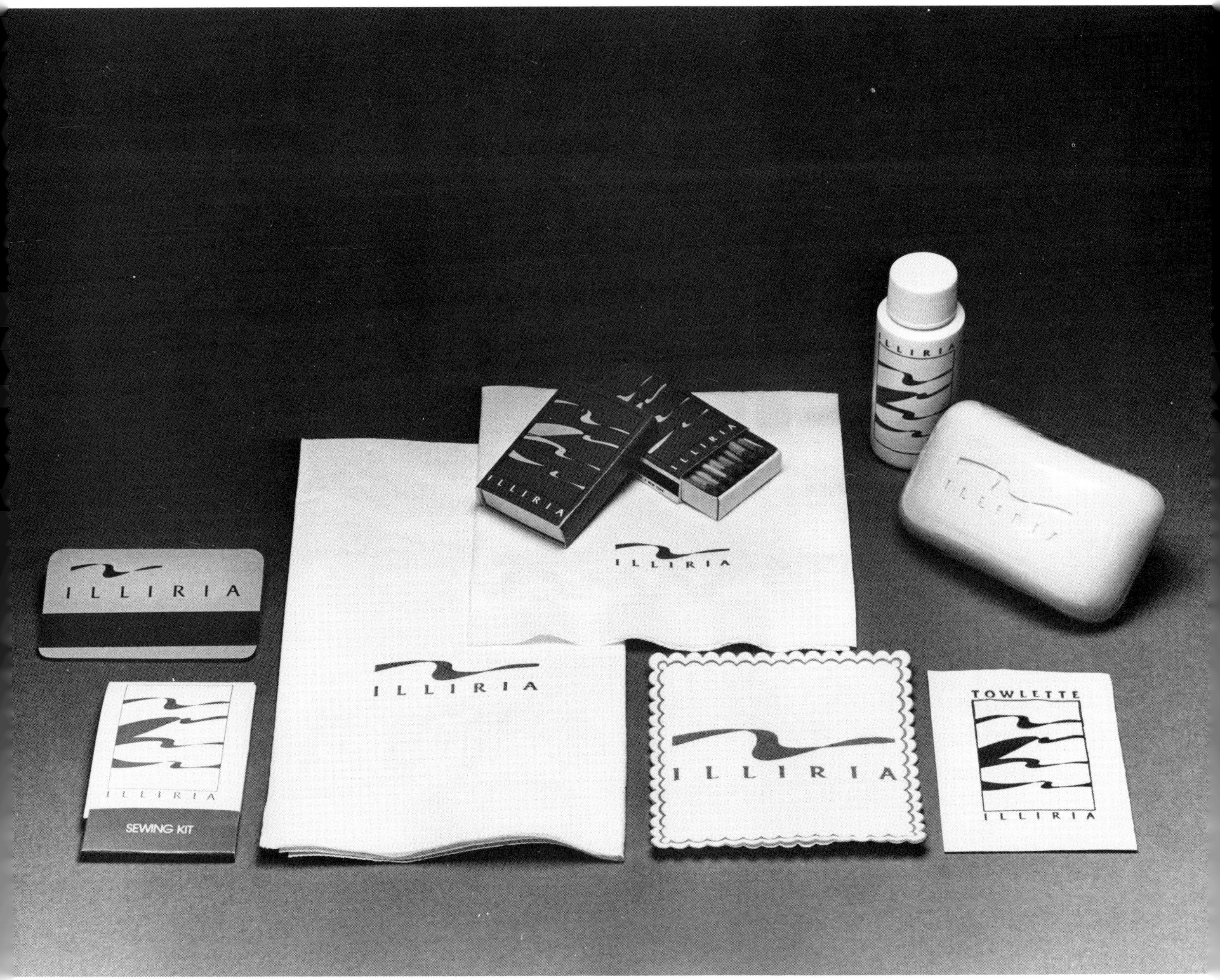

SELF-PROMO

652
Douglass Grimmett Designer
Big City Design Studio
Douglass Grimmett Client
New York NY

653
Gary Ludwig, Art Niemi, Paul Hodgson Designers
John J. Wood Photographer
Bruce Philp Copywriter
Fifty Fingers Inc. Client
Toronto, Canada

654
Patrick Florville Designer
Florville Design & Analysis Studio
Patrick Florville Client
New York NY

655
Brian A. Griffin Illustrator
Illustrations Done Client
Washington DC

654

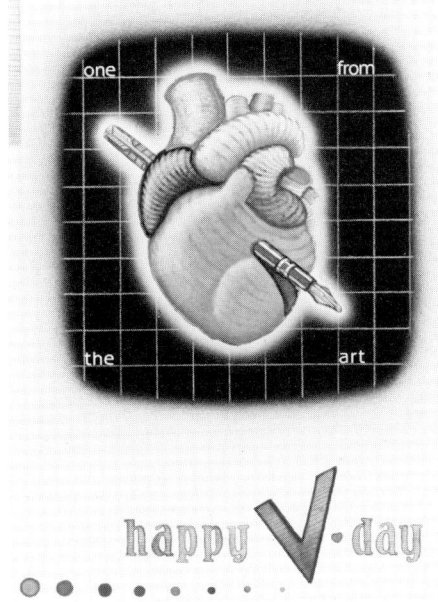

655

656
John Kneapler Designer
John Kneapler Client
New York NY

657
Sandra R. Bluett, Debi L. Paine Designers
Larry Paine & Associates Design Studio Client
Bethesdal MD

658
Michael Stelzer Designer
Noble & Assoc. Agency
Chris Fowler & Michael Stelzer Client
Springfield MO

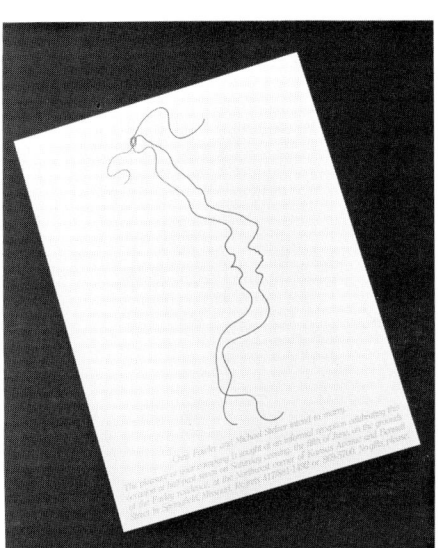

659
Gary Schenck Designer
Schenck Design Associates, Inc. Client
Dallas TX

660
Joep Dovianus Art Director
Rob Bogerd Photographer
Loebas H.M.C. Oosterbeek Copywriter
Spic 'n Span Client
Amsterdam, Holland

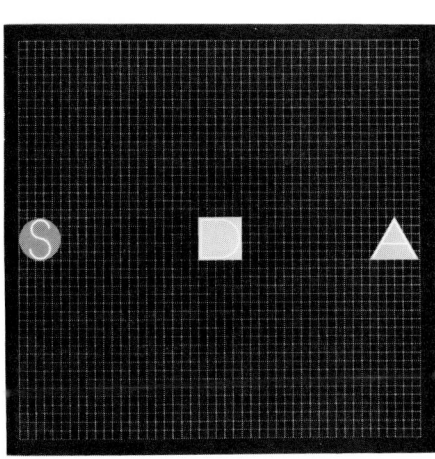

 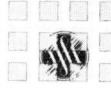 

IN AN EXPANSIVE GESTURE   WILLIAM ALLEN AND ASSOCIATES   HAS MOVED TWO BLOCKS WEST   WE CAN BE FOUND AT   THREE HUNDRED EAST PIKE SEATTLE WA 98122 206 621 9933

661
Bob Grindeland Designer
William Allen & Associates Client
Seattle WA

662
John Coy Designer
Coy, Los Angeles Client
Culver City CA

663
Kris Busa Designer
Cricket Press, Inc. Typographer
Gallagher & Morton Client
Rockport MA

664
Joe Shyllit Art Director
Ron Hills Illustrator
Terry Collier Photographer
Jerry Kuleba Copywriter
Enterprise Advertising Agency
Rosnick Productions Client
Toronto, Canada

665
Richard Loomis Art Director
Carl Howard Photographer
Evans Garber & Paige, Inc. Studio
Mohawk Paper Mills, Inc. Client
Utica NY

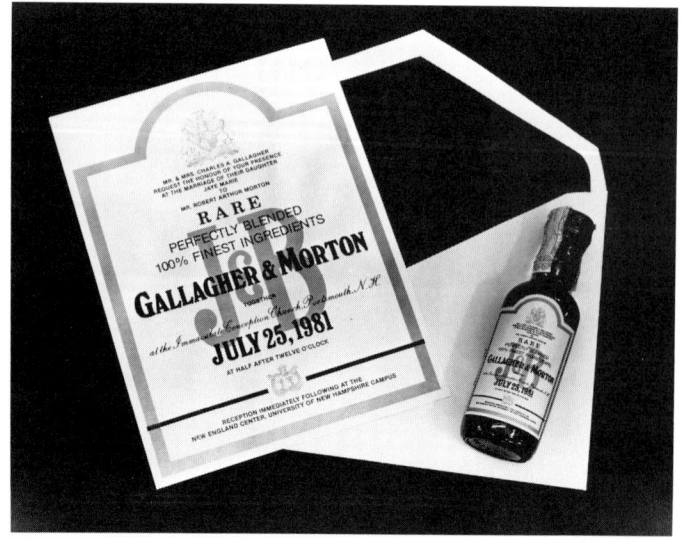

665

666
Dvaid Sykes Art Director
Kris Busa Illustrator
CYRK Inc. Production House
Jacob's Pillow Dance Festival Client
Cambridge MA

667
S. Payne Art Director
Gerhard Sxcheidle, Rudolph Janu
  Photographers
Michael Steinberg Copywriter
Bonnell Design Associates Studio
R/Greenberg Associates Inc. Client
New York NY

668
Ken White, Harold Burch Designers
Greg Zajack Photographer
Ron Roman Copywriter
Aldus Type Studio, Ltd. Typographers
Ken White Design Office, Inc. Client
Los Angeles CA

669
Daniel Haberman Designer
Isadore Seltzer Illustrator
**Royal Composing Room, Inc., Finch, Pruhn
  & Company, Inc., A Horowitz & Sons,
  Rae Publishing Co., Inc.** Production
  Houses
Royal Composing Room, Inc. Client
New York NY

670
Joep Dovianus Art Director
Louis van der Star, Charles van Hoften
  Photographers
Loebas H.M.C. Oosterbeek Copywriter
Spic 'n Span Client
Amsterdam, Holland

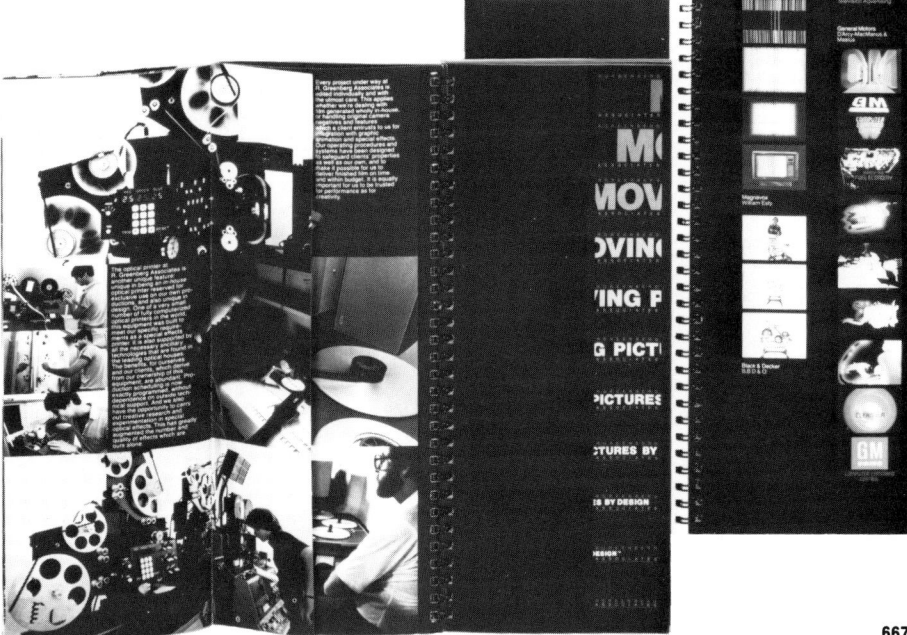

667

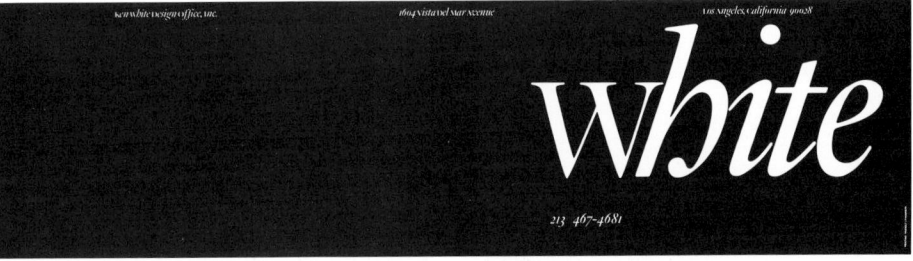

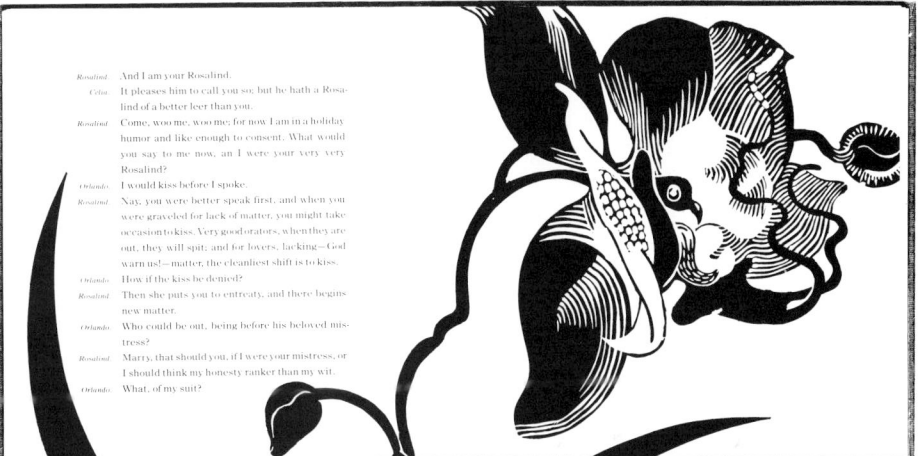

669

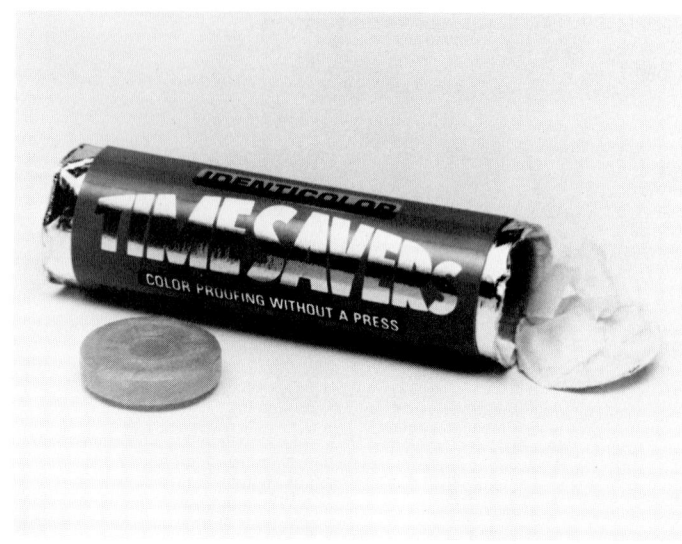

671
Serge Bevil, Peter Campbell, Ross Wittenberg Designers
Serge Bevil Designs, Inc. Client
New York NY

672
Gregory Cutshaw Designer
Dayton Typographic Service Client
Dayton OH

673
Robert Burns Art Director
Paul Browning Designer
Burns, Cooper, Hynes Ltd. Client
Toronto, Canada

674
Tom Antista Designer
Rusty Kay and Associates Client
Santa Monica CA

675
Constance Kovar Designer
Constance Kovar Graphic Design Inc. Client
Woodbury NY

676
Stan Chrzanowski Designer
Graphics West Inc. Client
Mission KS

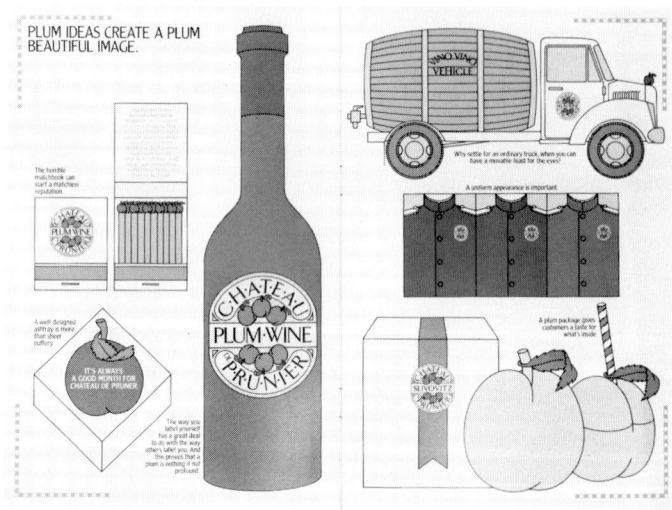

677
Cheryl Heller Art Director
John Gatie, Charlie Hoar Illustrators
Jack Richmond Photogapher
HBM Design Group Client
Boston MA

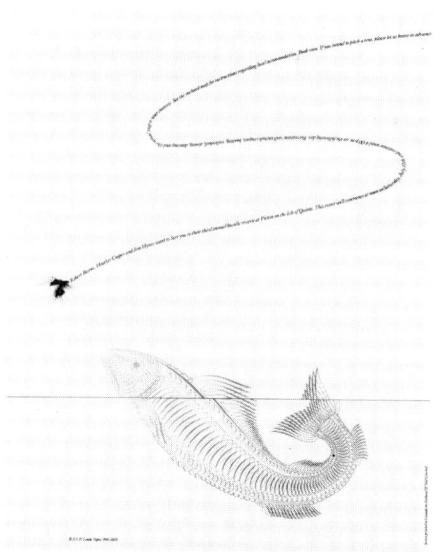

673 674 675

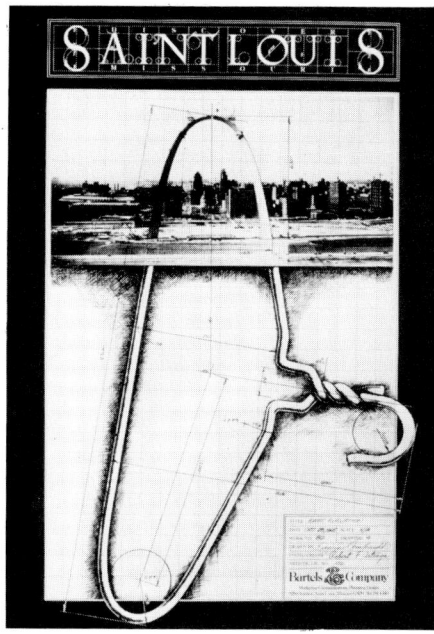

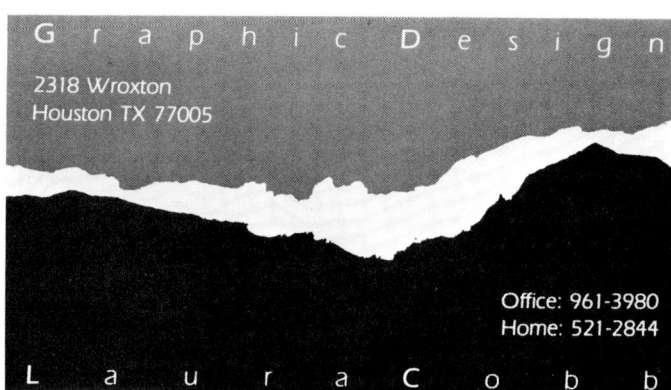

678
David Bartels Designer
Siegfried Reinhardt Illustrator
Robert Arteaga Photographer
Michael Simpson Typographer
Bartels & Company Client
St. Louis MO

679
Laura Cobb Designer
Laura Cobb Client
Houston TX

680
Jim Novotny Client
Jerry Della Torre Photographer
Jim Novotny Design Client
Bridgewater NJ

682
Jowill Woodman Illustrator/Client
Brooklyn NY

683
Thomas Esser Designer
Iris Studios Client
Hays KS

684
Trina Swerdlow Illustrator
Trina Swerdlow Client
Studio City CA

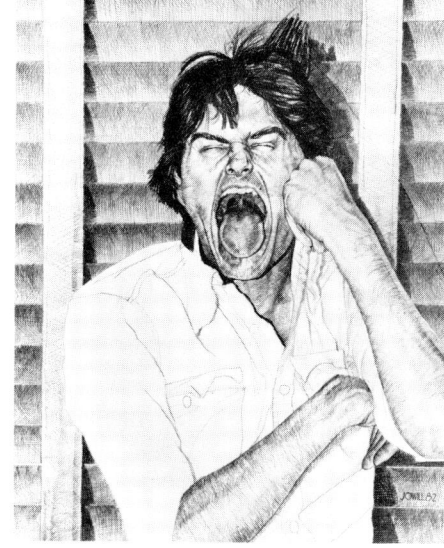

681
Jowill Woodman Illustrator
Jowill Woodman Client
Brooklyn NY

680

MARTY UMANS
PHOTOGRAPHY REPRESENTED BY MICHAEL HOEYE • (212) 362-9546

685
Leslie Morris Designer
Marty Umans Client
New York NY

686
Richard Foster Photographer
Richard Foster Photography, Ltd. Client
Chicago IL

687
Phil Bauer Art Director
Tony Sollecito, Carol Sollecito
   Photographers
Imahara & Keep Advertising Client
Santa Clara CA

688
William R. Goes Photographer
Mel's Lithoplate Service Printer
Goes Photography Client
Chicago IL

689
David Russell Miller Photographer
Larry Westdal Graphics
MillerImages Studio
Rapid Typographers Typographers
Oakland CA

690
Allison Seifer Art Director
Leslie Priggen Photographer
Leslie Priggen Client
New York NY

689

691
Larney Walker Designer
Gordon Meyer Client
Chicago IL

692
Richard Foster Photographer
Richard Foster Photography, Ltd. Client
Chicago IL

693
Vic Mazurkiewicz Designer
Nancy Rica Schiff Photographer
Nancy Rica Schiff Client
New York NY

694
Steve Rousso Art Director
Allen David Photographer
Garrett/Lewis/Johnson Client
Atlanta GA

695
O Paccione Photographer/Client
New York NY

696
David Gauger, Mark Decena Designers
Kevin Yarbrough Copywriter
Ernie Friedlander, Peter Oglivi
 Photographers
Gauger Sparks Silva, Inc. Client
San Francisco CA

697
Joe Feigenbaum, Doug May, Jason Calfo
 Designers
Carnase, Inc. Client
New York NY

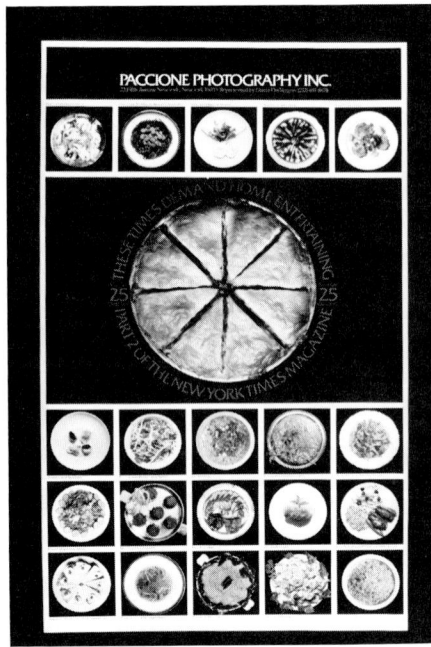

698
Brian D. Fox Designer
B.D. Fox & Friends, Inc. Client
Los Angeles CA

696

697

698

699
John Kane, Roger Sametz Art Directors
James Scherer Photographer
Sametz Blackstone Assoc. Client
Boston MA

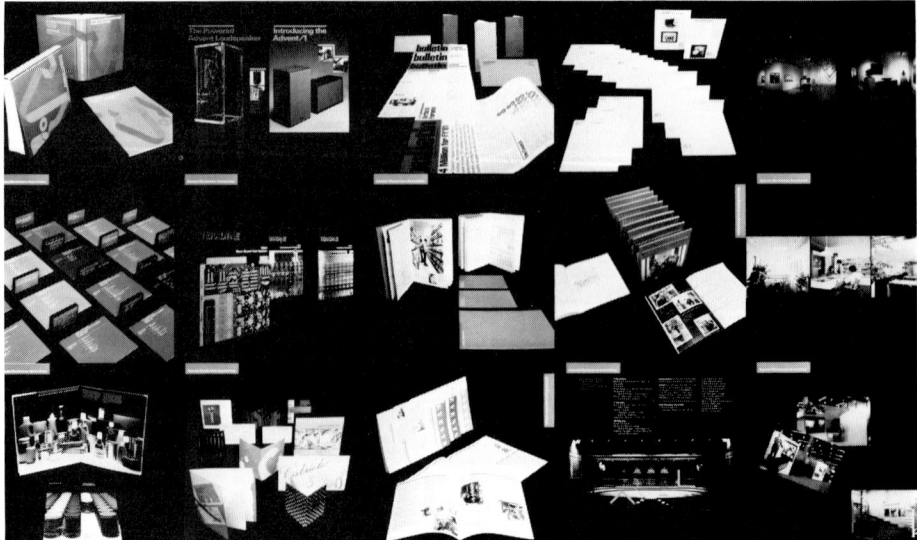

699

700
Ralph Casado Designer
Ralph Pagano Photographer
H & T Manufacturing Production House
Promotion Solutions, Inc. Client
New York NY

703
Oswaldo Miranda Designer
Miran Client
Curitiba, Brazil

701
Bob Muller, Diane Danheiser Art Directors
Jim Hunt Illustrator
Gallagher Group, Inc. Client
New York NY

704
Don Trousdell Designer
Jim Waldron Copywriter
McDonald & Little Agency
23 Skiddo Client
Atlanta GA

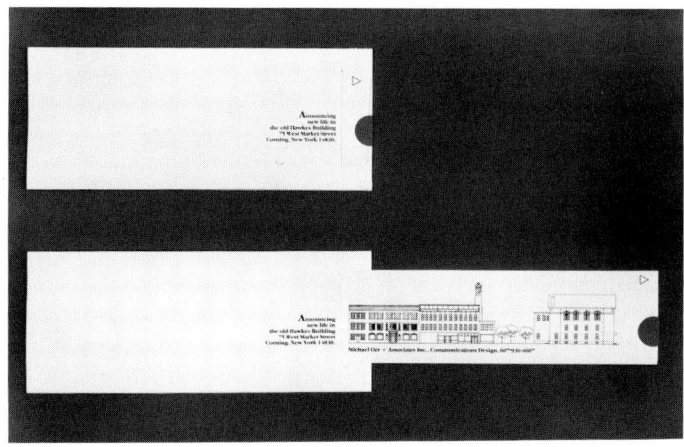

702
Michael R. Orr, Marcia Chadwick Designers
Michael Orr & Associates Client
Corning NY

705
Richard Foster Photographer
Richard Foster Photography, Ltd. Client
Chicago IL

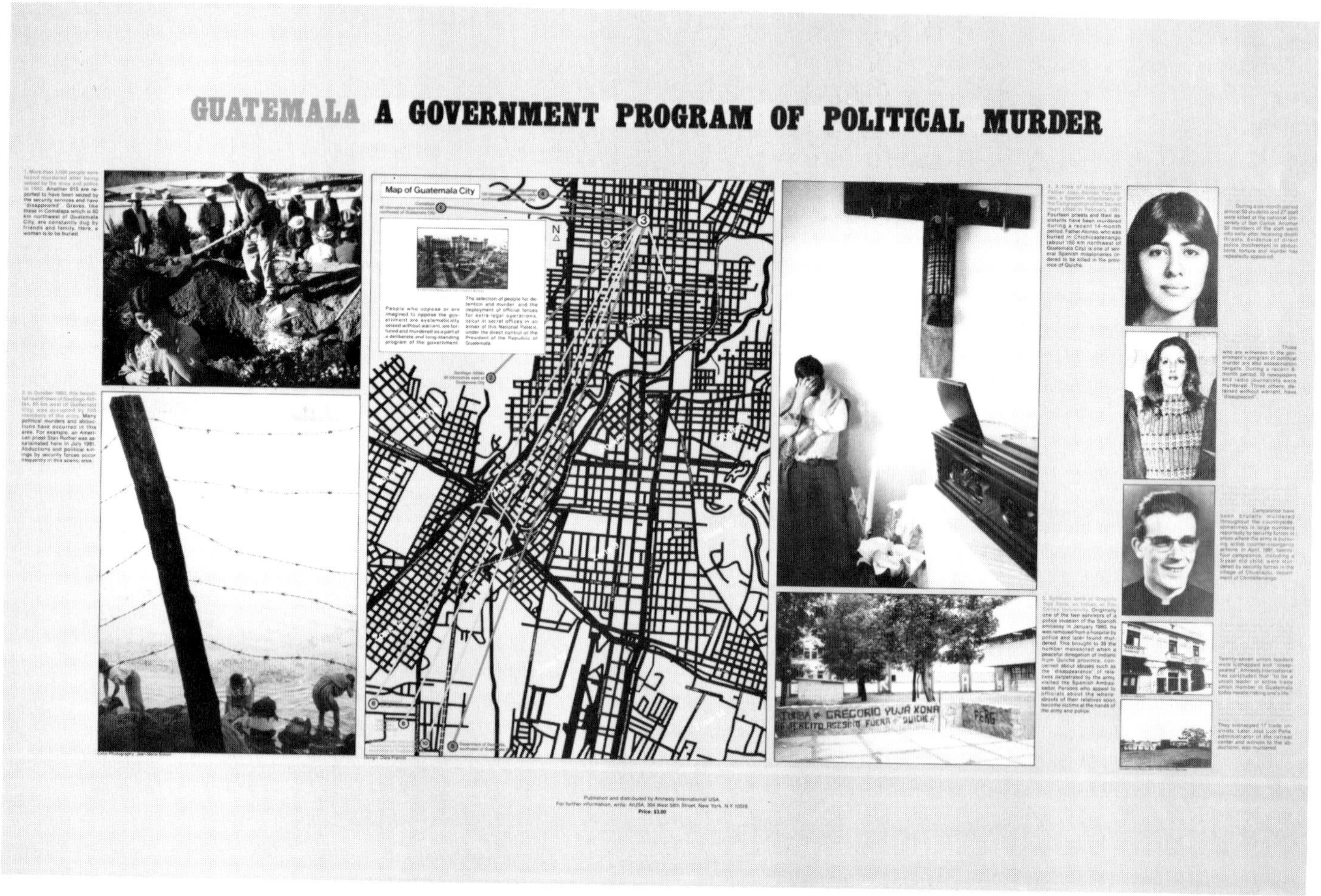

PUBLIC SERVICE

GUATEMALA A GOVERNMENT PROGRAM OF POLITICAL MURDER

706
Clare Francis Art Director
Jean-Marie Simon Photographer
Amnesty International Client
New York NY

709
Wayne D. Gibb Art Director
Ken Light Photographer
Northwestern Graphics, Digi-Type Inc.
  Production
California Human Development Corp. Client
Santa Rosa CA

710
Peter Chan Art Director
David McGrath Creative Director
Ralph Steadman Illustrator
Ken Wheat Copywriter
Ayer Barker Agency
Save the Children Fund Client
London, England

711
Gerry Rosentswieg Art Director
Jeff Corwin Photographer
The Graphics Studio Studio
Brakeley, John Price Jones, Inc. Agency
Hollywood Presbyterian Medical Center
  Client
Los Angeles CA

708
Roy Podorson Art Director
Ron Burkhardt Copywriter
NYC Client
Yonkers NY

707
Terry Paul Penrod Art Director
Robert J. Culpepper, Jr. Copywriter
Culpepper & Associates Agency
Georgia Museum of Art Client
Houston TX

713
John McIntyre Creative Director
Arnold Wicht Designer
Rudi von Tiedemann Photographer
Tim Heintzman Copywriter
Camp Associates Advertising Ltd. Agency
Ministry of the Attorney General Client
Toronto, Canada

714
Jori Svard Art Director
Kaj G. Lindholm Photographer
Sinikka Mykkanen Copywriter
Advertising Agency HPV Oy Agency
Oy ALKO AB Client
Helsinki, Finland

709

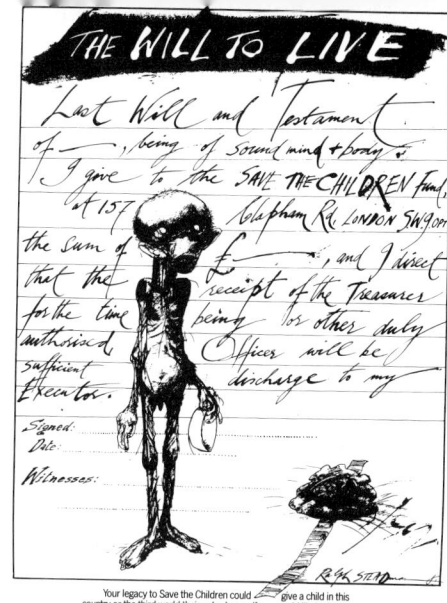
710

711

712
Bill Freeland Art Director
Angela Cocchini-Griefen Designer
LaGuardia College Client
Long Island City NY

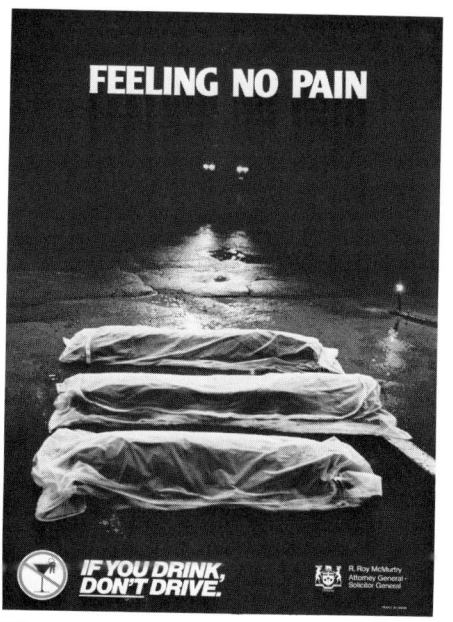
713

714

FILL IN THIS SPACE.

Please send me more information free of charge about College Answer Plan.

Name _____
Address _____
 Street City State Zip Code
Business Phone _____ Home Phone _____
 Area Code Area Code
Write: College Answer Plan, Citibank, N.A., P.O. Box 543, Tarrytown, N.Y. 10591
or call (800) 431-1042

We'll send you the best way to prepare for your child's education.

Easier said than done, right? But giving your child a college education is the most important gift you'll ever give him. And the most expensive too. But thanks to Citibank now there's a way you can prepare for it—*The College Answer Plan*. It's a unique and comprehensive program that makes the most of your money and your child's future.

First, we start you on a high yield savings program.* And as soon as your account starts to build and earn even higher interest rates, then it really starts to add up. Especially when all your interest can be tax free to you. So the sooner you start saving, the more interest you'll start earning. And by the time your child is ready to go to college, your investment will be too.

What's more, *The College Answer Plan* can help you and your child pick just the right school. And with our nationwide search, we can locate scholarships to save you even more money. So stop wondering how you'll be able to provide for your child's education. And call us at **(800) 431-1042** for information. Or send in this coupon. It may be one of the few things you'll have to cut out to secure your child's future.

*Federal regulations require substantial penalties for early withdrawals.

COLLEGE ANSWER PLAN. CITIBANK
THE CITI NEVER SLEEPS.
Citibank, N.A. Member F.D.I.C.

  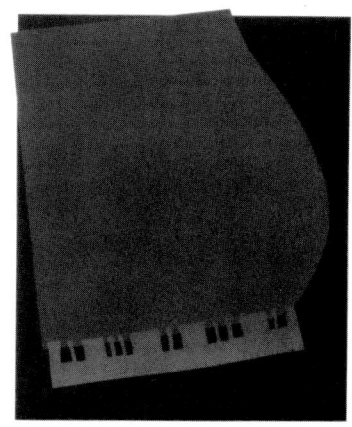

715
Gary Goldsmith Art Director
Micheal Pateman Photographer
Diane Sinnott Copywriter
Doyle Dane Bernbach Agency
Citibank Client
New York NY

716
Mark Oliver Art Director
Davies & Oliver, Inc. Agency
Haagen Printing Client
Santa Barbara CA

717
Roy Marshall Art Director
Colleen Brescia Photographer
Luyk Advertising Agency
NY State Health Department Client
Albany NY

718
Sandra Fryrear Art Director
Ann Marie Gerage Illustrator
Leonard G. Styche & Assoc. Inc. Studio
NYC Dept. of Environmental Protection Client
New York NY

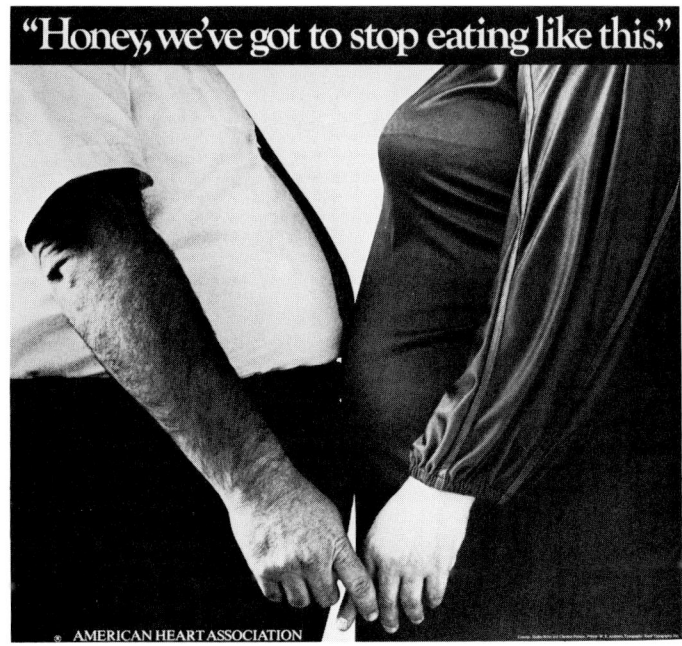 

719
J. Clarence Poisson/Shelley Buber Designers
American Heart Association Client
New York NY

TELEVISION GRAPHICS

720
Jim Denney Designer
WYES-TV Client
New Orleans LA

721
Percy Powers Art Director
KXAS-TV News Client
Fort Worth TX

722
An-Khang Vu-Cong Art Director
NBC Client
New York NY

723
Alan Eastman Art Director
ABC's World News Tonight Client
New York NY

724
Jim Denney Designer
WYES-TV Client
New Orleans LA

720

721

722

723

724

725
An-Khang Vu-Cong Art Director
NBC Client
New York NY

726
Nancy Foley Art Director
Robert R. Sanders Illustrator
KATU TV2 Portland, Oregon Client
Denver CO

727
Robert R. Sanders Designer
KECH 22 TV Salem, Oregon Client
Denver CO

728
Marian Levine Art Director
Phil Nee Photographer
Good Morning America-ABC-TV Client
New York NY

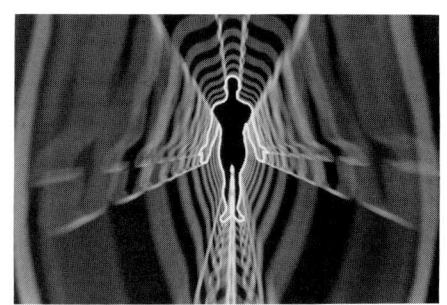

729
Trix Rosen Art Director
Roy Ruan Type Designer
WNBC-TV News 4 NY Client
New York NY

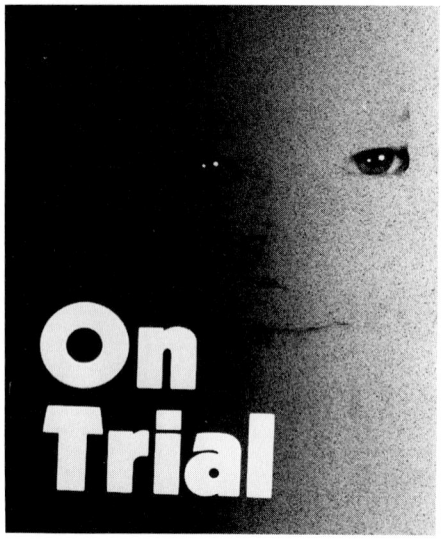

730
Tracy Ann Brown Art Director
WNBC-TV News 4 NY Client
New York NY

731
Bari Gilbert Art Director
WNBC-TV News 4 NY Client
New York NY

732
Roy Ruan Art Director
WNBC-TV News 4 NY Client
New York NY

733
Trix Rosen Art Director
WNBC-TV News 4 NY Client
New York NY

734
Gwen Gipson, Gerry Monley Art Directors
WXYZ-TV, ABC in Detroit Client
Southfield MI

TV / FILM Consumer SINGLE UNIT

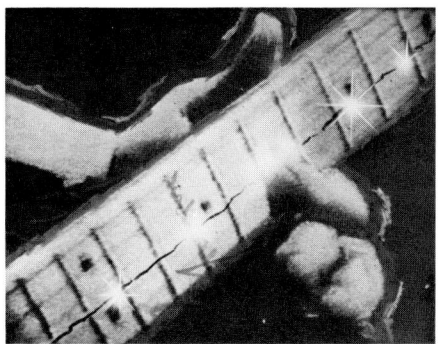

735
Peter Loft Designer
Black Swan Editing
Optimation Inc. Production House
David/Joseph & Assoc. Client
Milwaukee WI

736
John Lucci Art Director
Jud Alper Copywriter
Sunlight Production House
Young & Rubicam Agency
Dr. Pepper Client
New York NY

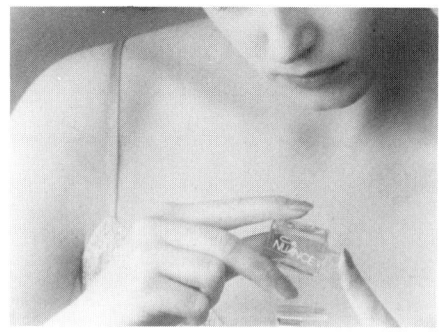

738
Ace & Edie Editor
Robert Elias Studio, Inc. Studio
Carlson, Liebowitz & Olshever, Inc. Agency
Merle Norman Cosmetics Client
Los Angeles CA

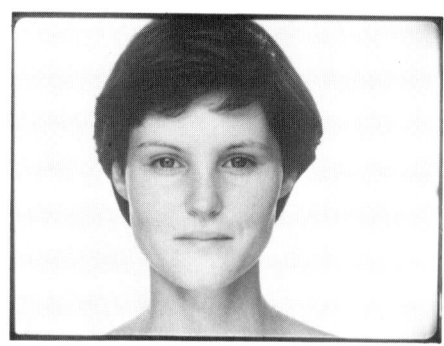
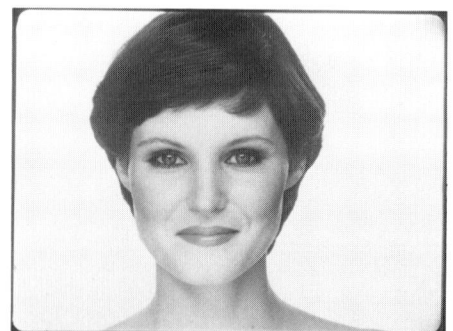

740
Sharon Spence Art Director
James Garrett & Ptrs. Production House
Kuper Hands (Pty) Limited Agency
Shoe Biz Client
Johannesburg, South Africa

737
Sarah Moon Photographer
John Paul Itta, Inc. Agency
Coty, Inc. Client
New York NY

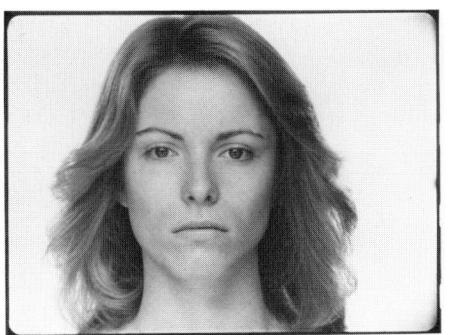  

739
Kathy O'Grady Art Director
Saks Fifth Avenue Client
New York NY

  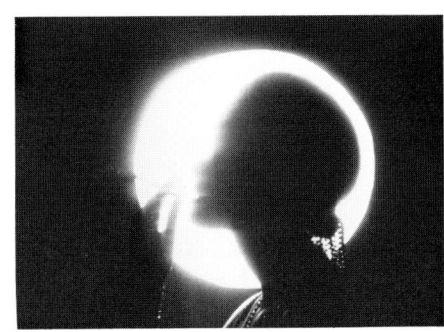

 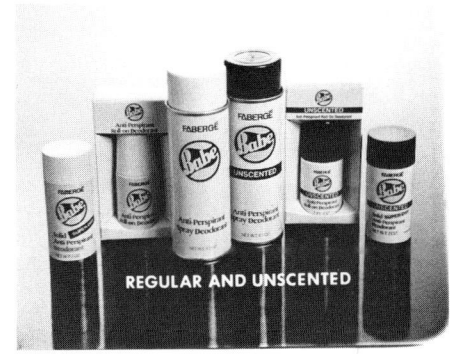

741
Irwin Goldberg Art Director
Ron Jacobs/Jaguar Productions Production House
Nadler & Larimer Inc. Agency
Faberge Client
New York NY

743
Fern H. Cohen Art Director
Klaus Lucka Director
Anne Cifu Copywriter
AC & R Advertising Agency
Laser Beams Sweatsuits Client
New York NY

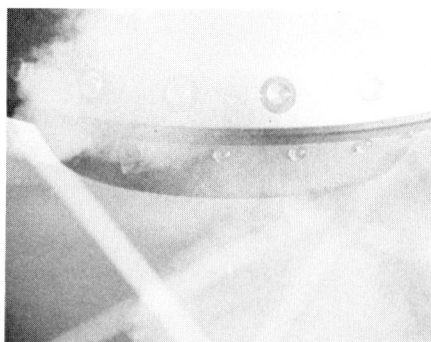
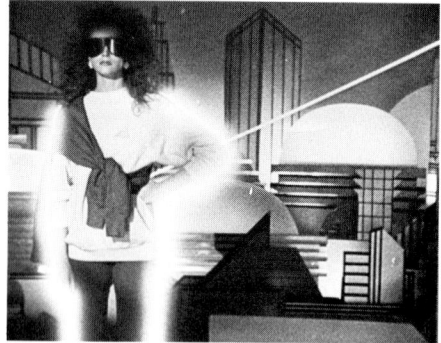
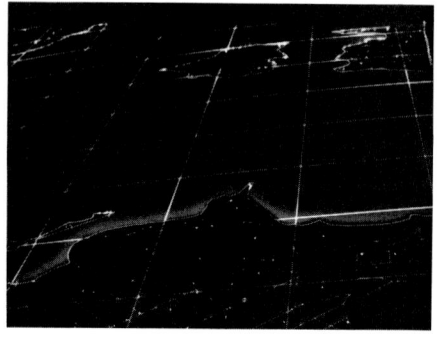
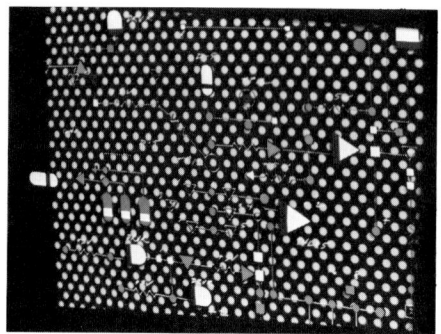
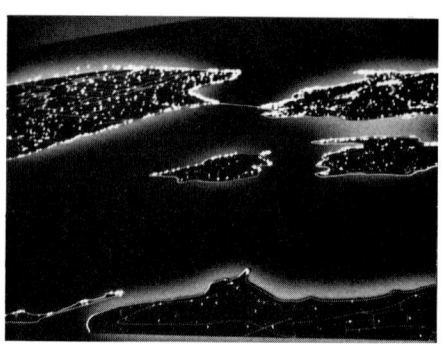

745
Steve Chase Art Director
Dieter Kaufmann Creative Director
Brian Quennell Copywriter
G. Anderson Advertising Agency
Rayovac Canada Client
Toronto, Canada

742
Randy Roberts Director
Richard Hollander Technical Director
Rick Ross Editor
Robert Abel & Associates Production House
Panasonic Client
Hollywood CA

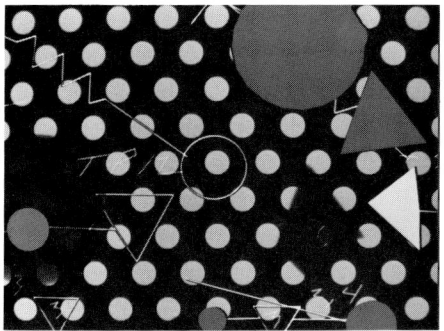 

744
Randy Roberts Animator/Director
Robert Abel & Associates Production House
TRW Client
Hollywood CA

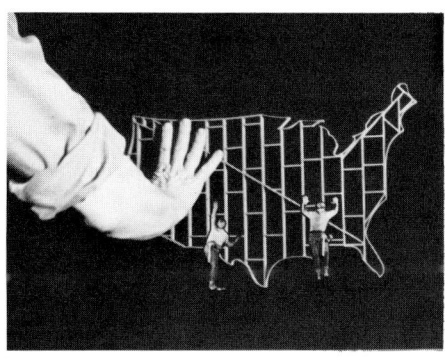 

746
Chris Blum Art Director
Maura Dutra, Con Pederson, Randy Roberts
  Animators
Rick Ross Editor
Robert Abel Director
Robert Abel & Associates Production House
Levi Strauss Client
Hollywood CA

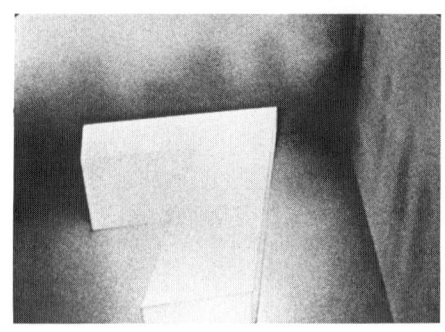

748
Jeff France Art Director
Bruce Mansfield Copywriter
AFI, Miami Production House
Lawler Ballard Advertising Agency
WLTY/FM Client
Norfolk VA

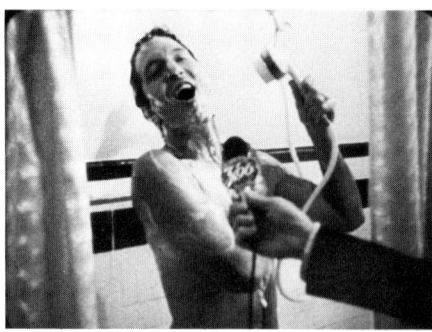

750
Terrance Iles Art Director
Bob Fortier Animator
William Lower Copywriter
Ousama Rawi Director
Scali, McCabe, Sloves (CDA) Agency
Ralston-Purina (Canada) Inc. Client
Toronto, Canada

747
Phil Silvestri Art Director
Rita Senders Copywriter
Della Femina, Travisano & Partners, Inc. Agency
WABC-TV Client
New York NY

 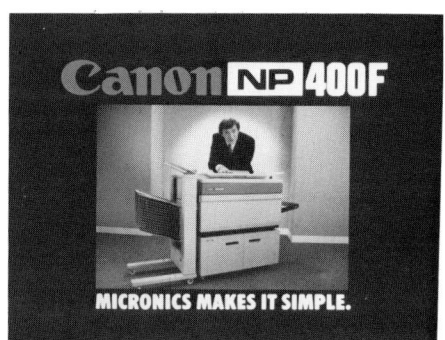

749
Michael Macina Copywriter
Makoto Hirano Producer
Dentsu Corp. of America Agency
Canon Copier Client
New York NY

751
Linda Morse, Clyde Hogg Creative Directors
B/H Productions, Inc. Production House
Bowes/Hanlon Advertising, Inc. Agency
Tindol Services, Inc. Client
Atlanta GA

752
Les Sharpe Art Director
Howard Smiedt Designer
Len Preskaw Copywriter
James Garret & Partners Production
Greysandton Agency
Cobra Brass Client
Sandton, S. Africa

754
Sue Wilson Art Director
Young & Rubicam, Inc. Agency
Lincoln Mercury Division Client
Detroit MI

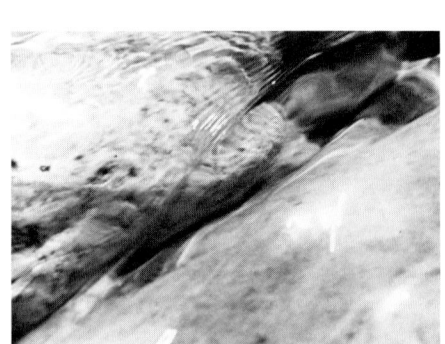

756
Frank Rizzo Art Director
Madelyn Miller Copywriter
Tracy-Locke/BBDO Agency
Phillips Petroleum Client
Dallas TX

753
John Paul Itta, Inc. Agency
Aer Lingus Client
New York NY

755
Robert Stevens Art Director
Robert Eberlein Producer
Stevens/Eberlein Productions Production
  House
Tri-Moto Client
Los Angeles CA

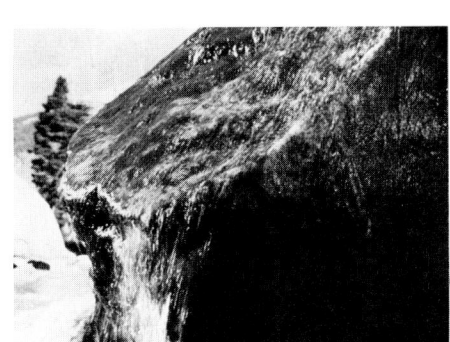

757
Dolphin Productions Production House
Bozell & Jacobs Agency
Sutan Plus Client
New York NY

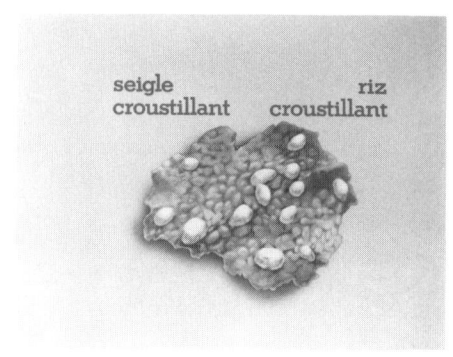

759
Bill Wurtzel Art Director
Hicks & Greist Agency
Villa Banfi Client
New York NY

761
P.R. Christensen Art Director
P.W.A. Film Productions Ltd. Studio
Brown, Christensen & Assoc. Ltd. Agency
NZ Wines & Spirits Ltd. Client
Auckland, New Zealand

758
Martin Shewchuk Art Director
Ed Nanni Creative Director
Bob Canning Director
Kathy Doherty Copywriter
Leo Burnett Company Ltd. Agency
Kellogg Salada Canada Inc. Client
Toronto, Canada

760
Bart Kuiper Art Director
The Filmworkshop Production House
Ogilvy & Mather B.V. Agency
Remia Client
Amsterdam, Holland

762
Bart Kuiper Art Director
The Images Film Company B.V. Production
Ogilvy & Mather, B.V. Agency
Koninklijke Verkade Fabrieken B.V. Client
Amsterdam, Holland

764
Dennis Bruce Art Director
Marty Myers Copywriter
Lesley Parrot Producer
The Gloucester Group Agency
Ciba Geigy Canada Ltd. Client
Toronto, Canada

766
John Cruickshank Art Director
George Anketell Copywriter
Ousama Rawi Director
Audrey Telfer Producer
Aisha Film Co. Production House
Maclaren Advertising Agency
Canadian General Electric Client
Toronto Canada

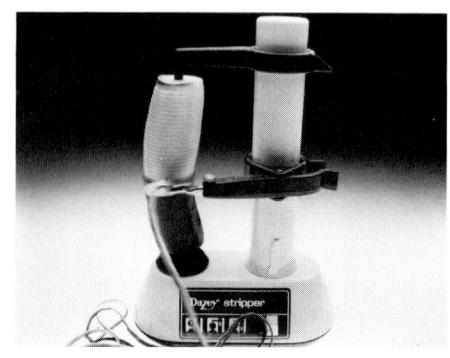

763
Ed Martel Art Director
John Eickmeyer Copywriter
Haboush Productions Production House
Tracy-Locke/BBDO Agency
Haggar Slacks Client
Dallas TX

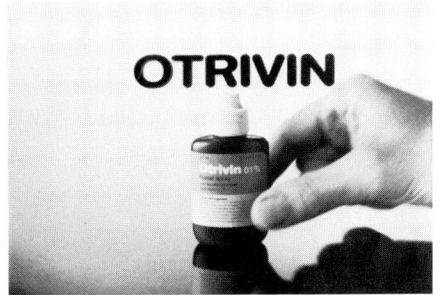 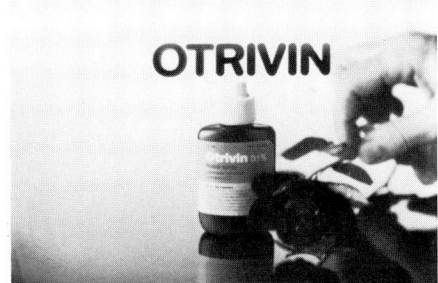 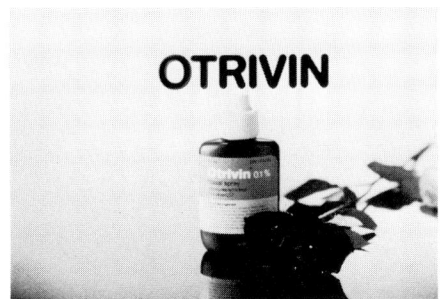

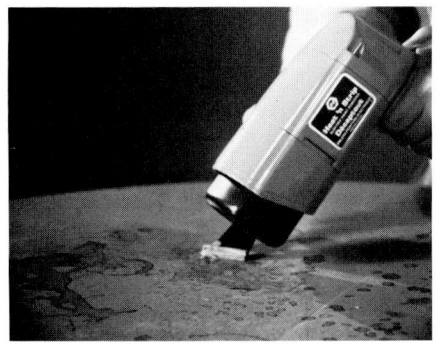 

765
Peter J. Tregale Creative Director
Tony Cooper Art Director
Fritz Spiess Photographer
Rick Okada Director
Paul Gottlieb Copywriter
Schulz Productions Production House
Black & Decker Canada Inc. Client
Toronto, Canada

767
Jim Wheeler Director
Debra Turpin Art Director
Mike Miller Producer
Guinotte Wise, Debra Turpin Writers
Wheeler Film Productions Production House
Studio in the Woods Agency
Dazey Products Inc. Client
Shawnee KS

768
Gary Goldsmith Art Director
Christine Osborne Copywriter
Mark Story Director
Doyle Dane Bernbach Agency
Polaroid Client
New York NY

Consumer Campaign

769
Mike Fromowitz, Gary E. Rouk, Bob Fortier Designers
Bob Fortier, Doug Martin Illustrators
George Morita, Nigel Dickson Photographers
Bob Mann Editor
Lorre Jensen Producer
Street Noise Prod., Rick Sherman Ptrs. Film Company Production Houses
Scali, McCabe, Sloves (Canada) Agency
Cadbury, Schweppes, Powell Inc. Client
Toronto, Canada

771
B.A. Albert Art Director
Jim Keithley Copywriter
Brian Cummins Director
N. Esserman Producer
Film Consortium Production House
Cargill, Wilson & Acree Agency
Krystal Restaurants Client
Atlanta GA

773
Charles Davidson Designer
Santiago Suarez Studio
Harry Viola Advertising Agency
Concord Watch Corp. Client
New York NY

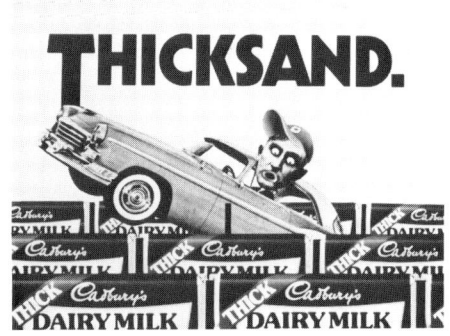

770
Bill Morden Art Director
James Bernardin Creative Director
Michael Stacker Copywriter
Dennis Plansker Direcxtor
Ed Krajewski Producer
Streetnoise/Toronto, EUE Screen Gems, Rabko Prod. Production Houses
Campbell-Ewald Co. Agency
Chevrolet Motor Division Client
Warren MI

772
Grace Sage Art Director
Jennie & Co. Production House
Grace Kent Sage Inc. Agency
Candie's International/El Greco Client
New York NY

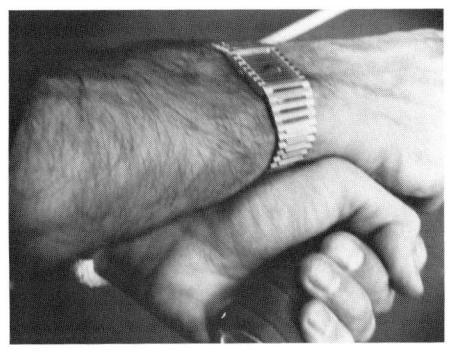

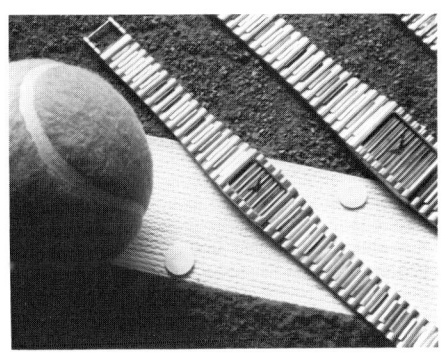

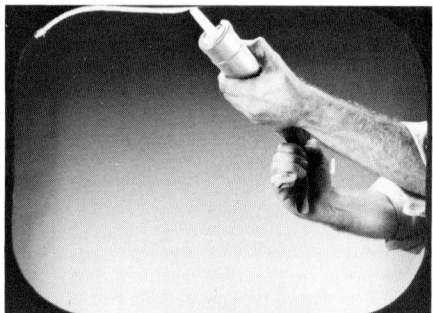
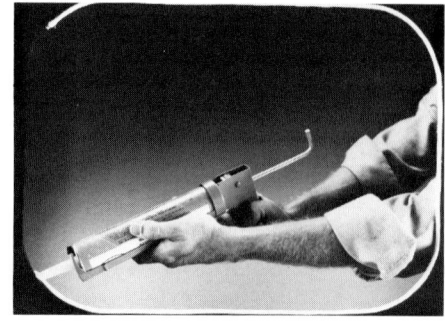

774
Peggy Cox Art Director
Robert Power Copywriter
Southwest Producers Services Production House
Arnold Harwell McClain & Assoc. Agency
Dallas Power & Light Company Client
Dallas TX

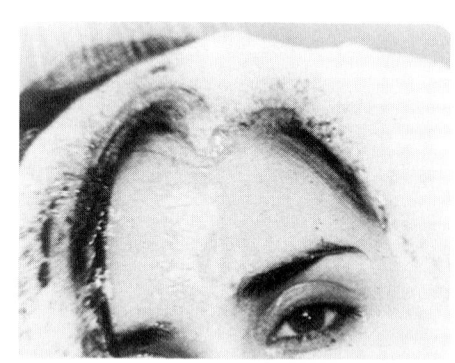

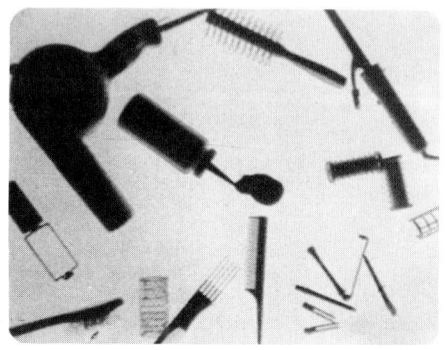

775
Len Favara Art Director
Peter Rogers Associates Agency
Vidal Sassoon Client
New York NY

776
Lloyd Allen Art Director
Graphoons Animators
Erik Perera Copywriter
Telemation Production House
Gerber Advertising Agency
Portland General Electric Client
Portland OR

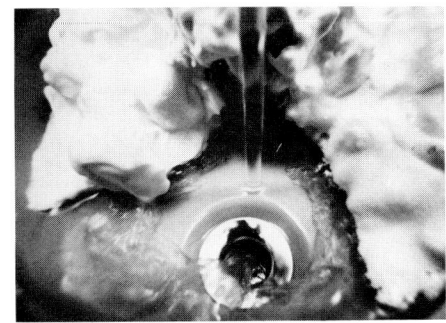
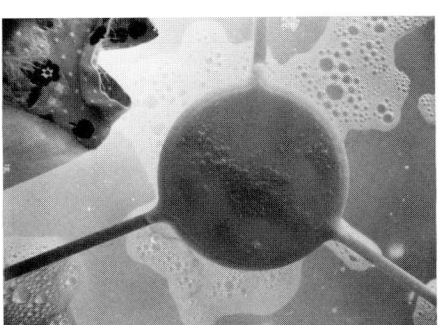
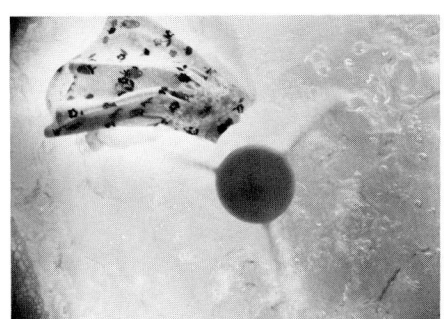
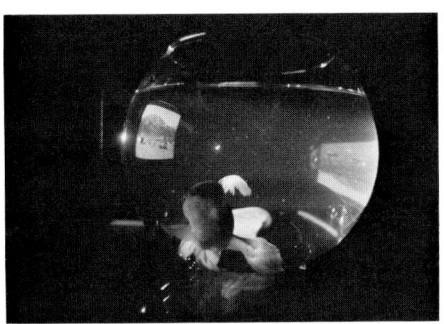
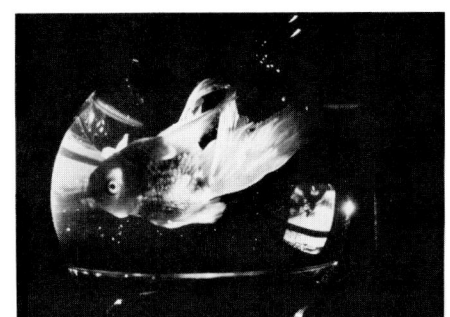
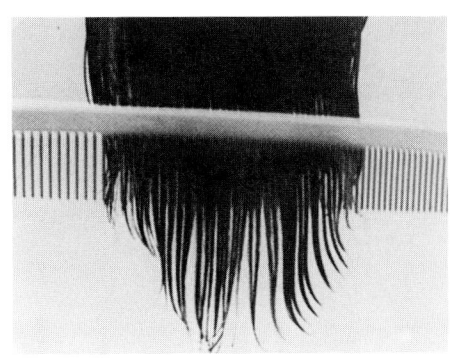

777
J.D. Magowan Art Director
Philo Pieterse Productions (Pty) Ltd.
  Production Houses
Grey Phillips, Bunton, Mundel & Blake
  Agency
Maister Directories Client
Johannesburg S. Africa

778
Mike Waterkotte Designer
Kim Stufflebeam, Steve Musgrave
  Illustrators
Kenetics, The Editings Exchange Animators
Bill Biagi, Chuck Kessler Photographers
Tom Wolferman Copywriter
Laurie Irwin Producer
Freese & Friends, Inc. Production House
Eisaman, Johns & Laws Agency
AAA-Chicago Motor Club Client
Chicago IL

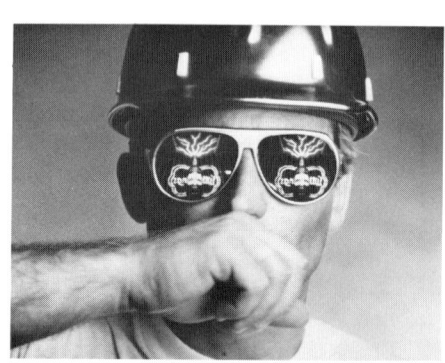

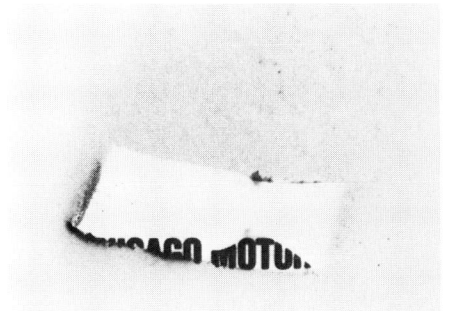

Richard Foster Films Photographers
Fahlgren & Ferris Client
Chicago IL

780
Earl Cavanah, Larry Cadman Art Directors
Scali, McCabe, Sloves Agency
Volvo of America Client
New York NY

782
Neil Joyce Creative Director
Oscar Grillo, Ted Rockley Animators
The Producers Production House
Connell, May & Steavenson Ltd. Agency
Michelin Client
London, England

781
Jeff Frame Art Director
Hellman Design Animators
Sue Fay Copywriter
Lawler Ballard Advertising Agency
Hall Pontiac Client
Norfolk VA

CORPORATE

783
Ben Somoroff Photographer
John Paul Itta, Inc. Agency
The Ahmanson Insurance Companies Client
New York NY

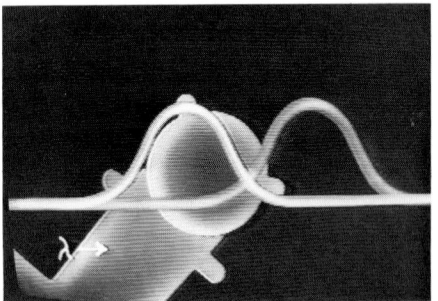 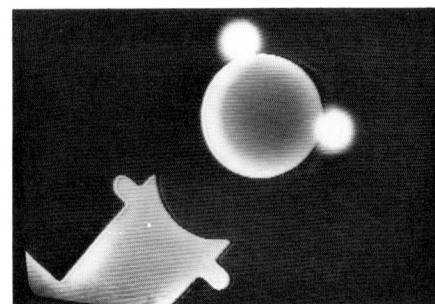 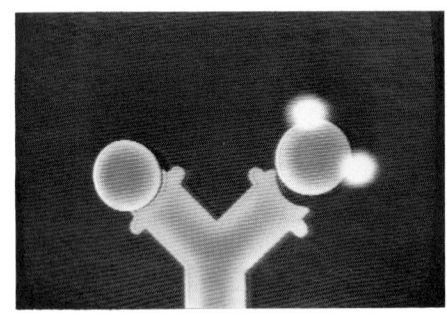

785
Gary Yoshida Art Director
Helmut Dorger Director
Bob Coburn Copywriter
Needham, Harper & Steers Agency
American Honda Motor Co. Client
Los Angeles CA

 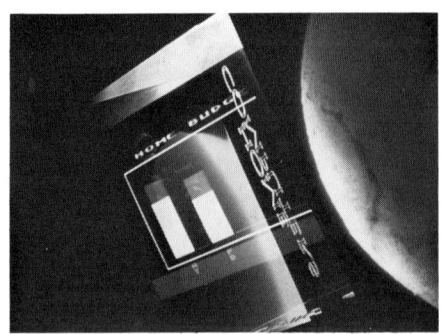 

787
Alan L. Brown Director
Frank Pfifer Cinematographer
John Komnenich Editor
Lee Earle Producer
Brown & Rosner, Inc. Production House
Simplot Client
Chicago IL

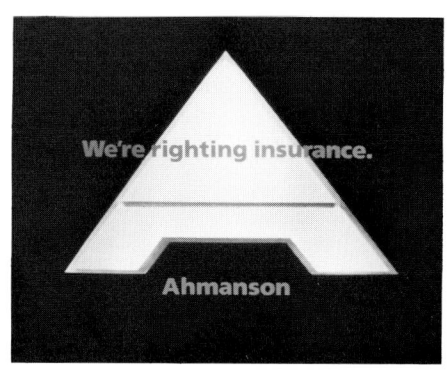

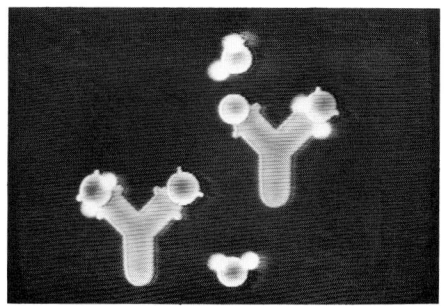

784
Dolphin Productions Production House
Gross Townsend Frank Client
New York NY

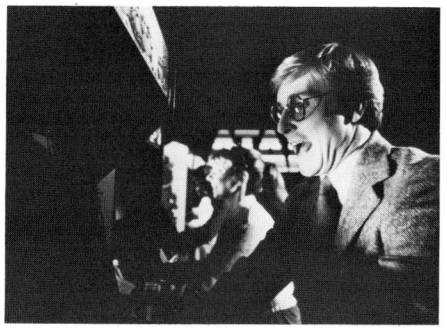

786
Richard Greenberg, Richard Marshall
  Designers
James Szalapski, Vinny Giordano
  Cameramen
R. Greenberg Associates, Inc. Production
  House
Young & Rubicam Agency
Atari Client
New York NY

PUBLIC SERVICE

788
John Evans Art Director
Allen Plane Director
Vis/Art Films Production House
California Dept. of Forestry Client
San Francisco CA

790
Barney Melsky Art Director
Lovinger Tardio Melsky Studio
U.S. Army Client
New York NY

792
Bill Valtos Creative Director
Karen Rizzo Designer
Ritter/Waxberg Production House
D'Arcy-MacManus & Masius Agency
Field Museum Client
Chicago IL

789
Gary Yoshida Art Director
Bob Coburn Copywriter
Jon Yarbrough Director
Summerhouse Films Production House
Needham, Harper & Steers Agency
American Honda Motor Co. Client
Los Angeles CA

791
John McIntyre Creative Director
Arnold Wicht Designer
Bill Martin Copywriter
Harry Lake Photographer
Camp Associates Advertising Ltd. Agency
Province of Ontario Client
Toronto Canada

Political

794
Tom Joyce Art Director
Allen Plane Director
Vis/Art Films, Inc. Production House
Daniel K. Whitehurst Client
San Francisco CA

Show Openings / Id's / Titles

795
Richard Greenberg, Randy Balsmeyer
  Designers
Randy Balsmeyer Animator
Vinny Giordano Cameraman
R. Greenberg Associates, Inc. Production
  House
Filmways Pictures Client
New York NY

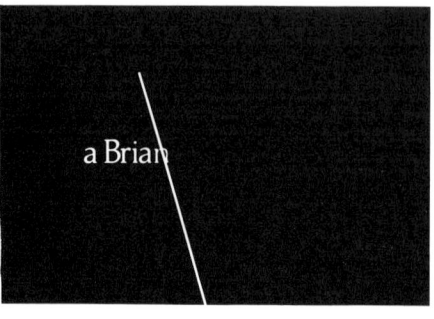 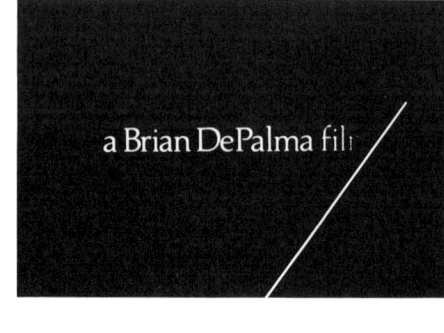

796
Dana Veirs, C.D. Taylor Designers
C.D. Taylor Animator
Klein Studio
Times-Mirror Cable Client
Los Angeles CA

Animation

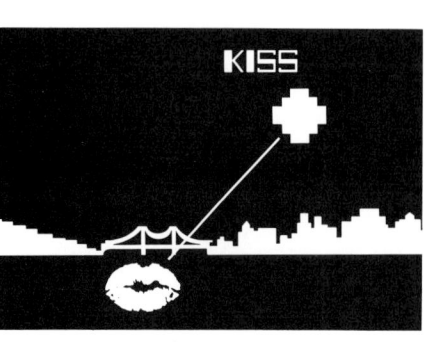

 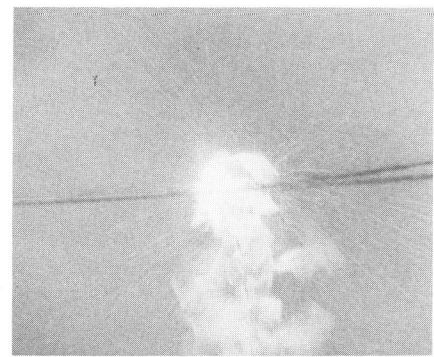

793
Oswaldo Mendes Filho Art Director
Mendes Publicidade Agency
Celpa Client
Belem Brazil

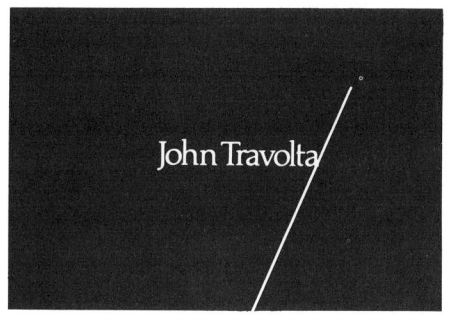 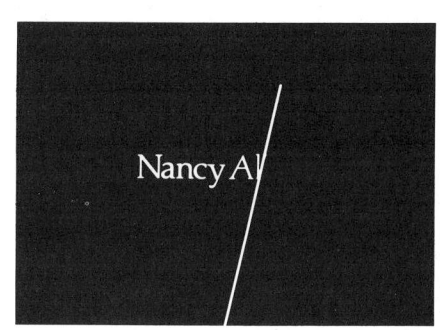 

797
Dolphin Productions
Ramm Advertising Agency
KISS/FM Client
New York NY

ANIMATION

798
Roman Mayer Art Director
Murray Skurnik Creative Director
Bill Feigenbaum, Roman Mayer Designers
Walter Wright Illustrator
Julie Begel Copywriter
Feigenbaum Productions Production House
Venet Advertising Agency
Pathmark Client
New York NY

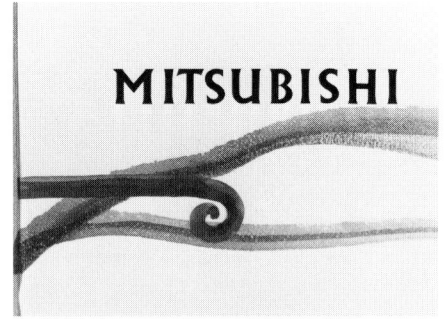

800
Ray Jacobs, Meryl Cohen
Stefan Gerber, Meryl Cohen Copywriters
Stefan Gerber, Ray Jacobs Producers
California Film Production House
Jacobs & Gerber Agency
WXYZ Newstalk Radio Client
Southfield, MI

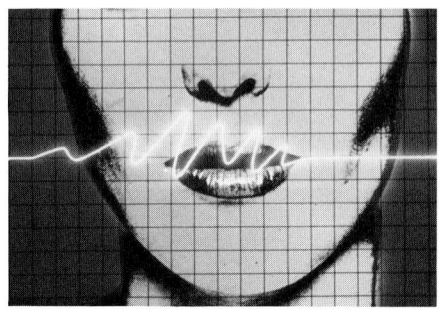

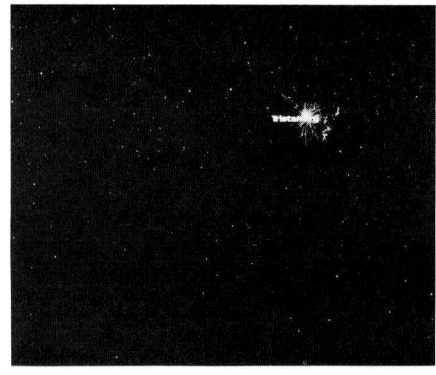

802
Elinor Bunin Designer
Elinor Bunin Productions, Inc. Production
Alvin H. Perlmutter/HBO Client
New York NY

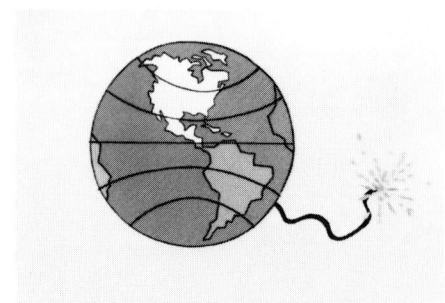

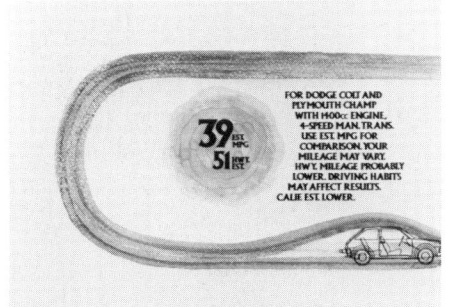

799
Chuck Dickinson Art Director
Paul Kim, Lew Gifford Designers
Alfred Eugster Animator
Albert Semels Photographer
Kim & Gifford Prods., Inc. Production House
Mitsubishi Client
New York NY

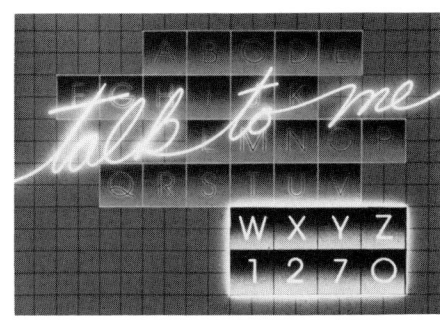

801
Joe Montgomery Art Director
I.F. Studios Production House
Arista Records Client
New York NY

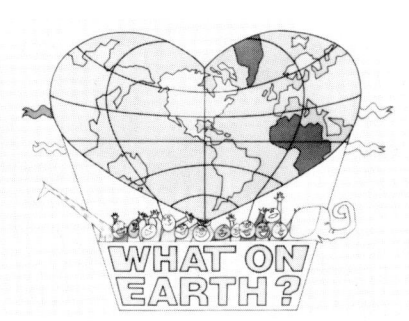

SPECIAL CREATIVE ACHIEVEMENTS

Ticor Mortgage Insurance Company

Report to Policyholders 1981

Art / Illustration

803
Andy Zito Illustrator
Jorge Alonso Art Director
Fotouhi Alonso Inc. Studio
Ticor Mortgage Insurance Co. Client
Los Angeles CA

804
Andrew Holmes Illustrator
George Noordanus Art Director
Gerrit Serne Photographer
Cream Creative Services Studio
Ogilvy & Mather BV Agency
Shell Nederlandse Verk. Mij. BV Client
Amsterdam, Holland

805
Tom Ingham Illustrator
Tom Staebler, Bob Post Art Directors
Playboy Magazine Client
Chicago IL

806
Don Trousdale Illustrator
William F. Finn, James L. Wilkins Art Directors
William F. Finn & Associates Studio
Stemco Inc. Client
Tyler TX

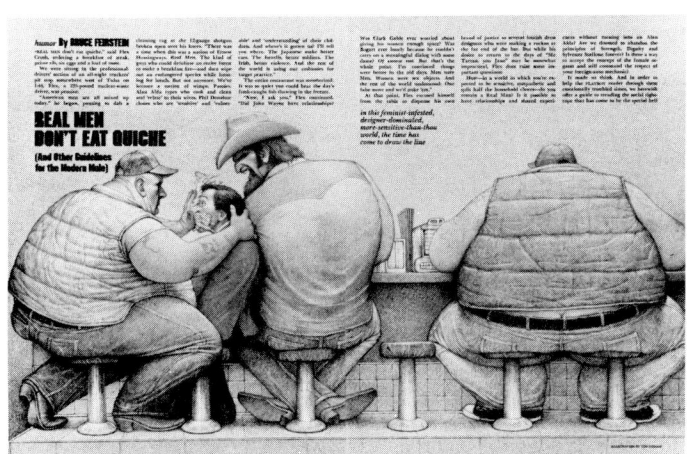

807
Heather Cooper Illustrator
Burns, Cooper, Hynes Ltd. Studio
Faber-Castell Client
Toronto, Canada

808
Mara Kalnins Illustrator/Client
New York NY

THE IDIOT

A portrayal of a truly beautiful soul.
In a nine-part television series, after the novel
by Dostoevsky ∽ Starring John Kurt and Lee Bates
Friday evenings on DBS, Channel Thirteen ∽
Beginning November 28

Masterworks Theatre
Hosted by Harrison Lloyd

SENCO

809
Wilson McLean Illustrator
Joe Brooks Art Director
Penthouse Client
New York NY

810
Dagmar Frinta Illustrator
Michael Grossman Art Director
National Lampoon Client
New York NY

811
Sue Coe Illustrator
Louise Kollenbaum Art Director
Dian-Aziza Ooka Designer
Mother Jones Magazine Client
San Francisco CA

812
G. Allen Garns Illustrator
Nancy Duckworth Art Director
New West Magazine Client
Los Angeles CA

813
Thomas Esser Illustrator
Iris Studios Studio
West '82, Art and the Law Client
Hays KS

814
Linda Crocket-Hanzel Illustrator
Greg Paul Art Director
Cleveland Plain Dealer Magazine Client
Romeo MI

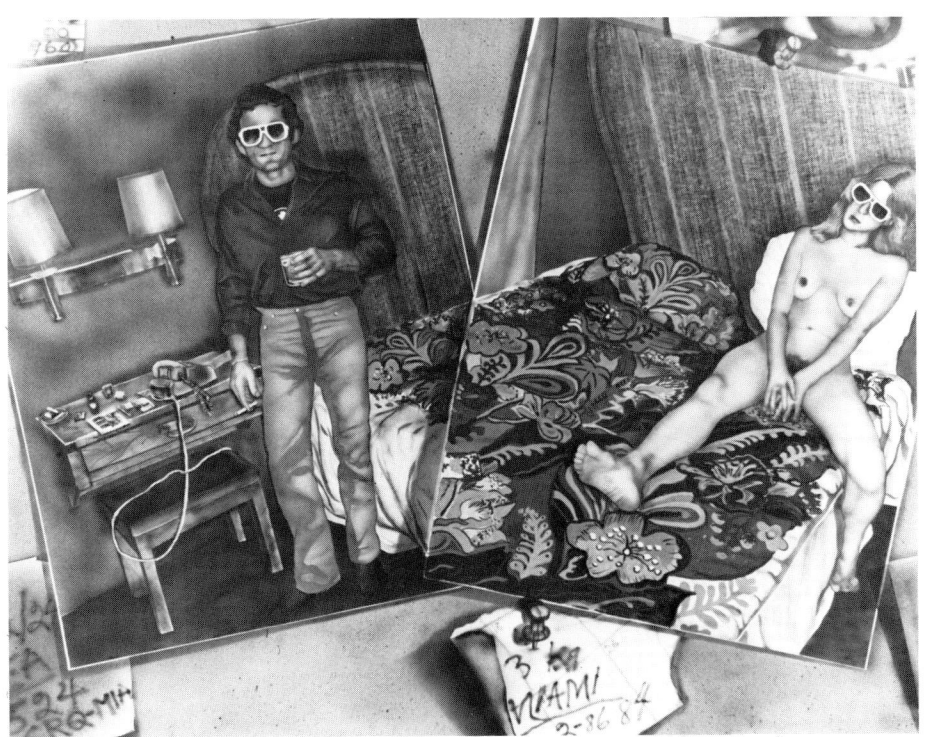

815
Melissa Grimes Illustrator
Jim Darilek Art Director
Texas Monthly Magazine Client
Austin TX

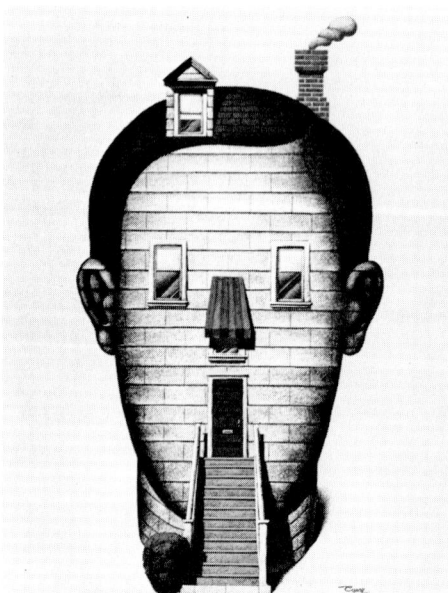

816
Tom Curry Illustrator
Robert J. Post Art Director
Charles A. Thomas Designer
Chicago Magazine Client
Chicago, IL

817
Christopher Bartlett Illustrator
Lois A. Toulotte, W. Michael Dunne Jr.
   Art Directors
Holtzman Gallery Towson State University
   Client
Towson MD

818
Heather Cooper Illustrator
Burns, Cooper, Hynes Ltd. Studio
Ruby Street, Inc. Client
Toronto, Canada

819

820

821

819
Marshall Arisman Illustrator
Joe Brooks Art Director
Penthouse Client
New York NY

820
Kim Lynch Illustrator
Robert Gassy Artist
Kim Mukerjee Photographer
Colin Anderson Art Director
Brand Management Pty. Ltd. Agency
Seapak Transport Services Client
Prahran, Australia

821
Braldt Bralds, Mary Zisk Illustrators
Frank Rothman Art Director
Science Digest Client
New York NY

822
Jerry Dillingham Illustrator
Rick Ferguson Art Director
Ralph Johnson & Associates Agency
Huyck Formex Client
Raleigh NC

823
Mike Quon Illustrator
Mike Quon Client
New York NY

824
Joel Resnicoff Illustrator
Yoshi Inaba, Tokyo Client
New York NY

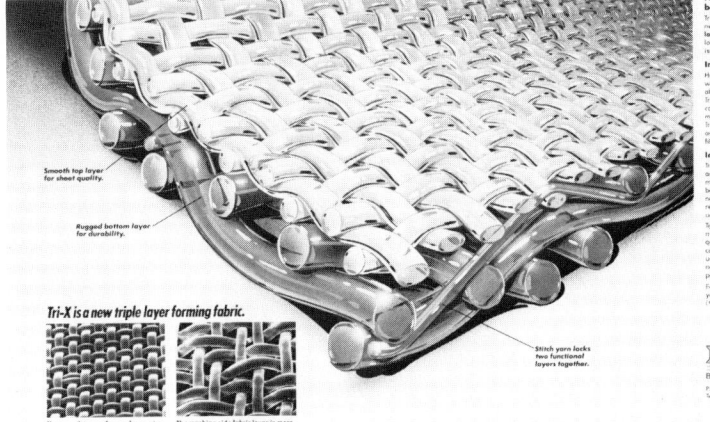

822

823

824

MY MISTRESS

*i'm happily married to the perfect woman—
so why am i in love with an imperfect one?*

fiction BY LAURIE COLWIN

825
Kinuko Y. Craft Illustrator
Tom Staebler, Kerig Pope Art Directors
Playboy Magazine Client
Chicago IL

826
Paul Hodgeson Illustrator
Art Niemi Designer
Quest Magazine Client
Toronto, Canada

827
Bob Heindel Illustrator
Richard Loomis, Robert Paige Art Directors
Evans, Garber & Paige Inc. Studio
Duofold Client
Utica NY

The art of feeling good.

Feel good about yourself. Let the classic quality of Duofold hug you in comfort. Express your individuality in a variety of authentic American stylings to fit the way you live: active tops, turtlenecks and long underwear for the entire family. Master the art of feeling good.

duofold®

©1981 Duofold Inc., Mohawk, N.Y. 13407   from Cluett

Making clothes that make a difference.

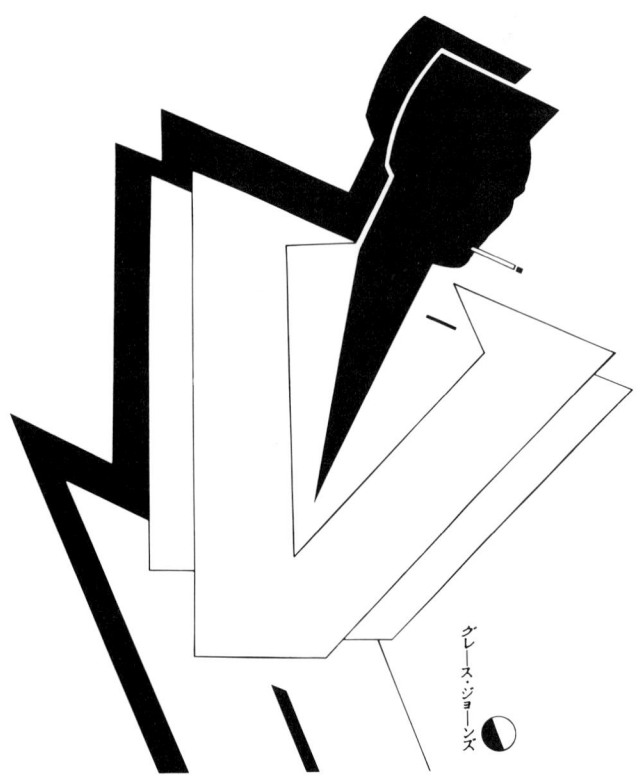

828
Greg Porto Illustrator
Grace Jones Client
New York NY

829
John Collier Illustrator
Alfred Zelcher Designer
Marcia Wright Art Director
Transworld Airlines Client
St. Paul MN

830
Vivienne Flesher Illustrator
Marcia Wright Art Director
The Webb Company Production
Transworld Airlines Client
St. Paul MN

831
Linda Crockett-Hanzel Illustrator/Client
Romeo MI

832
McRay Magleby Designer
Brigham Young University Client
Provo UT

833
Hans Herst, Harold Zellman Illustrators
Zellman/Herst Architects Studio
Marketing Plus Production House
So. California Early Music Soc. Client
Los Angeles CA

835

834
Don Weller Illustrator
Chris Poisson Art Director
Chuck Vadun Copywriter
Kaufman, Lansky, Baker Agency
E.F. Hutton Life Client
San Diego CA

835
Fred Otnes Illustrator
Alan Peckolick Art Director
Frank Moscati Photographer
Lubalin Peckolick Associates Studio
Grupo Industrial Alfa Client
New York NY

836
Franklin Shaw, Cathy Chou Illustrators
L. Dean Woolever, Thomas J. Castle Art Directors
Media Production, Nat'l Inst. for the Deaf
Joan Forman, John Albertini Clients
Rochester NY

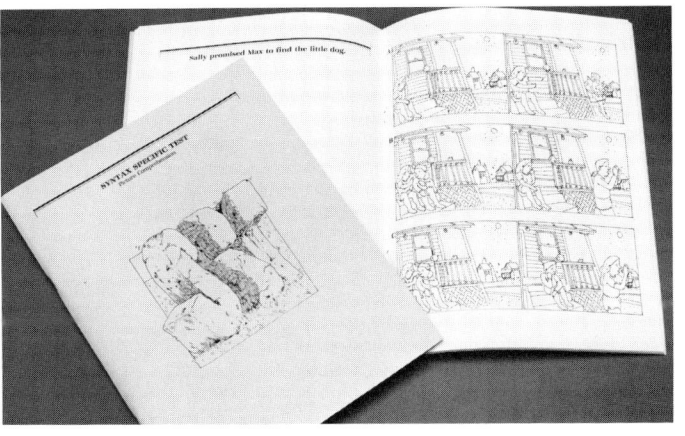

PHOTOGRAPHY

840
Archie Lieberman Photographer
Russ Hirth Art Director
Karen Kelley Copywriter
Carr Liggett Studio
Grumman Flxible Corp. Client
Cleveland OH

837
Al Satterwhite Photographer
Zoom Client
New York NY

838
Charles Moretz Photographer
John Graham Designer
Graham-Solano/Boston Agency
Port Authority of NY & NJ Client
New York NY

839
Robert Llewellyn Photographer
Thomasson-Grant Publishing Client
Charlottesville VA

GETTING THERE
A PEOPLE'S VIEW OF URBAN MASS TRANSPORTATION

A photographic exhibition by noted Chicago photojournalist, Archie Lieberman. *Archie Lieberman*

Chicago Marriott Hotel - Chicago Ballroom/Salons F, G & H, October 9 -11, 1981.

Sponsored by the Grumman Flxible Corporation in cooperation with the Chicago Transit Authority.

841
Philip Tsiaras Photographer
Theodore Kalomirakis Art Director
Greek Accent Client
New York NY

842
Ron Appelbe Photographer
Edyce Hall Art Director
R.J. Reynolds Inc. Producer
Winston-Salem Arts Council Client
Winston-Salem NC

843
Tony Giglio Art Director
William Edward Smith Photographer
Twin Arts, Inc. Studio
Camara 35 Client
New York NY

844
John Goodman Photographer
Tyler Smith Art Direction Studio
Ray Welch, Geoff Currier Copywriters
Welch Currier Smith Agency
Louis Client
Boston MA

842

846

845
Michael N. Paras Photographer/Client
Astoria NY

847

846
Bill King Photographer
Roger Schoening Art Director
Andrea Robinson Beauty Editor
American Vogue Client
New York NY

847
Hans Namuth Photographer
Richard Haymes & Co. Studio
Rapoport Print Corp. Production
Leo Castelli Gallery Client
New York NY

848
Josh Mitchell Photographer
Doug Joseph Designer
Robert Miles Runyan & Associates Studio
Texas Western Dev. Inc. Client
Los Angeles CA

849
Bill Farrell Photographer
Dick Lopez Designer
Dick Lopez Inc. Studio
Sterling Roman Press Client
New York NY

850
Sandy Stewart Photographer
George Dila Creative Director
Steve Spurgeon Art Director
Murlin/Dila Advertising Agency
Citizens Bank of Aurora Client
Englewood CO

851
Loren McIntyre Photographer
Barbara DiLorenzo Art Director
A R & H Advertising Agency
Peru Tourism Client
New York NY

850

We're supporting the worldwide search for new reserves through our offshore petroleum services division which has had a record setting year.

852
Lou Jones, Alex MacLean Photographers
Frank Glickman Designer
Anne Booth Archival Research
Frank Glickman, Inc. Studio
Massachusetts Port Authority Client
Boston MA

853
Arthur Meyerson Art Director
Kenny Ragland Designer
Baxter & Korge Studio
Houston Natural Gas Client
Houston TX

854
Al Fisher Photographer
Mark Kent Art Director
Calderwood & Pieg Illustrators
Banks & Company Studio
Cole-Haan Client
Boston MA

855
Bob Murray Photographer
Richard Weigand Art Director
Kim Hastretler, Branka Milotinovic, West Murray Editors
Bob Murray Studio
Hep Cats Client
New York NY

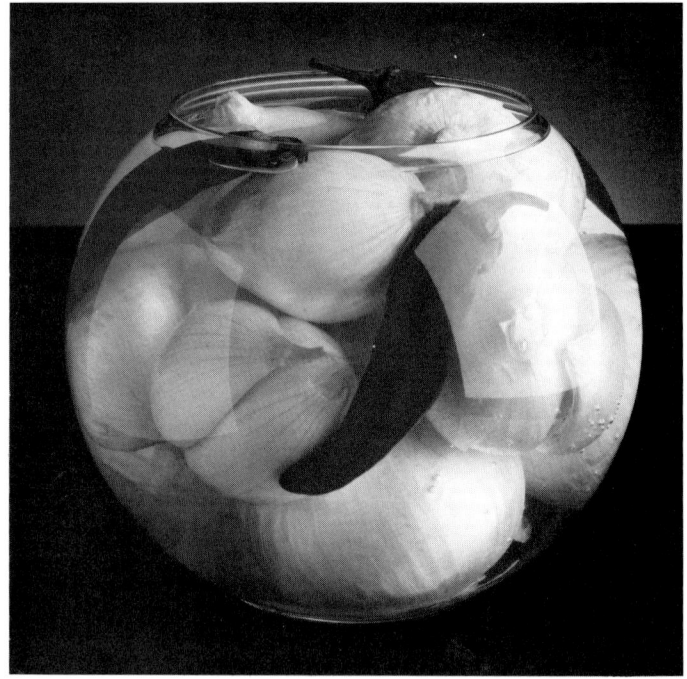

856
Victor Scocozza Photographer
Forgione International Confections Client
New York NY

857

857
Bret Lopez Photographer
Keith Bright Art Director
Julie Riefler Designer
Bright & Associates Studio
Saga Corproation Client
Los Angeles CA

858
Charles Gold Photographer
Laura Vergano Art Director
Lynn Stiles, Ann Conlon Copywriters
Lord, Geller & Einstein Agency
Hilton International Client
New York NY

859
Victor Scocozza Photographer
Good Housekeeping Magazine Client
New York NY

860
Nora Scarlett Photographer/Client
New York NY

861
Robert Stevens Photographer
Rick Besser Designer
Robert Miles Runyan & Assoc. Studio
Knudsen Client
Los Angeles CA

862
Diane Padys Photographer
Marcia Wright Art Director
Barbara Koster Designer
Susan Massey Stylist
Trans World Airlines Client
St. Paul MN

863
William Coupon Photographer
Leonard Mizerek Designer
Mizerek Design Inc. Studio
Scandinavian Foundation Client
New York NY

Portraits from Lapland/1982

1982
April

Sunday	Monday	Tuesday	Wednesday	Thursday	Friday	Saturday
				1	2	3
4	5	6	7	8	9	10
11	12	13	14	15	16	17
18	19	20	21	22	23	24
25	26	27	28	29	30	

864
Toppy Edwards Photographer
David M. Seager Designer
Anne D. Kobor Illustrations Editor
National Geographic Society Client
Washington DC

TYPOGRAPHY

865
Alan Peckolick Designer
Lubalin, Peckolick Assoc. Studio
Mobil Oil Company Client
New York NY

866
Gary Goldsmith Designer
Shawne Cooper Copywriter
Doyle Dane Bernbach Agency
Volkswagen Client
New York NY

867
Erkki Ruuhinen Designer
Anderson & Lembke Oy Agency
Finnish Marketing Federation Client
Helsinki, Finland

Ra bbit

868
Andy Edwards Designer
Sue Gregerowski Typographer
Douglas & Barry Studio
BBDO Marketing & Advertising Agency
Liberty Life Client
Johannesburg, S. Africa

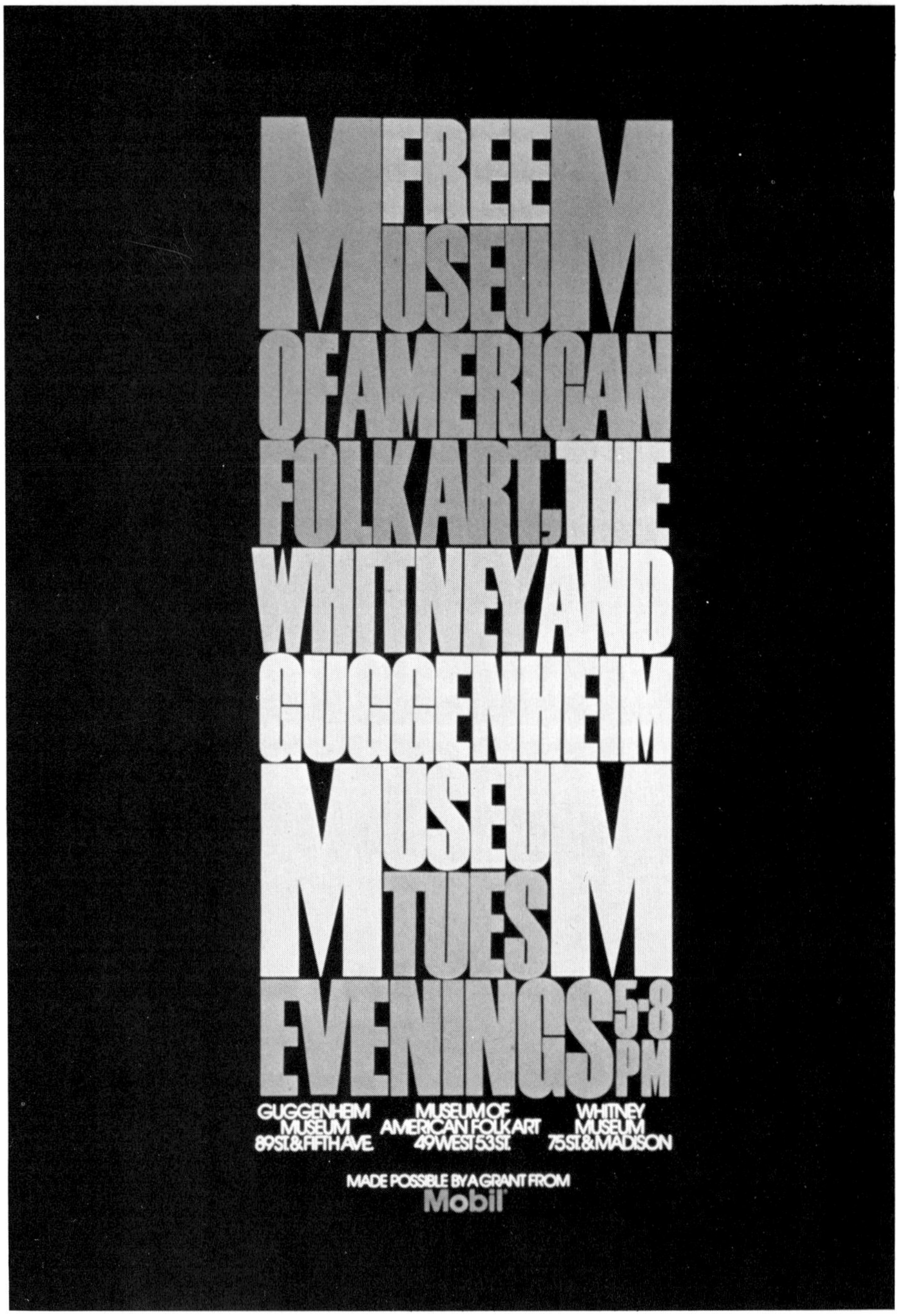

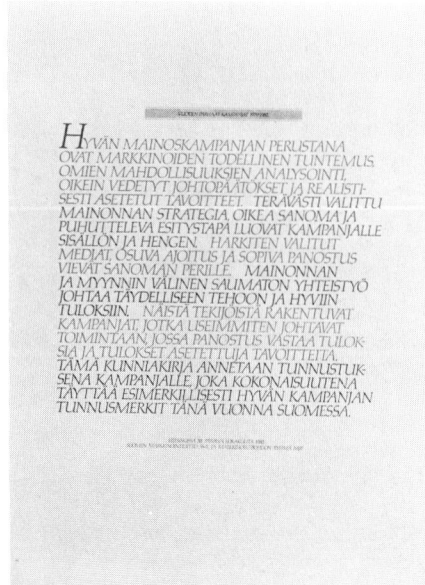

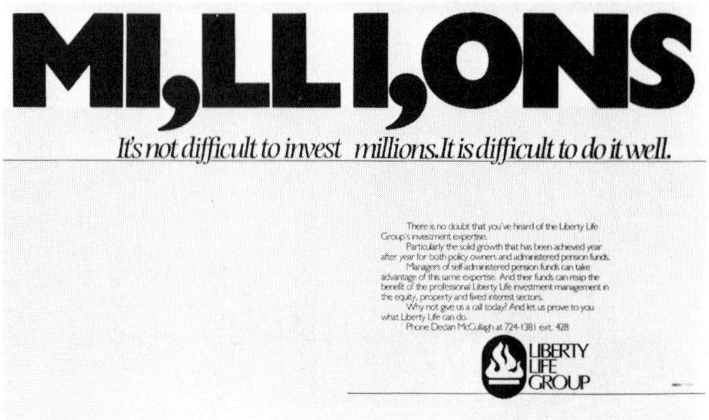

869
Debra Alt-Turpin Art Director
Studio in the Woods Studio
Hyatt Regency Kansas City Client
Kansas City MO

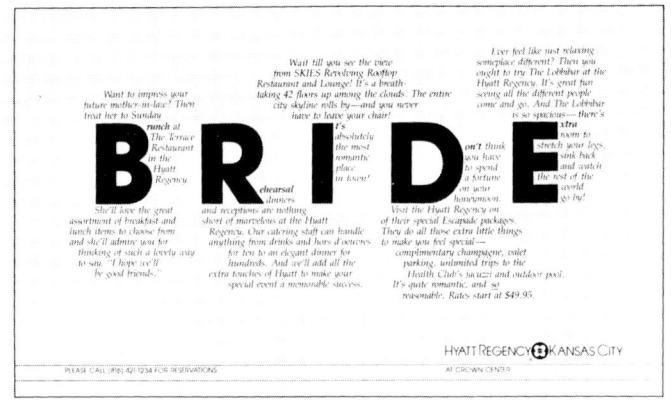

870
Jack J. Podell Director
Donna Tashjian Photo Editor
Anthony Monahan Editor
Robert Woolley Illustrator
American Bar Assoc. Press Client
Chicago IL

871
Oswaldo Miranda Designer
Umuarama Agency
Bamerindus/Grafia Client
Curitiba, Brazil

As Leo Burnett, himself, said, "There is nothing so dramatic as the truth simply told."

In 1979, our agency reorganized itself to be in a strong position to meet the challenges our clients and our industry would face in the 1980's.

In the past two years, we have worked hard and long doing what we know best: advertising our clients' products. The rewards have been many, with continual growth from our existing clients, and the addition of new clients who also believe advertising makes a sound and fundamental contribution to the growth of their businesses. These include: *The Adams Distillers Group Ltd., Boyle-Midway Canada Ltd./ Ltée, Les Biscuits David, Canadian Tampax Corporation Ltd., Les Aliments F.B.I. du Canada Ltée, Fuji Photo Film Canada Inc., Hotels Régent International, International Maple Syrup Institute, Mitchum-Thayer Ltd., Joseph E. Seagram & Sons Limited, Spillers Foods Limited and VISA.*

The simple truth is we are proud of what we've done and where we are going. And we still believe the best advertising for Leo Burnett is being run by our clients.

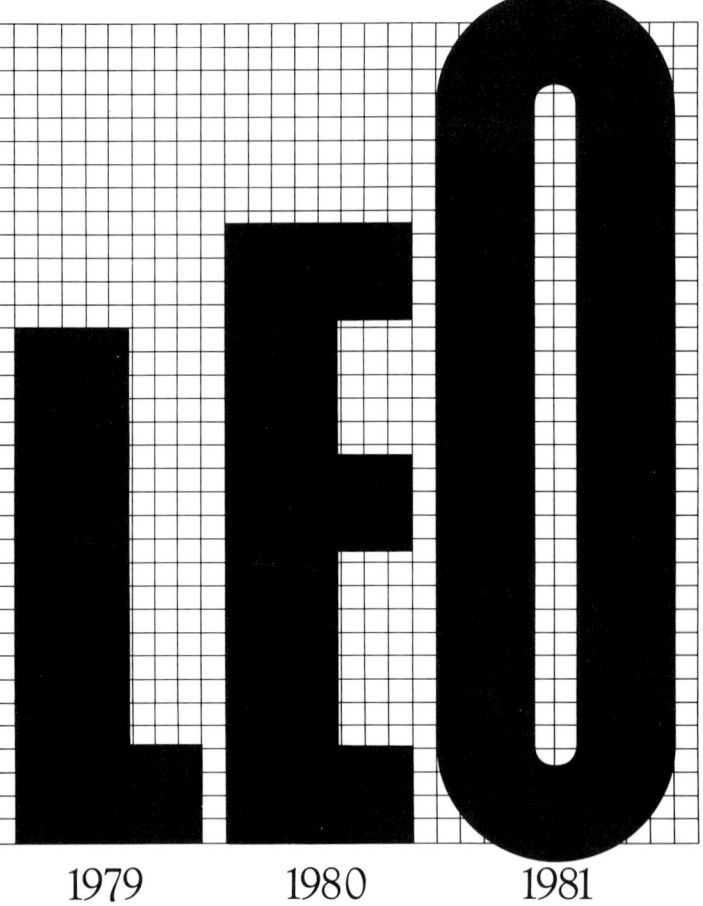

The Adams Distillers Group Ltd.
Allstate Insurance Companies of Canada
Barreau du Québec
Beecham Products Overseas
Benson & Hedges (Canada) Inc.
Boyle-Midway Canada Ltd./Ltée
Les Biscuits David
Canadian Tampax Corporation Ltd.
Les Aliments F.B.I. du Canada Ltée
Fuji Photo Film Canada Inc.
Hotels Régent International
International Maple Syrup Institute
Kroehler Mfg. Co. Limited
Kellogg Salada Canada Inc.
The Maytag Company
Memorex Canada Limited
Mitchum-Thayer Ltd.
Nissan Automobile Company (Canada) Limited
Pillsbury/Green Giant Canada Limited
Procter & Gamble Inc.
RCA Limited
Joseph E. Seagram & Sons Limited
Spillers Foods Limited
Star-Kist Foods Inc.
Société Radio-Canada
Union Carbide Canada Limited
Vigoro
VISA

Leo Burnett Company Ltd.
TORONTO · MONTREAL · VANCOUVER

872
Martin Shewchuk Designer
Ed Nanni Creative Director
Kathy Doherty Copywriter
Cooper & Beatty Ltd. Typesetting
Leo Burnett Company Ltd. Client
Toronto, Canada

873
Mark Simkins Art Director
Harry De Zitter Photographer
Chris Marrington Copywriter
Fine Geffen Simkins Marrington Studio
Kymmene Star Client
Johannesburg, S. Africa

874
Dave Reed Designer
Howard Frank Art Director
Leona Schaller Copywriter
Reed Kaina Schaller Advertising Agency
T.I. of Hawaii Inc. Client
Honolulu HI

875
Rick St. Vincent Designer
Len Egol Advertising Mgr.
St. Vincent, Milone & McConnells Agency
Dorr-Oliver Inc. Client
New York NY

876
Bob Salpeter Designer
E.F. Hutton Client
New York NY

877
John W. Douthwaite Designer
J.B. Rogers Co. Client
Huntington Beach CA

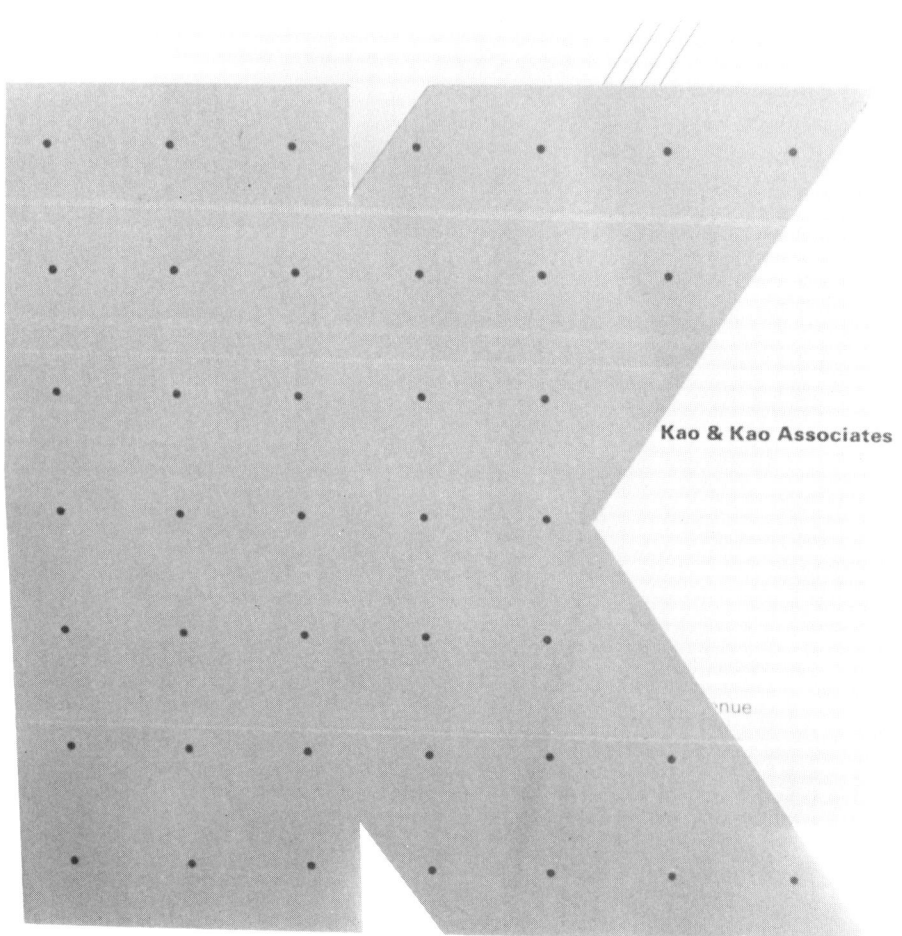

878
Kelly Kao Designer
Kao & Kao Associates Client
New York NY

879
Rob Hugel Designer
Melissa Brown Copywriter
Herman Miller Inc. Client
Zeeland MI

"Participation requires information." Rational participation in the workplace, in the community, in the world, in our own lives, depends on the thorough and thoughtful gathering of information. The MacNeil/Lehrer Report is thoughtful, thorough, and unique in television reporting: It is the only television news program that devotes a full half-hour program to a single issue. Viewers report finding interest in issues they had no interest in before, and seeing pros and cons they hadn't suspected. How many act on their new interest? That's harder to know. But without interest, there would be no action. Herman Miller is proud to sponsor The MacNeil/Lehrer Report on WGVC.

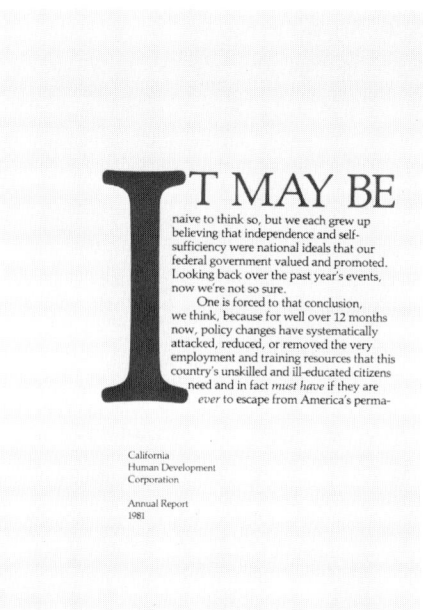

880
Wayne D. Gibb Art Director
Ken Light Photographer
California Human Development Corp. Client
Santa Rosa CA

881
Christos Peterson Designer
Book-of-the-Month Records Client
New York NY

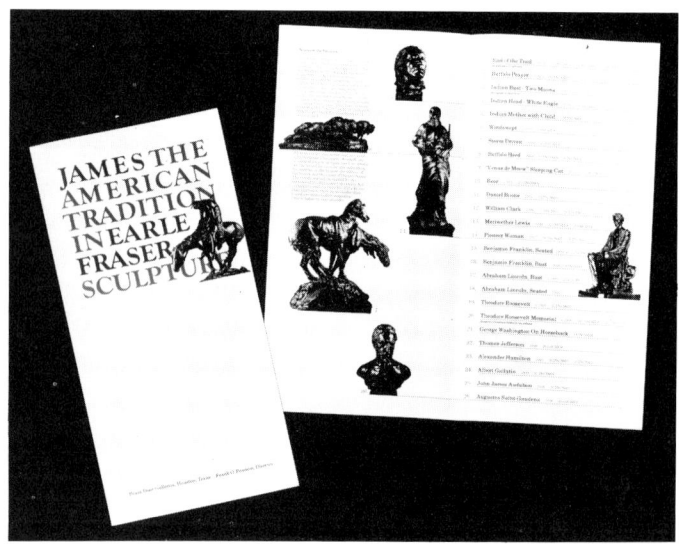

882
Kenneth R. Hine Designer
The Competition Studio
Syracuse University Art Collection/Brass Door Galleries Houston Client
Syracuse NY

883
Phyllis Schefer Designer
Ron A. Albrecht Art Director
Essence Magazine Client
New York NY

884
Norm Ung, Ron Coro Art Directors
Stan Evenson Design Inc. Designers
Elektra/Asylum Records Client
Los Angeles CA

885
Kathleen Sullivan Kaska Art Director
Brown & Rosner Inc. Studio
Ladendorf Bros. Printer
Kathleen & Robert Kaska Client
Chicago, IL

886
Gene Bradford Design Studio
Sandcastle Advertising Agency
Cicoil Client
Studio City CA

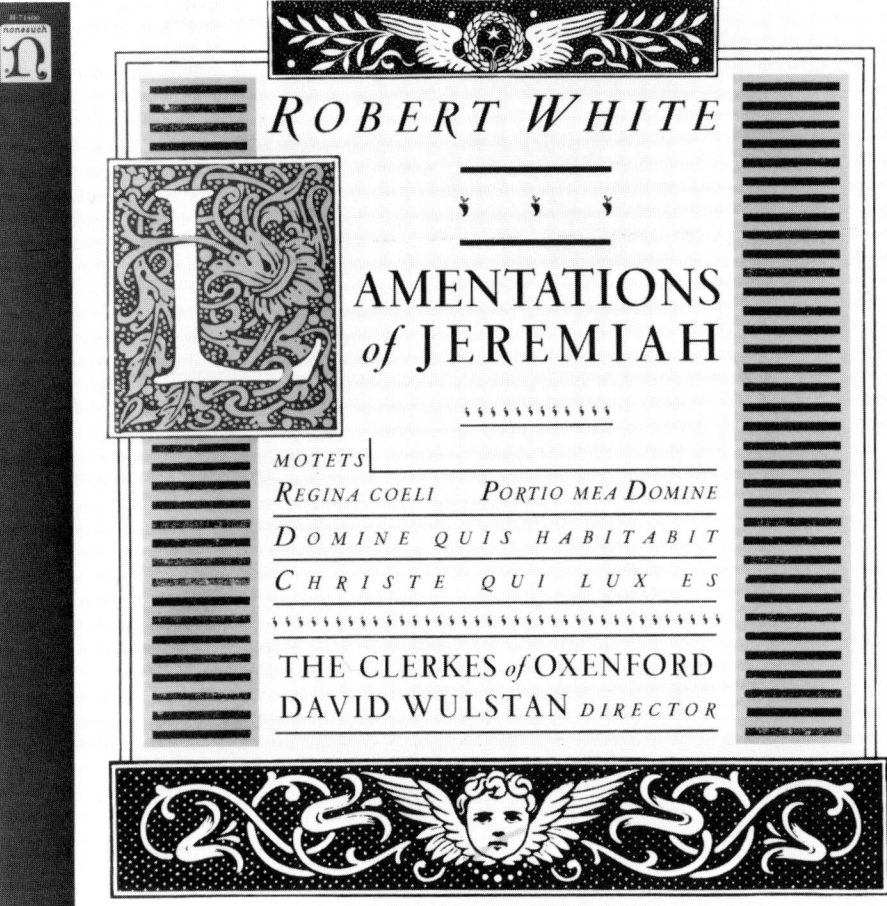

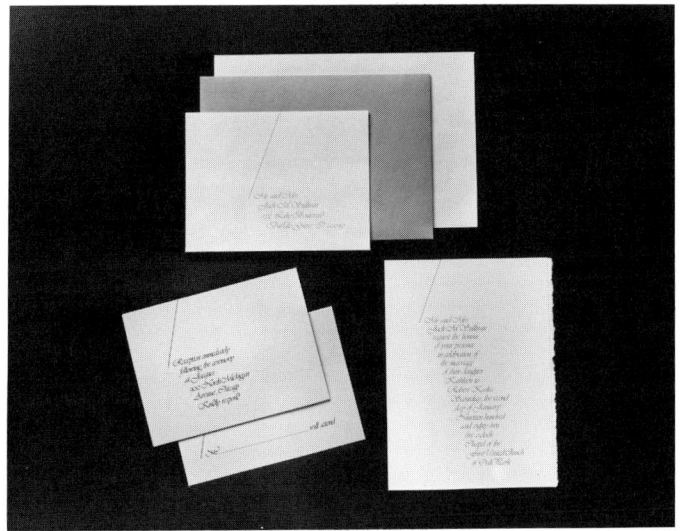

885

Buckminster Fuller observed that, near the turn of the century, the average lifetime distance a person traveled was 30,000 miles. Now it is common for people to travel millions of miles, for pleasure or to carry out their responsibilities in this "swiftly emerging spherical world city." And yet man is still unable to realize himself as "being already a world man." The technologies that have led to global communications, travel, and awareness have also led to a degree of global interdependence new in our experience. Weather in Europe affects grain prices and thus the income of American farmers; politics in Palestine show up in tomorrow's Dow-Jones. **Understanding the global community requires information. Herman Miller is pleased to sponsor the MacNeil/Lehrer Report on WGVC.**

herman miller

887
Rob Hugel Designer
Melissa Brown Copywriter
Herman Miller Inc. Client
Zeeland MI

888
Richard K. Manigault Designer/Client
Bronx NY

889
Andree Cordella Designer
George Petrakas Photographer
Gunn Associates Studio
Henry Reeves & Associates Agency
Inspeech Inc. Client
Boston MA

890
Bob Celander Designer
Sharon Kirk Copywriter
Young & Rubicam/Zemp Agency
Holiday Inn Client
St. Petersburg FL

891
Jean Larcher Designer
LaTaste-Odim Client
LaCelle St. Cloud, France

Harold Burch Art Director
Art Paquette, Richard Shaeffer Copywriters
Ken White Design Office, Inc. Studio
Aldus Type Studio Ltd. Client
Los Angeles CA

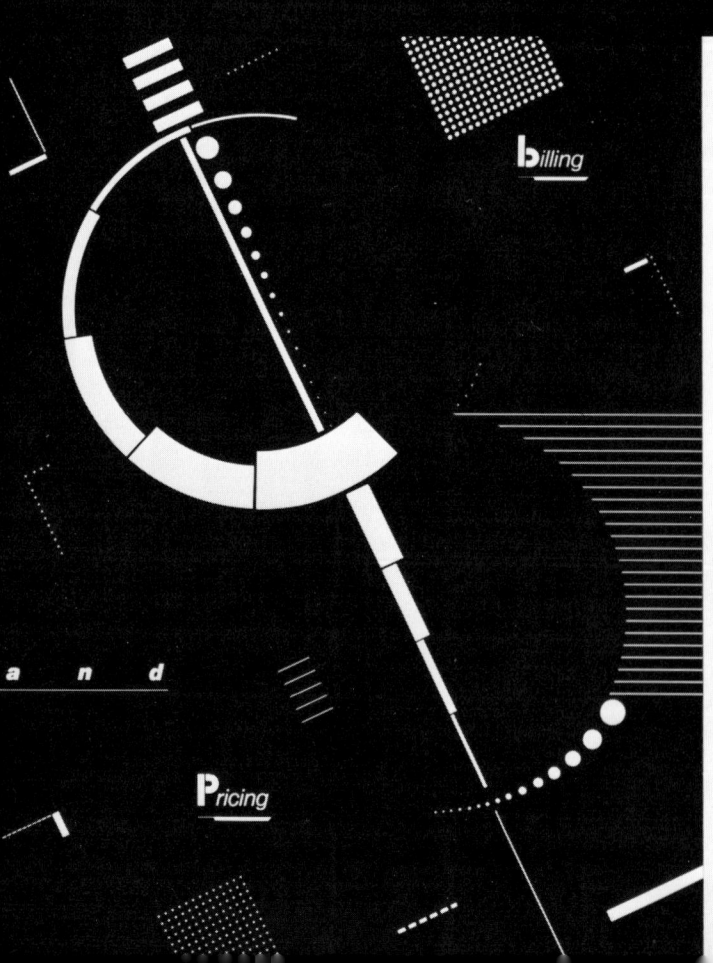

Accounting Department:
934-1179 is the direct line to our accounting department; use this number between 8 a.m. and 4:30 p.m. to request prices or for any billing inquiries. If you provide us with our job number, we can usually reply to price requests within several hours.

Billing Procedures:
Most typesetting jobs are billed after seven days of inactivity. Invoices are provided in quadruplicate and are accompanied by proofs of all work performed. Whenever practical, the cost of the original composition and any subsequent additions and/or alterations are itemized on the invoice. Reproduction proofs are itemized separately from composition costs in order to help provide an accurate breakdown of contributing cost factors.

Type forms are held six months after invoicing. To help defray storage and handling costs, a nominal charge is made for any forms "picked up" from jobs that have been closed (invoiced) for more than 15 days.

The Color Comp Machine:
A subsidiary of Aldus Type Studio, work produced by the Color Comp Machine will either be billed to you direct on a Color Comp invoice (if no typesetting is involved) or the charges can be incorporated into an Aldus invoice. The price will be the same no matter which method of billing is used since no markup is added to Color Comp charges billed through Aldus. The advantages of direct Color Comp billing are quicker billing and a lower per-job minimum charge (the Color Comp job minimum is less than half of the minimum we must charge for typesetting services).

Sales Ta%

Sales Tax: Unless we have a valid resale card in our possession, sales tax will be charged on all typography and film work. Separate resale cards are required for Aldus Type Studio and the Color Comp Machine in order to get direct billing from the Color Comp Machine.

We are obliged to charge sales tax on any work that is obviously not for resale (such as house ads, stationery, etc.) whether or not we have a resale card on file.

Terms: We expect payment in 30 days or less from the date of invoice; a 2% discount may be taken if payment is postmarked within 10 days from the date of our invoice. To expedite approval payment of invoices in order to take advantage of the 2% discount, we suggest stamping invoices with the date received.

Credit: We offer three basic types of accounts: C.O.D., Limited Credit, and Open. C.O.D. is a necessity for transactions with accounts that have not established credit with us, but because it is inconvenient for all concerned we try to put new accounts on a "Limited" or "Open" status as soon as possible. When adequate credit information is not available, such as in the case of a new business, we can extend "Limited" credit. A monthly ceiling is put on your account and if the billing (including work in progress) exceeds the credit line, we will ask for a partial payment to limit our risk. After three months the limit can be raised; after six months the account will be put on "Open" status if all payments have been made as agreed. Accounts with questionable credit will be accepted on a retainer basis only.

893
Kerry Polite Designer
Polite Design Studio
Route 66 Client
Philadelphia PA

896
Steven Liska Designer
Liska & Associates Studio
Deborah Riley Photostylist Client
Chicago IL

893

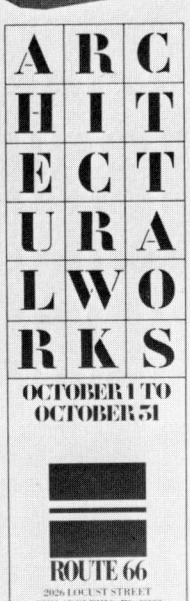

894
Michael Williams Designer
Anthony Garner Photographer
Hurst Printing Production
Shreveport Advertising Federation Client
Shreveport LA

895
Stuart Bresner Art Director
Mathieu, Gerfen & Bresner, Inc. Agency
Glenmore Distilleries Client
New York NY

894

897
Jack J. Podell Director
Donna Tashjian Photo Editor
Robert Woolley Illustrator
American Bar Association Press Client
Chicago IL

898
Mare Earley Art Director
Expertype Inc. Production
Entree Magazine Client
New York NY

902

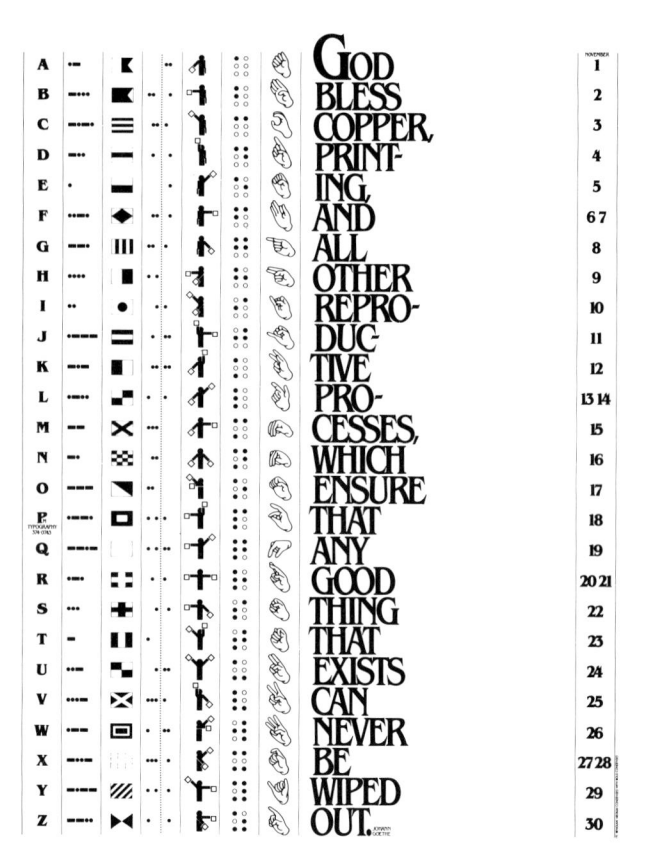

899
Paul Sinn Designer
PM Typography Production
Galarneau, Deaver & Sinn Studio
PM Typography Client
Palo Alto CA

900
Kurt Tausche Art Director
Warren Hanson Illustrator
Leslie Trinite Clark Copywriter
Great Faces Typographer
Brandt-Barringmann Inc. Agency
KSTP-FM Client
Minneapolis MN

901

901
Thomas Q. White Designer
Murrie White Drummond Lienhart Studio
California Dreamers Client
Chicago IL

902
Bryan L. Peterson Designer
Brigham Young University Client
Provo UT

903
Laurie Rosenwald Designer/Client
New York NY

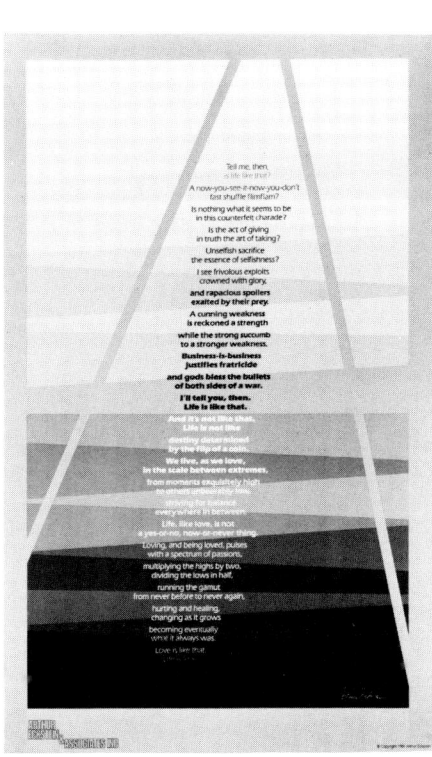

904
Christ Polito, Michael Doret Designers
Bartels & Co. Studio
The Hanley Partnership Agency
Anheuser-Busch Inc. Client
St. Louis MO

905
Arthur Eckstein Designer/Client
New York NY

906
Bjarne Norking Art Director
Alcantara Machado, Periscinto Comunicacoes Ltda Client
Sau Paulo, Brazil

907
Chris Poisson Art Director
Elizabeth A. Flynn Acct. Executive
Kaufman, Lansky, Baker Agency
Group W Cable Client
San Diego CA

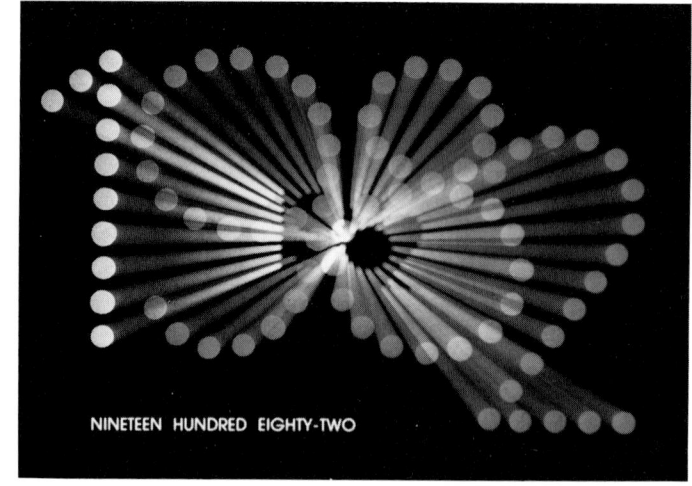

908
Dolly Altamuro Designer
Tony Til Photographer
TV Guide Magazine Client
Radnor PA

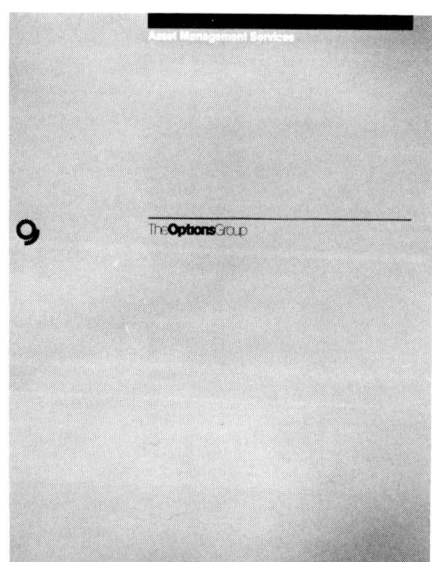

909
Bill Davis Designer
Stanford Golob Photographer
Doremus Design Studio
The Options Group Client
New York NY

910
Al Foti Designer
Geoffrey Gove Photographer
MD Magazine Client
New York NY

RADIO

911
DRACULA
SOCRATES
LAWRENCE OF ARABIA
Tricia Falcaro Creative Director
Mathieu, Gerfen & Bresner, Inc. Agency
Great Waters of France Client

912
EARN WHILE YOU BURN
Richard Andre Creative Director
Fred Arthur Productions Production House
Hart/Conway Company, Inc. Agency
Columbia Banking Client

913
BACK TO SCHOOL PENCILS
Cathedral Sound Studio Production House
Wolkcas Advertising Agency
Schatz Stationery Client

914
ACE INVADERS
Lawrence D. Senten Creative Director
D'Arcy-MacManus & Masius Agency
Ace Hardware Corporation Client

915
DIE FLEDERMAUS
SHORT SEASON
SEASON
Cynthia Hartwig Creative Director
Sharp, Hartwig & Vladimir Agency
Seattle Opera Client

916
KICK-ME RADIO
Daniel Goldstein Copywriter
King Productions Production House
Dancer Fitzgerald Sample, Inc. Agency
Barclays Bank of California Client

917
SIMPSON'S SECRET
Roger Myers Copywriter
Studio One Production House
Burch Myers Cuttie, Inc. Agency
Crain's Chicago Business Client

918
THE CRUISE/BASKIN
Irwin Goldberg Creative Director
Nadler & Larimer Inc. Agency
Hart Schaffner & Marx Client

919
YOUR GIFT IS INSTRUMENTAL
Howard Halaska Creative Director
McDonald & Little Agency
Atlanta Symphony Orchestra Client

920
WOMAN
William S. Babcock Creative Director
The Process Production House
The William Babcock Agency Agency
Heritage Motors Client

INDEX

A

A C & R Advertising, 56
A. Horowitz & Sons, 669
A & M Records, 275
A R & H Advertising, 851
AAA-Chicago Motor Club, 778
Aapiset Oy, 636
ABC Art Dept., 626
ABC Television Network, 626
Abel, Robert, 746
Abgell, Primo, 336
Abraham, Guenet, 269
Abromowitz, Jerry, 106
Absolut Vodka, 31
AC & R Advertising, 743
Accudart, 549
Ace & Edie, 738
A.D. Magazine, 314
Adam, Filippo & Moran, 516
Adamjee, Farzana, 385
Adams, Jon, 635
Adao & Eve, 526
Adelson, Richard, 240
Admatch Corp., 614
Admissions Office, Emory University, 645
Adolescent Records, 282, 288
Advertising Agency HPV Oy, 714
Aer Lingus, 21, 753
AFI, Miami, 748
After Six, 236
Agranat, June, 204
Agu Sport BV, 371
Aguas Minerales, 329
Agway, 127
The Ahmanson Insurance Companies, 783
A.I. Friedman, Inc., 68
Aisha Film Co., 766
Alan Wood Graphic Design Inc., 506
Albano, Tom, 73
Albert, B.A., 771
Albertini, John, 836
Albrecht, Ron A., 472, 883
Alcantara Machado, Periscinto Comunicacoes Ltda, 44, 906
Alderman's, 204
Aldus Type Studio, Ltd., 668, 892
Alexander, Al, 459
Alexander Communications, 301
Alexanian, Nubar, 432
Alfonso Capetillo y Asociados, 421, 504
Alfred A. Knopf, 263
All Brand Importers, 128
Alleghany Pharmaceutical Corp., 4
Allen Advertising, 388
Allen, Lloyd, 776
Allfonso Capetillo y Asociados, 504
Allmanna Brand, 389
Almaden Vineyards, 47
Alonso, Jorge, 411, 803
Alper, Jud, 736
Altamuro, Dolly, 908
Alt-Turpin, Debra, 869
Alvin H. Perlmutter/HBO, 802
AMAX Inc., 396
Amenola, Judy, 446
Amerada Hess, 415
America Illustrated, 302, 489
American Bar Assoc. Press, 870, 897
American Broadcasting Co., 226
American Cancer Society, 428
American Express/Air New Zealand, 5
American Heart Association, 719
American Honda Motor Co., 785, 789
American Hospital Supply Corp., 439
American Lamb Council, 54
American McGraw Marketing Communications, 382
American Savings Bank, 530
American Vogue, 846
AMF, 51, 81
Amies and Associates, 8
Amikin (Bristol Laboratories), 178
Amiran Corp., 67, 207
Amity Leather Products, 325
Amnesty International, 706
Amstar Corporation, 410
Anchorage Restaurant, 145
Anderson, Colin, 820
Anderson, Jack R., 569, 593
Anderson, John H., 173
Anderson & Lembke Danderydsgatan, 117, 228, 622
Anderson & Lembke Oy, 157, 188, 867
Anderson, Lynne, 252
Andresakes, Ted, 217
Andrew Quady Vineyards, 327
Angeli, Primo, 511
Anheuser Busch Inc., 144, 904
Ankers, Robert, 141, 172
Anketell, George, 766
Ann Taylor, 233
Another Season, 568
Ansearch, Inc., 575
Antista, Tom, 140, 563, 674
Appelbe, Ron, 842
Apple Computer Magazine, 461
Arias, Mauricio, 461
Arisman, Marshall, 272, 458, 819
Arista Records, 801
Arnold Harwell McClain & Assoc., 554, 774
Arnold, M., 398
Arnold Schwartzman Prod. Inc., 561
Aronson, 104
Aronson, Mark, 86
Art Direction, 291
Art Directors Club, 442
Art Institute of Chicago, 379
Art 'Y Fact, 642
Arteaga, Robert, 678
Arthur Eckstein, 905
The Associated Press, 420
Associates Corp. of North America, 438
Astra Trading Corp., 375
Atari, 786
Atco Records, 283
Atkins, Richard, 633
Atlantic Aviation, 193
Audio Dynamics Corp., 372
Audubon, 560, 651
Aurness, Craig, 398
Austopchuk, Christopher, 277, 285
Avco Community Developers, 509
Avedon, Richard, 34
Avenue Magazine, 310
Avery, Franklin, 383
Avon Books, 255, 261
AWE/Gebers, 248
AYC Graphics, 349
Ayer Barker, 710
Ayeroff, Jeff, 275

B

BA Capital Corp., 211
Badler, M., 396
Baehr, Richard, 192
La Baguette Bakery, 53
Bailey, Ken, 124
Bailey, Phil, 440
Bain, Joanna, 295, 491
Baker, Strandel, 144
Ballantine Books, 241
Ballotta Napurano & Co. Inc., 85
Balsmeyer, Randy, 795
Balterman, Lee, 194
Bamerindus/Grafia, 871
Banburry, Dale, 425
Banco B.C.H., 421
Banco de Occidente, 590
Baney, Gutzmer Inc., 514
Banfield, Elliott, 238
Banks & Company, 43, 65, 854
Barber, Ray, 506
Bard, Rachel, 593
Barker, Kent, 475
Barnard, John, 614
Barnes & Company, 286
Barnes, Jeff, 301
Barnett, David, 227
Barnett, Dennis, 227
Barr, Eli, 324
Barre, Richard, 199
Bartels & Company, 678, 904
Bartels, David, 144, 678
Bartlett, Christopher, 817
Barton, Gladys, 70, 538
Bascove, 242, 257
Basile, Matt, 6
Bassano, Donna, 355
Bates, Al, 339
Bates, David, 439
Battista, Albert J., 448
Bauer, Dana, 334
Bauer, Phil, 687
Baum, Stan, 70
Baxter & Korge, 853
BBC Enterprises, 643
BBDM, Inc., 100, 168
BBD&O, Inc., 7, 108, 113, 606
BBDO Marketing & Advertising, 30, 346, 868
B.D. Fox & Friends, Inc., 555, 698
Beauchamp, William C., 118
Beaudoin, Danielle Roy, 23, 583
Beck, Arthur, 55
Becker Bishop Studios, 125
Beeson, Chuck, 275
Begel, Julie, 798
Begley, Peter, 89
Behaeghel, Julian, 359
Bell, Lisa, 39
Beltran, Felix, 528
Benchmark, Inc., 406
Bender, Bob, 94
Bender, David, 100
Bender, Hickson, 95
Benes, Michael, 617
Benihana of Tokyo Inc., 393
Benoit, Judy, 439
Benstock, Bonni, 74, 154
Benton & Bowles, 51
Berg, John, 270
Berg, Linda, 127
Bergengron, Ake, 114, 170
Bergman, Beth, 271
Bergman, Louise, 517
Bergsoe 11/s, 392
Bergthold, Fillhardt & Wright, 125
Berk, Marvin, 132
Berkley Books, 246
Berman, Maira, 287
Bernard: Design, 614
Bernardin, James, 770
Bernie Barnett, 599
Bernitt, Mary K., 625
Berry Gross Inc., 523
Bertoli, Barbara, 261
Bescia, Colleen, 717
Besser, Rick, 418, 861
Bevil, Serge, 671
Bevins, Keith, 333, 334
B.F. Goodrich, 57, 143
B/H Productions, inc., 751
Biagi, Bill, 778
Bice, Paul, 418, 582, 589
Bick, Linda, 374
Bick, Ted, 374
Bieber, Tim, 167
Bierman, Kerry, 439
Big City Design, 652
Bill Blass, 13
Binder, Andrea, 531
Biotech Capital Corporation, 413
Birdsong, David, 535
Black Belt Karate, 580
Black & Decker Canada Inc., 765
Blair, Gail, 575
Blake, Charles, 137, 639
Blakemore, Lynn, 80
Blanch, Andrea, 9
Blank, Ronald M., 405
Blasutta, Mary Lynn, 486
Bleinberger, Stephen, 155
Bliss, Tony, 46
Bloch, Bruce, 56
Bloch, David, 408
Bloch Graulich Whelan Inc., 408
Block, Stuart, 149
Bloom Industrial Advertising, 115
Bloomingdale's, 352
Bloor Publishing, 295, 491
Bluebell Creameries, 339
Bluett, Sandra R., 657
Blum, Chris, 746
Blum, Connie, 75
Blumenthal, David, 236
Boa Design Inc., 615
Boating, 464
Bob Murray, 855
Bogerd, Rob, 660
Bokuniewicz, Carol, 274, 291, 552, 560, 651
Bollinger, Steve, 645
Bombay Gin, 50
Bonk, Cinda Katz, 367
Bonnell Design Associates, 667
Book-of-the-Month Records, 881
Boone, Joe, 176
Booth, Anne, 852
Borders, Perrin & Norrander Inc., 595
Borgen, Susan, 551, 584
Borin, Nancy, 625
Borrell, Peter, 251
Boucher, John, 209
Boussac of France, 120
Bowes/Hanlon Advertising, Inc., 751
Bowman, Lynne, 125
Bozell & Jacobs, 75, 757
Braids, Braldt, 821
Brakeley, John Price Jones, Inc., 711
Brand Management Pty. Ltd., 820
Brandsteder Electronics BV, 11
Brandt-Barringmann Inc., 135, 900
Brandtner, Al, 518
Branigan, John D., 189
Branson/IPC, 125
Brasch, Gary, 123
Brass Door Galleries Houston, 882
Bratt, Meredith G., 540
Braverman, Al, 459
Brazeal, Lee, 377
Brennan, Steve, 178, 387
Bresner, Stuart, 76, 328, 895
Brewer, Art, 8, 14
Brezden, Jurij, 40
Brickel Assoc. Inc., 122
Brier, David, 525
Brigham Young University, 134, 224, 832, 902
Bright & Associates, 363, 857
Bright, Keith, 857
Broderick, Edwards, 410
Bronstein, Steve, 31
Brooks, Joe, 809, 819
Brown, Alan L., 787
Brown, Christensen & Assoc. Ltd., 761
Brown, Christensen & Assoc. Ltd./New Zealand, 5
Brown, George E., 424
Brown, Lance, 339
Brown, Laura, 238
Brown, Leifer + Slatkin, 512, 587
Brown, Melissa, 879, 887
Brown & Rosner Inc., 166, 367, 787, 885

Brown, Tracy Ann, 730
Browning, Paul, 673
BRT, 208
Bruce, Dennis, 764
Bruce Kravetz, 383
Bruce, Sally Anderson, 88
Bruner-Johns, Sally, 477
Bruun, Claus, 392
Buber, Shelley, 719
Buchanan, Yvonne, 405
Bugbee, Robin A., 551, 584
Bullen, David, 268
Bulloch, Chris, 593
Bundzak, Bill, 565
Bunin, Elinor, 802
Burch, Harold, 585, 668, 892
Burch Myers Cuttle, Inc., 149, 640
Burch, Ralph, 149, 640
Burkart, Wayne, 300, 473
Burkhardt, Ron, 708
Burleigh, David, 26
Burns, Cooper, Hynes Ltd., 347, 522, 594, 673, 807, 818
Burns, Jerry, 110
Burns, M., 591
Burns, Robert, 522, 594, 673
Burson-Marsteller-Paris/France Cartes, 225
Burstein, Naomi, 415
Burton Advertising, 509
Busa, Kris, 663, 666
Bush, Gabby, 79
Butz, Roger, 334
By Design, 575

C

C. Genuzio/Myron Taplin, 186
Cabana, Seguin-Design Inc., 23, 429, 583
Cabarga, Leslie, 521
Cable Marketing Magazine, 465
Cadbury, Scheppes, Powell Inc., 769
Cadman, Larry, 780
Cahan, Catherine, 306, 483
Calderwood & Pieg, 854
Caldwell, Bill, 160
Calfo, Jason, 507, 697
California Dept. of Forestry, 788
California Dreamers, 901
California Film, 800
California Human Development Corp., 709, 880
Callahan, T.J., 163
Callaway, Peggy, 485
Camara 35, 843
Camargo-Weight Watchers, 84
Cambridge Oil Co., 523
Cameron, Janet, 309
Camp Assocs. Advertising Ltd., 46, 713, 791
Campbell, Peter, 671
Campbell-Ewald Co., 770
Campbell-Mithun, 73
Canadian General Electric, 766
Canadian/Schenley, 76, 328
Candemeres, Georgia, 478
Candie's International/El Greco, 772
Canniff, Bryan, 464
Canning, Bob, 758
Canon Copier, 749
Capezio Ballet Makers, Inc., 60
Carbarga, Leslie, 335
Cargill, Wilson & Acree, 771
Carl Mosander, 636
Carlin, Adrienne Y., 349
Carlton Centre Merchants Assn., 79
Carmen Amoras Cabrera, 557
Carmine, 603
Carnase, Inc., 507, 697
Carnase, Tom, 507
Carney, Jo Ann, 640
Carol Clayton & Associates, 520
Carolina Arts Magazine, 477
Carothers, David, 483
Carpelis, Irene, 467
Carr Liggett, 182, 840

Carr Liggett Inc., 126
Carroll, Phil, 278, 279, 281, 289
Carron Design, 326
Carron, Ross, 326
Carson, Charles, 247
Carson Pirle Scott & Co., 15
Carter, Bunny, 374
Carter, David E., 174
Carton y Papel de Mexico s.a. de C.V., 362
Cartwright, Reg, 11
Carugati, Eraldo, 292
Casado, Ralph, 700
Casthay Pacific Inflight Magazine 'Discovery,' 321
Castle, Thomas J., 836
Caswell-Massey Co. Ltd., 348
Cathay Pacific, 497
Cato Yasumura Behaeghel, 359
Cat's Paw Heel & Soles, 155
Cavanah, Earl, 780
Cavedo, Brent, 215
CBS Advertising & Design, 217
CBS Photo, 217
CBS Records, 97, 162, 270, 277, 285, 286
CBS Television Stations, 217
CCA Marketing Communications, 384
Cefadyl/(Bristol Laboratories), 387
Celander, Bob, 890
Celanese Corporation, 449
Celanese Fibers Mktg.Corp., 605
Celpa, 793
CEMA, 508
Le Centre Sheraton Montreal, 101
Ceremony Inc., 518
Chadwick, Marcia, 702
Chambers, Tom, 304
Champion International, 452
Chan, Maxi, 600
Chapman, Denise, 377
Characters, 222
Charbonnneau, Jim, 46
Charles Stark Draper Labs, Inc., 427
Chase Manhattan Bank N.A., 450
Chase, Steve, 745
Checkman, Sheryl, 435
Chen, James, 199
Chen, Peter, 710
Chenoweth Ellis & Faulkner, 136
Cheryl Lewin Design, 519, 634
Chesebrough-Pond's (Canada) Inc., 25
Cheung, Alice, 349
Chevrolet Motor Division, 770
Chiat Day, 38
Chicago International Film Festival, 158
Chicago Magazine, 292, 479, 816
Chicago Talent Inc., 301
Chirando, Rich, 180
Chou, Cathy, 836
Chris Fowler & Michael Stelzer, 658
Christensen, Anna Amabile, 574
Christensen, P.R., 5, 761
Christenson, Lyn, 430
Christer, Alm, 16
Christiansen, Jack, 112
Chrzanowski, Stan, 676
Chu, Hoi Ling, 505, 537
Chuldenko, John, 482
Chung, Cliff, 569
Church, Stanley, 631
Chust, Ramon, 44
Chwast, Seymour, 145, 254, 277
Ciba Geigy Canada Ltd., 764
Ciba Pharmaceuticals, 609
Ciba-Geigy, 90, 187, 632
Cicoil, 886
Cifu, Anne, 743
Cincinnati Enquirer Magazine, 312
Cinema Projects Inc., 573
Cipriani, Robert, 427

Citibank, 198, 419, 641, 715
Citizens Bank of Aurora, 850
City Slickers, 354
Clarity Coverdale Advertising, 599
Clark, Leslie Trinite, 900
Clemente, Tom, 159, 252
Cleveland, John, 404
Cleveland Plain Dealer Magazine, 814
Clifton, David, 194
Cline Inc., 164
Cobb, Laura, 679
Cobra Brass, 752
Coburn, Bob, 785, 789
The Coca Cola Company, 55
Coca-Cola USA, 635
Cocchini-Griefen, Angela, 712
Coderre, George, 150, 320, 480
Codex, 197
Coe, Sue, 811
Cohen, Fern H., 743
Cohen, Meryl, 800
Cohn, Ric, 20, 624
Cointreau America, 131
Cole-Haan, 65, 854
Collet, Bernard, 225
Collier, John, 62, 829
Collier, Terry, 664
Collins, Paul, 600
Colombian Coffee, 18, 105
Columbia Record & Tape Club, 70
Commercial Bank of Kuwait, 391, 423
Communications Design, 195, 629
The Company Store, 521
The Competition, 882
Comus Music Theatre, 522
Conceptual Resources, 91
Concord Watch Corp., 773
Congdon, Todd, 48
Conlon, Ann, 858
Connell, May & Stevenson Ltd., 782
Connolly, John, 114
Conran's, 634
Consolidated Cigar, 34
Consolidated Foods Corp., 581
Constance Kovar Graphic Design Inc., 675
Contarsy, Ron, 360
Continental Identification Products, 129
Continental Insurance, 146
Continental Tires West Germany, 28
Conwell, Joe, 110
Cook, Jamie, 219, 612
Cooke, Martin, 131
Cooney, Robert, 444, 649
Cooper & Beatty Ltd., 872
Cooper, Eckstut Assoc., 192
Cooper, Heather, 347, 807, 818
Cooper, Shawne, 84, 866
Cooper, Tony, 765
CooperVision Pharmaceuticals, 627
Copmpany, Paul Deur, 209
Coppins, Charlie, 182
Corbett, David, 259
Cordella, Andree, 889
Corfman, Stan, 484
Cornerstone Magazine, 309
Corning Designs, Ltd., 22, 333, 334
Coro, Ron, 271, 272, 273, 276, 280, 884
Corpcom, Inc., 396, 416
Corpcom Services, 449
Corporate Annual Reports, 409
Corporate Graphics Inc., 415, 433
Cortani, Brown, Rigoli, 112
Cortani, Roger M., 112
Corwin, Jeff, 711
Cos & Co. Hot Air Balloon Flights, 544
Coty, Inc., 737
Coupon, William, 863
Cousins Properties Inc., 110

Coverdale, Jac, 599
Cowart, Jerry, 512, 587
Cox, Jim, 38
Cox, Peggy, 774
Coy, John, 165, 327, 379, 633, 662
COY, Los Angeles, 165, 327, 379, 662
Crabtree & Evelyn, 347
Craft, Kinuko, 255, 825
Crafton Graphic Co., Inc., 201
Craig, John, 481
Crane, Ferris W., 354
Crawford, Elaine, 600
Crawford, Robert, 264
Cream Creative Services, 804
Creative Education, Inc., 156, 258
Creative Images Inc., 132
Creative Services, Inc., 436
Crestar Ltee., 356
Cricket Press, Inc., 663
Crifo, Paul, 163
Crockett-Hanzel, Linda, 284, 814, 831
Crofton, Chris, 103
Cromwell Paper, 86
Crosby, Bart, 581
Cruickshank, John, 766
Cuisine Magazine, 487
Culen-Eckrote, Susan, 627
Cullen, Jane, 431
Culpepper & Associates, 707
Culpepper, Jr., Robert J., 707
Cummins, Brian, 771
Cunningham, David, 340
Cuoio, 43
Currier, Geoff, 844
Curry, Tom, 816
Curtiss-Wright Corp., 405
The Curwen Press, 423
Cutshaw, Gregory, 517, 672
Cygnus, 74
CYRK Inc., 666

D

D Magazine, 475
Dadds, Jerry, 388
Dahlgren, Steven, 440
Dai Nippon Printing, 381
Daimler-Benz (S.A.), 591
Dall, Julian, 69
Dallas, Donald, 502
Dallas Power & Light Company, 774
Dallas Tomlinson & Assocs. (Pty) Ltd., 87, 502
D'Amanda, Kathy, 398
Dancer Fitzgerald Sample, Inc., 47, 142, 148
Danheiser, Diane, 701
Daniel K. Whitehurst, 794
Danielle Prosciutto, 186
Dankovich, Nick, 482
D'Arcy-MacManus & Masius, 792
Dare Foods Ltd., 77
Darilek, Jim, 490, 495, 815
David, Allen, 694
David Brier Design Works, 525
David E. Carter Corporate Communications, 174
David Olson Design, 566
David Torme Design, 430
David Wenman Associates, 10, 120
David Wright & Associates, 138
David/Joseph & Assoc., 735
Davidson, Bruce, 433
Davidson, Charles, 773
Davies & Oliver, Inc., 716
Davis, Bill, 909
Davis & Burton Contractors, Inc., 174
Davis, Curtis, 226
Davis, Ed, 298
Davis, Joseph, 308
Davis, Steve, 102
Davison Chemical, 388
Dawkins, Lee, 407

Day, Bob, 26, 324, 444
Dayton Typographic Service, 672
Dazey Products Inc., 767
de Harak, Rudolph, 189
De Krig Advertising, 588
de Lange, Jack, 71, 221, 371, 425, 620
De Plano, Marco, 613
De Zitter, Harry, 3, 873
Deahl, David, 300
Deborah Riley Photostylist, 896
Decena, Mark, 172, 235, 696
Decter, Naomi, 575
Deere & Company, 300, 473
DeGroat, Diane, 244
del Rio, Raul, 148
Della Femina, Travisano & Partners, Inc., 747
Della Torre, Jerry, 680
Della-Vedova, Rod, 295, 491
Denney, Jim, 720, 724
Denny, Don, 215
Dentsu Corp. of America, 74, 154, 749
DeSieno, John, 503
The Design Company, 541
The Design House Inc., 350
The Designory, 218
DeSpigna, Tony, 239
Despo, Karen, 617
Detroit Renaissance, 130
Deutsche Shell AG, Hamburg, 547
Dever, Jeffrey L., 494
Devino, Anthony, 478
Devino, Frank M., 455
Devlin, Tom, 1
DeZitter, Harry, 30
Di Giorgio Corporation, 434
Diagnostics & Designs Inc., 369
Diamond Art Studio Ltd., 573
Diana Garcia de Tolone Design, 524
Dicianni, Ron, 311
Dick Davis, 543
Dick Lopez Inc., 849
Dickinson, Chuck, 799
Dickson, Nigel, 769
DiDonato, Josephine, 162
Dieler, Stephen, 33
Diener/Hauser/Bates, 163
Different Points of View Restaurant, 597
Diggs, Eric, 222, 414
Digital Equipment Corporation, 617
Dila, George, 850
Dillingham, Jerry, 822
Dillon, Leo & Diane, 261
Dillon Read & Co., Inc., 407
DiLorenzo, Barbara, 851
Dimke, Hans-Peter, 469
Dingus McGee's, 629
Dipak, S.A., 524
Disario, George, 440
Diseno y Communicacion SA, 548
Dispenza, Emil, 26
Dividend Development Corp., 172
Dixon, Maynard, 299
DLS Communications BV, 71, 221, 371, 425, 620
Doherty, Kathy, 758, 872
Dolby, John, 100, 168
Dollens, Dennis, 27, 119, 229
Dolphin Productions, 757, 784, 797
Don Sparks Photography, 205
Donald, Chuck, 629
Donghia, 2
Donovan & Green, 122, 192, 208
Donovan, Michael, 122
Donovan, Mike, 462
Doremus Design, 909
Doret, Michael, 335, 904
Dorfman, Bob, 355
Dorfsman, Lou, 217
Dorger, Helmut, 785
Dorr-Oliver Inc., 82, 875

Douglas & Barry (Pty) Ltd., 69, 868
Douthwalte, John W., 877
Dovianus, Joep, 660, 670
Dow Jones & Company, Inc., 412
Downer, Gregory, 322, 474
Downey, Mike, 346
Doyle Dane Bernbach, 18, 84, 89, 105, 106, 598, 715, 768, 866
Dr. Pepper, 736
Drake Hotel, Chicago, 73
Drennan, Fran, 382
Dresser Industries, 123
Duckworth, Nancy, 460, 812
Dudash, Michael, 250
Dudeck, Diane F., 437
Duevell, Bill, 626
Duevell, William, 626
Duffy, Richard, 175
Dugan, Joan, 88
Duke, Dana, 407
Dunn, Carol L., 394
Dunne, Jr., W. Michael, 817
Duofold, 827
Dupey, Ken, 355
Durham Industries Inc., 373
Durrance, Dick, 48
Dutra, Maura, 746

E

Earl Lyon, 565
Earle, Lee, 787
Earley, Mare, 898
Eastman, Alan, 723
Eberlein, Robert, 755
Eckstein, Arthur, 905
Ed Gallucci/Freelance Photographer Guild, 609
Edelstein, David, 625
Edelstein-Borin Advertising, 625
The Editings Exchange, 778
Edwards, Andy, 30, 868
Edwards, Graham, 362
Edwards, Greg, 431
Edwards, Toppy, 864
Edwin, Randye E.K., 373
E.F. Hutton, 616, 876
E.F. Hutton Life, 834
Eggerding, Marty, 312
Egol, Len, 875
Ehrenstrahle Co. Ltd., 114, 170
Eickmeyer, John, 763
Eisaman, Johns & Laws, 778
Eiseman, Jr., Fred B., 321
Eisenman & Enock Inc., 27, 119, 229
Eisenman, Stanley, 27, 119, 229
Eisenstaedt, Alred, 48
Ekberg, Gunnar, 212
Electro Rent Corporation, 418
Elektra/Asylum Records, 271, 272, 273, 276, 280, 884
Elfenbein, Paul, 413
Elfwendahl, Tord, 389
Eli Lilly, 433
Eli Lilly Dista Products, 83
Elinor Bunin Productions, Inc., 802
Emmi, Frank, 626
Emphasis (Hong Kong) Ltd., 321, 497
Empire State Plaza Convention Center, 503
Eng, Ed, 462
Engel, Mort, 163
Engh, Barbeau, 172
Engle, Bob, 315
Enhammer, Gosta, 212
Enterprise, 367
Enterprise Advertising, 664
Enterprise Press/Smithsonian, 378
Entheos, 260
Entree Magazine, 898
EPSCO Incorporated, 402
Dr. Ernest Nagamatsu, 637
Escobedo, Louis, 329
Escobedo, Michael, 509

Eskind Waddell, 401
Essence Magazine, 472, 883
Esser, Thomas, 683, 813
Esserman, N., 771
Ethier, Robert, 429
Eucalyptus Tree, 388
EUE Screen Gems, 770
Eugster, Alfred, 799
Evans, Garber & Paige Inc., 358, 665, 827
Evans, John, 788
Expertype Inc., 898
Exxon Chemical, 462
Eye Institute of New Jersey, 500

F

Faber-Castell, 807
Faberge, 741
Fahlgren & Ferris, 779
Fairchild, Paul, 437
Famuliner, Cathy L., 213
Famuliner, Jody, 213
Fantasy Records, 279, 281
Farr Company, 398
Farrell, Bill, 849
Farrelly, Frank, 50
Favara, Len, 2, 13, 775
Fay, Sue, 781
Faye, Ming, 497
Fazio, Joseph, 99
Fearon O'Leary, 152
Feigenbaum, Bill, 798
Feigenbaum, Joe, 697
Feigenbaum Productions, 798
Fellerman, Stan, 618
Felsen, Sidney B., 165
Ference, Richard M., 462
Ferguson, Rick, 822
Ferrari, Stephen, 407
F.H. Hayhurst Co. Ltd., 25
Fiberglas Canada Inc., 401
Fibre etc. Weaving Guild, 534
Ficho & Corley, 340
Field Museum, 792
Fieldmark Media Inc., 323
Fifty Fingers Inc., 151, 451, 653
Filho, Oswaldo Mendes, 793
Fili, Louise, 237
Filicori, Mauro, 324
Filicori Visual Communications, Inc., 324
Filitalli/Film Stable, 499
Fill, Louise, 264
Fillhardt, Charles, 125
Film Consortium, 771
Filmways Pictures, 795
The Filmworkshop, 760
Finch, Pruhn & Company, Inc., 669
Fine Geffen Simkins & Marrington, 17, 873
Finn, William F., 806
Finnish Marketing Federation, 867
First L.A. Bank, 404
Fiscal Agency for the Farm Credit Banks, 397
Fischer, Carl, 6
Fisher, Al, 43, 65, 204, 427, 854
Fisher, Doug, 94, 376
Fitch, Steve, 281
Flaherty, Jim, 50
Flannery, Catherine, 427
Flesch, John A., 338
Flesher, Vivienne, 830
Flood, Brian, 617
Flora, Robert, 493
Florville Design & Analysis, 562, 654
Florville, Patrick, 562, 654
Fluor Corporation, 453
Flynn, Elizabeth A., 907
Focar, Mike, 419, 641
Fodor's Travel Guides, 259
Foerstal, Tom, 164
Foley, Nancy, 726
Fontecha Tajon, Edward, 595
Footwear News Magazine, 298, 476
Fordyce, Randy, 525

Foreman, Michael, 391
Forgione International Confections, 856
Foriotte, Nicolas, 465
Forman, Joan, 836
Formento Cultural Banamex A.C., 223
Forsythe, Kathy, 384
Fortier, Bob, 750, 769
Fosshag, Bengt, 316
Foster, Richard, 686, 692, 705
Foti, Al, 469, 910
Fotouhi Alonso Inc., 803
The Foundation of the Dramatists Guild, 132
Fountain, Michael, 335
Four Leaf Towers, 62
Foutouhi Alonso, Inc., 411
Fox, Brian D., 698
Fox, Kara, 555
Fox River Paper Company, 390, 621
France, Jeff, 748, 781
Frank Glickman, Inc., 852
Frank, Howard, 874
Freeland, Bill, 712
Freeman, Huenick, Zilbert Inc, 390
Freeman,a Huenink, Zilbert Inc. (Staff), 621
Freese & Friends, Inc., 778
Freis, Jay, 404
French Advertising Inc., 605
French, Helaine, 605
French, Lanny, 625
Freyer, Tom, 47
Frick, Rosslyn, 487
Fried, Richard, 108
Friedland, Jim, 332
Friedlander, Ernie, 696
Frieza, Jay, 430
Frinta, Dagmar, 237, 463, 634, 810
Frolick, Stuart I., 452
Fromowitz, Mike, 769
Frost & Associates, 577
Frost & Buchholz Graphic Design, 577
Frost Lighting Co., 586
Frost-Buchholz, Tricia & Bill, 577
Frye-Sills Inc., 54
Frykholm, Stephen, 129, 422
Fryrear, Sandra, 718
Fuchs, Bernie, 51
Fujitsu Kogyo Inc., 350
Furman, Michael, 118
Fury, Jerry, 599

G

G. Anderson Advertising, 745
GAF Broadcasting Inc., 454
Gahr, David, 162
Gair, Alan, 77
Galarneau, Deaver & Sinn, 899
Galaxy Records, 278
Galbraith, Ford, 595
Galerie Nina Dausset, 542
Gallagher Group, Inc., 701
Gallagher & Morton, 663
Gallo, Susan B., 476
Gamache, John, 440
Gamma One, 72
Gandy, Skip, 464
Garber, Ira, 36
Garberr, Thomas, 358
Garcia de Tolone, Diana, 524
Garcia-Luna, Jose A., 223
Garland, Albert N., 317
Garland, Michael, 307
Garner, Anthony, 894
Garns, G. Allen, 812
Garrett/Lewis/Johnson Inc., 110, 694
Garrido, Hector, 373
Garvey, Becky Adolphson, 171
Gassy, Robert, 820
Gatie, John, 677
Gauger, David, 141, 172, 235, 696

Gauger Sparks Silva, Inc., 141, 172, 235, 696
Gay, C., 591
Gear, 203
Geering, Martha, 288, 458
Geldutis, Audrey, 615
Gellen, Alex, 579
Gemini G.E.L., 165
Gene Bradford Design, 886
Genentech, Inc., 424
General Business Corp.(Pty) Ltd., 502
General Electric Company, 361
Generra, 625
Genrad, Inc., 446
Gentry, Don, 172
Geo Vann, 115
George de Gennaro Studio, 633
George E. Browne & Associates, 424
Georgia Museum of Art, 707
Gerage, Ann Marie, 718
Gerber Advertising, 776
Gerber, Stefan, 800
Gersin, Robert P., 361
Gersten & Meyers Inc., 330
Gerstner, John, 473
Geurts, Arie J., 366, 406
GGK-Dusseldorf, 153
GGK/Germany, 28
Giambattista, Gerry, 529
Gianninoto Associates, 345
Giant Eagle, 40
Gibb, Wayne D., 709, 880
Gifford, Lew, 799
Giglio, Tony, 843
Gilbert, Bari, 731
Gililland, Ed, 540
Gillette Espanola, 370
Gillis, Vickle, 31
Gioffre, Rocco, 460
Giordano, Vinny, 786, 795
Gipple, Patricia, 302, 489
Gips + Balkind + Associates, 152, 431, 536
Gips, Philip, 431
Gipson, Gwen, 734
Girvin, Tim, 195
Giuccione, Tony, 455
Glaser, Byron, 156
Glaser, Milton, 62, 159, 248, 314
Glasheen Advertising, 357
Glasheen, Pete, 357
Glenmore Distilleries, 895
Glickman, Frank, 852
The Gloucester Group, 77, 764
Goedicke, Hans, 11, 52
Goes Photography, 688
Goes, William R., 688
Gold, Charles, 858
Goldberg, Irwin, 741
Goldenberg, Carol, 244
Goldsholl Associates, 194
Goldsholl, Morton, 194
Goldsmith, Gary, 715, 768, 866
Goldstein, Dan, 47
Golob, Stanford, 189, 909
Gomes de Lima, Deilon, 44
Gomez, Ignacio, 142
Good Housekeeping Magazine, 859
Good, Jan, 397
Good Morning America-ABC-TV, 728
Goodman, John, 844
Gordon Meyer, 691
Gottlieb, Paul, 765
Gove, Geoffrey, 910
Gov't. of the Northwest Territories, 395
Grace Jones, 828
Grace Kent Sage Inc., 772
Grade A Graphics, 383
Graham, Bill, 168
Graham, Diana, 152, 536
Graham, John, 838
Graham-Solano/Boston, 838
Graphic Comm., 224
Graphic Communications-B.Y.U., 134
The Graphic Expression, Inc., 407

Graphic Solutions, Inc., 227
Graphics 3, Inc., 619
Graphics Plus, 446
The Graphics Studio, 711
Graphics West Inc., 676
Graphoons, 776
Graulich, Irwin N., 408
Great Faces, 900
Greek Accent, 841
Green-Armytage, Stephen, 409
Greenberg, Richard, 786, 795
Greene, Joy, 67, 207
Greenfield, Lois, 60, 489
Greengage Associates, Inc., 37
Greenspun, Mark, 205
Gregg Div. McGraw Hill Book Co., 253
Gregorowski, Sue, 346, 868
Greig, Art, 618
Greiman, April, 320
Greltzer, Mark, 623
Gremmler, Paul, 168
Grey Advertising, 57
Grey Phillips, Bunton, Mundel & Blake, 3, 53, 777
Greysandton, 79, 752
Grid Systems Corporation, 511
Griffin, Brian A., 655
Griffiths, Ken, 114. 170
Grillo, Oscar, 782
Grimes, Melissa, 815
Grimm, Linda, 447
Grimmett, Douglass, 92, 652
Grindeland, Bob, 661
Grohe, Stephen, 617
Gross, Cy, 457
Gross Townsend Frank, Inc., 627, 784
Grossman, Michael, 294, 810
The Ground Up, 550
Group W Cable, 907
La Groupe D'Animation Urbaine de Montreal Inc., 583
Gruen, John, 263
Grumman Energy Systems Co., 180
Grumman Flxible Corp., 840
Grupo Chihuahua, 638
Grupo Industrial Alfa, 835
Guedes, Omar, 24
Guerard, James, 453
Guerts, Arie J., 590
Gulf Canada, 451
Gullstrand, Marten, 212
Guma Rubber Footwear Ltd., 506
Gunn Associates, 169, 402, 889
Gunsaullus, Marty, 400
Gustafson, Denys, 536
Gutman, Harry, 202, 386, 445
Guy Romain A.I.A., 562

H

H & T Manufacturing, 700
Haagen Printing, 716
Haber, Merrill, 266
Haberman, Daniel, 669
Haboush Productions, 763
Hackett, Dan, 40
Haddon, B., 591
Haft, Harris, 357
Hagger Slacks, 763
Hakkinen, Olavi, 16
Hale, Butch, 438
Haligman, Matt, 598
Hall, Edyce, 185, 842
Hall, Joan, 283
Hall, Ken, 236
Hall Pontiac, 781
Hallakorpi, Arto, 636
Halpin, Denise, 543
Halt, James, 604
Hamel, Diane J., 602
Hammermill Paper Co., 604
Hammermill Papers Grp., 108
Hammond Farrell Inc., 104, 116
The Handler Group, Inc., 648
Handler, Mark L., 648
The Hanley Partnership, 144, 904

Hannibal Records, 274
Hans Gelden Hairstylist, 71
Hanson, Warren, 900
Harbor, Don, 80, 183
Harcomm Assocs., 204
Harcourt Brace Jovanovich, 242
Hardin, Russell, 147
Harold Danko, 525
Haroutiun, Georges, 295, 491
Harper's Bazaar, 493
Harper's Magazine, 293
Harris & Harris Ltd., 578
Harris, Ronald G., 294
Harrison, Peter, 426
Harry Knox & Associates, 494
Harry Murphy & Friends, 341, 533
Harry Viola Advertising, 773
Hart, David G., 544
Harter Corp., 94
Hartig, Karl, 416
Hartzell, Dave, 126
Harvey, Ross M., 395
Harwell, Barbara, 554
Hastretler, Kim, 855
Hausman, George, 606
Haven, Paul Randolph, 14
Hawk-James, Charma, 15
Haworth, Bob, 115
Haworth, Inc., 209
Hawton, Bob, 25
Hayes, Geoffrey, 50
Hayes, Pat, 541
Haymes, Richard, 650
Hayward, Bill, 474
HBM Design Group, 197, 432, 677
HBO National Sales & Planning, 227
The Hearst Corp., 459
Hearst Publishing, 467
Hecht's, 147
Heckman, Gordon, 262
Hedrich-Blessing, 194
Heid, Patti, 495
Heimall, Bob, 290
Heindel, Bob, 827
Heindel, Robert, 417
Heintzman, Tim, 46, 713
Held, Rainer, 64
Heller, Cheryl, 197, 432, 677
Heller, Shelley, 57, 143
Hellman Design, 781
Hellmuth, James, 205
Hemmer, William, 136
Henry Reeves & Associates, 889
Henry Wolf Productions, 236, 305
Henschel, K.W., 316
Hep Cats, 855
Heritage Bank, 535
Herlin, Robert M., 619
Herman, Del, 367
Herman Miller, Inc., 422, 879, 887
Hermsen Design Associates, 329
Hermsen, Jack, 329, 501
Hern, Robert, 340
Heron, Joseph, 560
Herst, Hans, 833
Hess, Richard, 319, 339, 452
Heyert, Elizabeth, 201
Hicks & Greist, 759
Hickson-Bender, 94
Higashi, Sandra, 196, 258
Higbee, Bob, 1
Hildmann Simon Rempen & Schmitz, 64
Hill, Chris, 403
Hill, John, 431
Hill & Knowlton Inc., 211
Hill, Roger, 77, 295
Hills, Ron, 46, 664
Hillsborough County Aviation Authority, 403
Hilton International, 1, 858
Hine, Kenneth R., 882
Hines, John, 438
Hinsche & Associates, 453
Hinshaw, Kirk, 148

Hirano, Makooto, 749
Hiro, 493
Hirth, Russ, 126, 182, 840
Hively, Charles, 96, 123, 145, 339
H.L. Chu & Company Ltd., 505, 537
HLR/BBDO, 16, 210, 214, 232
HLR/BBDO, Artillerigatan, 231
Hoar, Charlie, 677
Hochbaum, Susan, 426
Hodgson, Paul, 151, 653, 826
Hodowsky, Steve, 198
Hoechst Fibers Industries, 61
Hoffman, Dave, 85
Hoffman, Steven, 249, 468
Hoffmann, Bob, 541
Hogg, Clyde, 751
Hoglund, Rudy, 305
Holiday Inn, 890
Holland Advertising Inc., 372
Holland, Christopher, 372
Hollander, Richard, 742
Holloway, Bill, 495
Hollywood Presbyterian Medical Center, 711
Holmes, Andrew, 296, 804
Hols Donatin Krachtbrokken, 63
Holtzman Gallery, Towson State University, 817
Homemaker's Magazine, 471
Homestake Mining Company, 417
Hon, Mel Po, 450
Honda, Ray, 511
Hopkins, Christopher, 78
Hornall, John, 593
Horner, Jack, 192
Horowitz, Ryszard, 61
Horvers, John, 141, 235
Hosaka, Mitsutochi, 381
Hotel Barmen's Association, 381
Hotel Europe, 72
Houghton Mifflin Company, 244
Housel Precision, Inc., 585
Housing Magazine, 308
Houston Natural Gas, 853
Howard, Carl, 665
Howard, Merrell & Boykin, 102
Hrynkow, Ray, 492
Hucknell, Nanette, 527
Huerta, Jerard, 639
Hugel, Rob, 879, 887
Huggett, Tony, 391, 423
Hughes, Mark, 18, 84, 105, 106
Hul-Uy, Bon, 192
Hundred Arrows Press, 299
Hunt, Jim, 701
The Huntley Hotel, 515
Hurst Printing, 894
Hutchins Y & R, 628
Hutt, Pat, 104
Huyck Formax, 822
Hyatt Regency Kansas City, 869
Hyland, Kathleen, 430
Hylton, John, 62
Hyma, Dan, 564

I

Iacobucci, Marci, 73
Iannaccone, Thomas, 476
IBM, 200
IBM World Trade, 179
Idaho Potato Commission, 164
Ide, Toshiaki, 254
I.F. Studios, 801
Iles, Terrance, 750
Illustrations Done, 655
The Images Film Company B.V., 762
Imahara & Keep Advertising, 687
Industry Week Magazine, 482
Infantry Magazine, 317
Ingersoll-Rand, 100, 168
Ingham, Tom, 805
Inouye, Carol, 255
Inouye, Yosh, 12
Inspeech Inc., 889
Institute of Trichology, 369

Intercon, 570
Intermarco Advertising, 131
Intermedics, Inc., 184
International Communications Agcy., 160
International Harvester, 176
International Legends, Inc., 582
Inventive Eye Ltd., 270
Inverness Int. Corp., 365
Ireland, Charles, 333, 334
Irion, Mitchell, 514
Iris Studios, 683, 813
Irving Bank Corporation, 399
Irwin Co., 95
Irwin, Laurie, 778
Izu, Kenro, 74, 864A

J

J & J Typography, 46
J. Walter Thompson, 19, 49, 340, 521
J. Winn/Powell, 349
Jaben, Seth, 468
Jack Lenoir Larsen, 202
Jackson, David, 428
Jackson, Herbert, 306
Jacobs & Gerber, 800
Jacob's Pillow Dance Festival, 666
Jacobs, Ray, 800
Jacoby, Konstantin, 153
Jaffee, Lee Ann, 307
Jakobson, Jonette, 243
James Garrett & Ptrs., 740, 752
James, Glen, 17
James McLoughlin Photography, 4
James Orlandi & Assoc., 413
Jann Church Adv. & Graphic Design, 531
Janu, Rudolph, 667
Jay, Alex, 241
J.B. Rogers Co., 877
J.D.N. Estudio de Fotografia S/C Ltda, 24
Jeanmard, Jerry, 377
Jeff Babitz Graphics, 314
Jefferies, C. Claudia, 400
Jefferies, Ron, 400
The Jeffries Association, 400
Jenks, David, 593
Jennie & Co., 772
Jensen, Lorre, 769
Jensen, Michael, 141
Jenssen, Buddy, 323
Jerrild, Asger, 386, 445
Jerry Cowart Design, 587
Jerry Pavey Design Studio, 397
Jett, Edward, 219, 612
Jewish Reconstruction Foundation, 527
Jim Novotny Design, 680
J.L.C. Enterprises, 592
JLO, 546
The J.M.Smucker Company, 435
Joel Goldstein Marketing Communications, 633
Johansson, Johnny, 190
John Anselmo Design Assoc., 515
John Casado Design, 148
John Cleveland Inc., 404
John H. Harland Co., 219
John Helney & Associates,Inc., 399
John Hornall Design Works, 569, 593
John J. Harland Co., 535, 612
John M. Alexander-Barre Adv., 199
John Paul Itta,Inc., 21, 737, 753, 783
John Waters Associates,Inc., 405, 447
John Weitz for Palm Beach, 35
John Wiley & Sons Inc., 251
Johnson, Bill, 286
Johnson & Johnson, 6
Johnson & Johnson, Orthopaedic, 118
Johnson, V. Courtlandt, 156
Johnson, Zsuzsa, 107
Johnston, Skip, 498
Jones, Arnold, 167
Jones, C., 591
Jones, Lou, 852
Jones, Mark, 511
Jones, Reginald, 434
Jonson Pedersen Hinrichs & Shakery, 412, 488
The Joseph Dixon Crucible Company, 355
Joseph, Douglas, 589, 848
Joseph, Maurice, 3443
Jowill Woodman, 681
Joyce, Nell, 782
Joyce, Tom, 794
J.P.U.S.A. Graphics, 309
Juhasz, George, 337
Just Imagine, 160
J.W. Morris Wineries, 326

K

Kabl Group, Inc., 88
Kaein, Henry, 221
Kaem, Henry, 425
Kaeser & Wilson Design Ltd., 378, 616
Kahn, Ina, 61
Kah-Nee-Ta, 595
Kainins, Mara, 808
Kaiser, Dick, 139
Kaiser Permanente Federal Credit Union, 195
Kaiser, Ursula, 471
Kalayjian, Vasken, 137, 639
Kaldewel West Germany, 64
Kalman, Tibor, 274, 287, 291, 560, 651
Kalomirakis, Theodore, 841
Kamarowsky,Leonid, 316
Kamasa Tools Ltd., 114
Kaminski, C., 591
Kane, John, 568, 699
Kao & Kao Associates, 878
Kao, Kelly, 613, 878
Kara Fox, 555
Kasica & Brown, Inc., 146
Kaska, Kathleen Sullivan, 367, 885
Kaskin, Ken, 594
Kate Communications, Inc., 648
Kathleen & Robert Kaska, 885
Katsui, Mitsuo, 381
KATU TV2 Portland, Oregon, 726
Katz, Arnold, 251
Kaufman,Lansky, Baker, 834, 907
Kaufmann, Dieter, 745
Kazal,Larry, 274, 552
KECH 22 TV Salem, Oregon, 727
Keenan,Larry, 111, 268, 424
Keithley, Jim, 771
Keller, Bjorn, 214
Kelley, Karen, 840
Kellogg Salad Canada Inc., 758
Kellog's, 340
Kemper, George, 462
Ken Dupey Graphics, 355
Ken White Design Office, Inc., 585, 668, 892
Kenetics, 778
Kennedy, Michael, 629
Kent, Mark, 43, 65, 854
Kernan, Sean, 72
Kessler, Chuck, 778
Kieffer-Nolde, Inc., 149
Kim & Gifford Prods., Inc., 799
Kim, Paul, 799
Kimball, Orin, 627
Kimberly Clark (Mexico), 366
Kimmich & Company, 88
Kines, Ken, 183
King, Bill, 846
Kirk, Sharon, 890
Kirkley, Kent, 490
KISS/FM, 797
Klanderman, Leland, 135

Klein, 796
Klein & Co., 587
Klein, Howard R., 323
Klemm, Horst, 79
Klose, Stanton, 341
Kneapler, John, 656
Knudsen, 861
Kobor, Anne D., 177, 864
Koenders,Louis, 30
Koepke, Gary, 427
Koke, Carl, 439
Koliha, Ron, 625
Kollenbaum,Louise, 319, 458, 811
Kominklyke Wessanen B.V., 425
Komnenich, John, 787
Kondo, Yukio, 146
Koninklijke Verkade Fabrieken B.V., 762
Koslow, Ed, 144
Koster, Barbara, 481, 862
Kostiainen, Ilmari, 188
Kosunen, Jorma, 32, 45, 59
Kovar, Constance, 675
Krackehl, Gene, 610
Krajewski, Ed, 770
Krimstein, Jordan, 73
Krimston, Wayne, 325
Kroutel, Pat, 216
Krystal Restaurants, 771
KSTP-FM, 900
Kubly, John, 33
Kuchera, John, 628
Kuiper, Bart, 42, 63, 296, 760, 762
Kuleba, Jerry, 664
Kunstschule Alsterdamm Hamburg, 547
Kuper Hands (Pty)Ltd., 69, 740
Kutza, Michael, 158
KVH/GGK International BV, 11, 52
KXAS-TV News, 721
Kymmene Star, 873
Kyosti Varis/VPV Oy, 133, 220
Kyser Industrial Corporation, 167

L

Labatt Brewing Company Limited, 23
Laboratorio de Diseno y Analisis de Mercado-CPM, 638
LaBounty, James, 492
Lacher, Roland, 153
LaCosta Products International, 364
Lacroix, Pat, 466
Ladendorf Bros., 885
LaGuardia College, 712
Lake, Harry, 791
Lallamant, Robert, 607
Lally, John, 603
Lally, McFarland & Pantello, 603
Lamothe, Jim, 262
Land, Sea & Air Development Corp., 516
Landes, Les L., 394
Landsberg, Steven, 89, 105, 106
Langerman, Stephen, 435
Langley, Stephen, 155
Lansdowne Marketing, 391, 423
Lantagne, Suzanne, 161
Lappen, Arlene, 498
Larcher, Jean, 542, 891
LaRocca, Jerry, 171
Larry Paine & Associates, 557
Larry Paine & Associates Design Studio, 657
Laser Beam Sweatsuits, 743
Laszio, 343
LaTaste-Odim, 891
Lathem, Charles, 438
Latino Americana Seguros S.A., 504
Lattari, Tony, 478
Laubach, Rainer, 57
Laurent, Christor, 170
Laurentano, Michael, 201
Laurie Rosenwald, 903
Lawhead Press, 216

Lawler Ballard Advertising, 80, 183, 748, 781
Lawrence, Diane, 273
Leber Katz, 624
Leber Katz Partners, 20
Lederer, Joe, 337
Lee, Chris, 182
Lee, Edward, 194
Lee, Jared, 104
Lee King & Partners, 86
The Lee Music Center, 559
Lee, Raymond, 12, 98
Leeds, Martin, 624
Lehigh/Autoscreen, 253
Leidel, Michael, 535
Leigh Memorial Hospital, 183
Leighton, Edward, 82
Leighton, Michele, 8
Leland Music, 368
Leo Burnett Company Ltd., 758, 872
Leo Castelli Gallery, 650, 847
Leober, Marie, 623
Leonard G. Styche & Assoc. Inc., 718
Leonhard, Colleen, 130
Leppert, Robert N., 382
Leslie Priggen, 690
Lesniewicz, Terry, 206, 508, 611
Lesniewicz/Navarre, 206, 508, 611
Less, Michael, 248
Lester, Steven, 39
Lever Brothers, 19
Levi Strauss, 746
Levin, Diane, 533
Levine, Joan, 47
Levine, Marian, 728
Levine, Steve, 132
Levitan, Rachel Schreiber, 166
Levitsky, Leonard, 238
Levy, Stan, 91
Lewin, Cheryl, 203, 519, 634
Lewin, Gideon, 13
Lewis, Sheldon, 553
Leyko, Rob, 372
Liberty Life, 868
Liberty Magazine, 494
Lieberman, Archie, 840
Lieberman, Jerry, 180
Liebert, Victor, 61
Lienhart, Jim, 304
Light, Ken, 709, 880
Light, White, 121, 179
Limbos, Pelayia, 311
Lincoln Mercury Division, 29, 754
Linda Crockett-Hanzel, 831
Lindgren, Torbjorn, 231, 232
Lindholm, Kaj G., 220, 714
Linton, David J., 441
Liska & Associates, 539, 896
Liska, Steven, 539, 896
LithoArt, 618, 864A
Litografos Unidos S.A., 638
Litton Business Furniture, 208
Lizotte, David, 169, 402
Llewellyn, Robert, 839
Lloyd, Susan, 56
Loebas H.M.C. Oosterbeek, 660, 670
Loeser, Judith, 239, 257
Loft, Peter, 735
Logan, David W., 580
Long Machinery, 171
Loomis, Richard, 665, 827
Lopes, David, 432
Lopez, Bret, 857
Lopez, Dick, 558, 849
Lord, Geller & Einstein, 858
Lord, Geller, Federico, Einstein, 1, 22
Lord, Sullivan & Yoder Adv., 94, 95, 376
Lorenz, Al, 152
Lou Grasso & Associates, 343
Louis, 844
Louis Benito Advertising, 403
Love, Reg, 607
Lovinger Tardio Melsky, 790
Lower, William, 750
Lowy, Patricia, 253

LTX, 169
Lubalin, Peckolick Assoc., 530, 835, 865
Lucci, John, 736
Lucka, Klaus, 743
Luckett & Slover Inc., 93
Ludwig, Gary, 653
Lund, Jack, 479
Luther and Pedersen, Inc., 166
Luyk Advertising, 717
Lynch, Kim, 820
Lynn Hollyn Associates, 265

M

M & Co., 92, 274, 287, 291, 552, 560, 651
Macdonald, Holland S., 97
Macina, Michael, 749
MacKinnon, Mark, 364
Maclaren Advertising, 766
MacLean, Alex, 852
Macmilan, Inc., 431
Maender, Rich, 55
M.A.G. Graphics Ltd., 295, 491
Magleby,McRay, 224, 832
Magowan, J.D., 777
Mahalanobis, Deb, 286
Maisel, Jay, 123
Makstaller, Jim, 406
Malcolm, Andy, 161
Mald, Lanca, 7
Malignon, Jacques, 233
Malish, Miro, 103
Manarchy, Dennis, 301
Mango, Joseph J., 143
Manheim, M., 398
Manigault, Richard K., 888
Mann, Bob, 769
Mansfield, Bruce, 748
Manufacturers National Bank, 66
Mara Kainins, 808
Marathon World, 484
Marbeth, 489
Marc O'Polo, 231
Marco, Phil, 109
Marge, Elias, 330
Margulies, Joel, 226
Marin Swim School, 553
Mark Color, 333, 334
Mark Wood & Associates, 344
Marketing Plus, 833
Marks, Elizabeth, 567
Marrington, Chris, 17, 873
Marshall, Diana, 218
Marshall III, Frank B., 454
Marshall, Lee, 648
Marshall, Richard, 786
Marshall, Roy, 717
Marshutz, Roger, 411
Martel, Ed, 763
Martex/West Point Pepperell, 201
Martin, Bill, 791
Martin, Doug, 769
Martin, Eva, 210, 214
Martin, John, 151
Marty Umans, 685
Marvy, Jim, 54
Maryland National Bank, 414
Maslen, Barbara, 243
Maslowski, Karl & Steve, 485
Massachusetts Port Authority, 852
Massey, Susan, 862
Massport, 432
Mathieu, Gerfen & Bresner, Inc., 76, 128, 328, 895
Matsumoto, Kenji, 418
Matsuno, Mark, 555
Matsushita, Yutaka, 350
Matsuura, T., 639
Matusek, Gary, 73
Mau, Bruce, 451
May, Doug, 697
Mayer, Roman, 798
Mayfair Sales, 17
Mayo, Donna M., 382
Mazurkiewicz, Vic, 693
The McCall Pattern Co., 478
McClain, Wilson, 434

McConnell, Keith, 344
McCormick & Co., Inc., 602
McDonald, James A., 107
McDonald & Little, 55, 704
McDougall, Cathy A., 382
McFarland, Jim, 603
McGinley, Marie, 204
McGinnis, George, 538
McGovern, Charles, 82
McGrath, David, 710
McGraw-Hill Book Co., 247, 266
McGregor Hosiery Mills, 12
McIntyre, John, 713, 791
McIntyre, Loren, 851
McKay, Donald N., 608
McKay, Jeffrey, 35
McKenna, Donald J., 394
McKenna, Mark, 80
McKim Advertising, 337
McKinney, Andrew, 437
McLean, Wilson, 809
McLeod, Bill, 46
McLoughlin, Wayne, 315
McMacken, David, 144
McMahon, Mike, 183
McMullan, James, 62, 276
McNamara Assocs., 130, 143
McNamara Studio, 57
McNeil, Ted, 109
MD Magazine, 469, 910
Measer, David, 604
Media Production, 836
Medical Economics for Surgeons, 313
Medical Laboratory Observer, 470
Medina, Fernando, 370, 510
Medisan, 232
Mednick, Seymour, 107, 644
Meir, Colin, 52
Melillo, Nick, 303
Melitta Inc., 330
Mel's Lithoplate Service, 688
Melsky, Barney, 790
Memoli, Anthony J., 592
Mendenhall Jones & Leistra, 167
Mendes Filho, Oswaldo, 526
Mendes Publicidade, 526, 793
Merck Pharmaceuticals, 346
Merle Norman Cosmetics, 738
Merrill Lynch, 613
Metropolitan Structure, 194
Metz, Frank, 245, 256
Metzdorf Advertising, 96, 123, 145, 339
Metzdorf, Lyle, 96, 339
Meyer, Gary, 461
Meyers, Les, 260
Meyerson, Arthur, 403, 853
Meyerson, Ron, 315
MGA, 518
Michael, Jan, 28, 64, 153
Michael John Assoc. Inc., 175
Michael M. Smit & Assoc., Inc., 173
Michael N. Paras, 845
Michael Norton Studioes, 136
Michael Orr & Associates, 702
Michaelis, Sylvain, 467
Michele Lee, 685
Michele Lee Designs, 572
Michelin, 782
Michienzi, Giulio, 604
Mickler, Horst, 338
Mietzelfeld, Mary, 265
Migal, Herbert, 202
Mike Quon, 823
Mikimoto (America) Co. Ltd., 74
Milani, Armando, 121, 179
Millennium Design Comm. Inc., 623
Miller, Dan, 443
Miller, David Russell, 689
Miller, Lisa, 168
Miller, Madelyn, 756
Miller, Mike, 767
Miller, Stuart, 155
Millerimages, 689
Milotinovic, Branka, 855
Ministry of the Attorney General, 713

Ministry of Tourism & Recreation Province of Ontario, 46
Minobe, Denise, 272, 273
Minor, Wendell, 245, 256
Miolla, Ralph, 342
Miran, 703
Miranda, Oswaldo, 703, 871
Miszewski, Sam, 176
Mitchell, Benn, 614
Mitchell, Josh, 848
Mitsubishi, 799
Mizerek Design Inc., 863
Mizerek, Leonard, 863
MK, MarknadsKommunikation AB, 32, 45, 59
MOAC/Continental Insurance, 444
Mobil Chemical Canada Ltd., 628
Mobil Oil Company, 865
Mocarski, David, 364
Mohawk Paper Mills, Inc., 665
Mok, Clement, 192, 208
El Molino, 501
Mollor, Diane, 594
Molyneux, Colin, 267
Momb, Kim, 141
Monahan, Anthony, 870
Monley, Gerry, 734
Monogram Models, Inc., 640
Montgomery, Barbara, 357
Montgomery, Joe, 801
Moon, Sarah, 736
Moor Life, 3
Moore, David, 489
Moore, Truman, 104
Moran, Dennis P., 516
Morden, Bill, 770
Moretz, Charles, 1, 838
Morgan, Tom, 267
Moriber, Jeff, 211
Morita, George, 769
Morphesis, Kathy, 271
Morris, David, 154
Morris, Leslie, 685
Morris, Michael, 329
Morrisons, 436
Morse, Linda, 751
Morton Advertising Inc., 171
Mosander, Carl, 636
Moscati, Frank, 835
Moscovitz & Taylor Adv. Inc., 101, 356
Moskowitz, Steven, 127
Moss, George, 442
Moss, Tobias, 68
Mother Jones Magazine, 319, 458, 811
Moy, Greg, 130
Muench, David, 123
Mukerjee, Jim, 820
Mullen, Enza, 57
Muller, Bob, 701
Munro, Gordon, 10
Munson, Don, 241
Munz, Stephen E., 470
Murlin/Dila Advertising, 850
Murphy, Harry, 341, 533, 553
Murray, Bob, 855
Murray, West, 855
Murrie White Drummond Lienhart, 325, 338, 901
Musgrave, Steve, 778
Mydlowski, Gene, 246
Myers, Marty, 77, 764
Myers, Roger, 149, 640
Mykkanen, Sinikka, 714
Mynster, Robert, 438

N

Nabisco Brands Inc., 343, 592
Nadler & Larimer Inc., 34, 741
Nakahara, Yasuharu, 381
Namuth, Hans, 847
Nancy Rica Schiff, 693
Nangle, Joe, 617
Nanni, Ed, 758, 872
Napurano, Joe, 85
Nardi, Bob, 100

National Distillers & Chemical Corp., 447
National Geographic Society, 177, 864
National Lampoon, 294, 498, 810
National Panasonic Svenska AB, 59
Nat'l Inst. for the Deaf, 836
Navarre, Al, 206, 508, 611
NBC, 722, 725
NBC Marketing, 639
NBC Sports, 137
Nee, Phil, 728
Needham, Harper & Steers, 785, 789
Neo-Art Inc., 353
The Nestle Company, 342
Neto, Jose Daloia, 24
Neuman & Bogdanoff, 519
Neumeier Design Team, 156, 196, 258, 520
Neumeier, Marty, 156, 196, 258, 520
Nevamar, 376
New Jersey Institute of Technology, 448
New West Magazine, 460, 812
New York Telephone, 250
Newcomb, John, 313, 470
Newman, Bob, 416, 571
Newman Design Assoc. Inc., 416, 571
The News Corporation Ltd., 426
Newspaper Advertising Bureau, 159, 252
Newsweek, 315
Newton Associates, 529
Nichols, Frank, 554
Nichols, Jack, 437
Nichols & Stone, 204
Nielsen & David Design, 364
Niemi, Art, 653, 826
Niki, 78
Nikosey, Kristen, 276
Niles, Nancy, 297
Nintendo of America Inc., 154
Nissen, Melanie, 275
NL Chemicals/NL Industries, 107
Noble & Assoc., 658
Nolte, Randolph, 28
Nolten, Nick, 346
Noonan, Julia, 330
Noordanus, George, 296, 804
Nora Scarlett, 860
Norden Laboratories, 75
Nordstrom/Cox Marketing, 428
Norking, Bjarne, 906
North Carolina Wildlife Resources Comm., 485
North Point Press, 268
Northwestern Graphics, Digi-Type Inc., 709
Norton, Mary Ann, 317
Norwich Eaton Pharmaceuticals Inc., 603
Novak, Karen, 596
Novotny, Jim, 680
NY State Health Department, 717
NYC, 708
NYC Dept. of Cultural Affairs, 254
NYC Dept. of Environmental Protection, 718
NZ Wines & Spirits Ltd., 761

O

Obremski, George, 310
O'Conner, Terry, 12, 556
O'Connor Helena, 556
Odette, Jack, 198, 419, 641
Odeven, C., 632
Odgis, Janet, 269
Off Shore Sportwear, 8
Ogilvy & Mather AB, 212, 389
Ogilvy & Mather BV, 42, 63, 296, 760, 762, 804

Ogilvy & Mather (Canada) Ltd., 103
Ogilvy, Steve, 122
Oglivi, Peter, 696
O'Grady, Kathy, 739
Ohio Magazine, 486
Ohyi, Atsutochi, 357
Okada, Rick, 765
Old, Anne A., 230
Old Fort Brewing Company, 337
Old Grand Dad, 48
Old, Patrick A., 230
Oldham, Sherri, 123, 145
Olin Corporation, 409
Oliver, Mark, 716
Olivetti, 9
Olivetti OPE, 121
Olson, David, 566
Omann & Co. Hair Designs, 541
O'Mara, Dann 515
Omfors, Eva, 389
Omni Magazine, 455
Omnibus, 161
Ontario Science Centre, 151
Ooka, Dian-Aziza, 282, 288, 319, 811
Opera News, 322, 474
Opper, Mary, 466
Optimation Inc., 735
The Options Group, 909
O'Reilly, Curvon, 119
Oroton/Whiting & Davis Co., 230
Orr, Mary Rudnicki, 141, 235
Orr, Michael R., 702
Orr, Norman, 112
Ortiz, Jose Luis, 546
Orzech, Michael, 197, 432
Osborn, Jim, 216
Osborne, Christine, 768
Ostrie, Barry, 399
Otnes, Fred, 835
Outcrop Ltd., 395
Ovesey & Company, Inc., 60
Ovesey, Regina, 60
Ovies, Joe, 116
Owens Corning Photo Services, 206
Owens-Corning Fiberglas Corp., 206, 611
Oxford University Press, 238
Oy ALKO AB, 714

P

Pabst Brewing Company, 336
Paccione, O., 695
Pacific Fabric Protection, 514
Package Design Council, 631
Padova, Ruben, 362
Padys, Diane, 862
Pagano, Ralph, 700
Paganucci, Bob, 90, 187
Paige, Robert, 827
Paine, Debi L., 657
Paine, Larry S., 557
Pakay, Sadat, 67, 207
Pakistan Design Institute, 385
Palmer, Gabe, 211
Palumbo Associates Inc., 360
Palumbo, Gary, 360
Palumbo, Graziano, 98
Panasonic, 742
Pantheon Books, 237, 264
Paquette, Art, 892
Paramount Pictures, 163
Paras, Michael N., 845
Paris, Jay, 486
Park Avenue Hotel, 630
Park Davis Pty. Ltd., 607
Parker, Bo, 192
Parker Brothers, 374
Parker, Douglas, 165
Parkhurst, Ken, 363
Parrish, Jr., George I., 49
Parrot, Lesley, 764
Pateman, Micheal, 715
Pathmark, 798
Patrick, Russell A., 227
Patrick SooHoo Inc., 637
Patterson, Gavin, 502

Paul Deur Company, 564
Paul, Greg, 297, 463, 814
Paul Haven Graphics, 14
Pavey, Jerry, 397
Paxit Pipekor, 87
Payne, S., 667
Paz, Andres Garcia, 548
Pearce, Michael, 111
Peckolick, Alan, 530, 835, 865
Pedersen, B. Martin, 412, 488
Pederson, Con, 746
Pederson, Roy, 708
Pellegrini & Associates Inc., 410
Pellegrini & Kaestle Inc., 505
Pellegrini, Robert, 410
Pennelton, Bruce, 85
Pennwalt Prescription Products, 99
Penrod, Terry Paul, 707
Pentagram Design, 426
Penthouse, 809, 819
Perera, Erik, 776
A Perfect Setting, 589
Performing Arts Journal Publications, 249
Perigee Books, 265
Persechini & Moss, 601
Pertengen, Gerard, 425
Peru Tourism, 851
Perweiler, Gary A., 7, 19, 108, 113
Pet Incorporated, 394
Peter Rogers Associates, 2, 13, 35, 775
Petersen, Paul, 128
Peterson, Bruce, 213
Peterson, Bryan L., 134, 902
Peterson, Christos, 881
Petrakas, George, 889
Petty, Steven O., 213
Pfeffer, Rubin, 242
Pfifer, Frank, 787
Pfizer Laboratories, 600
Pharmavite Corporation, 181
Phase II, 168
Philip Morris Design Group, 215
Philip Morris U.S.A., 215
Phillips, Ardison, 327
Phillips, Melanie, 39
Phillips Petroleum, 756
Philo Pieterse Productions (Pty) Ltd., 777
Philp, Bruce, 653
Phyllis Persechini/Steven Cerasale, 601
Picker International, 182
Piedmont Industries, 536
Pierce, John, 126
Pilgreen, John, 27, 119, 229
Pilon, Michel, 471
Pinsler, Jacklin, 581
Pittston Coal Co., 175
Pizza Time Theatre, 437
The Plain Dealer Magazine, 297, 463
Plane, Allen, 794, 788
Plansker, Dennis, 770
Playboy Magazine, 456, 805, 825
PLM Pac, 212
Plotkin, Barney, 330
Plummer, Bill, 308
Pluzynski & Associates, 332
PM Typography, 899
Podell, Jack J., 306, 483, 870, 897
Pohjola-Yhtiot, 188
Pointe Comunications, 597
Poisson, Chris, 834, 907
Poisson, J. Clarence, 719
Polansky, Alan, 388
Polaroid, 768
Polich Creative, 559
Polich, Gary G., 559
Polite Design, 893
Polite, Kerry, 893
Politiken, 646
Polito, Christ, 904
Pollack, Mark, 202
Polygram Records, 290
Pope, Kerig, 825
Porin Jazz 66 ry, 133

Port Authority of NY & NJ, 838
Port Miolla Associates Inc., 342
Port, Paul, 342
Portengen, Gerard, 71, 221
Porter, John, 54, 262
Porto, Greg, 828
Portland General Electric, 776
Post, Art, 805
Post, Robert J., 292, 479, 816
Postmark Atlanta, 635
Power, Robert, 774
Powers, 135
Powers, Percy, 721
Prah, Andre, 630
Presentation Services Grumman Aerospace Corporation, 180
Preskaw, Len, 752
Press Brenner Communications Inc., 537
Prestige Records, 289
Price Waterhouse, 386, 445
Priggen, Leslie, 690
Primo Angell Graphics, 336
Print Resources, 377
Pripps Brewery, 32, 45
Pritzker, Tom, 449
The Producers, 782
Profancik, Larry A., 176
Progressive Architecture, 150, 320, 480
Promotion Solutions, Inc., 700
Province of Ontario, 791
The Prudential Assurance Company, Ltd., 429
Pruitt, David, 330
Purina Belgium, 359
Push Pin, 254
Putnam, Jamie, 279, 281, 289
PW Incorporated, 176
P.W.A. Film Productions Ltd., 761
Pyro Energy Corp., 213

Q

The Quaker Oats Company, 338
Qually & Co., Inc., 124
Qually, Robert, 124
Quennell, Brian, 745
Quest Magazine, 466, 826
Quon, Mike, 823

R

R. Greenberg Associates, Inc., 667, 786, 795
R. Rafkin-Rubin Inc., 413
R.A. Cooney, Inc., 191, 444, 649
Rabko Prod., 770
Radke, Richard, 131
Rae Publishing Co., Inc., 669
Ragland, Kenny, 853
Ralph Johnson & Associates, 822
Ralph Keefe, Inc., 574
Ralston-Purina (Canada) Inc., 750
Ramirez, Luis E., 638
Ramm Advertising, 797
Random House, 269
Random House/Vintage, 239
Rapid Typographers, 689
Rapoport Print Corp., 847
Rawl, Ousama, 750, 766
Raymond Lee & Associates, 12, 98
Rayovac Canada, 745
RCA Records, 284
R.E. Dietz Company, 358
Redding, Sue, 597
Reed, Dave, 874
Reed Kaina Schaller Advertising, 874
Regis, Toni Santo, 312
Reinhardt, Siegfried, 678
Reliance Insurance Co., 644
Remia, 760
Remington, 335
Rene Sheret Design, 398, 570
Resler, Gred, 535

Resnicoff, Joel, 824
Ress, Erica, 6
Restaurant il Contane, 546
Restivo, Leonard, 234, 380
Rettich, Linda V., 251
Reynolds, Paddy, 282
Rich Melman, 124
Richard Foster Films, 779
Richard Foster Photography, Ltd., 686, 692
Richard Haymes & Co., 650
Richard K. Manigault, 888
Richard Maymes & Co., 847
Richards, Jim, 252
Richert, Ruthann, 108, 113, 606
Richmond, Jack, 197, 677
Rich's Department Stores, 551
Rick Sherman Ptrs. Film Company, 769
Riddell, Larry, 330
The Ridge Tool Co., 126
Riefler, Julie, 857
Rigelhaupt, Gail, 648
Riser, Art, 219, 535, 612
Rishko, Cyndi, 26
Ritta & Associates Inc., 549
Ritter/Waxberg, 792
River Tower Assoc., 189
Rizzo, Frank, 756
Rizzo, Karen, 792
R.J. Reynolds Inc., 842
R.J. Reynolds Industries, 185
R.J. Reynolds Tobacco Co., 26, 331
RJR MacDonald, Canada, 624
RJR-NOW Cigarettes, 20
RL, 500
Robert Abel & Associates, 742, 744, 746
Robert Amon + Associates, 558
Robert Cipriani Associates, 427
Robert Elias Studio, Inc., 738
Robert Miles Runyan & Assocs., 33, 181, 418, 582, 589, 848, 861
Roberts, Cheryl, 36
Roberts, Randy, 742, 744, 746
Robins, Larry, 89
Robinson, Andrea, 846
Robinson, Bennett, 415, 433
Rockley, Ted, 782
Rockmore, Patty, 56
Rocky Boots, 216
Rodin, Christine Olympia, 97
Rodriguez, Marcos, 223
Rogers, Randy, 377
Roland Corporation, 58
Roman, Ron, 668
Ron Chereskin, 56
Ron Jacobs/Jaguar Productions, 741
Ronn, Johan, 231
Rose, Blaine, 441
Rose, Susan, 19, 521
Rose, Uli, 35
Rosen, Mike, 116
Rosen, Trix, 729, 733
Rosengarten, Mindy, 26
Rosenthal, Herbert M., 442
Rosentswieg, Gerry, 711
Rosenwald, Laurie, 352, 903
Rosner, Gene, 166
Rosnick Productions, 664
Ross, Rick, 742, 746
Rossum, Cheryl, 412
The Rotarian Magazine, 311
Rothmann, Frank, 496, 821
Rothovius, Iska, 250
Rouk, Gary E., 769
Rousso, Steve, 110, 694
Route 66, 893
Rowe, Michael, 573
The Rowland Co. & The Scotch Whisky Information Center, 191
Royal Composing Room, Inc., 669
RSR Associates, 173
Ruan, Roy, 729, 732
Rubin, Randee R., 413
Ruby Street, Inc., 818
Rudd International, 205

Rudd, Virginia, 72
Rudolph de Harak & Assoc., Inc., 189
Rumrill Hoyt, 127, 335
Russini, Ralph, 516
Rust, Deborah, 293
Rusty Kay & Assocs., 140, 563, 674
Ruuhinen, Erkki, 157, 188, 867

S

Sabado, Ray, 593
Sabinson, Kay, 225
Saga Corporation, 857
Sage, Grace, 772
Sakmanoff, George, 402
Saks Fifth Avenue, 234, 380, 739
Saksa, Cathy, 239
Salas, Ricardo, 421
Sally Bruner-Johns Design Studio, 477
Salo, Wayne, 163
Salpeter, Bob, 200, 876
Salvato & Cove Associates, 443
Salvato, Guy, 443
Sametz Blackstone Associates Inc., 568, 699
Sametz, Roger, 699
Sampo Mutual Insurance Co., 532
Samsonite, 49
San Francisco Zoo, 148
Sandcastle Advertising, 886
Sanders, Jr., George W., 240
Sanders, Rita, 747
Sanders, Robert R., 726, 727
Sandford, John, 439
Sandi Smith, 138
Sandmeyer's Bookstore, 513
Sandpiper Condominiums, 564
Sanson, Jeff, 115
Santa Barbara Designs, 199
Santiago Suarez, 773
Sarapociello, Jerry, 68
Sargent, Peter, 363
Satterwhite, Al, 41, 81, 837
Save the Children Fund, 710
Savings & Loan News, 304
Sawyer of Napa, 235
Sawyer, Vickie, 398, 570
Saxton Communications Group, Ltd., 448
S.C. Peach Council & Promotion Board, Inc., 567
Scali, McCabe, Sloves, 780
Scali, McCabe, Sloves (Canada), 769
Scali, McCabe, Sloves (CDA), 750
Scandinavian Foundation, 863
ScanDutch I/s, 392
Scarff, Michele, 103
Scarlett, Nora, 860
Schaefer, Carol, 647
Schaeffer Boehm Ltd., 647
Schaller, Leona, 874
Schechter, Alvin H., 331
The Schechter Group, 331
Schefer, Phyllis, 468, 883
Schenck, Gary, 659
Schenk Design Associates, Inc., 659
Scherer, James, 699
Scherzi, James, 358
Scheuer, Glenn, 7
Schiff, Nancy Rica, 693
Schilperoort, Mindy, 593
Schlachter, Trudy, 270
Schlosser, C.J., 545
Schmek, Heidi, 420
Schmidt, George, 99
Schoening, Roger, 846
Scholler Chemicals, 529
Schon, Julia, 478
Schoonover, Jan, 459
Schorre, Charles, 62
Schrager, Beverly, 409
Schulz Productions, 765
Schumacher, 203

Schwartz, Daniel, 280
Schwartzman, Arnold, 561
Schwarz, John, 332
Science Digest Magazine, 496, 821
Scocozza, Victor, 856, 859
Scott, Denis, 124
Scudellari, R.D., 263
Scullin, Terry, 108, 113, 606
Seager, David M., 177, 864
Sealy Mattress Company, 599
SeaPAK Transport Services, 820
SeaQuest, 505
Sebastian, James, 201
Sebastian, Liane, 513
Seelig, Barry, 631
Segal, Bonnie, 571
Segal, Leslie, 409, 416
Seifer, Allison, 690
Seldon Laboratories, Madrid, 528
Seltzer, Isadore, 669
Semels, Albert, 799
Sendra, Jaime A., 501
Seppo Holopainen, 636
Serge Bevil Designs, Inc., 671
Serne, Gerrit, 296, 804
Sessions, Steve, 62, 377
Setteducati, Mark, 375
Setzke, Gerd F., 547
Seymour, Ron, 166
Shadursky, Claudia, 615
Shaeffer, Richard, 892
Shaffer, Stan, 472
Shakespear, George, 413
Shalit, Randi J., 500
Sharpe, Bill, 422
Sharpe, Les, 752
Shaver, Freda, 80
Shaw, Franklin, 836
Shayne, Sharon, 550
Shell Canada Ltd., 103
Shell Nederlandse Verk. Mij. BV, 42, 296, 804
Sheret, Rene, 398, 570
Sherwin Williams, 89
Sheumaker, Craig, 417
Shewchuk, Martin, 758, 872
Shibata, Hiroshi, 74
Shiffman, Tracey, 165
Shoe Biz, 740
Shorter, Jeanne, 135
Shortt, Gary, 130, 143
Showtime Entertainment, 538
Shreveport Advertising Federation, 894
Shu-Sun, Cheung, 351
Shyllit, Joe, 664
Sibert, Gregg, 191
Sickenberger, Barbara, 439
Sidewalk Art Festival, 136
Sieber & McIntyre, Inc., 99
Sierra Designs, 141
The Signal Companies, 400
Siliconix, Inc., 112
Silva, Larry, 235
Silva, Leslie, 403
Silvestri, Phil, 747
Simhoni, George, 25
Simkins, Mark, 873
Simmons, Eric, 169
Simms & McIvor, Inc., 118
Simon, Jean-Marie, 706
Simon & Schuster, 245
Simon & Schuster/Wanderer Books, 243
Simplot, 787
Simpson, Michael, 678
Sims, Jim, 534, 635, 899
Sinnott, Diane, 715
Sirotin, Nick, 100
Siskind, Stewart, 189
Sivonen, Matti, 133
Sizemore, Tom, 300, 473
Skeji, Michael, 404
SKF JBD AB, 170
Skioldebrand, Erica, 117, 228, 622
Sklad Inc., 615
Skosbergh, Ulf, 56
Skrebneski, 158

Skurnik, Murray, 798
Slas, Ricardo, 504
Sliva, Karl, 46
Slover, Susan, 93
The Small Things Company, 341
Smiedt, Howard, 79, 752
Smit, Michael M., 173
Smith, Joseph, 509
Smith, Larry, 55
Smith, Richard, 632
Smith, Tyler, 36, 186, 233
Smith, William Edward, 843
Smith-Avery, Tracey, 383
Smitherman Graphic Design, 299
Smith's Vitamins, 344
Smithsonian Magazine, 623
So. Calif. Antique Motorcycle Club, 140
So. California Early Music Soc., 833
Sollecito, Carol, 687
Sollecito, Tony, 687
Solna Offset AB, 228, 622
Somoroff, Ben, 783
Soos, Anita, 72
Sorensen, Mogens, 392
Sortino, Steve, 333, 334
Souter, Michael, 195
Southwest Producers Services, 774
Southwest Truck Body, 173
Southwick, 36
Spaulding, Denise, 174
Spectra II, 465
Spectrum Composition Svcs., 452
Spence, Sharon, 69, 740
Spic 'n Span, 660, 670
Spiess, Fritz, 765
Spizzari, Charles, 176
Spring Magazine, 468
Sprinz, Yolanda, 398
Spurgeon, Steve, 850
Squashic, Lauren, 184
SS Design & Production, 351
St. Agnes Outreach, 517
St. Gillian, 10
St. Joseph Hospital, 443
St. Vincent, Milone & McConnells, Inc., 82, 875
St. Vincent, Rick, 875
Stacker, Michael, 770
Staebler, Tom, 456, 805, 825
Stahl, Nancy, 342, 412
Stan Evenson Design Inc., 884
Standart, Joe, 201
Stanfield's Limited, 98
Star, Black, 483
The Stat Store, 92
Steadman, Ralph, 710
Steele, Kim, 415
Steelograph Co. Inc., 202, 386, 445
Steigman, Steve, 84, 105
Stein, Larry, 90
Steinberg, Michael, 667
Stellenbosch Farmers Winery, 30
Stello, Jr., Ralph, 465
Stelzer, Michael, 658
Stemco Inc., 806
Stendahls, 646
Stendahls Vasagatan, 190, 630
Stendig International Inc., 93
Sterling, Joe, 439
Sterling Roman Press, 849
Stern, Laszlo, 631
Stevens, Robert, 38, 218, 755, 861
Stevens/Eberlein Productions, 755
Stewart, Brenton, 115
Stewart Mosberg Design Associates Inc., 373
Stewart, Sandy, 850
Stichting Stoffenbeurs Amsterdam, 620
Stiles, Lynn, 858
Stimson, Fred, 434
Stone, Pete, 595
Story, Beth, 405

Story, Mark, 768
Stow/Davis, 119
Strathmore Press, 579
Street Noise Prod., 769
Streetnoise/Toronto, 770
Streger, Sharon, 146
Strickland, Danny, 219, 612
The Stroh Brewery, 106
Student Lawyer, 306, 483
Studio in the Woods, 767, 869
Studio L, 126
Studiographix, 438
Stufflebeam, Kim, 778
Sudler & Hennessey, 607
Sugar, Jim, 177
Summerhouse Films, 789
Summit Books, 256
Sun Chemical Export Corp., 91
Sun Company Inc., 441
Sunbreaker Surfware, 14
Sunlight, 736
Susan Bennis/Warren Edwards, 27, 229
Susan M. Love, 569
Susan McCarthy, 571
Susan Moore Lawyer, 566
Sutan Plus, 757
Sutherland, Eric, 650
Svard, Jori, 714
Svenska Film Institute, 157
Swack, Terry, 568
Swan, Black, 735
Sweet-Wyatt, Robin, 9
Swerdlow, Trina, 684
Swope, Martha, 489
Sxcheidle, Gerhard, 667
Sykes, David, 666
Sylvania, 598
Syntex, 430
Synthesis, 513
Syracuse University Art Collection, 882
Szalapski, James, 786

T

Tachna, Rebecca, 243
Tai-Keung, Kan, 351
Talarczyk, Robert, 83
Taller Agricola Mexicano, 548
Talmatch, Herb, 34
Tanaka, Tetsuya, 393
Tandom Computers, 111
Tani, Dennis, 181
Tanner, Steve, 138
Tapp, Eddie, 39
Tardiff, Melissa, 457
Tarkett, 16
Tarkett AB, 210, 214
Tarry O Communications Inc., 556
Tashjian, Donna, 870, 897
Tassian, George, 406
Tate, Don, 338
Tausche, Kurt, 135, 900
Taylor, Bob, 340
Taylor, C.D., 796
Taylor, Clare, 101, 356
Taylor, Josh, 348
Taylor/Johnson Petrocap, 539
TBWA, 31, 50
Tcherevkoff, Michel, 487
Team, Virginia, 286
Tedesco, Michael, 193
Tegopen (Bristol Laboratories), 608
Telemation, 776
Telfer, Audrey, 766
Tell, Goran, 210, 214
Templeton, Susan, 436
Texaco, Inc., 324
Texas Monthly Magazine, 490, 495, 815
Texas Western Dev. Inc., 848
Texsteam, 96
Thermador, 633
Thomas & Betts Corp., 85
Thomas, Charles A., 816
Thomas J. Lipton Inc., 345
Thomasson-Grant Publishing, 839

Thomson Industries, 116
Thursby, Steve, 25
T.I. of Hawaii Inc., 874
Tiani, Alex, 146
Ticor Mortgage Insurance Co., 803
Tieman, Michael, 337
Til, Tony, 908
Time Magazine, 305
Times-Mirror Cable, 796
Timken, 113
The Timken Company, 406
Timmins, William F., 435
Tina Lepera, 588
Tindol Services, Inc., 751
Tipton, Judy, 624
Tobin, Michael, 549
Tomlinson, David, 87
Tonkovich, Debbie, 593
Topczewski, Mark, 578
Tora, Shinichiro, 381
Torme, David, 430
Torres, Javier, 223
Totaro, Charles, 361
Toulotte, Lois A., 817
Town & Country Magazine, 457
Townsend, William G., 629
Toyota, 142
Trace Elements Design, 383
Tracy, Tom, 125
Tracy-Locke/BBDO, 756, 763
Trainer, Kathleen, 199
Trans World Airlines, 481, 829, 830, 862
Travel Dynamics Inc., 649
Tregale, Peter J., 765
Tremblay, Jean, 23
Trenter, Bo, 228, 622
Trepal, Lad, 126, 182
The Trimensa Company, 363
Trimensions, Inc., 627
Tri-Moto, 755
Trina Swerdlow, 684
Trojan Properties Inc., 531
Trousdale, Don, 806
Trousdell, Don, 704
Troxell, Deborah, 644
TRW, 744
Tsiaras, Philip, 841
Tucker, Bill, 86
Tulip Time Festival, 129
Tureck, Karen, 253
Turner Broadcasting, 39
Turner, Graham, 31
Turner, Pete, 427
Turpin, Debra, 767
TV Guide Magazine, 908
Twin Arts, Inc., 843
Tyler, Harry, 87
Tylor Smith Art Direction Inc., 36, 186, 233, 844
Type House & Durograph, 545
Typehouse, 422
Tyrrell, Bob, 40

U

Uchida of America Corp., 357
Udcoff, Barry, 73
Uhlig, Grace, 217
Ulrich, Mark, 443
Umuarama, 871
Unangst, Andrew, 120
Ung, Norm, 273, 280, 884
Unigraphics, 417, 434
Union Carbide Canada, 594
United Paper Mills Ltd. Jamsankoski, 220
United States Post Office, 41
United States Virgin Islands, 37
Upper & Lower Case, 488
Urban, Timothy E., 390, 621
U.S. Army, 790
U.S. Invest, 196

V

Vadun, Chuck, 834
Valtos, Bill, 792
van der Star, Louis, 670
Van Dyken, Pam, 129
Van Epps, Susan, 141
van Hoften, Charles, 670
Vanessa Jewelry, 351
Vanity Fair, 647
Vareltzis, Raon, 609
Varis, Kyosti, 133. 220, 532
Vartanian, Hrair, 318, 440
Vartoogian, Jack, 489
v.d. Vlugt, Will, 63
Veer Corporation, 385
Veirs, Dana, 796
Veistola, Jukka, 499
Veistola Oy, 499
Venet Advertising, 798
Venn, Bill, 607
Vergano, Laura, 858
Viacom International Inc., 408
Vias y Transportes, 510
Vibert, Arthur, 86
Victory Optical/Geoffrey Beene, 360
Vidal Sassoon, 775
View Magazine, 307
Viking Press, 240
Villa Banfi, 759
Vintage, 257
Virginia Port Authority, 80
Vis/Art Films, Inc., 788, 794
Visser, Cor, 221, 371, 620
Visual Services Inc., 592
Volkswagen, 866
Volkswagen do Brasil S.A., 24, 44
Volkswagen Germany, 153
Vollers, William, 88
Volpe, Rocco, 118
Volpi, Larry, 49
Volvo of America, 780
Volvo RS, 190
Von Kaenel, Axel, 95
von Tiedemann, Rudi, 713
Vuarnet, USA, 33
Vuchinich, Andrew, 48
Vu-Cong, An-Khang, 722, 725

W

WABC-TV, 747
Waddell, Malcolm, 401
Waites, Raymond, 203
Waldenbooks, 610
Waldman, Chuck, 369
Waldron, Jim, 704
Wales Tourist Board, 267
Walker, Larney, 691
Walker/Group Inc., 551, 584
Wallace/Church Assoc., 631
Wallack, Bob, 365
Wallack & Harris, Inc., 365
Wallack, Sherry Berne, 91
Waller, Jr., David B., 642
Walther, Marianne, 359
Waltsman, Michael, 513
Wang Laboratories, 318, 440
Wanner, Wayne, 39
Ward, Robin, 643
Warkulwiz Design, 576
Warkulwiz, Robert, 576
Warner Brothers Records, 287, 302
Wasserman, Barbara, 439
Waterkotte, Mike, 778
Waters, John, 405
Watson, Bob, 467
W.B. Doner & Co. Advertising, 40
Weaks, Bob, 75
The Webb Co., 481, 830
Webster, D.J., 18
Webster, Robert, 602
Weedy, Theresa, 279
Weisz, Thomas J., 121, 179
Weisz/Greco Inc., 121, 179
Welch Currier Smith, 844
Welch, Ray, 844
Welgand, Richard, 855
Weller, Don, 368, 834
Wendover Associates, 632
Wenman, Carol, 10, 120
Wenman, David, 10, 120
Wessanen Meel B.V., 221
West '82, Art and the Law, 813
Westdal, Larry, 689
Western Landscape Construction, 139
Westin Hotels, 593
Westlin, Claes, 389
Westvaco, 109
Westworld Publications, 492
Wheat, Ken, 710
Wheeler Film Productions, 767
Wheeler, Jim, 767
White, John, 262
White, Ken, 668
White, Thomas O., 901
Whitehead, John, 183
Whitmore, Ken, 181
Wicht, Arnold, 46, 713, 791
Wick, Walter, 313
Wieland, Don, 143
Wilcox, Shorty, 416
Wilkerson Advertising, 58
Wilkerson, Jim, 58
Wilkins, James L., 806
Wilkinson, Bill, 623
Wilkinson, Chuck, 99
Wilks, Darrell, 49
Willardson & White, 78
William Allen & Associates, 661
William Esty Co., Inc., 26
William F. Finn & Associates, 806
William Kreysler & Associates, 533
Williams, Carl, 566
Williams, David, 485
Williams, Harry, 267
Williams, Michael, 894
Williams, Richard, 137
Williams, Sherri, 215
Williamson, John, 395
Wilson, Anna Lee, 378, 616
Wilson, Bob, 395
Wilson, Steven S., 260
Wilson, Sue, 29, 66, 754
Winckler, Torbjorn, 190, 630
Wing, Frank, 434
Winston-Salem Arts Council, 842
Wirsbo Bruks AB, 117
Wirtschaftswoche, 316
Wise, Guinote, 767
Witherspoon, Kendall L., 428
Wittenberg, Ross, 671
WLTY/FM, 748
WNBC-TV News 4 NY, 729, 730, 731, 732, 733
Wojdyla, David, 588
Woldin, John, 109
Wolf, Bruce, 203
Wolf, Henry, 236, 305
Wolf, JoAnn, 9
Wolf, Marv, 398
Wolferman, Tom, 778
Wolfhagen, Bill, 96
Wolin, Ron, 142
Wolman, Baron, 278
Wong, Peter, 497
Wong, Ronald, 331
Wood, Alan, 506
Wood, John J., 653
Wood, Tom, 436
Woodlan, Don, 80
Woodman, Jowill, 681, 682
Woods, Earl, 209, 422
The Woods Group, 222, 414
Woodward, Fred, 475
Woody Pirtle Inc., 554
Woolever, L. Dean, 836
Wooley, Robert, 870, 897
Woon, Kay, 424
World Typeface Center Inc., 507
Woudt, Jan, 221, 425
W.R. Grace & Co., 102
Wright, David B., 138
Wright, John M., 178, 387
Wright, Marcia, 481, 829, 830, 862
Wright, Walter, 798
Wunderman Ricotta & Kline, 70
Wurtzel, Bill, 759
WXYZ Newstalk Radio, 800
WXYZ-TV, ABC in Detroit, 734
WYES-TV, 720
Wylie Wilson & Munn, 111

Y

Yamaha Motor Corp., 38
Yamaha Parts Distributors Inc., 218
Yamasaki, Paula, 637
Yamashita, Mike, 497
Yankee Books, 262
Yarbrough, Jon, 789
Yarbrough, Kevin, 172, 696
Yasumura & Assoc., 67, 207
Yasumura, Muts, 67, 207
Yates, R.H., 382
Yeates, Stephen, 98
Yoshi Inaba, Tokyo, 824
Yoshida, Gary, 785, 789
Yoshida, Zengo, 353
Yoshikawa, Joy, 541
Young, Frank, 60
Young, James, 598
Young President's Organization, 606
Young & Rubicam, 6, 29, 48, 66, 130, 736, 754, 786
Young & Rubicam/Zemp, 890
Youngblood, Margaret, 225
Your Corporate Look, 442

Z

Zabe, Lichael, 638
Zabe, Michel, 223
Zabol, Myron, 491
Zajack, Greg, 668
Zambelli, Michael, 360
Zanetti, Gerald, 47
Zangenberg, Dorte, 646
Zash, Jane, 122
Zeitgeist/Houston, 213
Zeitsoff, Elaine, 137
Zelcher, Alfred, 829
Zellman, Harold, 833
Zellman/Herst Architects, 833
Zeltsoff, E., 639
Zenn Graphic Design, 353
Zisk, Mary, 821
Zito, Andy, 633, 803
Zographos, Paula, 415, 433
Zolan, Russell, 496
Zoom Magazine, 303, 837

Nos.

23 Skiddo, 704